MW00323910

Compassionate Stranger

IRISH STUDIES

James MacKillop, *Series Editor*

Mrs. Asenath Nicholson. From a drawing by Anna Maria Howitt.

Compassionate Stranger

Asenath Nicholson and the Great Irish Famine

MAUREEN O'ROURKE MURPHY

Syracuse University Press

In memory of my parents
Bernard J. O'Rourke
(1909–2006)
and
Louise Sawner O'Rourke
(1917–2008)

Maureen O'Rourke Murphy is the Joseph L. Dionne Professor of Curriculum and Teaching in the School of Education at Hofstra University, in Hempstead, New York. A past president of the American Conference for Irish Studies and a past chair of the International Association for the Study of Irish Literatures, Murphy was one of the six senior editors of the prize-winning *Dictionary of Irish Biography* published in nine volumes and online by the Royal Irish Academy and Cambridge University Press in 2009. Murphy directed the New York State Great Irish Famine Curriculum Project (2001), which won the National Conference for the Social Studies Excellence Award in 2002; she was the historian of the Irish Hunger Memorial in Battery Park City. She is currently the historian, with John Ridge, of the Mission of Our Lady of the Rosary/Watson House Project.

Murphy edited *Irish Literature: A Reader* (1987, rev. ed. 2006), with James MacKillop. She also edited Asenath Nicholson's *Annals of the Famine in Ireland* (1998) and *Ireland's Welcome to the Stranger* (2002). She edited Annie O'Donnell's *Your Fondest Annie* in 2005. She has been awarded honorary degrees by the State University of New York at Cortland and by the National University of Ireland.

Contents

Illustrations

ix

Maps

Acknowledgments

IN THE AUTUMN OF 1965, I climbed up to Roger McHugh's office on the top of University College Dublin's old building at Earlsfort Terrace to ask him whether he would take me on for a master's degree. I told him I thought I would like to look at fiction and travel writing in Ireland before the Great Irish Famine. Leaning back in his chair, he said, with a twinkle in his ice-blue eyes, "Did you ever hear of an American traveler called Asenath Nicholson?" I had not, so I went right to Hodges Figgis, where I found a copy of *Ireland's Welcome to the Stranger* (1847) for five shillings. When I got home, I opened the book and began a relationship with Nicholson that has lasted nearly fifty years. She has been full of surprises, has left me baffled and exasperated, but she has never disappointed me.

Not only have I been blessed with an entrancing subject, but I was doubly blessed with generous friends and helpers who shared the trail from Chelsea, Vermont, to the site of Nicholson's unmarked grave in Brooklyn's Green-Wood Cemetery. The staff at the old Irish Folklore Commission, located in those days at 82 St. Stephen's Green—Kevin Danaher, Anraí Ó Braonáin, Seán Ó Suilleabháin, and Tom Wall— provided me with a copy of Nicholson's second Irish book, *Lights and Shades of Ireland* (1850), and directed me to the books that contextualized Nicholson's Irish writings. The books and manuscripts are now housed in the National Folklore Collection that Ríonach Uí hÓgáin directs at the Delargy Centre, University College Dublin.

Later that fall, when I visited Janet Carroll, who worked part-time at the Quaker Library in Eustace Street, I met Olive Goodbody, who remembered seeing a drawing of Nicholson, the drawing that is the frontispiece of this book. Janet Barcroft, who could trace her Barcroft roots to William Barcroft, a corresponding member of the Central Relief Committee of the Society of Friends, was tolerant about the line of Nicholson-related books that trailed around the walls of our sitting room at 41 Waterloo Road. F. M. "Buzz" Carroll, Anne Francis Cavanaugh and Frank Phelan, Donla Ui Bhraonáin, Robert and Norma Rhodes, and Roger and Ginny Rosenblatt were early encouragers during my Dublin year.

When I returned to the United States and had the opportunity to give a paper about Nicholson at the 1977 meeting of the American Conference for Irish Studies in Williamsburg, Virginia, the talk brought new supporters, including Jim MacKillop, who urged me years later to bring this book to Syracuse University Press. The same spring, my late sister-in-law, Kate Murphy, found a copy of Nicholson's *Loose Papers* for a dime in a secondhand bookstore in Salem, Massachusetts. Those occasional writings provided my first insight into Nicholson's life after she left Ireland; it suggested that it might be possible to write a life of Nicholson.

During my teaching career at Hofstra University, research leaves and presidential and School of Education research grants provided opportunities to consult the Archives of the South Presentation Convent in Cork; the British Library; the Capuchin Archives at St. Mary of the Angels, Dublin; the County Clare Library in Ennis; the Crawford Gallery, Cork; the Irish Architectural Archive; the Libraries of the Society of Friends in Dublin and London; the National Gallery of Ireland; the National Library of Ireland; the National Maritime Museum, Liverpool; the National Portrait Gallery, London; and the Trinity College Dublin Library. John T. Cooper, the owner of the Dairyman's Cottage on the Isle of Wight, permitted me to make a copy of Nicholson's entry in the cottage guest book.

In the United States, I found resources about Nicholson and her contemporaries at the American Antiquarian Society Library; the American Irish Historical Society Library; the Amherst College Special Collections; the Chelsea, Vermont, Library; the Essex County

Collection in Keene Valley, New York; the Essex County Historical Society; the Library of Congress; the Manuscript Division of the Boston Public Library; the New Britain, Connecticut, Library; the New Haven Historical Society; the New-York Historical Society Library and Archives; the New York Public Library; the Oberlin College Archives and Special Collections; the Oneida County, New York, Archive and Library; Rutgers University Seminary; and the Swarthmore College's Library of the Society of Friends.

The late Jean Hatch Farnham, a descendant of Asenath Nicholson's brother David Hatch, and her cousin Kay Hatch Campbell shared Hatch family history with me. Margaret Bartley provided me with information about the Nicholson family and photographs of family gravestones; Rachel Arciniega, a descendant of Norman Nicholson's brother John, filled in valuable dates in the Nicholson chronology. Connie Hedren Fitz's master's thesis, "Asenath Hatch Nicholson: An Unknown American Author," supplied information about Nicholson's later years.

All Great Irish Famine researchers are indebted to R. Dudley Edwards, T. Desmond Williams, and their essayists who contributed to *The Great Famine* (1956) and to Cecil Woodham-Smith's pioneering *The Great Hunger* (1962). I owe special thanks to a later generation of famine scholars for their scholarship and for their interest in the Nicholson project: Gordon Bigelow, Mary E. Daly, James S. Donnelly, Margaret Kelleher, Christine Kinealy, Cormac Ó Gráda, Robert Scally, and Kevin Whelan and the collections of famine documents edited by John Killen, Noel Kissane, Cathal Póirtéir, and Liam Swords.

Friends who joined the long-running Nicholson hunt include Joan DeStaebler, Henry Farrell, Michael and Rhona Kenneally, Joann Krieg, Joe Lee, Robert Lowery, Larry McCaffrey, Lucy McDiarmid, James McGuire, Maureen Milletta, Janet Nolan, Michael and Donna O'Rourke, Peter O'Rourke, John Ridge, Ann Saddlemyer, Catherine Shannon, Julius Sherman, Alan Singer, Karin Spencer, and Mary Helen Thuente. Friends and family who did not live to see this book finished include Adele Dalsimer; Emmet Larkin; Gus Martin; Éilis McDowell; Roger McHugh; Máire and Jack Sweeney; Jude Uí

Fhatharta; my parents, Bernie and Louise O'Rourke; and especially Don Murphy.

Diana Ben-Merre, Margaret MacCurtain, Donna O'Rourke, Mary Helen Thuente, Donla Uí Bhraonáin, and the scholars who evaluated the manuscript for Syracuse University Press demonstrated the valuable part that critical readers play in bringing a book from manuscript to print. Their careful and candid comments are reflected in the pages of *Compassionate Stranger*.

I am grateful to Antony Farrell, Brendan Barrington, and Siobhán O'Reilly of Lilliput Press, which published Nicholson's *Annals of the Famine* (1998) and *Ireland's Welcome to the Stranger* (2002). Antony has generously allowed me to use material published in the Lilliput editions in *Compassionate Stranger*.

A late grace note was meeting Donnacha Dennehy, who has set a Nicholson text to music for a song cycle titled "If He Died, What Then?" He promises more Nicholson music, the appropriate coda for the life of a joyful hymn singer.

Finally, my gratitude to Syracuse University Press begins with my old friend James MacKillop. We worked together on two editions of our *Irish Literature: A Reader* for the press, and he encouraged me to offer *Compassionate Stranger* to acquisitions editor Jennika Baines, who has worked efficiently and courteously with me to bring the book to print.

Abbreviations

Annals	*Annals of the Famine in Ireland*
IWS	*Ireland's Welcome to the Stranger*
LP	*Loose Papers*
LS	*Lights and Shades of Ireland*
Nature's	*Nature's Own Book*

Chronology

1792   February 24: Asenath Hatch born to Michael (ca. 1747–1837) and Martha Rice Hatch (ca. 1747–1837) in Chelsea, Vermont.

1807   District 2, Chelsea, lists a fifteen-year-old scholar in Michael Hatch's household.

1808   According to *Nature's Own Book*, Asenath Hatch was teaching in her own school by the age of sixteen.

1812   Norman Nicholson (NN) and David Hatch enlist in their own local militia units during the War of 1812.

1823   Asenath Hatch opens a school in Elizabethtown, New York.

1826   A local deed establishes that Asenath Hatch was married to NN, a widower with three children. Death of Henry Nicholson, NN's youngest child.

1829   The Nicholsons leave Elizabethtown and settle in New York City.

1830   Death of Michael Hatch in Chelsea at the age of eighty-three. David Hatch builds a cottage that has become the home of the Chelsea Historical Society.

1831   NN (merchant) is listed as the householder at Third Avenue and Sixth Street. Asenath Nicholson (AN) is listed as a schoolteacher. Nicholson hears Sylvester Graham lecture and gives up coffee, visits her mother in Vermont, and travels west along the Erie Canal. There is a cholera epidemic in New York City from July through September.

1833   The Nicholsons open their Graham Boarding House at 79 Cedar Street.

1834   The Nicholsons move their Graham Boarding House to Wall
       Street and Broadway.

1835   The Nicholson Graham Boarding House moves to 118 William
       Street. AN, not NN, is listed as proprietor. Wilbur and Whipple
       publish *Nature's Own Book*.

1837   Martha Hatch dies in Chelsea, Vermont, at the age of ninety-one.

1839   NN dies in Canton, New York, at the age of fifty-four.

1840   The 1840 Census lists AN as the householder at 21 Beekman
       Street.

1842   AN is listed as a widow living at 26 Beekman Street.

1843   AN moves to 65 Barclay Street.

1844   AN sails for Liverpool aboard the *Brooklyn*; the ship arrives in
       Liverpool on June 12.

       June 15: AN lands in Kingstown, travels by train to Dublin, and
       meets Miss H, her "first constant friend."

       July: AN travels from Dublin to Tullamore, Kilbride, Arklow, the
       Vale of Avoca, Rathdrum, Kilbride, Glendalough, and Dublin.

       August: AN travels from Dublin to Kilkenny, Johnstown, Url-
       ingford, Ballyspellin, the Colliery, New Birmingham, Grange,
       Kilcooley, Thurles, Cashel, Clonmel, Dungarven, Cappoquin, and
       Mount Melleray.

       September: AN travels to Youghal, Lismore, Cappoquin via Dun-
       garven, Clonmel, Cappoquin, Urlingford, and Thurles.

       October: AN leaves Thurles for Urlingford, Roscrea, Borris-in-
       Ossory, Roscrea, and Birr.

       November: AN travels to Galway through Birr and Loughrea. She
       leaves Galway and returns toward Urlingford through Oranmore,
       Loughrea, Killimor, Banagher, Birr, and Roscrea.

       December: AN continues from Roscrea to Urlingford and leaves
       for Dublin via Durrow, Abbeyleix, Maryborough, Stradbally, Athy,
       Kilcullen, and Naas.

1845   January 9: AN leaves Dublin for Wicklow, Wexford, Wateford,
       Clonmel, Cork, Cahir, Michelstown, Fermoy, Rathcormac, Water-
       grass-Hill, and Glenmore.

February: AN travels to Cove, Ringacoltig, Cork, Blarney, Cloyne, Rockview, Carrigacrump Quarry, Bandon, Cork, Bantry, and Glengarriff.

March: AN continues through the Southwest, visiting Kenmare, Killarney, Ross Island, Torc Cascade, Muckross Abbey, Killorglin, Bay of Ross, Mountain Stage, Cahirciveen, Valentia Island, Ballybrack, Derrynane, Ballinskellig Bay, Killoyra, Beaufort, Killarney, and the Gap of Dunloe to Hyde Park.

April: AN leaves Dinis Island, Killarney, and travels to West Kerry via Tralee and on to Ventry, Dingle, Dunquin, and returns to Dingle and Tralee before crossing the Shannon at Tarbert. AN goes through Limerick, Ennis, Gort, Oranmore, Galway, Oughterard, Recess, and Derrnavglaun to Clifden, Letterfrack, Tully, Omey, and Claddaghduff and leaves Clifden via Oughteerard and Galway for Tuam, Westport, and Croagh Patrick.

June: AN spends most of June in Mayo: Newport, Achill Sound, the Achill Mission at Dugort, Slievemore, Axhill Sound, Newport, Westport, and Castlebar. She visits Sligo, Glencar, and Carrick-on-Shannon on her way back to Dublin.

August: AN leaves Dublin for Belfast and visits Scotland—Glasgow to Dunbarton Castle and Inverness.

1846   January: Glasgow.

May: Londonderry.

Summer: Malahide and Dublin.

December 7: James Webb's home, DeVesci Lodge, Carrickbrennan Road, and Upper Monkstown Road.

A second edition of *Nature's Own Book* is printed in Glasgow for private circulation by William Brown.

1847   February: AN writes letters to the *New York Tribune* and to the *Emancipator*, appealing for help in relieving the Irish poor.

February 27: AN writes a second letter to the *New York Tribune*.

April: AN meets William Bennett at Richard Davis Webb's home in Dublin.

June 10: AN dates the preface of *Ireland's Welcome to the Stranger*. Printed by Webb, the book is published by Gilpin in London.

July 6: AN leaves Dublin for Belfast. AN stays with the Hewitsons in Rossgarrow, County Donegal, and travels on the Gweedore and Dungloe.

August 3: AN write to William Bennett. The letter is published in *Howitt's Journal*. AN visits Arranmore and Gweedore.

September 1: AN's "Destitution in Arranmore, Co. Donegal," is published in the *Londonderry Journal and Tyrone Advertiser*.

Fall: AN spends the rest of 1847 in Mayo—Newport, Achill Sound, Belmullet, Rosport, and the Erris peninsula.

December 2: AN's letter "Distress in Erris" appears in the *Tyrawly Herald and Sligo Intelligencer*.

1848   January: AN works among the poor in Achill and stays in Achill Sound and Newport.

February: AN spends the month in Ballina, where she meets Richard Davis Webb.

AN leaves Ballina for Castlebar.

Spring: AN travels from Castlebar to Louisburg, Murrisk, Tuam, and Galway.

June: AN arrives in Cork and stays until September, visiting Blarney, Castlemartyr, and Spike Island.

October 22: AN leaves Ireland from Dublin. She stays with Richard and Elizabeth Bennett at their home near Regents Park.

1849   April 5: AN leaves from London Bridge for Paris via Boulogne.

April 14: AN returns to Boulogne.

May 8: AN writes to William Goodell from 9 Elizabeth Terrace, Liverpool Road, London.

Late spring: AN visits Herefordshire and John Bunyan's cottage near Elstow.

July: AN travels from London to Southampton en route to the Isle of Wight. On the Isle of Wight AN visits West Cowes, Newport, Carisbrooke, Braiding, Arreton, Newport, Ryde, Needle Rock, and Newport.

July 21: AN signs the guest book at the Dairyman's Cottage.

1850   August 21: The *Illustrated London News* reports "Departure of English Members of the Peace Conference for Frankfurt-on-Main." AN in one of the delegates. She joins excursions to Heidelberg and Wiesbaden.

        Lights and Shades of Ireland is published by Stoneman, Paternoster Road, London.

1851   UK Census lists "Elizabeth" Nicholson in the home of Thomas Elgie, 119 Westgate, Thirsk, Yorkshire.

        April 1: American edition of *Lights and Shades* is published in New York by E. French, 135 Nassau Street, with an introduction by Joshua Leavitt.

        May 1: AN is present for the opening of the Crystal Palace Exhibition in Hyde Park, London.

        Winter 1851–52: AN visits Bristol. David Hatch dies in Chelsea at the age of seventy-five.

1852   April 30: AN arrives in New York aboard the *Cornelius Grinnell*.

1853   *Loose Papers; or, Facts Gathered during Eight Years Residence in Scotland, England, France and Germany*, printed by John A. Gray, 95–97 Cliff Street, New York, is sold at the American and Foreign Anti-Slavery Office, 48 Beekman Street.

1854   AN moves to 95 Erie Street, Jersey City, New Jersey.

        Winter 1854–55: AN experiences old spinal complaint.

1855   May 15: AN dies at 95 Erie Street. Her death certificate lists the cause of her death as typhoid fever.

        May 16: AN's funeral at the Dutch Reformed Church on Erie Street, Jersey City. Internment in Green-Wood Cemetery, Brooklyn.

Prologue

"NO, MRS. NICHOLSON, there is no letter here for you from America."

"I am sure a letter from New York was forwarded from Urlingford. May I see the postmaster?"

Robert Persse came from his office to see a woman wearing spectacles, dressed in a bonnet and a polka coat and carrying a parasol and large bearskin muff.[1] She explained that she had left Roscrea on October 29, 1844, and walked seventy miles from Roscrea in anticipation of receiving a letter from New York with funds for her that were forwarded from Urlingford. She arrived in Galway on Friday, November 5, with but four shillings and sixpence. If there was no letter, she would have to walk back to Urlingford. Mr. Persse told her that no letter had arrived.

Nicholson returned Monday morning. The post was scheduled to arrive at 11:40, but, once again, there was no letter for her. Although the sun set at 4:08 on that winter evening, Nicholson decided that she could not delay and set off on the road back to Urlingford. She trudged through the desolate countryside, slipping in the mud and clay track to Oranmore. Determined to reach Loughrea by evening, she plodded on for four miles until she sat down against a stone wall to rest her blistered feet and to wonder whether she would go on. She looked west toward the Atlantic, toward the life she had left in New York among her prudent friends, clergymen, and reformers who had warned her about her reckless plans to walk among the Irish poor.

> I there saw cheerful fires lighted; I saw friends gathered around them;
> I heard them say, "I wish I could see what Mrs. N. is doing tonight.

By this time she believes we told her the truth when we advised her to stay at home, and keep out of difficulties which she must unavoidably meet in a land of ignorant, reckless strangers. Pity she could not find enough Irish in New York to keep her busy, without going to that land of darkness. Well! She always would have her own way, and she must abide the consequences." I saw too my own once happy parlour lighted, and the books gathered for the evening: and did I wish to draw around the table, and participate in the enjoyment? I did not. No, I did not. Should I sleep the sleep of death, with my head pillowed upon this wall, no matter. Let the passer-by inscribe my epitaph upon this stone, fanatic, what then? It shall only be a memento that one in a foreign land loved and pitied Ireland and did what she could to seek out its condition. (*IWS* 2002, 135–36)

What were the forces that shaped the life of Asenath Nicholson and that informed her sense of divine mission to relieve the suffering of the Irish poor during the Great Irish Famine (1845–52)? An early influence was her plainspoken father, who shared his compassion for the Irish poor with his children. Nicholson's training and experience as a schoolteacher in rural Vermont and New York, in both Elizabethtown and New York City, established her principles about what schools owe their young students. When she became a health reformer, her study of nutrition gave her the practical experience that she used later to run her own soup kitchen in Dublin's Liberties. The austerity of her childhood on the Vermont frontier prepared her for the hardships of her travel through Ireland before the famine and for the deprivations of her life in Erris in the winter of 1847–48, the most wretched place in famine-stricken Ireland. Nicholson's commitment to social reforms, particularly to temperance and abolitionism, linked her to circles of activists in Ireland and England and provided outlets for her journalism and established the networks that she used to appeal to readers to contribute to famine relief. She wrote *Ireland's Welcome to the Stranger: or, Excursions through Ireland in 1844 and 1845, for the Purpose of Personally Investigating the Condition of the Poor* (1847) to raise awareness of the conditions in Ireland before the famine and *Annals of the Famine in Ireland in 1847, 1848 and 1849* (1851), which was published first as part 3 of *Lights and Shades of Ireland* (1851), to bear witness to famine suffering. When her mission was over, she spent four more years abroad before returning to New York in 1852, where she spent the remaining three years of her life. Nicholson's account of Ireland before the Great Irish Famine has been widely praised for the way it enlarges our understanding of Ireland in the 1840s. She not only recorded that history, but also helped to shape the history of those years.

The challenges of telling Nicholson's story were two: to reconstruct her life from the very few clues in her own narrative, in her other published writings, and in the scant sources that document her life and to contextualize her life in the history of the times—in Vermont, in New York, in Ireland, in Britain, and on the Continent. Mysteries remain, but they do not diminish the appreciation of this extraordinary woman and of her self-appointed mission to the Irish poor.

Compassionate Stranger

1

Puritan Beginnings on the Vermont Frontier

ON MAY 11, 1840, nearly 450 members of the American Anti-Slavery Society left Boston and boarded the chartered steamboat *Rhode Island* to travel to the meeting of the society at the Fourth Free Church in New York City. The delegation, organized by abolitionist William Lloyd Garrison, included a large number of women. They were headed for a showdown between the Tappan brothers' evangelical wing of the society and Garrison's more militant and radical contingent.[1] Tensions in the organization had been exacerbated by Garrison's introduction of women's rights into the abolitionist agenda in 1839, an issue that Arthur Tappan called "a tin can tied to the tail of anti-slavery" (Wyatt-Brown 1969, 173). When the Garrisonites carried the vote to seat Abby Kelley as a member of the society's business committee, Lewis Tappan, who had interpreted the American Anti-Slavery Society Constitution (1833) as allowing women to be *members* of the society but not to conduct the *business* of the society, left the organization with his supporters for the alternative American and Foreign Anti-Slavery Society.[2]

Asenath Nicholson's temperance boardinghouse had been the place that residents, including the Tappans, William Goodell, Joshua Leavitt, and others, discussed the plans that led to the founding of the New York and later the American Anti-Slavery Society.[3] Nicholson appears not to have been drawn to feminism; indeed, she quoted passages from Solomon and passages from Saint Paul's letters to Titus (11:4–5) that link woman's salvation to the discharge of her Christian duties to home and family. Her life, however, was never constrained by those conventions.

The American Anti-Slavery Society schism corresponded with the end of Nicholson's period of intense reform activities in New York City. She appears to have closed her temperance and vegetarian Graham Boarding House in 1842, the year *Longworth's American Almanac* listed her as the widow of Norman Nicholson. Friends had died or moved out of the city. She wound up her affairs in New York in the spring of 1844. It was time for her to realize her long-cherished ambition: to visit the Irish poor. What provided the stamina and self-sufficiency for a fifty-two-year-old woman to take on the physically demanding requirements of this singular journey? In part, it was her childhood in Chelsea, Vermont, a village carved out of the dense hardwoods and pine forests of the New England frontier in the White River valley of eastern Vermont, where she was born on February 24, 1792, the youngest child of Michael Hatch (1748–1830) and Martha Rice Hatch (1746–1837).

On August 4, 1781, the Republic of Vermont granted a charter for 23,040 acres of uncharted land north of Tunbridge to West Lebanon tavern keeper and land speculator Bela Turner and a group of seventy men who had acquired the land "for settling a New Plantation," a town they call Turnersburgh (Chelsea Historical Society 1984, 4, 277; see also Comstock 1944, 5–6). The charter promised that lands leased to settlers would require that occupiers would build a house that was at least eighteen square feet and cultivate at least five acres, and it called for families to settle on the land within four years (Chelsea Historical Society 1984, 4). Nicholson's parents were not listed among the names in the charter; however, because Chelsea was not actually settled until 1784, the Hatches could be considered a pioneering family in Chelsea. The town's Founder's File (1780–1858) lists a Michael Hatch of Ackworth, Cheshire County, New Hampshire, arriving on June 7, 1788, the year that the town's name was changed from Turnersburgh to Chelsea.[4]

Michael Hatch probably belonged to the group of pioneers headed by Thomas and Samuel Moore and Asa Bond who arrived from Winchester, New Hampshire, and settled in the center of what would become the village of Chelsea. While the Town of Chelsea records report that Hatch came from New Hampshire, Michael Hatch may have joined the other settlers there before they headed west to Vermont, because Hatch family tradition describes Michael and Martha Hatch as traveling to Vermont from Connecticut with their son David (1775–1851) and Peggy De Jersey, a woman who may have been a servant (Chelsea Historical Society 1984, 5).[5] The explanation for the different accounts may be that Michael Hatch spent the summer of 1788 felling the ash, beech, birch, and maple, the hemlock, pine, and spruce, clearing the underbrush from his land, and building a basic log cabin, work that was necessary before he could bring his wife and family to Chelsea. Michael Hatch's family probably came in the early spring of 1789, in time to plant their crops of wheat, rye, and oats. They walked or rode the nine miles north along the First Branch of the White River from Tunbridge, the closest settled village to the south, carrying their belongings on ox-drawn sleds or pack horses or on their backs.[6]

What was Michael Hatch's background, and how did it influence his youngest daughter? Kaye Hooley's history of Jacob Hatch and his descendants provides some information about Michael Hatch and his forebears.[7] According to her research, Michael Hatch descended from old New England stock. Merchant Thomas Hatch settled in the "Two Mile" section of Scituate, Plymouth Colony, about 1638. His son Michael Hatch (1712–84) married Priscilla Sprague of nearby Hingham in Scituate, Massachusetts, on February 10, 1732.[8] Priscilla Sprague's paternal grandmother was descended from Richard Warren (d. 1628), who arrived in Plymouth aboard the *Mayflower*. Michael Hatch, their ninth child and fourth son, was born in Scituate on July 21, 1748. Sometime between 1770 and 1774, the Hatches moved west from Scituate to Spencer, a town near Worcester, Massachusetts, where Michael and Priscilla died in 1784 and 1798, respectively. Michael and his brother John Hatch (1751–?) joined Captain Ebenezer Mason's company of fifty-six Minute Men who marched to Cambridge on April 19, 1775 (Draper 1860, 274). Michael served thirty days of active duty.

Asenath Hatch Nicholson's mother, Martha Rice, was born in Spencer, Massachusetts, on June 14, 1746. Rice is a common surname among the early settlers of the Worcester area. Michael and Martha were married in Worcester on October 13, 1773. According to Hooley, the Hatches probably left Spencer between 1777 and 1782, because Michael was living in Sturbridge, Massachusetts, when his father Michael's estate was probated in 1784. Michael Hatch headed north to the Vermont frontier four years later, in 1788.[9]

The first Vermont census of 1791, the year before Asenath's birth, lists the 227 residents of Chelsea by head of household. Michael Hatch's entry lists three males over the age of sixteen, two of whom were Reuben (1774–?) and David (1775–1851); three males under sixteen, Benjamin (1782–1843), Jonathan (1784–?), and Michael (1786–?), and four females, Martha (1777–1874), Sarah (1779–?), Rhoda (1782–?), and Peggy De Jersey (*Heads of Families at the First Census* 1903, 30).[10]

When a daughter was born the following year (1792), she was given the name Asenath. Although Asenath is an unusual name today, the Hatches often chose it for their daughters. Hatch family genealogy lists four other Asenaths in her own generation, and there are two Asenaths buried in Chelsea's Old Cemetery: Asenath Sanborn, who died in 1869, and her daughter Asenath, who died at twenty-one in 1852.[11] The name Asenath would prove prophetic. In the book of Genesis (41:45, 50–52, 46:20), the Pharoah gave Joseph an Egyptian wife called Asenath (she who belongs to or is the servant of Neith), daughter of Potiphera, priest of On (Heliopolis).[12]

By the time Asenath Hatch was born, her family was probably living in a log cabin roofed with elm or black ash bark.[13] It would have had a brick and stone fireplace with iron pots and kettles hanging from an iron crane.[14] Years later, in 1849, the chimney nook in John Bunyan's cottage in Elstow reminded her of her childhood home. "In the opposite corner was a little niche, under the long mantelpiece, evidently intended for a seat, where, in olden times, the contending urchins of a farmer's log cabin in New England were struggling to secure a warm seat for the winter's evening" (*LP* 1853, 196).

The Hatches' cabin would have been the center of Martha Hatch's world, the domain of the wife of a subsistence farmer. Her duties included managing the stock, the dairy, and the orchard; producing cloth and clothing from their sheep; bread making; sugaring; and soap making (Dodge 1987, 89–90). Aptly named for the Martha of the New Testament, when she died in 1837, at the age of ninety-one, Martha Rice Hatch left her daughter a model of persistent hard work and self-sufficiency, qualities essential for surviving in the early days of a pioneering community that practiced "warning out," a custom of discouraging settlers who were thought to be a burden on the community. The practice was serious enough to have been declared illegal in the town of Chelsea in 1817 (Chelsea Historical Society 1984, 7; Comstock 1944, 7).

Later, in 1847, when Nicholson was working among the poor of Dublin, she was grateful for her mother's example:

> Never before in all my privations in Ireland, had I tested the value of being early trained under the discipline of a rational mother, who fitted me, when a child, for the exigencies of life, who not only by precept taught me, that in going through the journey of this world I would meet with rough roads and stormy weather, and not always have a covered carriage, that sometimes I should have a hot supper, sometimes a cold one, sometimes a welcoming greeting and sometimes a repulsive one; but she had instructed me too, by precept and example, that my hands were to be employed in all that was useful and that idleness was both disgraceful and sinful. (*Annals* 1998, 53–54)

Nicholson reported in her 1846 edition of *Nature's Own Book* that her mother said, "The sun never looked down upon me in bed, when I was well" (35).

Nicholson was also influenced by her independent Yankee father, and she inherited her father's reputation for frank speech. In Thomas Hale's "Historical Address" to celebrate the centenary of Chelsea in 1884, he recalled a famous encounter, a Chelsea legend, between "Uncle Mike" Hatch and the governor of Vermont, Martin Chittenden (1763–1840).[15] Hatch was drawing a sled load of logs in deep snow. He was overtaken by a man driving a two-horse team who demanded that Hatch "turn out" and let him pass. Hatch told him that it was impossible and to wait until he reached his home, which was just ahead. The traveler insisted on trying to pass and found himself buried in deep snow. Hatch helped him out but told the driver that he was a fool and should not be let out on the road. "Perhaps," said the traveler, "you don't know that I am Governor Chittenden." "No, I don't," replied Uncle Mike. "Had I known it, I might not have spoken just as I did. But I can't in conscience take anything back!" (Centennial Committee 1884, 120).

The habit of direct speech lived in his daughter, who reported that her outspoken way frequently got her into trouble, including expulsion from the Protestant missionary colonies at Ventry and at Achill. Nicholson realized that her speech could cause trouble, but she insisted on using her plain speaking to press her issues of human rights and even human survival. With her own self-deprecating humor she warned the unnamed recipient, probably William Bennett, of her October 30, 1847, letter from Belmullet, County Mayo, that she would "be applying some of those 'offensive points' in my character which I so eminently possess," and in her frank way she called for land reform and employment opportunities rather than charity for the suffering Irish (*Annals* 1998, 100).[16] Nicholson realized her frank speech could get her into trouble, but she insisted on using her confrontational speech to address issues of human rights—later of human survival. Her outspokenness lasted a lifetime. In his appreciation of Nicholson written after her death, Henry Clubb described her friend William Bennett, "her best friend in England . . . [who] often reconciled to her those who had been offended by her style of address" (Clubb 1855, 31).[17]

The 1800 Vermont census reveals an expanded Hatch household: two males between the ages of ten and sixteen (Jonathan and Benjamin), two between the ages of sixteen and twenty-six (Reuben and David), and a man over forty-five (Michael Hatch). The females included a girl under ten (Asenath was eight), three women between sixteen and twenty-six (Martha, Sarah, Rhoda), one woman between twenty-six and forty-five who may have been Peggy De Jersey, and one woman over forty-five (Martha Rice Hatch) (*Heads of Families at the Second Census* 1938, 86).

David Hatch married Olive Wright (1777–1862) on September 7, 1800, in Chelsea. They may have set up their own household that year.[18] David and Olive's descendants lived on in Chelsea for six generations; they became some of the town's most prominent citizens.[19] Asenath Hatch's commitment to education and to Christian evangelism persisted into later Hatch generations. Two later Hatches were Christian missionaries. Franklin Samuel "Frank" Hatch (1846–1907), a Congregationalist minister, went to India with the YMCA, and Susan Hatch Mahoney (c. 1852–1948) was a missionary teacher in South Africa.[20]

David Hatch is listed among the Chelsea men who responded to the call when the British invaded New York in the War of 1812. The Chelsea Company started for Plattsburgh, but most did not arrive until the battle, fought on September 11, 1814, was over (Chelsea Historical Society 1984, 300).[21] Had David Hatch reached Plattsburgh in time, he would have fought with the foot soldiers of Captain John Calkins's company of Elizabethtown, New York, a unit that included Sergeant Norman W. Nicholson, the man who would marry his sister Asenath.[22]

The Vermont of Nicholson's girlhood was in the throes of social reform and religious fervor. The Hatches were probably members of Chelsea's Congregational Church, which was founded on April 10, 1789.[23] The congregation selected the conservative, zealous Rev. Lathrop Thompson as Chelsea's first pastor. He served six years, Asenath Hatch's impressionable childhood years between seven and thirteen. Installed in 1799, he was dismissed by his congregation in 1805.[24]

The Hatches' Christianity was broader than the Congregationalist doctrines of covenant and personal salvation, which emphasized Bible reading, individual freedom, and local congregational authority. The Hatches provided examples of tolerance and charity to their children. Michael Hatch "hung no Quakers, nor put any men in a corner of the church because they had a colored skin"; he also told his children that "the Irish are a suffering people, and when they come to your doors, never send them empty away" (*IWS* 2002, 1). Where would Michael Hatch have met the Irish? The seventeenth-century records for the town of Scituate, Massachusetts, mentions stolen Irish children working as indentured servants (Pizer 2004, 329). While Irish immigrants did not arrive in large numbers in Scituate until the nineteenth century, Michael Hatch may have known the descendants of these early indentured Irish in Scituate.

Hatch certainly would have met the Irish in Worcester, the descendants of Scottish planters in the Londonderry area who objected to paying tithes to the Church of Ireland and emigrated to Boston in 1718 and moved west. William Lincoln, the nineteenth-century Worcester historian, described the hostile experience these immigrants from Northern Ireland met in Worcester. "They were everywhere abused and misrepresented as Irish, a people then generally but undeservedly obnoxious" (1837, 48–49). Lincoln mentions that the Scots Irish were accompanied by "a few of the native Irish Young family who first introduced and planted here the useful potato" (1837, 49). There may have been Irish in Chelsea. Certainly, they were there by the middle of the nineteenth century, because the 1860 Chelsea census lists seven Irish-born males (Barron 1984, 89, table 5.8).

Nicholson's mother was equally charitable. Martha Hatch "remembered the poor and entertained strangers; hated oppression, scorned a mean act and dealt justly by all" (*IWS* 2002, 6). Much later Asenath described her mother's generosity to the poor with an allusion to Hebrews 13:2: "Be not forgetful to entertain strangers: for thereby some have entertained angels unaware." These words were to have a special resonance for her daughter during her later travels through Ireland when she found that the Irish poor lived the Gospel.

In 1811, when Asenath Hatch was nineteen, the Reverend Frederick Plummer brought the "Christians" to Chelsea. A passionate preacher and hymn singer, he attracted a large congregation and built a meetinghouse. The Christians later became the Methodists, and they held their first services in 1825 with a circuit-riding preacher; a minister was appointed for Chelsea in 1839 (Chelsea Historical Society 1984, 59). Based on her later practice of seeking out Methodist and

Baptist preachers and attending their services, it may be that Asenath was one of Plummer's converts. In any case, it would have been her introduction to evangelism. The Hatch children grew up in Chelsea village during its boom years when the population grew from 800 to 1,800 to its peak of 1,959 in 1840. After 1840 Chelsea's population declined until it leveled off at about 1,000 at the turn of the twentieth century. It remained an agricultural community of about two hundred farms (Barron 1984, 55).[25]

While Asenath Hatch Nicholson enjoyed robust health in her middle years, her letter of April 20, 1833, the first of the "Certificates," or testimonials, in praise of Sylvester Graham's vegetarian regime, the appendix to her second edition of *Nature's Own Book* (1846), describes Nicholson as a sickly child, the youngest child in the family who was kept in school longer than her siblings: "From infancy, my health was delicate, and violent fits of sickness were my lot through my whole childhood. Being inclined to study, I was kept constantly in school, and when at a proper age placed from home. Applying myself closely to study, exercising but little and eating the most hearty food, I was afflicted with a lassitude, especially through the summer, which kept me low, and unable to sit up through the middle of the day" (*Nature's* 1835, 52).

The expression "placed from home" usually means a girl placed into service; however, Asenath Hatch was probably referring to her career in Chelsea as a schoolteacher. In her case, "placed from home" may have meant that she boarded with farmers' families. The experience of living with different families in varied circumstances and becoming part of their households would have served her well in later years when she stayed in Irish rural cottages.

In Chelsea's early years of rapid growth, residents who had come from the settled towns of Connecticut and New Hampshire were concerned with providing schools for Chelsea's children. Asenath Hatch probably attended Chelsea's earliest school, the "schoolhouse on the branch" (Chelsea Historical Society 1984, 17). In 1801 eleven school districts and a grammar school in Chelsea village were established; in 1807, when Asenath was fifteen, Michael Hatch was listed as living in

District 2 (Chelsea Historical Society 1984, 280). Early on, Chelsea drew its teachers from their own school districts, but accounts of the village school do not explain how young teachers like Asenath Hatch were trained for the classroom. Later, Chelsea teachers may have been educated at Thetford Academy, Vermont's oldest private academy, but it was not founded until 1819. It is likely, then, that Asenath Hatch went to the grammar school in Randolph Center or was trained as an apprentice teacher, or as a monitor, in a District 2 school. She tells her reader in *Nature's Own Book*, that she began teaching at the age of sixteen (1808) in one of the schools in her own district (1835, 52).

The District 2 schoolhouse, the village school in Chelsea, did not open until 1811, the year work began on the present Congregational Church (Chelsea Historical Society 1984, 107). It would have been a simple structure, not the more imposing building dating to 1870 that reflected the importance the town gave to education. An old photograph of the renovated school shows the white-clapboard two-story building with a square tower. A porch at the gable end of the school facing the road shelters a central window and doors at each end of the building. It is very similar to the Methodist church that was built next to the Hatch homestead on the east side of Chelsea's Main Street, but the church had no porch.

The old Chelsea Academy built in 1852 has a Greek Revival facade, a pediment, and a portico with balustrade supported by four Doric columns. The academy provides a balance to the Chelsea village green, a gem of New England vernacular architecture that was placed on the National Register of Historic Places in 1983. The closest thing we have to a description of the District 2 schoolhouse was written in the 1850s by E. D. Redington, who described "the large room on the first floor of the old village school building . . . with a desk for the teacher at the south end and a great wood stove near the center" (Chelsea Historical Society 1984, 108). Asenath Hatch's school day was probably similar to her contemporary Emma Willard's.[26] There were Bible readings, lessons from Webster's *Spelling Book*, mathematics, geography, grammar, and needlework for older girls, who learned to hem towels and stitch samplers (Griffiths 1947, 8).

Later, Nicholson mentioned the titles and authors of works that influenced her as a young woman teaching children in rural Vermont. Like most of her contemporaries, she was raised on the Bible and on John Bunyan's *Pilgrim's Progress*, but in her later writing she mentions other works that moved that impressionable girl. Some were sufficiently important to her to be sites of pilgrimages when she visited Britain. Leigh Richmond's story "The Dairyman's Daughter," from *Annals of the Poor* (1814), a classic of Victorian pious literature, was a favorite book.[27] When she visited the Dairyman's Cottage on the Isle of Wight on July 21, 1849, she wrote in the guest book, "I find myself in the cottage where the Dairyman's Daughter died and the associations of youth again rekindle that which so vividly awaked on reading the touching sketch of her humble yet exalted life."[28]

Hannah More also influenced Asenath Hatch.[29] Both women started as schoolteachers; both shared a commitment to education and social equality, so Nicholson would have approved of More's *Strictures on the Modern System of Female Education* (1799). When Nicholson spent the winter in Bristol in 1851–52, she set out, unsuccessfully, as it turned out, to visit the sites associated with Hannah More in the area. While she praised Belfast's Linenhall Library for not having a single work of fiction among its eight thousand volumes, Nicholson herself read fiction with pleasure (*Annals* 1998, 79). Visiting the Scottish Highlands in August 1845, she recalled how she was enthralled by Sir Walter Scott's novels. "I was now in the region of scenes rendered sacred by those who have greedily devoured the fascinating descriptions of Walter Scott. Loch Lomond was but five miles in advance; and here, at the age of sixteen, I had formed picture after picture of undying beauties in the graphic delineations of 'Lady of the Lake'" (*LP* 1853, 67). She could have read *The Lay of the Last Minstrel* (1805) at sixteen (1808), but *The Lady of the Lake* was not published until 1810. The confusion is understandable because of the extraordinary success of *The Lady of the Lake*; by 1836 the book sold no fewer than fifty thousand copies.[30] Whenever she read Scott, she would have been taken by his romantic tales such as *Rob Roy*, tales often inspired by the stories of the country people he met while traveling through the Highlands.[31]

In the general preface to *The Waverly Novels* (1829), Scott acknowledged his debt to Irish writer Maria Edgeworth, whose portrayal of national character inspired him to try to capture Scottish Highland character in his fiction.[32] Curiously, Nicholson never mentions Edgeworth. No doubt she would have been tempted to call in at Edgeworthstown on her journey from Sligo to Dublin in June 1845, but she traveled by boat on the Grand Canal, a route that took her from Carrick on Shannon west of Longford through the midlands to Dublin. She certainly would have heard of the Edgeworths' reputation as improving, responsible, resident landlords. Maria Edgeworth herself managed her father's estates and used her experience visiting tenants' cottages in her novels and didactic writing. If she had read them, Nicholson would have approved of the essays Edgeworth wrote with her father, *Practical Education* (1798) and her own *Essays on Professional Education* (1809), and she would have found Edgeworth's *Castle Rackrent* (1800) a powerful moral tale of the failure of Irish landlords to take responsibility, observations that Nicholson herself made during her Irish travels.

Later, during the Great Irish Famine, Nicholson would have heard from her friends on the Central Relief Committee (CRC) of the Society of Friends about Maria Edgeworth's efforts to secure public works projects and other forms of relief for her tenants and about her concern that such measures not compromise tenants' dignity. Edgeworth's correspondence in the Famine Papers in Ireland's National Archives demonstrates a stewardship that Nicholson would have admired. When the *Macedonia* arrived with relief supplies from the United States, it carried food for both Edgeworth and Nicholson. Finally, Nicholson took pains to tell readers of *Annals of the Famine* about the women who worked among the poor during the Great Irish Famine. Why did she not mention someone as active in famine relief as Edgeworth?

Nicholson admired Scott's fellow poet Robert Burns enough to make a trip to Ayrshire, southwest of Glasgow, to Burns Cottage, the poet's birthplace near the River Doon in Alloway, where she confessed to having a certain nostalgia for the elegiac "The Banks of O'Doon,"

(1783), a poem Burns set to music. Nicholson had loved the song since she was a girl, so she sat down and sang a valedictory, "Ye banks and braes of bonny Doone," in memory of Miss Kennedy, the beautiful young woman who was seduced and abandoned by McDoual of Logan (*LS* 1850, 126).

She read the poetry of the popular nineteenth-century poet Felicia Hemans (1793–1835), who is probably best known for "Casabianca" ("The boy stood on the burning deck").[33] Describing the ancient two-handled sword associated with the Irish pirate queen Granuaile that she saw in the Howth castle, Nicholson misquoted, without attribution, the last stanza of Hemans's "The Sword of the Tomb: A Northern Legend" in her essay "Grana-uille and Her Castle." Nicholson changed the wording from "Sigurd's breast" to "Astmon's breast":

> That sword its fame had won
> By the fall of many a crest;
> But its finest work was done,
> In the tomb of Astmon's breast.
>   (*LP* 1853, 23)

Nicholson's admiration for Hemans's poetry was shared with her contemporary Horace Greeley.[34] Greeley said Hemans's poems were the first that awakened him to the power of poetry, and, in his enthusiasm, he placed her work alongside Lord Byron, Sir Walter Scott, and Edward Bulwer-Lytton. Greeley's biographer James Parton reminded his mid-nineteenth-century reader that poetry need not be of high literary value to make its mark on an impressionable adolescent (1855, 64).

When Nicholson needed to describe the young man who kept her from drowning on a dark, stormy November night in 1844, she turned to Henry Wadsworth Longfellow's lines from "Footsteps of Angels," "with a slow and noiseless footstep comes that messenger divine" (*LS* 1850, 48). As Nicholson had authors who were important to her throughout her life, as was her wont, she had writers she actively disliked. She confessed that she found Dickens "too tinctured with national prejudice" for her taste (*LP* 1853, 142), and when a "pert" Scot asked Nicholson what she thought of Mrs. Frances Trollope's

Domestic Manners of the Americans (1832), Nicholson replied that she had never read the book.[35] When the Scot quoted Mrs. Trollope's observations to speak of the "ignorant, filthy Irish" in America, Nicholson rounded on him: "He was told that the highest classes of the Irish who resided in America were the most intelligent and accomplished of any foreigners who visited our shores; and the lower classes, when treated kindly, were the most civil, and rose into respectability much more rapidly than any other nation" (*LP* 1853, 142). Although Nicholson allowed that Mrs. Trollope's description of chewing and spitting tobacco was accurate, she found that Scottish snuff takers were every bit as disgusting.

In addition to her teacher training and her spiritual and secular reading, Nicholson was a musician. Her fervent hymn singing probably started during her girlhood when Rev. Frederick Plummer organized a school to teach singing to his congregants. Singing was not only a form of prayer for Nicholson, but also a way for her to express the joy of the moment or to keep her spirits up. As she walked through Ireland, she often sang hymns like her favorite, Thomas Hasting's "Majestic Sweetness Sits Enthroned."[36] Although Nicholson was modest about her own abilities, she does tell her reader that gentlemen visiting Killarney hid in the rocks to hear her sing and praised Nicholson's sweet hymn singing to others (*IWS* 2002, 265). She also played the piano; she tells her reader that when she stayed with the curate and his wife in Clifden, County Galway, she was grateful when, thinking she would be lonely, they left her the key to their piano. "This little act of kindness said more for their true Christian hospitality towards a stranger, than money would have done" (*IWS* 2002, 300).

In the second edition of *Nature's Own Book*, Nicholson says she started to teach at sixteen (1808), and she described herself as putting in long days during the summer terms. It was the custom in Chelsea, as well as in other New England school districts, to employ women for the summer term only so that they did not have to endure the difficult winter travel and strenuous fire-building chores (Chelsea Historical Society 1984, 48). Asenath's contemporary Emma Willard also taught only during the summer, while men took the winter terms.

Despite what must have been fairly short sessions, Asenath's associates spoke of her effectiveness in the classroom. In his introduction to the American edition of *Annals of the Famine* (1851), J. L. (Joshua Leavitt) described Nicholson as "a native of Vermont, where she is extensively known, (by her maiden name of Hatch) as an able teacher" (1998, 23). Two generations later when she was long gone from Chelsea, in his address celebrating the Chelsea Centennial in 1884, Thomas Hale, who was taught by Nicholson when he was a schoolboy in 1815, remembered her as a "famous teacher" (Centennial Committee 1884, 78).

Given her success as a teacher, it may come as a surprise to hear that her dedication took a toll on her health. In "Certificate," her only sustained autobiographical statement, Nicholson described the poor diet, the lack of rest and exercise, and the coffee drinking that resulted in digestive problems, nervousness, heart palpitations, and high blood pressure (*Nature's* 1835, 53). A doctor advised that a boarding school might ameliorate her health complaints; this advice may have prompted her to leave Chelsea. Running a boarding school gave her the opportunity, "constantly observing some hundreds of scholars," to develop insights into the nutritional habits and academic performance of her pupils. After a few years, the physical complaints returned, and a sensible and sympathetic physician suggested that she relocate; thus, as she wrote to Sylvester Graham in 1833, she "came to this city" in May 1829.[37]

A reader of the autobiographical "Certificate," a testimonial letter in Sylvester Graham's *Asculapian Tablets*, is led to believe that Nicholson's health crisis took her directly from Chelsea to New York City. She does not mention the life-changing stop along the way: her years in Elizabethtown, New York, and her marriage to Norman Nicholson. There is no record of exactly when Nicholson went west to Elizabethtown, but, according to H. P. Smith, she was running a boarding school on Water Street by 1823 (Hand 1906, 490).[38] This Champlain Valley town, nicknamed "Pleasant Valley," the county seat of Essex County, is built on the east bank of the Boquet River in the lee of the high peaks of the Adirondack Mountains. The midway stop on the stage route between Westport and Lake Placid, the town is about a hundred miles north of Albany. Richard Lockhart Hand described Edward Tendean's "Hat Shop" as "the place where a private school was sometimes kept and religious services held at times"; however, in 1825 Samuel Williams was the hatmaker on Water Street in 1825.[39] The Baptists may have met at the school because there is a note in the Elizabethtown Baptist Church records that mentions a vote taken on April 5, 1823, "to leave the Church records with Sister Hatch so long as Church meetings are held at her house" (G. Brown 1905, 310).

Asenath Hatch met Norman W. Nicholson (1785–1839) in Elizabethtown. He was born to the farmer and blacksmith John Nicholson and his wife, Sarah Steele Nicholson, in 1785 in New Hartford, Litchfield, Connecticut.[40] By 1801 he had moved to Elizabethtown, possibly from Dorset, Vermont, where he served as the town's first postmaster.[41] A sergeant in Captain John Calkins's 37th Regiment of Infantry that fought in the Battle of Plattsburgh during the War of 1812, he was the unit's quartermaster (*Military Minutes* 1901, 1695).[42] Nicholson shared a law practice with Ezra C. Gross; both men served as justices of the peace in Elizabethtown.[43] Nicholson was also a town inspector between 1818 and 1820.[44] Norman Nicholson appeared on the 1820 Elizabethtown census as head of household that included three female members: a child under ten (Pluma), an adolescent under sixteen, and a young woman under twenty-six (Harriet Nicholson). He also was active in the Elizabethtown Congregational Church; his brother-in-law Dr. Alexander Morse was one of the church's organizers, and, in 1821, Nicholson himself was listed as one the church's thirty-two members (G. Brown 1905, 104–5). He later served as the first clerk of the church. His son George Sidney Nicholson continued the family tradition, serving as the treasurer of the Congregational Church in 1885.

Norman Nicholson's wife Harriett Frisbie Nicholson died on February 11, 1824. She was twenty-six.[45] A widower with three children who lived near Nicholson's school on Water Street, it is likely that his two older children, Pluma (1815–60) and George Sidney (1817–92), attended Miss Hatch's school. No doubt looking for a mother for his children, Nicholson married Asenath Hatch sometime after February 1824 and before April 6, 1826, when an Essex County deed lists Norman Nicholson and his wife, Asenath, as the individuals who sold a lot of one-third of an acre to Ira Marks for $550. Apparently, Norman and Asenath Nicholson had no children of their own. Aside from a single mention of the difficulties of being a stepmother, Nicholson never mentions Norman Nicholson's three children. She must have cared for her young stepson Henry Clinton Nicholson, who died at the age of seven years and seven months on February 3, 1827. Like his mother, he is buried in the Old Post Cemetery. Years later in Dublin, when the contents of Nicholson's trunk that was left with her landlady were robbed and sold, Nicholson missed only a silver spoon, "a blessed companion—it had become part and parcel of myself. Besides it was a true born American, and had an indenture made by an agonized child when in the act of taking medicine. Sacred relic!" (*Annals* 1998, 171). Was the child perhaps little Henry Nicholson?

Pluma, who never married, died of consumption at the age of forty-five in her brother George Sidney Nicholson's home on Water Street in Elizabethtown.[46] Perhaps George had returned to the home he had occupied as a boy. He lived until 1892 and is buried with his wife, Louisa Windsor Drown, and six of their twelve children in Elizabethtown's Riverside Cemetery.

Norman Nicholson may have married Asenath Hatch so that his children would have a stepmother, but the Nicholsons appeared to have shared an interest in the politics of the day. Records of appointments for town clerk, for constables, for school inspectors, and for highway supervisors made by Norman Nicholson when he served between 1822 and 1827 as one of Elizabethtown's three justices of the peace are preserved in the Essex County clerk's office, but Nicholson had political ambitions beyond Elizabethtown. Early in their marriage Norman Nicholson was the Clintonian nominee for clerk of Essex County. On the state level, the Clintonians backed Governor DeWitt Clinton, who opposed Martin Van Buren's Republican machine known as the Albany Regency or the Bucktails because they wore bucks' tails on their hats.[47] Local politicians like Gross and

Nicholson certainly would have objected to the Bucktails' patronage system, a system tied to the Masons that included the men on the Council of Appointments, which controlled most of the state's local offices. While Norman Nicholson had been a founding member, in 1818, of the Valley Lodge No. 314 of Freemasons, like other Clintonians, he may have become disenchanted with Freemasonry's Masonic privileges—the administrative appointments and bank-lending practices that favored insiders.[48]

The populist Anti–Mason Society became a political party in 1828, two years after William Morgan, a disgruntled Mason from Batavia, New York, published Masonic ritual secrets; his body subsequently turned up in the Niagara River. The event led to a steep decline in Masonic lodges, from 480 in 1826 to 22 in 1827, and it precipitated a campaign for banking reform in the state. Elizabethtown was not spared Masonic politics. In his *History of Essex County*, H. P. Smith reported that while the anti-Masonic excitement was very great in the town, he believed that no Mason renounced his allegiance; however, he wrote elsewhere that the Baptists were taken up with the Masonic question (1885, 320, 491). A meeting was held at the Baptist Church on April 10, 1828, to "investigate the principles of the institution of Masonry." The anti-Masonic forces were led by Captain John Calkins, the surrogate of Essex County. Whether "Sister" Hatch was still an active member of the Baptist congregation and may have taken an active role in this inquiry, the inquiry was so divisive that the church broke up in 1830 (H. Smith 1885, 491).[49]

While Elizabethtown debated Masonry in Essex County, the anti-Masonic forces in the state were drawing up charges against the Masons and pledging not to support Masons for public office. The movement developed into a political party under the leadership of Thurlow Weed, the editor of the anti-Masonic *Albany Evening Journal*. When Nicholson found her voice as a reforming journalist, it may have, in part, resulted in the anti-Masonic party's success at the poll in 1828, when Solomon Southwick, the anti-Mason candidate, received 33,345 (12 percent) of the popular votes for governor of New York; thirty-three anti-Masons were serving in the state legislature by 1833.

The anonymous author of Nicholson's obituary in the *New York Tribune* said of the efficacy of her anti-Masonic journalism, "It was *her* pen chiefly that made Solomon Southwick's paper, *The Albany Register*, the dread of the Masonic fraternity, and she became, as she believed, the object of long-continued and secretly conducted espionage and persecution on that account" (May 18, 1855). Nicholson did not write articles for Southwick's *Albany Register*; instead, she wrote for his *National Observer* (Albany). Although there are no signed Nicholson contributions to the *Observer*, the diction and references to particular passages of scripture in this unsigned letter from Essex County, dated March 13, 1828, are certainly hers, and it establishes Nicholson as an amazingly sure and confident polemicist:

> Mr. Southwick—Sir:
>
> There is a great hue and cry raised among us respecting the persecution which Masonry endures, the brotherhood giving the "grand hailing sign of distress" in every corner of our streets; and to borrow the words of another looker-on, must suppose, "all Bedlam or Parnassus was let out!" You, sir, they tell us, have set a political engine in motion, which has so frightened ignorant old men and silly women, that this fair handmaid to religion, can no longer sleep in our churches, without the past bitter persecution. The truth is this: some of us have had the daring boldness to read a little, and, on examining the tinseled lady, we do not altogether like her form and texture. She appears upon minute inspection to be "full of men's bones, and all manner of hypocrisy." She likewise proves fully to us, the truth of Timothy's words—viz—men shall be heady, high-minded, proud, false accusers having a form of godliness but denying the powers thereof. Masonry has long shrouded herself in the mantle of religion, enveloping ministers and private Christians, dazzling the multitude with her popish parade until she began to boast sitting godless of nearly the whole world. But the impious transaction at Batavia has "digged a hole in this world," and for further particulars, read the eighth chapter of Ezekiel. The Illuminists of France with their password—"crush the wretch" might

well claim affinity to these midnight conspirators; and it is from these abominable dens have issued our legislators, our rulers—and must be spoken, our ministers. Yes, many had, and still are renovating this well dressed popery with all the zeal of a St. Paul going with letters to Damascus. Many have been duped into a belief that Masonry is good, because so many ministers are members: but what are ministers? They are men with like passions of ourselves—some fond of popularity, some of filthy lucre and many "run before they are sent." Where there is any natural or moral impossibility that even the tongues of ministers, inured to such horrid oaths, as Mason take, should "madly defend them" by repeating the like: many a long sigh is drawn among us, because ministers who are Masons are treated with such disrespect. Let us examine—"Render unto Caesar the things that are Caesar's." If ministers are set as lights, as teachers, as guides, and have embraced sentiments, which to them are so peculiarly sweet, why hide this "candle under a bushel." If this be a part of their religion, why not preach the whole truth? If it be no, what right do they have to do it, it must necessarily follow that, if they are set as guides and connecting themselves with a secret clan of murderers, they are not entitled to equal respect with the ignorant and open immoral. Be not deceived: the lightness with which the ministers treat the murder of Morgan, is sufficient to strip them of all the dignity which was ever attached to their office.

To conclude, we do not suppose, sir, we have advanced anything new, our Only object is to show that Masonry possesses the same malignant spirit among us, as at the rest, that storm is loud, and Satan comes out with great rage because (we hope) his time is short.

We cordially wish your paper all possible success, as we are only 'Entered Apprentices.' Our desire is "light" and be assured it will be read with avidity until we see the Masonic inquisition, with all its implements of torture in full operation.

An excerpt from a letter written the following year, on May 27, 1829, also probably by Nicholson, titled "The Cloven Foot Out for Essex County," addressed the politics of the anti-Masonic movement and the antipathy of the writer toward Edwin Croswell, the editor of the *Albany Argus* and state printer:

> The Republicans of Elizabethtown are anti-Masonic almost to a man except for a few who have had the misfortune to get the cable-tow around their necks what Mr. Croswell may say is contrary not withstanding; and it is true that anti-Masons did prevent the election of one double-dealing jack as justice of the peace last fall, who declared himself an anti-Mason, and received a nomination from them, and at eve of the election, lent his name to the Masons and received the votes of both parties on the first day of the election and was defeated the last two days. It is by double-dealing fraud and deception that Masons sustain themselves. At the last town meeting they spent much time and rum, and brought forward even minors and Masons in this way did obtain a small majority. We counted 77 anti-Masonic votes out of 184 in this town. It was Masons who commenced the attack on people in this place, and they will repel the assault to their dishonor and shame. In one year past, in spite of their threatening and persecution, seventy-seven Freemen have declared themselves free and will ever be ready to sustain their rights.
>
> Now Mr. Southwick, since you and our old friend Croswell are neighbors, and follow the same profession, so have the goodness to tell him that he says that the anti-Masonic party is either the old or new federal party, because we do know, it cannot convert a republican into a federalist, to express himself against secret societies, kidnapping and murder and in favor of equal rights, and lest Mr. Croswell may say that we are ignorant on the subject, tell him likewise that we read his paper and of course cannot be misinformed. This kind of logic does not satisfy community; they are in fact what Mr. Croswell says they are, the old federal party. If the sage state printer does not stop his calumnies and abuse against his old republican friends, he may find himself out of the frying pan into the fire. More hereafter from Elizabethtown.
>
> An Anti-Mason

This letter suggests that Croswell was something of a bête noire for Nicholson and that she may have been the author of a number of critical, unsigned articles responding to Croswell and to articles in the *Argus* that appeared in the *Observer* in 1829.

Nicholson's anti-Mason journalism may have come with a price in a town that had experienced active hostility about the anti-Masonic agitation. The experience of John Calkins, the Elizabethtown anti-Mason agitator, may have been a cautionary tale for the Nicholsons. When the Masons regained their control, it was said that Calkins was "run out of town" (G. Brown 1905, 319).[50] If Asenath Nicholson was involved with the local Baptist investigation of the Masons as well as writing for Southwick, the Nicholsons may have been pressured to leave Elizabethtown. We know from an Essex County Poll List that Norman Nicholson was in Elizabethtown in 1829; however, Ezra Gross's sudden death on April 9, 1829, a political as well as personal loss for Norman Nicholson, may have led to their departure from Elizabethtown. Nicholson herself makes no mention of local politics. Instead, she attributed the move to New York to her health. She describes herself as suffering from the clinical symptoms associated with the kind of illness, labeled hysteria, that was common among middle-class women in the nineteenth century. If this was the case with Nicholson, what were the causes? Was it her anti-Masonic crusade? Did her reforming journalism interfere with her school? Was her marriage troubled? Did she find the burden of stepchildren overwhelming? Perhaps, as earlier, it was a sensible and sympathetic physician who advised a change.

Nicholson told the diet reformer Sylvester Graham that she "came to this city" in May 1829.[51] The following year, in the 1830 census, Norman Nicholson was listed as a merchant and head of household in New York City's Ninth Ward. He would have been about fifty years old, and he had given up his life as a successful lawyer and civic leader in Elizabethtown for a new start in New York City. He had uprooted his children who had lost their mother and their little brother within five years. This decision to come to New York may have caused later stress in the Nicholson marriage. The 1830 census and New York City directories list Norman Nicholson as head of household until 1835, but he seems to have maintained his ties with Elizabethtown. Neither Norman Nicholson nor his children appeared to have settled in New York, but for Asenath Nicholson, the city was a new beginning. She arrived as a teacher, but she became a reformer, an abolitionist, a writer, and an advocate for the Irish poor.

2

Social Gospels, Garrets, and Cellars
The New York Years, 1831–44

WHEN NICHOLSON ARRIVED in New York in 1829, she was thirty-seven years old. She had been a wife and a stepmother of three children for three or four years; she had been a very successful schoolteacher and had achieved some notoriety as a journalist who had fearlessly challenged the Masonic hegemony. Although she may have been harassed and hounded, she had found that she had a persuasive pen and that there would be other causes to champion. She started her New York life in her household at 3 Sixth Avenue, a house on the eastern edge of the city's Ninth Ward, in her familiar role as a teacher in charge of her own boarding school.[1] The 1830 census numbered three boys and four girls five to fifteen years old living at Nicholson's. Two youngsters were the Nicholsons' teenagers; the others may have been Nicholson's pupils.[2] She was identified as a schoolteacher just once, in Thomas Longworth's *Longworth's American Almanac, New York Register and City Directory* for 1831–32, but by that time she was writing for the weekly *Genius of Temperance* (1830–33), edited by the abolitionist and temperance advocate William Goodell (1792–1878), who had come to New York in 1830. He edited the *Genius* with Prudence Crandall (1803–90), the Quaker schoolteacher credited with the first integrated classroom in the United States. Nicholson was one of their contributors.[3] When Goodell later started the *Female Advocate* (1832–33), with his wife, Clarissa Cade Goodell, a founding member of the Female Moral Reform Society, Nicholson became one of their principal writers.[4]

24

Her work with Goodell may have been her introduction to a circle of clergymen and reformers with whom she would be associated in New York in the 1830s: Charles Wheeler Denison, Sylvester Graham, Horace Greeley, Simeon Jocelyn, John M'Dowall, Arthur and Lewis Tappan, Joshua Leavitt, and Henry Clarke Wright.[5] These ten men shared similarities with Nicholson. Nine were born and or reared in stern, serious New England households; four men shared Nicholson's Congregational background, and four were raised as Presbyterians. Seven started life working as apprentices in the trades or in business. At least six struggled with periods of failure. Six were ordained ministers, while three others were active in Christian reform organizations. Six of the men were active in temperance organizations; eight of the ten men were ardent abolitionists. Like Nicholson, all were evangelical Christians who believed that the commitment to reform causes was the way to personal salvation. They inherited that shared sensibility of salvation from the eighteenth-century Puritans' recognition of covenant, the "cornerstone of the Congregational church in New England," that informed the early settlers' "errand into the wilderness," a theological and political compact fundamental to establishing a just, religious society in New England (Miller 1956, 21). These nineteenth-century New England reformers were united in their uncompromising principles and sustained focus on social reform. Although Nicholson shared their commitment and vision, her challenge was to be accepted into their society. Her solution was as original as it was providential.

When the Nicholsons arrived in New York in 1829, the city, which had experienced a population increase, was on the brink of a decade of growth and change. The population grew from 152,000 to 242,000 from 1820 to 1830; it increased during the next decade by nearly another 150,000 residents, to 391,000. The Port of New York's "forest of masts" was located along the East River, and the old elite residential neighborhoods surrendered to the demand for the commercial premises in the city center; the city began its move north. The Nicholsons' boardinghouses met the housing demand for the young men who came to seek their opportunities in New York.

Nicholson's initiation into active reform work probably began with her involvement with John R. M'Dowall, a sensitive, high-strung young Presbyterian minister who went to New York in September 1830 to work among the poor and to establish a Sunday school in the Five Points, the densely packed slum at the intersection of Baxter, Park, and Worth Streets in the city's notorious Sixth Ward. His real mission, however, was rescuing fallen women. M'Dowall accepted silk importer, reformer, and philanthropist Arthur Tappan's invitation in 1831 to be chaplain of the New York City Magdalen Society. M'Dowall had worked for Tappan in Rhode Island as an agent for the American Tract Society in 1829.[6] M'Dowall began to work to reform "the depraved and abandoned females of the city" with a zeal that was surpassed only by his morbid fascination with vice (Wyatt-Brown 1969, 65). It was probably Joshua Leavitt, editor of the *New York Evangelist*, who warned its readers that unless something was done immediately for the estimated 10,000 prostitutes in the city, "multitudes will be immolated on the altar of the destroying demon of debauchery."[7] M'Dowall answered the call, and Nicholson was probably one of the individuals who gathered to pray with him before going into the Five Points.[8]

The same year that M'Dowall founded his Magdalen Society, William Goodell invited New England temperance crusader and dietary reformer Sylvester Graham (1794–1851) to lecture in New York in June 1831. The visit by the man Ralph Waldo Emerson called "the apostle of bran and pumpkins" transformed the Nicholsons' lives. Graham appeared at Clinton Hall, the venue for public lectures and mass meetings named for New York governor DeWitt Clinton that was located at the corner of Nassau and Beekman Streets. As the general agent for the Pennsylvania Temperance Society in 1830, Graham had found his vocation as a health reformer and had developed into a compelling speaker. He believed that man's and woman's fall in the Garden of Evil was not only spiritual but physical. He called for abstinence from tea, coffee, and hot chocolate; a vegetarian diet; early rising and bedtime; daily bathing with cold water; regular exercise; and sexual hygiene.

It is likely that Nicholson heard Graham when he gave his first New York lecture on June 9, 1831, a lecture that "ladies as well as gentlemen attended" and found highly interesting.[9] His round face with a crown of curls around his high forehead, his steady gaze, his straight nose, and his firm mouth combined with his gift for passionate, extemporaneous oratory would have made Graham a success as a public lecturer on any number of subjects, but his message about dietary habits and sexual practices was riveting to his listeners. Women were known to faint when they heard his sexual advice. He argued that marital excess was as bad as masturbation or even adultery and that sexual activity, even sexual excitement, could lead to pain and disease (Nissenbaum 1980, 30). Graham advised abstinence. After 1834 he toned down his sexual advice and, instead, concentrated on his vegetarian diet regime.

Graham's message affected Nicholson profoundly. Describing an experience like Saint Paul's on the road to Damascus, Nicholson summoned the words of the prophet Habakkuk, "I *heard and trembled* (3:16)," which described the moment that she was converted to Graham's reform regime. "The torrent of truth poured upon me, effectually convinced my judgment and made me a convert" (*Nature's* 1835, 53). A strict temperance observer since childhood, her own demon was caffeine—coffee—not alcohol. When Graham preached that caffeine too was unnatural and was poison to the system, she gave it up immediately and described the cold-turkey withdrawal symptoms she suffered the next day during Sunday services. "*That* Sabbath will never be forgotten: a numbness and stupor came over me, and during the morning service I actually feared my rash resolve would cost me my life" (*Nature's* 1835, 54). She suffered a further fortnight of acute discomfort before her body adjusted to the Graham regime.

Caffeine free, she set off with a basket of provisions: apples and crackers, presumably Graham crackers, by steamboat for Vermont to visit her family in Chelsea. Her father had died the summer before (August 1830), in his eighty-third year. He is buried in Chelsea's Old Cemetery on the Main Street hillside. His tall gravestone is decorated with the traditional mortuary motifs of the times: a funeral urn framed by a weeping willow. The epitaph is a quatrain from Samuel Woodworth's "On the New Year":

> Incessant rapid roll the wheels of time
> Year after year in swift succession speeds
> How short man's race from infancy to prime
> From prime how quickly decrepit age succeed.
> (*Ladies' Literary Cabinet* 1820, 57)

Nicholson's mother, Martha Hatch, lived on for another seven years, probably in her son David Hatch's household. After Nicholson's visit, David Hatch built a new home in 1836 on the site of the old Hatch homestead at the north end of Chelsea's Main Street, now State Highway 110. Known locally as the Hatch House, the structure still stands beside a wood-frame one-and-a-half-story cottage, the home of the Chelsea Historical Society. Its gable faces Main Street, and its front door faces the Hatch House. Hatch may have built the cottage for his widowed mother or for one of his children. In addition to visiting her mother, Nicholson would have become acquainted or reacquainted with David's children: Harriet (twenty-nine), Samuel (twenty-five), Susan (twenty-three), Olivia (twenty), Lucia (seventeen), and Caroline (twelve). The three younger girls would die as young women, between June 1841 and February 1843.

Refreshed by her visit to Chelsea, Nicholson returned to New York and set off again by boat through the recently opened Erie Canal to the west. One of her stops would certainly have been the Oneida Institute, located along the canal in Whitesboro, a village four miles west of Utica in the Mohawk Valley, the heartland of the "Burned-Over District," the area of central New York west of Albany that experienced fervent evangelical revivalism in the first half of the nineteenth century (Cross 1950, viii).[10] Founded by Rev. George Gale in May 1827 as the Oneida Academy, the school prepared young men in the "Presbygational" tradition, the combined efforts of the Presbyterians and Congregationalists to train missionaries to work with Charles Grandison Finney to minister to settlers in the newly opened territory of the Western Reserve.[11] The academy became chartered as the

Oneida Institute of Science and Industry in 1829 (Sennett 1956, 79, 81, 87, 88).[12] By the time Nicholson arrived in 1831, the institute campus was situated on more than one hundred acres bordered by Main Street and the Mohawk River and by Ellis and Ablett Avenues in Whitesboro village, and their campus had grown to three large buildings: a cupola-capped two-story central hall flanked by two identical three-story buildings, probably student rooms.

To reduce the cost of attending the institute, the school combined study and manual labor, thereby making education available to poor boys. The founders also believed that such a regime helped students fight temptation with physical exercise. Later, in 1833, radical abolitionist Beriah Green succeeded Gale and served as the institute's president until it closed in 1844 for financial reasons, caused, in part, by the New York Anti-Slavery Society's failure to pay the institute for the printing costs of their paper *Friend of Man*. Under Green's leadership, the institute became a center for immediatists, the abolitionists who advocated an immediate end to slavery; it was the position that would be supported by the New York State and the American Anti-Slavery Societies. The institute educated the sons of radical reformers, including abolitionist Lewis Tappan's, with free black men. Nicholson could not have failed to have been impressed by the institute.

When she returned to New York from her journeys to Vermont and to the west in the late summer or early fall of 1831, she became a Grahamite reformer who promoted the regime in a temperance and vegetarian boardinghouse where Grahamite principles could be lived and tested. A notice announcing the opening of the Nicholsons' Graham Boarding House appeared in the *Genius of Temperance* on September 14, 1831: "A BOARDING HOUSE will be opened on the 20th at No. 3, 6th Avenue on GRAHAM's Plan of Living. Gentlemen wishing to avail themselves of this opportunity will be furnished with comfortable rooms and lodgings at two dollars per week." The advertisement ran through the autumn and winter of 1831: November 9, December 7, 14, and 28. During that time, she may have helped M'Dowall produce *Magdalen Facts* (1831), his pamphlet designed to warn New Yorkers of the vice in their city.

Graham returned to New York in the winter of 1831–32 to give two series of lectures at Clinton Hall and at the Mulberry Street Baptist Church and, no doubt, to inspect the Graham Boarding House. In January 1832, Nicholson organized her Graham Boarding House and wrote her treatise on vegetarianism titled *Nature's Own Book*.[13] The spring of 1832, however, was dominated by the Asian cholera pandemic that had started in India and spread westward to Europe and to Canada and south through Albany to New York City. New York mayor and diarist Philip Hone left a harrowing account of the news from Albany that the disease had reached Montreal with the arrival of Irish emigrants aboard the *Carrick*.[14]

Hone reports in his diary the first case of cholera in New York on June 26 and the spread of the disease through the city in July: 411 new cases between July 14 and 16 with a mortality rate of more than 50 percent (234 of 411). Those people who could, fled the city and stayed away until the danger was declared over at the end of August. By then 3,527 deaths had been recorded for the three months (July–September), with the highest mortality in the Five Points area, where many Irish immigrants lived. According to Hone's September 20, 1832, diary entry, the Irish not only suffered most but were also responsible for the plague (1927, 1:73).

While New Yorkers waited for cholera to reach the city, there were conflicting opinions about how best to protect residents from the disease. Graham believed he had the solution. In March 1832 he gave a series of talks called "Science of Human Life" in which he announced he would address the prevention and treatment of cholera.[15] More than 2,000 crowded into the Mulberry Street Baptist Church to hear him. According to Graham, healthy people could withstand the disease, but people whose organic systems had been so seriously impaired by prolonged exposure to artificial stimulation were incapable of responding in a natural way when irritated (Nissenbaum 1980, 94). M'Dowall had a similar opinion. He believed that licentious persons would be the most likely to be victims of the disease (Nicholson 1838, 198). A believer, Nicholson stayed in New York during the epidemic when most people fled. William Goodell sent his wife and children out of the city while he boarded with the Nicholsons (In Memoriam 1879, 24).

The following year the May 1833 *Longworth's Directory* lists Norman Nicholson as the proprietor of the Graham Boarding House at 79 Cedar Street at the corner of Nassau Street.[16] Nissenbaum describes Graham's boardinghouses as opening in 1833 under his name but not under his direction (1980, 142); he calls it "a private residence that had been converted into a temperance hotel where men, not women, could go for the Graham cure."[17]

One gets some sense of the regime at Nicholson's Boarding House from Sylvester Graham's "Rules and Regulations of the Temperance Boarding House in the City of New York" that appears as the preface to Nicholson's second edition of *Nature's Own Book*, a treatise on the Grahamite regime. Graham's rules included the hours for sleeping (10:00 p.m.) and waking (4:00 to 5:00 a.m., varying with the season), the kind of mattresses to be used (firm), and the direction that the window should be opened (from the top) at night, meal hours (dinner at 1:00 and supper by common agreement), and the approved diet for meals: raw fruits and vegetables and coarse-ground bread made from unbolted flour, daily washing with cold water, outdoor exercise, and the cultivation of a cheerful disposition.

In her comments to the "Rules," Nicholson took a harder line than Graham. Although he discouraged meat, he allowed the occasional use of one kind of meat (rarely pork), cooked simply in its own juices. Nicholson denounced any meat eating as promoting moral obtuseness and irrationality and cited Genesis to support her argument that flesh eating was not only unnecessary and unnatural but also at odds with Divine law (*Nature's* 1835, 29).

Graham allowed that the sweetest and best butter might be used sparingly but never so as it could be melted. Graham called butter "questionable"; Nicholson prohibited it, citing the work of physiologist Dr. William Beaumont to bolster her argument (*Nature's* 1835, 31).[18] Years later, Irish Quaker diarist Alfred Webb recalled her warnings about butter and the mischief his cousins practiced on their American visitor: "Butter was her peculiar aversion. She told a story of her or some friend examining the intestines of some deceased patient and finding them choked with butter. Our 'Dunville' cousins there in the North considered she ate too many gooseberries in their garden and used to pull them, filled them with butter and replaced them on thorns on the trees in hopes she would light on them."[19]

Graham also advocated a simple diet, counseling that mixed dishes should be avoided and that a variety of dishes should be eaten from meal to meal. Nicholson called for a disciplined palate, discouraged mixing food at the same meal, and encouraged limiting one's appetite and occasionally fasting. On a spiritual level, these measures reflected her maxim that "our bodies are a living sacrifice" (*Nature's* 1846, 14, 23, 96). On a practical level, she used a majority rule by the boarders to establish what limited varieties of food would be offered at a particular meal "to protect the keeper of the house from unreasonable and capricious demands," adding that "the capriciousness of boarders know[s] no bound if indulged" (*Nature's* 1835, 24).

Nicholson cited Deuteronomy 23:10–15 in her interpretation of Graham's rule about cleanliness: a cold wash daily and a tepid bath once a week and three times a week in summer, and she added her own directives about housekeeping, especially the requirement that the kitchen be kept clean. "A dirty kitchen is like a dirty heart" (*Nature's* 1846, 57, 58). To Graham's recommendation that boarders cultivate cheerfulness, Nicholson added a quotation from Scottish lawyer and phrenologist George Coombe, urging the habit until "the heart feels a happy content in all the vicissitudes of life" (*Nature's* 1835, 38–39).[20] Nicholson commented in great detail about the Graham regime: temperance, diet, sleeping conditions, cleanliness, and exercise; however, a woman of her times and sensibilities, she was absolutely silent in *Nature's Own Book* about Graham's advice about sexual practices, the subject of his *Lectures to Young Men on Chastity* (1834).

William Goodell's biographer described the reformers living at the Graham Boarding House after the 1832 cholera scare: "It was at this time that Mr. Goodell, together with Lewis and Arthur Tappan, and other temperance reformers became interested in the lecture of Sylvester Graham and partially followed his teaching, giving up tea, coffee, meats, and high seasoning and using the unbolted (or Graham) flour bread.[21] They boarded for a considerable time at the Graham boarding house kept by Mrs. Nicholson, at which Horace Greeley, then a bashful young man, saying little or nothing imbibed anti-slavery principles from the conversation of those around him" (In Memoriam 1879, 25).

William Goodell's testimonial letter for Nicholson's second edition of *Nature's Own Book* describes living at Nicholson's for two years, probably 1833 to 1835. Greeley's biographer James Parton describes Greeley's conversion to Grahamism and how Greeley found his way to Nicholson's because it was run on Graham principles (1855, 149). Living at Nicholson's, Greeley must have overcome his bashfulness, because he met his schoolteacher wife, Connecticut-born Mary Young Cheney, there. They were married on July 16, 1836 (Parton 1855, 165).

Encouraged by Joshua Leavitt's promise to assist him, M'Dowall replaced the *Magdalen Tracts* (1832) with its emphasis on fallen women with *M'Dowall's Journal* (1833), a publication that sought to rid the city of vice by publishing the names of the prostitutes' patrons in its pages. He knew this initiative would put him at risk; "gentlemen of high standing" whom he had met in his researches in houses of prostitution had "sworn revenge if he ever exposed their character" (Nicholson 1838, 207). Nicholson would have been reminded of her own harassment when she attacked the Masons. A New York grand jury called *M'Dowall's Journal* a public nuisance; politicians and the popular press demanded its suspension. When the *Journal* ran out of money later in 1833, printer Daniel Fanshaw pledged the financial support to continue the *Journal* to the end of the year (Nicholson 1838, 216).[22]

While the M'Dowall crisis developed, Nicholson's Graham Boarding House became the center of an even more controversial reform movement, the New York Anti-Slavery Society. William Tyler's October 10, 1833, letter to his brother Edward provides details about life in the Nicholson Graham Boarding House that the Amherst College tutor observed when he stayed with the Nicholsons while visiting New York:

> But I forgot to tell you where I put up in the city. You have heard of the Graham Boarding House, & what they live on there. I went immediately to that house & engaged board and lodging over the Sabbath. That I was to be served with no tea or coffee, I learned from a sign in front of the house which contains the following inscription, "Temperance Boarding House. No Alcohol, Tea or Coffee." Soon after entering the house, I found that the "Tabu" which proscribes tea & coffee extends also to chocolate, hot water & all other hot drinks. The only bread stuff used is coarse wheat meal unbolted & unsifted. Of this they make their bread & their crackers & their puddings & their gingerbread, and they *would* make their pies of it if they *ate* any. Samp is a common dish. Ripe fruit of some kind is always on the breakfast table. *Something warm* is always provided in the morning. If they do not have a warm wheat or Indian pudding, a tepid gruel is prepared to drink.
>
> The only other drink is cold water or milk. The Boarders in this establishment are not only Grahamites but Garrisonites—not only reformers in diet, but radicalists in Politics. Such a knot of Abolitionists I never before fell in with. Slavery, colonization, constitute the unvarying monotonous theme of their conversation expect that gives place to an occasional comment on their peculiar style of living. Arthur Tappan, Goodell, & Dennison are the most prominent characters. Arthur Tappan, you know, as a zealot in everything good, in some things bad and in many things indifferent. You may be at a loss to reconcile his choice of so frugal a boarding house with the known extravagance of the furniture & style of living at his own house, but remember the *wife* rules *at home*. Goodell is Editor of the Genius of Temperance & of the Temperance Agent-Dennison, of the Emancipator. Both are flaming abolitionists. Garrison & Leavitt are sometimes at the Graham House & then only the presence of Mr. Thatcher is wanting to complete an Editorial corps, as unique

as radical, and as uncourteous, as the world ever saw. (Le Duc 1939, 190–91)

Tyler identified Charles Wheeler Denison, William Goodell, and Arthur Tappan as Nicholson's boarders. Denison edited the *Emancipator* in 1833–34; Goodell would edit the American Anti-Slavery Society's *Emancipator and Journal of Public Morals* in 1834–35, and Arthur Tappan would shortly found and serve as the first president of the New York Anti-Slavery Society. "Mr. Thatcher" is probably a reference to Benjamin Bussey Thatcher, a historian and antislavery advocate but not an abolitionist.[23]

Just a week before Tyler wrote his letter, Philip Hone wrote in his diary on Thursday, October 3, 1833: "A notice appeared in the papers of yesterday signed by Joshua Leavitt, Wm. Goodell, Wm. Green, Jr., John Rankin and Lewis Tappan, calling a meeting of the 'Friends of Immediate Abolition of Slavery in the United States' at Clinton Hall last evening. I expressed great dissatisfaction that the Hall should be let without my approbation for any purpose not immediately connected with the objects of the institution, and my decided opposition to its being used for the agitation of this most mischievous question" (1927, 1:102).

In his study of Lewis Tappan, *Lewis Tappan and the Evangelical War against Slavery*, Bertram Wyatt-Brown suggests that Hone disliked the Tappans because they criticized his part in the city's monopolistic auctioneering system and that there was a resentment of New England reformers, particularly by the Tammany leaders, who had attacked the Tappans' support of M'Dowall (1969, 68). To avoid a confrontation at Clinton Hall itself, the Tappans quickly moved the abolitionist meeting to the Tappan-funded Chatham Street Chapel. While the Tappans and their associates quickly adopted a constitution for the New York Anti-Slavery Society and elected Arthur Tappan its president, their adversaries adjourned to Tammany Hall, where they assembled under the chairmanship of General Robert Bogardus to pass their own resolutions condemning the abolitionists (P. Hone 1927, 1:102).[24] Although there was no violence that night, a line was drawn between the abolitionists and their opponents that warned that further confrontations would not be peaceful.

Later in 1833 or in early 1834, the Nicholsons left Cedar Street for another premises at the corner of Wall Street and Broadway. Paul F. Berdanier's etching based on a sketch by Hugh Reinagle depicts that corner from the front of Trinity Church in the winter of 1833–34. Four-story buildings combining commercial and residential premises face one another across Wall Street.[25] In the foreground of Reinagle's sketch, a horse-drawn sleigh moves north on Broadway, outpaced by a dandy in a cocked hat driving his lady in a cutter with a bird carved on its prow. It is a lively street scene of promenading New Yorkers: men in silk hats and tail coats and women in broad-brimmed hats and tight-waisted coats and dresses; men buy and transport wood; dogs race with horses in the snow-covered street. Wall Street was still residential; however, the thirties brought changes: commercial premises were moving into the ground floors and leaving the upper stories for offices and what Charles Lockwood called "fashionable boarding houses" (2003, 25). The entire area would be swept away by the great fire of 1835.

In the spring or summer of 1834, Elihu Parsons Ingersoll, a Graham disciple who later became the first professor of sacred music at Oberlin, visited Nicholson's Boarding House. Perhaps he had come to New York to call on Oberlin benefactor Arthur Tappan to discuss an impending crisis at the Lane Seminary.[26] As part of the plan to evangelize the Western Reserve, Arthur Tappan gave the money to found the Lane Seminary near Cincinnati. In the spirit of their benefactor, the Lane students formed an antislavery society in 1834 that called for an appeal to slaveholders through the Gospel. They also began to implement practical antislavery principles such as starting a school for African Americans in Cincinnati.[27]

While Cincinnati simmered, tension over abolitionists' activities was increasing in New York. Resentment mounted against the Tappans and their abolitionist cause through the spring of 1834. By then there was not only a New York State Anti-Slavery Society but also an American Anti-Slavery Society, with Arthur Tappan president of the national as well as the state organization. By the summer of 1834, there were riots in the city, and Lewis Tappan's home was attacked on July 7 (Wyatt-Brown 1969, 117). Hone believed that the abolitionists' meetings sparked the riots.

> There has been of late great excitement in consequence of the proceedings of a set of fanatics who are determined to emancipate all of the slaves by a *coup de main*, and have held meetings in which black men and women have been introduced. These meetings have been attended with tumult and violence, especially one which was held on Friday evening at the Chatham Street Chapel. Arthur Tappan and his brother Lewis have been conspicuous in these proceedings, and the mob last night, after exhausting their rage at the Bowery Theatre, went down in a body to the house of the latter gentleman in Rose Street, broke into the house, destroyed the windows and made a bonfire in the street. The police at length interfered, rather tardily, I should think; but the diabolical spirit which prompted this outrage is not quenched, and I apprehend we shall see more of it. (1927, 1:134)

Mayor Cornelius Lawrence put the city under martial law and called up the militia; however, it was known that the rioters would be handled with leniency (Wyatt-Brown 1969, 118). A mob of some two thousand from the Five Points attacked black churches and the homes of African Americans in the Five Points and on Mulberry Street. They also rampaged down to Hanover Square and to the Tappans' business premises, a three-story granite building at 122 Pearl Street, near Hanover Square. Knowing that they could not count on the militia, Arthur Tappan distributed arms to his clerks and friends who stood by them (Ziegler 1992, 61, 184n8).[28]

One friend was Rev. Simeon Jocelyn, minister to an African American congregation in New Haven, Arthur Tappan's closest friend, and the man Lewis Tappan credited with his conversion to abolitionism. In 1828 Arthur Tappan had purchased Samuel B. Morse's house on Temple Street in New Haven; Simeon Jocelyn was a neighbor. Tappan spent weekends in New York with his family but kept his Rose Street home in New York open. Rev. Simeon Jocelyn, who had come to New York for the abolitionist meeting, was in the Tappans' store on the night of the riot. He later recalled, "I was in the store part of the time, and also mingled with the crowd and heard the mutterings. 'These Tappans Arthur and Lewis always making trouble; they tried to get up Sunday mail laws, now they are engaged in abolition acts. It is time they were stopped'" (Tappan 1870, 222).

M'Dowall was also advised for his own safety to leave his home and to take down the sign from his office. He followed the advice but traveled around the city with the mob. When they reached M'Dowall's office, they left it saying, "This is M'Dowall's—ah, he's a *poor devil*— we won't hurt him" (Nicholson 1838, 233). It was a moment of respite for poor M'Dowall, who had been arraigned by the Third Presbytery on June 2, 1834, to answer charges about his *Journal* that included "financial mismanagement, unministerial conduct, misrepresentation and slander" (H. Davis 1990, 88).

There is no indication that the Nicholsons were subject to the rioters' wrath. Nicholson did not mention the trouble when she wrote to her fellow Vermonter and reformer John Jay Shipherd, president of Oberlin College.[29] Her letter of July 15, 1834, may have been prompted by Ingersoll's earlier visit; her purpose was to congratulate Shipherd: "The name [Oberlin] had ever been pleasant to me but have had no opportunity of learning its true history till Mr. Ingersoll visited my house. What you are doing there eternity will tell and O that your boarders may be enlarged, your means and zeal increased till your principles shall encompass the earth."[30]

She saw in Oberlin the application of her credo of "temperance in all things." The letter gushed with the enthusiasm of a convert. Ingersoll later wrote a Graham testimony, a letter to the *Graham Journal* in 1837, telling readers how he had conquered his appetite for butter, which he loved "as a drunkard does his brandy" (*Graham Journal* 1 [1837]: 143–44; *Nature's* 1835, 16; Fletcher 1971, 325). Oberlin adopted the Graham regime. David Campbell, who also operated a Graham Boarding House and edited the *Graham Journal of Health and Longevity* during its three years of publication (1837–39), became a steward at Oberlin with the responsibility of running the college dining hall along Grahamite principles.

When fiery British abolitionist and orator George Thompson visited the United States from September 1834 to November 1835, the unity of the abolitionist movement was tested.[31] Thompson had come to challenge the American attitude toward abolitionism that lagged behind the more progressive British, who had abolished slavery in 1833. Arthur Tappan cautioned that a public forum for Thompson would be imprudent; however, the Garrisonites, and even Lewis Tappan, thought Arthur's reticence was timid (Wyatt-Brown 1969, 132). Nicholson was an admirer of the charismatic Thompson. Years later, writing from Belmullet, County Mayo, on October 30, 1847, to her friend and benefactor William Bennett, she spoke about her sense of outrage about the suffering Irish poor. "I would take some half-dozen of your George Thompsons—if so many truly independent members you have—and would transport them through the waste lands of Erris, and seat them snugly around a boiler [a soup boiler] under full play" (*Annals* 1998, 97). In the end, Arthur Tappan's caution was justified when Thompson had to escape from a Boston mob aboard a packet to New Brunswick (Rice 1968, 13).

Thompson's presence in the United States through November 1835 exacerbated the strain between Tappan's cautious approach to abolitionism and William Lloyd Garrison's more radical campaign. All three men were immediatists who did not subscribe to the American Colonization Society's plan to resettle slaves in Africa. Instead, they advocated integrating slaves into a biracial society, but they differed about means. Tappan, a moderate immediatist, believed in using the political system to achieve abolitionists' ends; the radicals rejected the political system as "morally compromising" (Ziegler 1992, 6).

Although Garrison thought Arthur Tappan tepid, the Tappans' abolitionist efforts could still incite a riot. Lewis Tappan's pioneering direct-mail campaign to send antislavery literature to southerners was intercepted in Charleston, South Carolina, on July 29, 1835, where a mob broke into the Charleston Post Office and burned the mailing. Effigies of Arthur Tappan, Garrison, and others were hanged on a mock gallows before a crowd of three thousand (Wyatt-Brown 1969, 149).

While the abolitionists and M'Dowall were coping with fresh crises, domestic life for the Nicholsons was marked by another move. It is uncertain just when the Nicholsons left Wall Street for 118 William Street, but Asenath Nicholson, not Norman Nicholson, is listed in *Longworth's* as the proprietor of the William Street Graham Boarding House between 1835 and 1838 (1841, 518). It would have been unusual enough for a married woman to be listed as the householder in *Longworth's*. What did it say about the Nicholson marriage? Had Norman Nicholson left the household? He had come to New York with a schoolteacher wife some five or six years earlier, but during their years in the city his wife had become in turn a dietary reformer, a boardinghouse keeper, a crusading journalist, and an abolitionist. They shared their home with evangelical clergy and moral reformers. We know that his children left the city to return to Elizabethtown before 1840. George Sidney Nicholson, who had worked for Horace Greeley in New York, is listed in the 1840 census as the twenty-six-year-old head of a household that included his wife, Louisa Drown Nicholson (twenty-four), and a son, George Henry, who was born in 1839.[32] Pluma probably went back to Elizabethtown with George. Did Norman Nicholson leave New York with his children? The only clue to Norman Nicholson's last years is the fact that his name was removed from the rolls of the Congregational Church in Elizabethtown in 1839, which was the practice of removing the name of a church member upon her or his death. According to Harold Jessup's "Family Group Sheet for John Nicholson," John's brother Norman Nicholson died in Canton, New York, on June 2, 1839. His final years remain a mystery.

The reason for the move to William Street is clear enough. It moved the Graham Boarding House closer to the Christian evangelical heartland of the city. Nassau Street, one block north of William Street, housed, in a single block, the American Bible Society (115), the City Temperance Union (135), the Board of the Foreign Missions (142), the American Anti-Slavery Society (143), the American and

Foreign Evangelical Society (145), the Female Moral Reform Society (149), the Home Missionary and the American Tract Society (150), and the Sunday School Union (152). Daniel Fanshaw's printing office, which supplied Bibles and tracts, was located on William Street.[33] The proximity to printing and reform offices meant that men such as Henry Clarke Wright and other agents of the American Anti-Slavery Society (48 Beekman Street) could live nearby at Nicholson's Boarding House. Some of the antislavery agents would have been trained at Oberlin College by Theodore Weld, a graduate of the Oneida Academy, who later married Angelina (Nina), the younger of the abolitionist, feminist Grimké sisters.

Nicholson's premises at 118 William Street was located next to the Rigging Loft (120), the site where Irish Palatine Methodists from County Limerick under the leadership of Philip Embury, his cousin Barbara Heck, and Captain Thomas Webb met in 1766 for their first worship service in America.[34] By 1846, 120 Williams Street housed engravers and printers Doty and Bergen in a two-story frame building, with their shop at ground level. The two windows in the gable of the house facing the street created a break in a fairly unified streetscape of federalist houses along the east side of William Street. An 1848 engraving of 118 William Street is valuable because it shows the commercial premises at street level and a doorway at the left side of 118, which was the entrance to Nicholson's Boarding House upstairs.

When Nicholson and her boarders were settling into 118 William Street, Daniel Alexander Payne (1811–93) visited after attending the meeting of the National Reform Society in Philadelphia (June 1–5, 1835). It was Payne's first visit north from his native South Carolina, and he probably visited Nicholson at the suggestion of Joshua Leavitt, who attended the Philadelphia meeting. While Payne's description is based on his memory of his visit to Nicholson forty years earlier, it is, nevertheless, the first contemporary description of Nicholson herself as she appeared in New York in the spring of 1835:

> On my return, I stopped in New York at Mrs. Asenath Nicholson's Graham's boarding house. This lady was a devout Christian, in deep

sympathy with every movement leading to the amelioration of the condition of colored people and to the uplifting of the condition of humanity in general. She was also a woman of intellect and culture, and has written a biography of the first pioneer in the efforts to reform the abandoned women of New York. She was, as might be expected, in deep sympathy with the Oberlin movement of that day. At her boarding house I met that gifted man Theodore Weld, one of the most eloquent of the anti-slavery lecturers. He invited me to the Shiloh Presbyterian Church where at the request of the pastor, I preached. (Payne 1969, 67)[35]

Payne later became a bishop of the African Methodist Episcopal Church and was a founder of Wilberforce University, becoming its first president in 1863, the first African American college president in the United States. Shortly after Payne's visit, Nicholson made a trip to Boston. She probably called on Rev. John Pierpont to present her corrected and expanded second edition of *Nature's Own Book*, published earlier that year by Wilbur and Whipple. The New York Public Library owns that presentation copy, dated Boston, June 13, 1835, with the following inscription:

> Hearing that you are an able advocate [of] temperance, I take the liberty to send you this work hoping when you [have] candidly criticised [it], [you] will pass judgment. Good sense may (?)
> Respectfully,
> Asenath Nicholson

John Pierpont (1785–1866) was the pastor of the Hollis Street Chapel, an "Evangelical Unitarian" Boston church that welcomed those individuals too poor to afford to buy a pew. Whereas Maria Chapman went to hear the transcendental abolitionist Theodore Parker preach, her sisters disliked his mysticism and went instead to Hollis Street to hear Pierpont, until he was dismissed for his abolitionist sermons (Taylor 1857, 53). Pierpont was another of the clergymen that Nicholson admired, a minister turned reformer whose zeal was his undoing. Born in Litchfield, Connecticut, and educated at

Yale (1804), Pierpont was called to the Hollis Street congregation in 1825.[36] His first years at Hollis Street, when he confined himself to his pastoral duties, were peaceful enough; however, he began to take an interest in other things. His congregation had no objection to his poems and hymns. They did not become alarmed when he began tinkering with inventions: stoves, screws, and razor straps. Even his interest in phrenology seemed innocuous. It was when he turned reformer and thundered from the pulpit about temperance, anti-Masonry, the militia law, imprisonment for debt, and, above all, abolitionism that his congregation objected to his replacing scripture with the social gospel. Anne W. Weston wrote her sister on February 12, 1837, that Pierpont "has come out boldly and decidedly" for abolitionism.[37] Two years later the "Proprietors of Pews" in the Hollis Street Meeting House met on October 25, 1839, to discuss Pierpont's controversial ministry, and the majority vote against him on September 30 (*Proceedings of a Meeting* 1839, 12–23; Chaney 1877, 37–42, 49).[38] Anne W. Weston reported to Deborah Weston on October 1, 1839, that Pierpont was dismissed.

When a fire on August 12, 1835, destroyed buildings on Ann, Nassau, and William Streets, the Nicholson Boarding House appeared to be spared. While owners of residences and businesses were assessing their fire damage, the *New York Sun* ran a story on August 26, 1835, that developed into their hoax about men on the moon. The *Sun*'s stunt may have been a distraction for New Yorkers while the controversy over abolitionism with its threat of violence continued in the city. The same day that the moon hoax started, Philip Hone wrote with approval about an antiabolitionist public demonstration planned for the next day. Hone planned to attend "to reassure the South" but also to prevent violence, because he believed that the racial situation in the city was voluble because "in the present state of feelings the least spark would create a flame in which the lives and property of Arthur Tappan and his associates would be endangered" (1927, 1:173).[39]

Tappan and his property were spared in August but not in the great conflagration that began at a quarter to nine in a warehouse across from Tappan's business at 127 Pearl Street on the night of December

16, 1835, and continued until noon the next day. The extreme cold froze the fire hoses, and the sharp wind spread the flames quickly through the densely settled downtown of wooden buildings, destroying more than fifty acres of stores and warehouses of the city's principal merchants. William James Bennett's aquatint and etching *View of the Great Fire in New York, December 16 & 17, 1835 as Seen from the Top of the Bank of America, Corner of Wall and William Streets* (1836) shows the vain efforts of firemen to contain the blaze while what appears to be hundreds of spectators watch the conflagration. The "burnt district," which smoldered for five months, was such a tangle of bricks, stone, and metal that streets were obliterated and property owners were hard-pressed to locate their own lots (Tappan 1870, 272). While Nicholson was safe enough at 118 William Street, her friend Arthur Tappan's business was a casualty. Tappan's staff and friends were able to save two-thirds of his goods, and he was opened by noon the next day, a gesture that gave courage to other New Yorkers who suffered similar losses; however, the fire resulted in insurance bankruptcies and tighter money in the short run and the financial crash of 1837 in the long run.[40]

Along with the fire and the economic disruptions, there were changes in Nicholson's own circle of friends. In 1836 William Goodell moved his family to Utica, New York, where he started editing the *Friend of Man*, the weekly journal of the New York Anti-Slavery Society that was printed by the Oneida Institute in Whitesboro. The prospectus printed in the first number promised that the *Friend* would be concerned with temperance, gaming, and war as well as slavery, "all enemies of our race, closely allied to slavery." While Nicholson adjusted to the loss of a steady friend like Goodell, a fresh crisis developed for M'Dowall. He retreated to the Oneida Institute while the Third Presbytery considered the charges filed against him. In the end, they suspended M'Dowall and closed his ministry on April 30, 1836. Complaining that Arthur Tappan abandoned him, M'Dowall succumbed to exhaustion and tuberculosis. One of the few who stood by him was Asenath Nicholson, the "compiler" of his life who described his death later that year on December 13. While Nicholson does not identify herself in a ministering role, she may well have been the friend who calmed him with a hymn, and it is likely that Nicholson was the friend M'Dowall was anxious to see in order to ask her whether he might convene a group in her back parlor to read the Bible: "I have thought of asking you this favor, should the Lord raise me from this bed of sickness, to allow me to meet a few Christian friends in your back parlor, and with them spend an hour in reading the Scriptures, and praying for a blessing and a descent of the Holy Spirit, *and to read the Bible without note or comment.* I have selected that room because of its retirement and many Christians who resort there" (Nicholson 1838, 357).

M'Dowall's legacy to Nicholson was his commitment to the Gospel: "How simple the gospel plan on missions: 'Go preach my Gospel, saith the Lord;' not go and form societies to support missionaries; but go ye who would form societies; go ye, also, and preach my Gospel— go *all* and preach: tell the story of a Savior's dying love. Bid rebellious man his rebellion cease. Tell him there is mercy—mercy for the relief of sinners" (Nicholson 1838, 357).

Nicholson's own later mission seems to be informed by M'Dowall's devotion to simply reading the scripture. Joshua Leavitt, another friend who never abandoned M'Dowall, gave the sermon at M'Dowall's funeral, held at the Broadway Tabernacle. Bible printer Daniel Fanshaw offered the M'Dowalls a place in the Fanshaw family vault to bury John M'Dowall. The generous, respected Fanshaw stepped forward again in 1847 when he took on the responsibilities of treasurer and agent for the funds collected by the abolitionist paper the *Emancipator* for Nicholson's famine work. In his editor's introductory note to Nicholson's March 3, 1847, letter from Dublin, Joshua Leavitt identified Nicholson as the author of the M'Dowall biography *Memoir and Select Remains of the Late Rev. John R. M'Dowall, the Martyr of the Seventh Commandment in the Nineteenth Century.* We can take Leavitt's word on this matter. He published the *Memoir* in 1838.

For Nicholson, 1837, her last year at 118 William Street, was a time of crisis: in her own life, in abolitionist circles, and in the life of the city. Her mother, Martha Hatch, died at the age of ninety-one.

Nicholson says she was ninety-two the last time she saw her, but she may have meant her mother was in her ninety-second year when Nicholson visited Chelsea in 1837, the year of Martha Hatch's death.

Arthur Tappan had his own business crisis in 1837. The city had barely recovered from the fire; money was tight. Tappan had lost southern customers, who objected to his abolitionist crusade. On the first of May, he announced his own failure with a debt of $1.1 million (Tappan 1870, 281). Philip Hone wrote about Tappan's failure with horror. Although he was not a Tappan admirer, the shock of Tappan's financial failure was a bad omen for the commercial life of the city. Within a week the Dry Dock Savings Bank failed, and on the tenth of May there was a run on the banks. For the next year, banks suspended species payment (1927, 1:257). Hone himself ended the year dangerously in debt (1927, 1:294). With Tappan's financial reversals came a loss in his personal power in abolitionist circles at a time when the movement was torn between his evangelical wing and the more radical Garrisonian wing. The tension was exacerbated by the introduction of women's rights into the abolitionist agenda, an issue Arthur Tappan called a "tin can tied to the tail of anti-slavery" (Wyatt-Brown 1969, 173).

During the abolitionists' crisis, in 1838, Nicholson moved her boardinghouse one last time, from 118 William Street to 21 Beekman Street. Beekman Street is one of the oldest streets in New York. It appears on a 1729 map showing the street running from the north end of Kip Street close to where it joined with Broadway to form the High Road to Boston to the waterfront; Beekman's Swamp lay to the north at the eastern end of the street. The street shared some characteristics with nearby Nassau Street: offices of attorneys and businesses involved with the publishing trade. Nicholson's premises at 21 Beekman Street occupied the south side of the street. An 1855 advertisement for Vernon's Paper Warehouse offers a glimpse of the premises.

The house appears to have been larger and grander than her William Street premises. There is an iron railing at street level, tall shuttered windows at the hall level, and four floors of smaller windows. There were a number of boardinghouses on Beekman Street in 1840. Sarah Church had a boardinghouse down the street at number 11, and Crooker's boardinghouse was at 45. Across the street there were boardinghouses at 52, 66, and 92 that were identified as belonging to the widow Cocks, J. Annin, and Coles, respectively.

Nicholson placed advertisements from the new location in August 1838 in the *Graham Journal of Health and Longevity*:

TEMPERANCE HOUSE, NEW YORK

The public are notified that the Temperance House 21 Beekman Street is open for the reception of such persons from abroad, as prefer a vegetable diet, and such as wish to make the experiment. Good accommodation will be given, and the latest and best works on Physiology provided to which all may have access gratuitously while remaining in the house.

A year later a smaller advertisement suggested that she was seeking additional boarders, perhaps on more flexible terms, because this noticed appeared in the Grahamite *Health Journal and Advocate of Physiological Reform* on July 29, 1839:

TEMPERANCE HOUSE

NO. 21 BEEKMAN STREET, NEW YORK

Transient boarders can be accommodated on reasonable terms. The house is kept on physiological principles.

The following month, in late August 1839, Nicholson's abolitionist friends rallied to the defense of the African crew of the Spanish slave ship the *Amistad*, who had mutinied. When the schooner appeared at the mouth of Long Island Sound, it was captured by an American cutter and towed to New Haven Harbor. On September 4, 1839, Simeon Jocelyn, Joshua Leavitt, and Lewis Tappan formed the *Amistad* Committee to defend the Africans. The case took two years to reach the Supreme Court when the *Amistad* Committee secured the legal services of John Quincy Adams, who won a favorable judgment for the *Amistad* crew; the slaves were repatriated to Africa in December 1841. William Cullen Bryant's sonnet "A Poem for Cinque" celebrated the nobility of the African leader of the *Amistad* mutineers.

Nicholson does not mention the *Amistad* case. What we know about her during that period is the information given in the US Census for 1840. "A. Nicholson" is listed as head of household for a premises in New York City's Fourth Ward. The household lists but does not name one male between fifteen and twenty and four females between twenty and twenty-five. (Nicholson employed Irish girls in her boardinghouse, some of whom were from near Urlingford, County Kilkenny.)

While Nicholson ran her boardinghouses, she visited the poor Irish of New York in their rickety tenements in the Five Points, the notorious slum that was located nearly at the junction of Mulberry, Orange, Anthony, Cross, and Little Water Streets in New York's Sixth Ward.[41] "It was in the garrets and cellars of New York that I first became acquainted with the Irish peasantry and it was there I saw that they were a suffering people" (*IWS* 2002, iii). Although Protestant missionaries were working in the district—the Central and Spring Street Presbyterians in the late 1830s and the Congregationalists in the late 1840s—Nicholson chose to work alone, as she later would work on her own in Ireland. In her Five Points work, she demonstrated that she was a cause person, not an organization person, satisfied to make her way alone, living the Gospel as she worked among the poor. Her preference for solitary work may be one reason she does not speak about people, particularly women, with whom she might be expected to have some affinity: health reformer Mary Gove Nichols and the teacher-abolitionist Weston sisters.[42]

Nicholson does not indicate that she was aware of the sympathy that feminist, literary critic, and social journalist Margaret Fuller (1810–50), her younger contemporary, had for the Irish poor in New York.[43] Nicholson never mentions Fuller, nor does Fuller mention Nicholson, but they must have been aware of each other through Nicholson's old boarder Horace Greeley.[44] Horace and Mary Greeley admired Fuller, whom Greeley recruited to write about literature and about social issues for the *Tribune*. When she moved to New York in December 1844, Mary (Molly) Greeley urged her husband to invite Fuller to live with them in the home along the East River near Turtle Bay. By that time Nicholson was in Ireland, so she may not have read Fuller's piece "The Irish Character" that appeared in the *Tribune* on June 28, 1845.[45] If she did read it, she would have concurred with Fuller's appreciation of the touching generosity of the Irish poor toward their families. Fuller equated their self-sacrifice with Irish romantic nationalism, explained their failings as "the faults of an oppressed race," and celebrated their family loyalties, their good humor, their wit, and their unquenchable hope (1855, 346).

Like Nicholson, Fuller was concerned about prostitution in New York. Fuller's pioneering *Women in the Nineteenth Century* (1845), published by Greeley, argued for women's social equality with men. Although Nicholson often quoted with approval Solomon's and Saint Paul's descriptions of "virtuous women and housekeepers," she lived her life as an independent woman who ran her own temperance boardinghouse and would travel alone in Ireland, in Britain, and on the Continent. She would also write books and organize her own relief program for the Irish poor. Both Fuller and Nicholson found their independence abroad. Nicholson went to Ireland in 1844; Fuller sailed for Europe in 1846. Both immersed themselves in social work abroad. Nicholson took on famine relief, and Fuller directed the Hospital of Fate Bene Fratelli during the French siege of Rome in 1849. Even after she went to live in Europe in 1846, Fuller continued to write for the *Tribune* until 1849, so she would have read the letters Nicholson wrote from famine-stricken Ireland in 1847. Fuller perished during her journey back to the United States from Italy on July 19, 1850, when the merchant ship the *Elizabeth*, having struck a sandbar off Fire Island, New York, was wrecked.

By the 1840s the Tappans' evangelical fortunes had fallen along with their finances, and the Garrisonites, supported by radical Quakers, gained control of the American Anti-Slavery Society. At the May 1839 meeting of five thousand abolitionists at the Broadway Tabernacle in New York, women's suffrage was again the issue, but the control of the organization turned on the vote that contributions from state associations to the national would be voluntary. The following May a Garrisonite contingent traveled from Boston to New York by steamer to the 1840 meeting of the American Anti-Slavery Society. This time Abby Kelley was seated as a delegate.

Lewis Tappan gave four reasons it was immoral for a lady to sit behind closed doors with gentlemen and resigned from the society (Wyatt-Brown 1969, 197). Nicholson would have stood squarely with the Tappans on the place of women in the antislavery movement. She believed that a woman's salvation depended on her faithful discharge of her Christian duties to her family and to her home. She marshaled Paul's letter to Titus, the dictum that women be "discreet, chaste keepers of the home" (2:5) and 1 Timothy 2:9–12, which counseled that a woman should show her goodness in her works, not usurp authority over a man, and be silent. On the other hand, Nicholson's widowhood was empowering. She traveled to Ireland and to Britain and Europe and became actively involved in a number of social causes. Her own reports of her plain speaking suggest she seldom practiced what she preached about suffering in silence.

Having left the American Anti-Slavery Society, the Tappans and about three hundred others joined the American and Foreign Anti-Slavery Society, an organization modeled on the British and Foreign Anti-Slavery Society that was founded in 1839 by Birmingham Quaker Joseph Sturge, a man who would be a great help to Nicholson during the time she spent in Ireland helping with famine relief. Sturge and Lewis Tappan became devoted friends, and it is probably through Tappan that Nicholson met Sturge.[46] The British and Foreign Anti-Slavery Society invited American abolitionists to meet their British counterparts in London for a meeting that was held June 12–23, 1840. William Lloyd Garrison visited Dublin after the London meeting with his friend Nathaniel Rogers. In Dublin he stayed with Quaker printer Richard Davis Webb, who became Garrison's closest European friend and in time became Nicholson's printer and her most trusted friend in Ireland.

In *Longworth's* for 1842, Nicholson is listed as the widow of Norman Nicholson living at 26 Beekman Street. In 1843 Nicholson moved to 65 Barclay Street, probably to Goss's Graham Boarding House.[47] The split continued among the abolitionists. Goodell resigned from the *Friend of Man* in 1842 and went west to Honeoye, New York, near Rochester, where he became pastor of a church he founded for congregants who shared his commitment to temperance and to abolitionism.

When the New York Anti-Slavery Society met at the Congregational Church in Utica from November 29 to December 1, 1843, Garrison tried to sow disorder among the members. He introduced the concept of disunion at the 1843 Massachusetts Anti-Slavery Society. The following year at the May 7–9, 1844, meeting of the American Anti-Slavery Society, he introduced a resolution that not only repudiated the Union but also repudiated the US Constitution with the slogan "No Union with slaveholders" (Garrison 1973, 118).

By 1844 Nicholson too was ready for a new challenge. Although she does not comment directly about the changes in the abolitionist movement, she would have been disappointed to see a cause that was so important to her riven by dissension and factionalism. She had talked of visiting Ireland in the late 1830s (*IWS* 2002, iv), so in 1844 when she was not only widowed but otherwise without ties to keep her in New York, she felt she could answer her Divine calling to work among the Irish: "The world was before me and all mankind my brethren. 'I have made you desolate. I want you for other purposes. Go, work in my vineyard was the Word.' I conferred not with flesh and blood" (*IWS* 2002, 1). Her mission? To bring the Bible to the Irish poor.

Map 1. Asenath Nicholson's tour of Ireland in 1844–45.

3

An Errand in the Wilderness
Nicholson in Ireland in 1844

NICHOLSON'S DECISION to go to Ireland was her own. She tells her reader in the preface to *Ireland's Welcome to the Stranger* that her mission to Ireland was informed by a long-standing interest in visiting the poor of Ireland. She heard no voices; instead, she explained that she acted in response to a message, a call that told her, "I have made you desolate. I want you for other purposes. Go, work in my vineyard" (*IWS* 2002, 2). Although she presents the lines as a passage of scripture, it appears to be a pastiche of Micah 6:13, "Therefore also will make thee sick in smiting thee, in making thee desolate because of thy sins," or perhaps 1 Timothy 5:5, "Now she that is a widow and, indeed desolate," and Matthew 21:28, "A certain man had two sons and he came to the first and said, "Son, go work today in my vineyard." The first said he would not, repented, and went to work.[1] There is also a suggestion of John 9:4, "I must work the works of Him that sent me while it is day; the night cometh, when no man can work."[2] Why did Nicholson create a text to support her action? She apparently wanted to create a rationale beyond her own interests, and, for her, such a rationale had to be couched in biblical language.

Although Nicholson is usually grouped with other nineteenth-century travelers who left accounts of Ireland in the years before the Great Irish Famine (1845–52), her intention was not to produce yet another book about Ireland; however, the famine prompted her to write *Ireland's Welcome to the Stranger* (1847) in order to provide a sympathetic account of the poor she met in Ireland in 1844–45 and to encourage active intervention to help the hungry.[3] She would have protested that she was not a travel writer; she was a missionary. She differed from the other Victorian women missionaries because she was an independent Bible reader (M. Russell 1994, 41–43). She moved about the Irish countryside, fearlessly enduring hunger, fatigue, pain, and uncertainty. Although she never claimed that she spoke with God, she frequently felt that she was sustained by Divine intervention. In that respect Nicholson shared a sense of Divine protection with her contemporary Harriet Tubman, who was said to have been saved from being captured by Divine Providence as she conducted slaves north on the Underground Railroad (Bradford 1961, 114).[4]

Nicholson prepared herself for her Irish journey by reading Samuel Hall and Anna Hall's lavishly illustrated three-volume *Ireland: Its Scenery and Character*, a county-by-county report of their visits to Ireland in the 1840s. It was clear that Nicholson had digested the book, and on two occasions in *Ireland's Welcome to the Stranger*, Nicholson refers directly to Mrs. Hall's description of Blarney and of Achill. Nicholson also read Charlotte Elizabeth's *Letters from Ireland, MDCCCXXXVII*, letters written "to remove an unfounded apprehension, or an unjust suspicion as to this lovely country and its interesting inhabitants" (1838, iv).[5] Elizabeth had lived with her first husband, Captain Phelan, in Kilkenny for "five years, three months" (1818–24), years of rural unrest (Ó Macháin 2004, 6–12). Nicholson knew Kilkenny from the girls she employed in her boardinghouses and planned to visit the ones who had returned to Ireland. She was no doubt cheered by Elizabeth's report that she was struck by the courtesy of the Irish "when they see it will not be coldly repelled" (1838, 77).[6] When Nicholson visited Kilkenny, she found that even Elizabeth's praise failed to do justice to her own experience (*IWS* 2002, 58).

Nicholson shared a sense of Divine mission with Charlotte Elizabeth, who described the launch of her literary career: "I now proceed to an interesting epoch in my life: the commencement of my literary labours in the Lord's cause. It marks very strongly the ever ruling-hand of Him who was working all things" (1838, 24–25). Charlotte

Elizabeth's literary labors were sectarian, whereas Nicholson's mission was evangelical but broadly Christian, with the Gospel of St. John, "In my father's house there are many mansions" (chap. 23), as her informing text.

Nicholson also attended to the practical details of her trip, identifying people she could contact in Ireland. Although she disliked letters of introduction for the dread of rejection they put on the person presenting the letter and the sense of obligation they put on the recipients of the letter, who often found it inconvenient to entertain a visitor, she did solicit and use letters of introduction to meet Irish people who shared her commitments to temperance, to abolitionism, to evangelical Christianity, and to universal peace (*IWS* 2002, 15). Her entrée to the Irish Quaker community through her friends in the American temperance and antislavery movements was especially valuable for her. William Lloyd Garrison may have provided the introduction to Dublin Quaker printer Richard Davis Webb, who became a close friend.[7] She appears to have lived with Richard and his wife, Hannah Waring Webb (1809–62), when she was finishing *Ireland's Welcome to the Stranger* during the late spring of 1847; Webb published the book the same year. That Nicholson would have sided with Goodell, with Leavitt, and with the Tappans during the American Anti-Slavery Society schism did not appear to have interfered with her relationship with the Webbs, who numbered William Lloyd Garrison among their closest friends.

Her letters in hand, Nicholson took leave of her clergy and reformer friends and boarded the *Brooklyn* on May 16 at Whitehall Slip, a place not far from the streets where she had lived and worked for more than a decade. She watched the spires of Trinity Church and St. Paul's Church recede as she sailed past the masts along the East River and then through New York's great harbor, with the city of Brooklyn on her left and the hills of Staten Island and the Atlantic highlands on her right until they reached the open sea.[8]

The *Brooklyn* was a 445-ton, three-mast, square-rigger Yankee trader.[9] Abel W. Richardson, one of the ship's owners, was probably the captain. He later sailed from New York to San Francisco in

1846 aboard the *Brooklyn* with "the *Brooklyn* saints," 238 Mormon men, women, and children.[10] Mormon historian Conway B. Sonne described Richardson as "a master mariner and a gentleman of fine moral character" (1987, 34). In 1844, at forty-six, he would have been six years younger than Nicholson. She wrote with approval that he often assembled the crew for prayers, thus proving that "a ship may be a temple of worship" and that his crew was treated with civility (*IWS* 2002, 8). When a Scottish woman traveling in steerage died one night, Richardson conducted the appropriate obsequies with readings from the scriptures and the prayers of Christian burial.

In Ireland Nicholson traveled second class as much for entertainment as for economy, but she crossed the Atlantic in cabin class with a shared bedroom and a common room for the two ladies and the seven other passengers who were traveling cabin class: the widow of an English clergyman who was traveling with her son and daughter, a returning Irishman, a naval officer, an American editor, and the Irish wife of the ship's mate. A week out of New York, the widow's dissolute son died of the effects of acute alcoholism.

Unpacking her parcels in her narrow cabin, Nicholson took courage from lines 108–11 from William Cowper's poem "On the Receipt of My Mother's Picture Out of Norfolk":

> My boast is not that I deduce my birth,
> from loins enthroned, and rulers of the earth
> but higher far my proud pretentions rise,
> The child of parents passed into the skies.[11]

Considering the assets that she would draw on for her Irish journey, Nicholson concluded that her New England parents and her early education had been the best preparation for her mission.

She shared her cabin with a Dublin woman who had lived in New York between 1839 and 1844 and was going home on business. The two women shared an active concern for the poor, and they regularly visited the steerage passengers. Other than Nicholson's two reported ship's deaths, the two-week crossing to St. George's Channel was peaceful. They reached the channel on June 5, and they docked in Liverpool on the twelfth. At 2:00 p.m. on June 14, Nicholson boarded one of the Admiralty packets that carried the mail between Liverpool and Kingstown. Normally, the journey took twelve hours; however, the tides delayed Nicholson's arrival in Ireland. The packet did not sail past the East Pier lighthouse and into Kingstown Harbor until five on the following evening. While they waited outside the harbor, Nicholson reviewed what she knew about the country. She recalled being told that "over this fair landscape hangs a dark curtain of desolation and death." The metaphor was a foreshadowing of the Great Irish Famine, which, in May 1844, was only seventeen months away.

The day Nicholson arrived, June 15, 1844, the *Freeman's Journal*, a journal that was in Dublin Castle's pocket from 1786 to 1809 but by the time of Nicholson's visit was supporting Irish nationalism, carried the news of the state trial against Daniel O'Connell for conspiracy, a charge connected with O'Connell's campaign for the repeal of the Act of Union (1800). The *Journal* described the "Liberator's" incarceration in Richmond Prison and the local efforts in Dublin and around the country to raise support for O'Connell by petitions and by contributions to his Catholic Rent, subscriptions that supported O'Connell's campaigns for Catholic Emancipation and for the repeal of the Act of Union. There were meetings of the Repeal Association in Dublin and efforts on behalf of the government to suppress the wearing of repeal buttons. Boys from the national school on Marlborough Street were dismissed for the same offense. There were the usual crimes: a man in Essex Street charged with the murder of his wife, a coroner's inquest about the murder of an infant who was thrown into a coal hole. There were market reports; there was foreign news, including the reports about sectarian riots in Philadelphia, and there were announcements of cultural and popular events: a performance, on horseback, of "The Grand Hussar Movement" followed by "Larissa; or, The Female Bandit" at the Olympic Arena of Arts on Lower Abbey Street, a procession of Dewhurst the Clown and his stable of highly trained cats from Beresford Street to Marlborough Street, a concert by Quinn, the Celebrated Harper of the Phoenix Tavern and Coffee House on D'Olier

Street, and the Royal Hibernian Academy's eighth annual exhibition at Academy House at 35 Lower Abbey Street.[12]

Nicholson's own first full day in Ireland set the tone for her travels around the country. She was curious; she was independent and resilient, and she demonstrated her penchant for losing things. Her first impression of the Irish, that they were honest, was established when an old man returned her misplaced pocketbook. She also managed to lose her keys and her train ticket. When she reached the city, she had a few false starts finding a place to stay before she settled down for her first night in Ireland in a Dublin back parlor.

She lost no time getting to know the city. She paid her shilling to visit the academy exhibition, where she was impressed most by a life-size bog oak statue, *Father Mathew Administering the Pledge to a Peasant*.[13] She visited the Linen Hall, where she met Richard Davis Webb's brother linen draper James H. Webb and reflected on the building, then desolate, that housed the Irish linen industry during Ireland's period of economic independence at the end of the eighteenth century. She preferred to visit institutions that provided various types of social welfare to visiting tourist attractions. She made a point to visit two British experiments in social legislation: the national school and the workhouse. Her tour of the North Dublin Union workhouse impressed her favorably and gave her the baseline from which to measure the workhouses of Ireland during the famine years when they were overcrowded and disease ridden.[14]

Though she disliked using letters of introduction, Nicholson presented her letters to Dublin contacts, who gave her a mixed response when she announced that she was in Ireland to visit the poor. The "Doctor M" who warmed to her and gave her practical advice was no doubt Richard Robert Madden (1798–1886), the historian of the United Irishmen. Nicholson and her friends Simeon Jocelyn and the Tappan brothers would have known Madden as the abolitionist who spent a year in the West Indies and later gave evidence in support of Cinque and the crew of the *Amistad*. He too attended the first Anti-Slavery Convention in 1840 (Wood 2009a).[15]

Christopher Fleming, the proprietor of the Old English Temperance Hotel at 6 North Wall, warned Nicholson that if she was in Ireland to see the poor, the rich would have nothing to do with her (*Dublin Almanac* 1845, 703). Fleming's caution was realized when Nicholson presented a letter to a Dublin woman from her sister whom Nicholson knew in New York and learned something about the matter of class in Ireland. She was told, "I am not partial because they keep up no distinction of rank and eat with their servants" (*IWS* 2002, 6). Invited to stay for dinner, Nicholson declined wine and meat. She was taunted into giving a defense of vegetarianism and then ridiculed by her hostess and her guests. Nicholson sputtered that their conduct "would have disgraced the lowest American table," picked up her shawl and bonnet, and left the house (*IWS* 2002, 17). She much preferred the hospitality of her first Irish cottage, the home of young girls who were employed in a sailcloth factory that she visited on Monday, June 17 (*Dublin Post Office* 1844, 382).[16]

It was in Dublin that Nicholson first talked with the working poor and learned the details of their struggle to survive and their complaint that there was no work for them. On her way to Phoenix Park one morning, she first saw people begging on the street. Wondering what could be done for the Dublin poor, she speculated that if fifty women with leisure were to mingle with the poor, to see who was able to work and what they might do, to determine the needs of those individuals who were limited by infirmity or age, and then, based on that knowledge, to provide some assistance, such informed women could provide much relief and hope.[17]

Nicholson used her time in Dublin to consider her first impressions of the city and of the Irish who helped her to plan her first visit into the Irish countryside where her work awaited. While she had spent her time in Dublin visiting her American reformers' friends and meeting others who shared her commitments to evangelical Protestantism and social reform, it was time to test her own ability to execute her mission independently. Having settled into comfortable and friendly lodgings in Dublin, she had to remind herself that comfort was not the reason that she came to Ireland. She would give herself the same stern advice in other places when she found friendship and hospitality that tempted her to delay her departure.

Early on July 2, Nicholson left the city's Grand Canal Docks in Grand Canal Basin, the deepwater docks at the mouth of the River Dodder, for her first excursion west to Tullamore, Queen's County (Laois), traveling fifty-seven miles along the Grand Canal by flyboat, a boat drawn by two or three horses that could travel nine English miles per hour.[18] Second-class passengers sat on benches on top of the box-shaped cabin. Her comments about her "aristocratic" fellow travelers suggested that she paid the seven shillings and sixpence for a first-class ticket. Their disparaging remarks about the Irish poor— their preference for beggary over work and filth over cleanliness—led her to conclude that it is axiomatic that we despise the ones we oppress (*IWS* 2002, 23).[19]

Nicholson frequently likened the Irish poor to the American slave; however, she recognized that the Irish were "subject to a virtual slavery, which is but a step in the advance of the condition of the American Negro" (*IWS* 2002, 72). In that respect, Nicholson would have agreed with Frederick Douglass, who argued that there was no similarity between the condition of the Irish tenant and the American slave:

> It is often said, by the opponents of the anti-slavery cause, that the "condition" of the people of Ireland is more deplorable than that of the American slave. Far be it for me to underrate the suffering of the Irish people. They had been long oppressed; in the same heart that prompts me to plead the cause of the American bondsman, makes it impossible for me not to sympathize with the oppressed of all lands. Yet I must say that there is no analogy between the two cases.
>
> The Irish man is poor, but he is not a slave. He may be in rags, but he is not a slave. He is still the master of his body, and can say with the poet, "the hand of Douglass is his own."
>
> The same scandal of kidnapping will long remain wholly monopolized by the American Congress. The Irishman has not only

the liberty to emigrate from his country, but he has liberty at home. He can write and speak, and cooperate for the attainment of his rights and the redress of his wrongs. (Douglass 1994, 422–23)[20]

When a priest in Cashel was among the first to inquire about American slavery, she told him simply, "I blush for my country" (*IWS* 2002, 77), and when she was asked why she was in Ireland rather than working for abolitionism in America, she responded, "I have done so, and it was a strong inducement to bring me to Ireland" (*IWS* 2002, 338). Having worked for abolitionism in a city that also discriminated against its Irish immigrants, she resolved to do what she could for the Irish poor.

She arrived in Tullamore on July 3 with letters from a woman in New York to her mother, a woman of education and sensibility who was abandoned by her husband after he had lost his money and her fortune. He fled to America, leaving her to struggle to raise her young family. Accompanied by the eleven-year-old twin daughters of the household, Nicholson visited the poor of the town.[21] She was impressed with the clean and tidy cabins of the poor, the securely cribbed pigs, and the contentment of the householders.

Nicholson's visits to the Tullamore workhouse helped to establish her habit of inspecting the union workhouses, jails, and other local institutions. Schools, however, told her the most about the quality of life for the poor in a town or region. A schoolteacher herself, she knew the qualities of a well-run classroom. Her experience with the Irish in New York convinced her that education was the most valuable preparation for emigration, and she looked for the knowledge and skills that would prepare immigrants for life in America. She noted that in Tullamore, children in the school she visited produced specimens of writing that honored their teachers.

Nicholson returned to Dublin by coach instead of by flyboat. Boarding her coach, she was surrounded by more than two hundred beggars hoping for a handout. Nicholson was unaccustomed to the ubiquitous Irish beggars. Later, when beggars surrounded her coach in Kilkenny, rather than calling them lazy and shiftless, as other travelers tended to do, she blamed the government's land policy, noting that in a time of neither "famine nor pestilence," there was a plague of beggars around visitors to the country. Other travelers, including Thomas Crofton Croker, Thomas Carlyle, Johannes Kohl, and Emily Taylor, were less sympathetic. Kohl found beggars hawking ballads at a fair in Kilkenny and begging women around his car to Waterford. Thackeray noted that the beggars were "more plentiful and loathsome at the Ballinasloe fair" and that "beggars swarmed in towns and followed his car." Leaving the beggars behind, Nicholson found two convicts sentenced to transportation among her fellow travelers and an unprepossessing man who proved to be well schooled in Irish history. He left her with a neat list of the towns between Tullamore and Dublin and the reminder not to judge a person based on first impressions.

She distinguished between beggars and another sector of the Irish poor: the unemployed, agricultural laborer. She met men carrying spades and hoping for work in Tullamore; on the way to the Barrack Lane depot in Ringsend, she observed nine migrant laborers making their way from Connacht to England for summer work. Aware of the amount of Irish unemployment and underemployment she witnessed and the desperation of the poor for work, she was critical when members of the upper class dismissed the Irish as lazy and eager to avoid work.

During the next few weeks in Dublin, Nicholson attended services in Ringsend with a young friend, possibly Elizabeth Horner, her "good friend" who lived on Dorset Street.[22] The church may well have been the Church of Ireland's Royal Chapel of St. Matthew because Nicholson described the devout behavior of soldiers of the queen's regiment who attended the service. Nicholson reported hearing a sermon appropriate for her mission that was based on Mark's Gospel 16:15, "Go ye into the world, and preach the gospel to every creature." The words would have been on her mind when she left the following day for her second trial run out of Dublin, a visit to County Wicklow. Armed with a letter from the son of the household, her destination was the home of a widow and her family near Arklow. The detail she provided that one of the widow's eleven children had drowned and been buried with his father in the local Kilbride grave-yard identifies the widow as Margaret Sherwood.[23] Invited by Mrs. Sherwood to spend a week, Nicholson took the opportunity to visit at least one of the three schools established by the earl of Wicklow and his wife, Cecil, countess of Wicklow. One of their seven daughters, perhaps a teacher, wrote juvenile religious fiction.[24]

Her visit to the school on the Wicklow estate established Nicholson's own litmus test for schools. Asked about her pupils' accomplishments, the teacher linked education and class. "They are educated according to their rank; they belong to the lower order and, reading, writing, arithmetic and a little knowledge of the maps is all the education they will ever need" (*IWS* 2002, 35). Nicholson refused to put limits on what a child could achieve; she believed that the distribution of talent was God's work. Although she differed with Catholics on the matter of theology and practice, she praised the Presentation nun who said of the three hundred poor children in her Dingle school, "Though they are the children of the poor, we do not know what station God may call them to fill. We advance them as far as possible while they are with us" (*IWS* 2002, 275). Nicholson's interrogation of teachers about the limits they put on their children's education would create trouble for her when she visited the Protestant missionary colonies at Dingle and Achill.

A carriage ride one evening through the mountains to Killahester and to the abandoned Wicklow gold mines where men worked alone, searching for nuggets, brought Nicholson to the cabins of the mountain poor. She noted that the poor who worked for farmers were better off than the ones who worked for the large landowners, who paid their laborers only ten pence a day and did not provide food. Passing a gate, she met a hungry man and his famished dog; she was haunted by that image of want in a season of plenty. It was a foreshadowing of what she would see within two years during the Great Irish Famine.

Leaving Wicklow, its scenery, and its pleasant peasantry, Nicholson regretted that she had listened to a New York friend who cautioned her to avoid politics. No doubt it was well-intentioned advice to a woman whose unpopular political views caused her to take stands and actions that were controversial, but she found repeal politics ubiquitous and irresistible. Even coaches were identified with the Radicals (Repealers) or the Conservatives. Nicholson rode with the Repealers. She told a Wicklow priest, "Ireland ought to be redeemed from her bondage and whether it be done by repeal or some other instrument, let it be done" (*IWS* 2002, 52–53). Nicholson's sympathy for repeal reflected her commitment to abolitionism, a sensibility that was reinforced by her Yankee republicanism. She certainly knew that O'Connell was an ardent abolitionist who was known to refuse to shake the hand of a slave owner. Ireland's national poet Thomas Moore considered O'Connell a demagogue who played to the crowd, but he shared O'Connell's nationalism and active commitment to abolitionism.[25] When Moore visited the United States in 1803–4, he wrote an unpopular criticism of American slavery, "To the Lord Viscount Forbes: From the City of Washington": "Where bastard Freedom waves / Her fustian flag in mockery over slaves" (1915, 116, lines 1–2), which was responsible for the hostile reception his *Epistles, Odes, and Other Poems* (1806) received in the country. In 1833, the year that the British Parliament passed the act that abolished slavery in most of the British possessions, Moore published his "Epistle of Condolence from a Slave-Lord to a Cotton Lord," a poem that satirizes the lord of the "white pickaninnies" of the "Satanic mills" of the British midlands as well as the slave owner (1915, 3).[26] While Nicholson does not mention Moore, she certainly knew, and no doubt admired, his work, which was the Irish counterpart of the Scottish romantics, whom she does mention: Robert Burns and Sir Walter Scott. A piano player and a fine singer, she might well have played and sung Moore's *Irish Melodies 2* (1806). Had she sung "The Song of Fionnuala" in her New York parlor, she might have reflected on the words of the song that merged slavery with repeal.[27]

Having explored Tullamore and Wicklow, Nicholson began to prepare for her ministry to the rural poor by going farther into the interior to visit the Irish poor in County Kilkenny. Again she used her letters of introduction, but this time she used them with confidence. Her contacts were the families of the nine Irish servant girls from near Urlingford who had worked in her Graham Boarding Houses in New York. She would be known and valued by the community, and it would be the base from which she could observe life in the Irish countryside. It was a sensible and safe decision.

She set off on Lammas Day. It was the first of August 1844, the first day of autumn in the old Celtic calendar and the traditional beginning of the harvest season. She took the horse-drawn flyboat to Athy, where she transferred to a car for the journey on to Kilkenny.[28] Sitting alone on the top of the car, she succeeded, unbeknownst to the driver, in inviting three lively little boys to sit up beside her, where they competed with each other to answer her questions about local life. A young woman who had been silent in the car arranged for Nicholson to have tea with a convent-educated widow who earned her living as a teacher when they stopped in the town of Kilkenny overnight. Nicholson noted with approval that the school was inter-denominational, with religious instruction provided for both Catholic and Protestant pupils.

Traveling to Johnstown by coach, a man guessed that Nicholson might have been Mary H.'s mistress, and he raised a cry that startled the driver and passengers. They stopped briefly in Johnstown, where a man who called himself a doctor offered to remove a wart from Nicholson's face. She declined.[29] As they walked from Johnstown toward Mary H.'s home, men, women, and children came out of their cabins to take her hand and welcome her.[30] Although Nicholson does not identify the town, chances are that Mary H.'s widowed mother lived in Mountfinn, in Urlingford parish.[31] As they walked, the "doctor's" car arrived, a kish or creel, to take her rather unceremoniously the rest of the way to the H household (Evans 1957, 70).

Nicholson's first night in an Irish cottage, her introduction to rural hospitality, was unforgettable, if uncomfortable.[32] She spent the warm summer evening tucked into a feather bed in the widow's tiny bedroom. The next morning Anne, one of her servant girls who had returned home from Nicholson's New York household and married, demonstrated the respect and affection Nicholson's girls had for her. Hearing that her old mistress had arrived, Anne walked all night to the H cottage and fell on Nicholson's shoulder and wept. Another measure of the local esteem for Nicholson was that on Sunday evening, after she had attended church in Johnstown, she was treated—reluctantly—to a dance in her honor held in a local field. She described the dress of the dancers, the men in corduroy breeches, blue jackets, and stockings, and the solemn hour of serious dancing presented for her pleasure, but like Charlotte Elizabeth, who wrote about the St. John's Eve celebration she attended in King's County, Nicholson was most impressed by the dignity and courtesy of the people of the parish. Nicholson's account reminds the reader of the popularity of dance as a form of local entertainment in prefamine Ireland.[33]

While Nicholson visited with Anne, Anne's sister left for America. Her departure included the traditional elements for nineteenth- and early-twentieth-century emigrants. They probably went on to Liverpool from London to get the ship for their transatlantic journey; she was going to siblings—two brothers and two sisters lived in New York, and she was given an "American wake" before she departed. Nicholson recorded the language of the laments for the departing girl that have become a trope in the literature of emigration: the *caoine*-like lament that equated emigration with death.[34] Nicholson observed but did not comment on the ambivalence that surrounded emigration. The experience that Nicholson's girls had with her in New York and the money they were able to send to their families demonstrated that even before the Great Irish Famine, the young people left in order for the family to survive.

Nicholson balanced her visit to the cabins of the parish with time spent with Urlingford "respectability." Again, New York opened doors, and Nicholson had the added cachet that she had employed Urlingford girls. Her warm reception from the gentry as well as from the country people is a measure of the ease with which Nicholson moved between big house and cabin and her gift for making friends. Of course, she first prompted a certain curiosity. Dr. White, the dispensary doctor on Sir William Barker's Kilcooley estate, whose daughter was home for a visit from New York, became a friend. Her little son "Yankee Doodle" was a poignant reminder of home. Nicholson said that for months, the doctor's home was her own, so she apparently stayed with the Whites during her two subsequent visits to Urlingford in October and in December.[35]

While Nicholson stayed on the Barker estate and attended the Protestant church there, she does not mention Sir William Barker (1795–1877), the orthodox, evangelical Christian who established himself as the master of the Orange lodge on his one-thousand-acre Kilcooley estate.[36] Nicholson would have heard that the Kilcooley house had been destroyed in a fire in 1839 after a woman with a child appeared at the door, asking for the butler Mr. Ashby, whom the woman identified as the father of her child. Barker fired Ashby, who packed the chimney with paper and set it afire. The house was destroyed. Barker had hoped to build a grand Palladian house to replace it, but he could afford only to replace the original house in 1843 (Neely 1983, 104).[37]

Nicholson also stayed nearby in a room overlooking the Urlingford fairgrounds along Lumper Lane. As she had experienced daily cabin life in Mountfinn, she had an opportunity to observe calendar customs and rites of passage during her stay in Urlingford town, including a fair and a wake. She saw her first fair on the fifteenth of August. She did not mention it, but the day would have coincided with the Feast of the Assumption, an important day for the Urlingford parish's Church of the Assumption, where the Virgin Mary was the patron of the parish and where the Lady Well, a venerated holy well, was situated beside the Togher Road on the way to Gortnahoe. Nicholson regarded these beliefs and practices as so much Roman superstition. Later she noted with approval that she thought the practices were discontinued.[38] What Nicholson did notice was that people had commented that the fair was peaceful and that she would see no fighting. Faction fighting had been a feature of Kilkenny life during an earlier period that was characterized by rural unrest (see Ó Macháin 2004, xi). Locals told her it was Father Mathew's temperance campaign that had brought sobriety and peace to fairs and patterns.

Nicholson befriended a Catholic middle-class draper with a shop along Urlingford's main street.[39] She admired the ninety-year-old mother of her host for her kindness and for her generosity to the workmen of the house and to the poor. When the old woman died, Nicholson described the wake and funeral with sympathetic attention to every detail. She also reported observing the same restraint brought by the absence of drink that she had found at the Urlingford fair.

Nicholson's first of three stays in Urlingford living in cabins and in the town gave her the opportunity to observe the habits of the rural Irish: their dress, cooking, and habits of cleanliness.[40] The standard varied, but Kilkenny people were not as impoverished as people elsewhere. She saw a gathering that she called a "faction"; however, what she describes was the practice of gathering to work together cooperatively to save a harvest, often with musicians playing to encourage the work and with communal meals provided by the landowner. The practice is usually called a *meitheal*, not a faction.[41] What she did notice about the Kilkenny countryman was his self-possession. She applied her own educational standards to the national schools in Urlingford and pronounced them more than satisfactory. She reported that she observed in one "the best specimen of reading I ever heard in any country."[42]

The brother of her Urlingford landlady invited Nicholson to spend a night at Urlingford Spa at Ballyspellin. Given her interest in holistic medicine, she visited not only the mineral waters in Ballyspellin but later Barter's Cold Water Establishment outside of Cork in 1845 and in 1848.[43] She observed at Ballyspellin that there was a well, but there were neither bathing facilities nor accommodations for visitors beyond a thatched cottage. By contrast, she found Barter's well organized and effective.

Nicholson also took advantage of the excursion from Urlingford to investigate the conditions of the working poor. She visited the coal mines at nearby New Birmingham, interviewing workmen along the way about their pay, "Eight pence a day, ma'am, and it's but a little of the time we get that," and their diet, "We eat potatoes when we can get 'em" (*IWS* 2002, 72). Writing of these times in *Ireland's Welcome to the Stranger* in the spring of 1847, she used these conversations to document the precariousness of life in the years leading up to the Great Irish Famine: the lack of employment, the poverty, and the dependence on a single food source.

Reluctant as she was to leave Urlingford, where she had come to stay with friends and where she made many more during her visit, a visit that included cooking her versions of healthy American food from *Nature's Own Book* for local families, she resolved to press on with her plans to see the rest of the country. Her friend the doctor's wife brought Nicholson the ten miles to her own sister's home in Thurles, County Tipperary, where, again, her hosts tempted her to stay longer while she observed the residents of the large and prosperous market town.[44] Her visit with her Catholic hosts, Mrs. W. and Mrs. B., was an occasion for Nicholson to begin to distinguish between their Catholic theology and practices, which she criticized, and their Christian charity, which she admired. She reported that Mr. B.'s well-meaning efforts to convert her to Catholicism were tempered with kindness (*IWS* 2002, 76). When her hosts took her to the ruins of Holy Cross Abbey, the Cistercian abbey on the bank of the Suir, four miles south of Thurles, she wrote respectfully that this "most venerable curiosity" she had yet seen gave her a glimpse of "the grandeur of the Romish church in Ireland's early history." She described the altars, the carvings, and even the remains of skulls and bones, but she did not mention the abbey's treasure, the relic of the true cross, believed to have miraculous powers, that drew pilgrims to the "Wood of the Cross" from around the county.[45] Although she would have heard of this tradition from her friends, Nicholson would have regarded beliefs about the efficacy of the true cross as so much popish superstition.

Nicholson's visit to Holy Cross prompted her to visit the monastery at Mount Melleray. She traveled by coach with a Catholic priest; he was one of a number of priests that Nicholson met who shared her views about slavery and the Irish poor. Her journey took her through Clonmel, the town associated with Charles Bianconi, the Italian traveling salesman turned entrepreneur who sent the public throughout rural Ireland on his Bianconi cars.[46] As Nicholson traveled around the country, he became her bête noire because she believed that he exploited his drivers as well as his passengers, the latter by charging add-on fees to their tickets.

At Mount Melleray, a monk received Nicholson in the Porter's Lodge, the site of the present reception center, where once again the New York address on her calling card brought a cordial welcome.[47] Nicholson highly approved of the monks' simple diet and their sleeping arrangements, a regime that was similar to that which she recommended in *Nature's Own Book*. The monks, for their part, saw Christ's example in her mission to seek out the Irish poor (*IWS* 2002, 80). Returning with a mountain woman the following Sunday for "a sermon in the chapel," a sermon given during a High Mass, she commented on the degree to which the ritual—the white-robed monks, the liturgical music, the incense—created "a grandeur" that could not "fail deeply to impress a credulous people"; however, the sermon on pride, with its careful attention to scripture and their shared commitment to humility and Christian charity, did not fail to impress Nicholson.[48]

She went to Cappoquin from Melleray, where she was told that the Irish member of Parliament (MP) Sir Richard Musgrave might be able to advise her about a packet of letters that she had paid for but failed to receive. While Sir Richard's granduncle Sir Richard Musgrave (1757–1818) was the author of the fiercely loyalist account of 1798 *Memoirs of the Different Rebellions in Ireland* (1801), Sir Richard, Fourth Baronet, was a liberal who supported Sharman Crawford's unsuccessful effort to abolish tithes and introduced, also unsuccessfully, measures to assist the able-bodied poor.[49] Her informant told her that Musgrave was "condescending in manner, peculiarly kind of heart, a true friend of Ireland and O'Connell and delights in doing good to Catholics, though himself a Protestant" (*IWS* 2002, 84).

Nicholson said that she went at their behest to Tourin House, Sir Richard's country home that was built in the ruins of a castle near Lismore, but he had gone to his home by the sea at Whiting Bay. Nicholson followed him, taking a steamer down the Blackwater to Youghal and walking the rest of the way, stopping en route to inspect the holy well of Saint Declan, the site of an annual pattern near Dysert Church at Ardmore Head. Always dismissive of such folk devotions as so much superstition, she noted that the bishop of the Diocese of Waterford and Lismore warned that no miracles could be expected and prohibited the gatherings. When she finally reached Sir Richard, he took her card, read her letter of introduction without comment, and told her curtly that he could give her no information on the matter of her missing letters. Although he did offer to give her something to eat, she said, "I am not hungry, sir," and departed (*IWS* 2002, 87). Unaware, perhaps, of the impression that the impromptu visit of a forthright American could have made on Sir Richard, as she returned from rebuff at Tourin House, she reminded herself that it was the *poor* she had come to see and that in the matter of courtesy, they failed to disappoint.[50]

Nicholson arrived back in Lismore in time for the celebration of O'Connell's release from Richmond Prison and his return to Dublin in triumph on September 6.[51] Bonfires on hilltops spread the news around the country that the Liberator was back. The night was spoiled for her because she managed to lose her glasses when she paused to admire the duke of Devonshire's Lismore Castle from the bridge over the Blackwater. When she joined a group celebrating near a bonfire to inquire whether her spectacles had been found, a countrywoman disparaged the effect of O'Connell's repeal of the Act of Union campaign on the local poor: "It's many a long day that we have been lookin' for that same to do somethin' for us, but not ha'p'orth of good has come to a cratur of us yet. We're aitin the pratee to-day, and not a divil of us has got off the rag since he begun his discourse" (*IWS* 2002, 90).[52]

Nevertheless, Nicholson found that only Father Mathew's campaign and O'Connell's absolute aversion to violence kept the passion for repeal peaceful. Speaking to workmen breaking stone on the road between Thurles and Urlingford a day or so later, she wondered if O'Connell could continue to restrain the agitation for repeal. Nicholson's musing was prescient. When the Young Irelanders staged a brief, unsuccessful rising in 1848, "the battle of Widow McCormack's cabbage patch," near Ballingarry, County Tipperary, about fifteen miles from Thurles, Nicholson was sympathetic about the causes that led them to that desperate action (*Annals* 1998, 119).

Near Clonmel she observed an old woman struggling to carry a sack of potatoes suspended by a rope across her forehead who told Nicholson that she raised six children after she was widowed. Three had disappeared abroad, and two who married in Ireland stayed away, perhaps fearing contact with her youngest child, who was dying of tuberculosis. It was not the last time that she would criticize the Irish for allowing their women to become beasts of burden. She later was outraged to observe a beautiful young woman near Cahirciveen, County Kerry, carrying a heavy basket of turf.

Returning along the road to Urlingford, she was mortified to be taken for a camp follower by an old man, who asked her, "Do ye belong to the army?" Her usual sense of self-deprecating humor abandoned her, and she could only "beg that he would think that I belong to that craft" (*IWS* 2002, 98). Cheered by a short stay with her Urlingford friends, she set out for Roscrea, where she would meet yet another friend, Father Theobald Mathew.

As early as 1840 Father Mathew had visited Roscrea, where he found a flourishing temperance society (Kerrigan 1992, 61). He returned on Sunday, October 27, for a two-day visit that began with temperance sermons at 8:00 and at 12:00. Nicholson attended both. She perceived some criticism of Mathew on the part of moderate drinkers, not drunkards, who charged him with political motives (*IWS* 2002, 110). Father Mathew's campaign may have had a political dimension. Paul Townsend has made a persuasive case in *Father Mathew: Temperance and Irish Identity* (2002) that Daniel O'Connell modeled his repeal campaign on Father Mathew's temperance campaign. O'Connell's appropriation of Father Mathew's organizational strategy may have been the basis of the charge that the Capuchin was political.

Nicholson sat up in the gallery on Monday morning to watch Father Mathew administer the pledge to the children of Roscrea, who promised to abstain from tobacco as well as from drink. Nicholson was able to reach him just as his coach was leaving. She pushed through the crowd, handed him a letter of introduction (probably from one of their mutual Quaker temperance friends, possibly James

Haughton or Richard Davis Webb), and told him that she hoped to see him in Cork.

Nicholson then set off on her most ambitious and worrying journey. Reduced to four shillings and sixpence, she walked some seventy miles to Galway in hopes of finding a letter with cash from New York, forwarded from Urlingford. She left Roscrea on October 29, stopping at Birr before walking north to Ballinasloe. Cabins were appreciably poorer west of the Shannon, and Nicholson despaired that bright, self-possessed children were consigned to their "rank" unless, of course, they emigrated to America. Ballinasloe friends of Dr. White's gave Nicholson lunch to accommodate him, but they said they could not give her a bed and that she would have to call the next morning to collect her parasol. Once again she found shelter in a cottage, where she paid four pence for her bed, her supper of crisp grilled potatoes, and careful instructions about the road to Galway: how to break up the journey and what to see on the way. It was another sign to her that she should avoid the middle class and gentry and seek out only the poor.

The conditions in Galway, as in most places in the West of Ireland, were more desperate than in the places Nicholson had visited. The wages for work—when it was available—could be as little as threepence a day, and the rents were high compared with a worker's wages. Her sympathetic interest in the stories and the circumstances of the people she met on the road was sometimes rewarded with practical help, including directions to a cabin where she would be welcomed. The woman of the house in a cabin near Loughrea handed Nicholson a Bible and asked her to read the story of the loaves and fishes. Because Nicholson did not impose her Bible reading on the Irish and instead waited to be asked, it was her first opportunity to read the Bible to the poor. She read the passage and continued to read until a simple Connachtman who was present said, "By dad, and why didn't we never hear the likes of that from the praist?" (*IWS* 2002, 123).

Convinced that watching people transact business offered an insight into their character, Nicholson watched the buying and selling of beasts and fowl at a fair in Loughrea on Thursday, November 7, from a vantage point in a teetotaler's public house. While Nicholson watched the locals, she complained that they stared, openmouthed, at her. A second night in Loughrea brought her another, larger, audience who had heard of the spontaneous Bible session and had come to hear Nicholson read again. Nicholson wisely chose to read stories from the Bible. Her audience was part of a culture that was rich in oral tradition; they would have been familiar with and would have enjoyed all types of fireside narratives, including saints' legends.

As usual, Nicholson followed her own course as a Bible reader, a course that differed from other Bible readers and evangelical Christians. Her choice of texts was instinctively ecumenical. Later, she often introduced the Bible by reading John 14:2, "In my father's house there are many mansions," to demonstrate that she was not a proselytizer. Other favorite texts, Matthew 25:35, "I was a stranger and ye took me in," and Hebrews 13:1–2, "Be not forgetful to entertain strangers: for thereby some have entertained angels unawares," honored the hospitality of those Irish who had welcomed her into their cabins. She used parables of charity: the widow's mite (Mark 12:41–43) and the Good Samaritan (Luke 10:33–37) to tell the poor that their hospitality was not only observing the mores of the Irish countryside but also living the Gospel.

Paddy, the man of the house, introduced the subject of the Virgin Mary the second night. While Nicholson recognized Mary as the mother of Jesus, she regarded the Marian Roman Catholic dogma of Mary's assumption into heaven and her intercessionary powers as idolatry.[53] In Loughrea Nicholson simply said there was no scriptural support for the adoration of Mary, and, it appears, the matter was dropped. In eastern Galway between Loughrea and Eyre Court, perhaps in the village of Killimor, a woman quizzed Nicholson about the Virgin Mary. Once again Nicholson answered that nowhere in the Bible were people told to worship Mary. One of the women present responded, "I told ye, ye couldn't confete with her."[54] Another woman present dismissed Nicholson's religious beliefs as a symptom of feeblemindedness: "There's no use talkin. She hasn't got sinse; that I see afore, poor thing. She'd never left so fine a country to be walkin' in this, if she'd the right sinse. Aw! She's cracked" (*IWS* 2002, 139).

Later, in Killarney when she followed a Bible reader who had distributed anti-Catholic tracts, Nicholson again had to explain her beliefs about the Virgin Mary. "This will cut the garment." She was told, "As ye think of the mother, so ye'd love the Son, and if yer tracts say nothin' of her, we would not read 'em" (*IWS* 2002, 230). In the areas where there were strong proselytizing efforts—places with missions such as Achill, Dingle, and Ventry—the question of belief in the Virgin Mary was a test of Catholic orthodoxy.

After her two nights of Bible reading in Loughrea, Nicholson moved on toward Galway. She was prepared to walk the eighteen miles, but nine miles into her journey, the post car stopped and offered her a ride for the price of a shilling. She reached the city at two o'clock on Friday, November 8, with just half a crown in her pocketbook. After settling into her lodging place, she went right to the post office, anticipating that her American letter had arrived. If there was no letter, she would have to walk back to Urlingford.

The Galway postmaster, Robert Persse, must have been astonished at Nicholson's appearance and at her story of walking from Urlingford to Galway; he gave her the bad news that her letter had not arrived (Pethica and Roy 1998, 57).[55] Disappointed but undaunted, she "perambulated the town, and saw what I could see, enjoyed what I could enjoy, and then went back to her lodgings for the night" (*IWS* 2002, 127). She inspected the harbor. Docks had been built, but the sight of just a few masts was a reminder of the lack of commerce in Galway in 1844.[56] Given her interest in visiting the cabins of the poor, it is odd that she did not mention the Claddagh, the fishermen's village across the Corrib from the town, a place she was sure to have investigated. Everywhere she went Nicholson complained that people followed her and stared at her. She left before seven to see the Galway cemetery, but spent the time there ducking behind tombstones to avoid a curious man who pursued her, gazing down at her from the tops of the stones. She regretted that she spoke no Irish and could not, therefore, explain her mission and satisfy his curiosity.

Returning to her lodgings, Nicholson saw another group of men, spades in hand, waiting expectantly, but not hopefully, for a day's work. Nicholson noticed them silent, hungry, and despairing, and though she stopped and tried to speak to them, she was so overcome with sadness, she was unable to speak. The desperation for work and the want of employment were becoming a leitmotif of her account of her travels. Writing *Ireland's Welcome to the Stranger*, she would have thought back to the stark memory of the unemployed as a harbinger of the Great Irish Famine.

Nicholson returned to the post office on Monday morning. The post was scheduled to arrive at 11:40, but when the car arrived there was no letter for her. Although the sun set at 4:08 on that winter evening, Nicholson decided her only course was not to delay but to retrace her steps to Urlingford. With little more than two hours of daylight, she left the house with a student lodger, who carried her basket and saw her safely through the outskirts of Galway to the Oranmore road. When she reached Oranmore, she found that the mention of America, in this case New York, again opened doors. Her Oranmore hosts had spent six years there, built their nest egg, and returned to establish a shop and a lodging house. They talked happily of the city through the evening and the next day, when rain prevented Nicholson from moving along. They refused to take a farthing for her lodging.

While there Nicholson studied the Connemara woman who was in the house to take care of a sick boy. A gawky, skittish woman who was painfully shy, she thwarted any attempt Nicholson made to befriend her. When she heard the Connemara woman singing in the traditional distinctive *sean nós* fashion, she laughed "unavoidably." "She dispraises me," the woman told her mistress and would not sing again. At that moment, Nicholson realized that the Connemara woman was a metaphor for the Ireland described by the travel writers who failed to look further than the poverty, the servility, and the strangeness of the mountain countrywoman to the nobility, kindness, and generosity of the Irish rural poor. The Connemara woman became for Nicholson the exemplar of that goodness.

She continued toward Urlingford from Loughrea to Killimor and from Killimor through Eyre Court to Banagher along muddy roads and through heavy rains. A kind Catholic family took her in, bathed her blistered feet, and listened to her read her Bible. They invited neighbors in to hear Nicholson read, paraphrasing Nicholson's own sense of mission, saying that she was inspired by God to come to Ireland to do good (*IWS* 2002, 141). She read to them by candlelight until after midnight. She went on to Birr, where she was turned away from a local castle, perhaps Edward G. Synge's Castle of Rathmore, "for hearing hireling Protestants preach and Father Mathew giving the pledge" (*IWS* 2002, 150), but then she was brought into a cabin and given the best that a widow, Mary Aigin (Eagan), had to offer.

Returning rain soaked to Roscrea after ten o'clock at night and finding no place to stay, Nicholson was rewarded for having given one of her little store of sixpence to a woman facing eviction. A woman who recognized Nicholson as the American lady who "kept a cabin over a poor woman's head" went back with her to a lodging house, where Nicholson was given a supper and offered a place to sleep in the only unoccupied space, a garret. She had "cast her bread upon the water." After paying threepence for the night, she had just threepence left. Looking at her last bit of money, still twenty-six miles from Urlingford, she assessed her condition: "A stranger in a foreign land; a female, alone, walking with but threepence in my possession, I did so, and the sight of the pennies, rude and ungrateful as it might be, caused me to laugh. What lack I yet? was my prompt reply and then I was happy that I had been compelled to test my sincerity in visiting Ireland, and my firm unwavering belief in the promises and care of God" (*IWS* 2002, 154). As if to demonstrate that care, the Quaker with whom Nicholson had stayed earlier recognized her and stopped and gave Nicholson a ride in his carriage to the house where she had stayed with the family of her friend Mr. C. from Urlingford. She was greeted by the son of the family, who told Nicholson that the errant American letter was waiting for her in Urlingford. It had not been forwarded because the seal had been broken, and Mr. C. thought it unsafe to forward it to Galway.

This episode was the second involving a long journey, a wild-goose chase, brought on by the British government's policies with regard to the Royal Mail. The first sent her off down the Blackwater to her unsatisfactory interview with Sir Richard Musgrave; the second sent her on a trip to Galway, where her expectation of a letter was thwarted by a broken seal.[57] On this occasion all ended well. She was given her letter and reunited with her friends Dr. White and his family, where she spent just a couple of days before leaving for Dublin via Durrow on December 4. She left the Whites very reluctantly for the last time. When she was rebuffed by the middle class or the gentry, she took it as a sign that she should visit only the poor that she had come to see. When she found welcome and friendship among the gentry and the middle class and was tempted to extend her stay with them, she took it as a test of her determination to accomplish that which she had set out for herself: to bring the Gospel to the Irish poor. She returned to her old lodgings in Dublin, where she was warmly welcomed and told she could stay on as long as she liked as a guest of the household.

What had Nicholson learned from her Galway excursion? What did the reader learn about her? Her faith sustained her in her time of need, and she believed that she traveled under a kind of divine protection that would carry her safely through the Irish countryside, where the generous poor would provide for her. The reader saw her doughty determination, her fearless curiosity about the places she visited, her gracious personality that observed the Irish people and their lives, and her commitment to read the Bible to those poor who welcomed her.

4

"A City on a Hill," 1845

NICHOLSON SPENT December 1844 in Dublin and began the new year in that city, a year that started with fresh hopes for Ireland. Tensions within O'Connell's Repeal Association had eased; Thomas Davis and his Young Irelanders continued to publish their celebration of Irish cultural nationalism in the *Nation*, and controversial legislation providing for nondenominational higher education was scheduled for consideration by Parliament in 1845. September would also bring the first report of the potato blight and the beginning of the Great Irish Famine, the event that would define Nicholson's relationship with the Irish poor. For Nicholson herself, it would be a year that would cause her to reevaluate her opinion about Catholics and Protestants in rural Ireland. As an independent Bible reader, she expected to be welcomed in the Protestant missionary colonies that she planned to visit in Kerry and in Mayo, but she was rebuffed, rebuked, and expelled. Although she continued to believe that knowledge of the Bible would turn the Irish from the superstitions of Rome, 1845 brought close friendship with Theobald Mathew, the Franciscan temperance crusader.

She confessed that she was reluctant to leave the Dublin friends who had befriended her and made her so comfortable, but her work awaited. She used some of her time in Dublin to gather Bibles and tracts from the Hibernian Bible Society for distribution to the Irish poor.[1] The clergyman who helped her get the Hibernian Bibles also supplied her with Bibles and tracts (*IWS* 2002, 299). She spent some time devising a way to bring her store of books around the country. Her solution was to carry a basket with pockets for tracts and two bags of Bibles that she fastened around her waist under her polka coat.[2] She also stashed books in the large black bearskin muff that she carried. Once she got to a destination, she took books from the bag, put them in her basket, and walked through the countryside with a testament in her hand. Sometimes she read; sometimes she sang hymns. And she complained that people stared at her!

Nicholson left Dublin for Wicklow on Thursday, January 9, 1845. This time she was more confident about her access to cabins. She was also more aware of the poverty and suffering in Protestant as well as in Catholic households that were the result of a lack of employment or a household crisis such as the illness of the family wage earner. The instances were not widespread, but she observed that the poverty was not connected with any wider want.

When she read the Bible, or especially when she distributed her Bibles, she discovered her Catholic audience demanded the Douay Version, which is what she read them.[3] On her first Sunday morning, the first really fine day that she had seen in months, she took off her bonnet, looked out over the sea, and sang her favorite hymn, "Majestic Sweetness Sits Enthroned":

> Majestic sweetness sits enthroned
> Upon our Sov'reign's brow;
> His head with radiant glories crown'd.
> His lips with grace o'erflow

When she finished the song, she was surrounded by mountain boys, who had run up the rocks to see who was singing. Pat, a laughing boy of ten, the son of the Roman Catholic lighthouse keeper, begged her to take him back with her to America.

While waiting in Wicklow town for Mrs. Baldwin, the hospitable young wife of lighthouse keeper Henry Baldwin, to return from church, Nicholson met some young people, including an Irish phenomenon that she had heard about, "shepherd boys . . . found reading and talking Latin" (*IWS* 2002, 165–66). Had Nicholson read William Carleton, she would have recognized that her "mountain linguist" carrying a copy of *The Iliad* was the Wicklow counterpart of Carleton's

Jemmy McEvoy ("The Poor Scholar"), Denis O'Shaughnessy ("Denis O'Shaughnessy Going to Maynooth"), or one of Mat Kavanagh's schoolboys ("The Hedge School"). She never mentioned Carleton by name, but perhaps she knew of his *Traits and Stories of the Irish Peasantry* and appreciated that the country people in his stories and novels were, like her own observations of Irish life, based on his intimate knowledge of Irish cabin culture and on his discovery that the rural poor were "a class unknown in Irish literature, unknown by their own landlords, and unknown by those in whose hands much of their destiny was placed" (1834, x).[4] Mrs. Baldwin encouraged her to visit the lighthouse under the rock on Wicklow Head. Although it ceased functioning as a lighthouse, its limestone caves created by the breakers crashing against the rocks had become a landmark. She also shared a meal of kale and potatoes with the merry schoolboy Pat's family, but his parents thought he was making a nuisance of himself and exiled him to the barn, where Nicholson visited him. She quite lost her heart to the spunky boy and confessed to shedding a "womanish" tear as she left Wicklow for Gorey. While waiting for the coach to leave, she gave an impromptu temperance lecture to punch-drinking travelers waiting for the coach. She discovered that when she couched her caution in language that related to the Last Judgment, it got their attention.

Nicholson's time in Wexford town included a visit to one of Wexford's five private schools, a Protestant school that may have been supported by Erasmus Smith funds. Nicholson observed that there were more Catholic students there and that they were more receptive to scripture than the Protestant children, who had a surfeit of Bible reading at home. Approving of the ecumenical school but curious about why Catholic parents sent children to a Protestant school, particularly in a town known for its sectarian history, Nicholson queried a Catholic mother, who said simply that she sent them there because it was the best school (*IWS* 2002, 169).

In addition to her school visit, Nicholson took time to inspect all of Wexford's institutions: the Franciscan church and St. Peter's College in Summerhill; she also noticed the Presentation convent nearby, and the residence of the Sisters of Mercy at the back of the college.

She visited the jail, which she observed to be clean and neat and where prisoners received training in the trades. She enjoyed the joke when one of the women thought that Nicholson was a new inmate. She approved when she saw women and girls, incarcerated for petty thievery, sewing and knitting, and she concluded that some of the prisoners were better off in jail than outside.

She finally made her way to the poorhouse. Built in 1842, with accommodation for six hundred, it was located on a hill north of the town. The matron asked Nicholson if she wished to be admitted. She laughed and said not at the moment but that she might ask to enter soon! She saw the children eat their dinner of three pounds of potatoes and a pint of buttermilk and pronounced the Wexford poorhouse clean and tidy with an adequate diet for its inmates. She objected only to the use of tobacco. An old lady begging for money to buy snuff prompted Nicholson to fume about the curse of tobacco and snuff in the country. She was treated civilly and shown what she asked to see, but here Nicholson met resistance to her mission for the first time. When she offered tracts to boys making shoes, an overseer refused them and sent her off to see their library. Then, she was politely, but firmly, shown the door.

During the time that Nicholson waited in Wexford for the packet to Waterford, she went to the Hermitage to visit the kindly Lady Neville, who became a model to Nicholson of what Irish titled landowners could be.[5] The adopted son of the household, who became a favorite, introduced Nicholson to his Catholic schoolmaster, a man who brought Oliver Goldsmith's "The Deserted Village" to mind. When Nicholson invited the schoolmaster to call, she was startled to hear him decline the offer, saying that he would be treated as a servant. Her hostess assured her that such treatment would be the case. Again and again, Nicholson would learn that class could be more limiting than religion in Ireland.

After a number of delays, Nicholson traveled on from Wexford by coach instead of by packet. She got a seat in a packed car to Clonmel. From there she left on a cold, snowy January 29 in a crowded, open Bianconi car, where a dog in a box overhead held on to Nicholson's shoulder or bonnet as the car lurched on toward Cork. They arrived at 9:00 in the evening. The next morning she sought Dr. George N. Watson, the Baptist minister. She spent the day with Watson's family and attended a prayer service at 6:30 in the evening at their Marlboro Street chapel. Dr. Watson recommended she lodge with a Mrs. Fisher, who did everything she could to ensure Nicholson a pleasant stay.[6]

Nicholson made a number of excursions from her base in Cork. She walked to Passage and spent a pleasant week with Dr. Maurice Power and his American wife, Catherine Louise Livingston, the daughter of Supreme Court justice Henry Brockholst Livingston of New York, their three daughters, and Power's mother in their water-side cottage in Ringacoltig, Cove.[7] She visited Blarney with her friend Mrs. Danker (Danckert?), where she was far more interested in Barter's Cold Water Establishment than in the celebrated castle and the Blarney Stone. She was so impressed with Barter's that she made it a point to visit the spa again when she returned to Cork in 1848. In Cloyne she met both silly, proud, nouveau riche heiresses, perhaps the daughters of the Allen family, who leased the bishop of Cloyne's palace and demesne, as well as true aristocrats, the noble, yet unassuming, family of Thomas Fitzgerald of Rockview (Fraser 1844, 247).

Her three weeks in Cork, however, were dominated by the figure of Father Mathew. She called on him at his house at 10 Cove Street on February 1, just two days after she arrived in the city. Father Mathew was just past the height of his power when Nicholson met him. A member of the Catholic aristocracy with a brother and a brother-in-law in the brewing industry, Father Mathew, a Capuchin friar, seemed an unlikely choice for president of the Cork Total Abstinence Society when he was asked to assume the post, in 1838, by the elderly Cork Quaker William Martin.[8] Martin, who served with Father Mathew on the Board of Governors of the Cork workhouse, knew that the Capuchin was aware of the problems of drink among the poor that he had served from 1814 to 1838 as parish priest. A visionary social worker, Father Mathew organized schools, coordinated welfare efforts, founded St. Joseph's cemetery for the Catholic poor of the city, and personally administered to the sick during the 1832 epidemic of Asiatic cholera in a large temporary hospital that he opened near the friary in Blackmoor Lane. The Capuchin won the hearts of the poor with his philanthropy and the respect of the city for his broad ecumenism. Father Mathew reluctantly accepted William Martin's call, and from April 10, 1838, until he died in 1856, worn out by debt and despair, Father Mathew's name was synonymous with total abstinence.

By the early 1840s, his temperance campaign had developed into a social movement, a movement that began as Daniel O'Connell was trying to build a political sense of confidence and self-respect among the Irish people. Nicholson heard about the difference that sobriety had made in the Irish countryside. By the mid-1840s, however, Father Mathew was beginning to have trouble balancing the demand of a campaign that he hoped to expand to Britain and to America but that also required his presence to reinforce the importance of keeping the pledge. While he was a gentle, modest man, his charisma was such that people believed that taking the pledge from him directly conveyed special blessings.

Other travelers had visited Father Mathew. Calling at his home in 1840, Samuel and Anna Hall found a plain, narrow house with a straw-covered floor on a side street near the old quays. There was little furniture in the room full of visitors and those individuals waiting to take the pledge. The Halls praised Father Mathew's work and followed the progress of his campaign throughout the country. Anna Fielding Hall made drink the subject of "It's Only a Drop," one of the stories in *Stories of the Irish Peasantry* (1839), her collection of moral tales.

William Makepeace Thackeray's contact with Father Mathew was brief; however, his impressions from the morning that they breakfasted together were perceptive and lacked the unsympathetic tone that marks much of his *Irish Sketchbook* (1843).[9] Describing Father Mathew as "exceedingly simple, hearty and manly," Thackeray judged him a reformer, not a politician: "Avoiding all political questions, no man seems more eager than he for the practical improvement of this country. Leases and rents, farming improvements, reading societies, music societies—he was full of these, and of his schemes of temperance above all" (1843, 66, 58).

German traveler Johann Georg Kohl, who observed Father Mathew giving the pledge at a mass meeting in Kilrush, County Clare, in the autumn of 1842, was stuck by the rapport he had with the crowd.[10] He traced the history of the temperance reform movement in Ireland for his German readers. While he was impressed with Father Mathew, he suggested the reform might not be lasting. Some pledge takers were insincere; others regarded the medals given to the faithful as having magical powers. Allowing for the temporary "totallers," Kohl did not fail to be impressed with the increase in orderly behavior in the Irish countryside, an improvement he attributed to Father Mathew.

Two period paintings depict Father Mathew as Nicholson would have known him in the mid-1840s: Joseph Haverty's genre painting *Father Mathew Receiving a Repentant Pledge-Breaker* (1844) and Edward Daniel Leahy's small portrait (1846). While Capuchins wore brown habits and hoods, in both paintings Father Mathew wears a white stock, his temperance medal, and a black coat.[11] In the Haverty painting, the viewer sees the repentant figure from the back, head bowed. A serious, compassionate Father Mathew in profile reaches out his hand to receive him. A worried wife weeps, while a wary child holds his father's elbow with his right hand and touches Father Mathew's fingers with his left hand. Leahy's painting portrays a handsome middle-aged man with a broad forehead, black curling hair, steady eyes under dark brows, a Roman nose, and a sensuous mouth. Nicholson could not help but find him attractive, and there may have been a certain frisson. After all, she had been attracted emotionally to clergymen during her New York years.[12]

Nicholson came to Ireland admiring Father Mathew. She had heard of him in America, as had poet John Greenleaf Whittier, who wrote Richard Davis Webb on December 30, 1841, that "there are no two men on the face of the Earth whose hand I would rather grasp than those of O'Connell and Mathew."[13] Having had the opportunity to observe him preach and administer the pledge in Roscrea, Nicholson regarded Father Mathew as a hero: "I had heard much of this man in my own country, but here I saw him, must acknowledge that he is the only person of whom I had heard much praise who ever met the expectation given. He more that met it; he passed it by. He was farther removed from all that could render him suspect than I had supposed, and I was convinced that acquaintance must remove all honest distrust" (*IWS* 2002, 111).

Acquaintance developed quickly into warm friendship. Nicholson and Father Mathew shared an inclusive Christianity. Mathew preached the Gospel of John 13:34–35, "That ye love one another; as I have loved you, that ye also love one another." Nicholson, who opened her Bible reading to the Irish poor with John 14:2, "In my Father's house are many mansions," observed that Father Mathew lived the Gospel. Sitting in a corner in his home, she watched the Capuchin receive those persons who arrived to take the pledge or to seek his advice or his help. Father Mathew invited her to dine the first night she called, and she was a guest at his table any night that she was in the city. On Shrove Tuesday, 1845, she met Father Mathew's brother Charles, an overseer in the Cork workhouse, and a nephew at dinner. Dining with Father Mathew was an experience that must have taken her back to the evenings she spent with her clergy friends in her parlor in New York.

After dining with Father Mathew on Shrove Tuesday, Nicholson witnessed the traditional custom of sending bachelors and spinsters to the Skellig Islands off the coast of Kerry. James Beale's painting *Skellig Night on the South Mall, 1845* depicts that night in Cork.[14] Revelers dance about the equestrian statue of King George II in a nightscape illuminated by bonfires; in the foreground dark figures stand in a cart. The Skelligs Eve custom was associated with the popular belief that because the monastic settlement on the top of Skellig Michael had not adopted the Julian calendar, those individuals who had not married by Shrove Tuesday could still be married on the Skelligs. Later in March, when Nicholson viewed the Skelligs from the road to Derrynane, she recalled the harassment of the hapless unmarried:

> This is the place to which the people of Kerry and Cork, on Shrovetide eve, amuse themselves by hunting out the old maids and widows,

putting them into carts, on asses, and all kind of ludicrous vehicles, to send them to Skellig-rocks. The streets of Cork were alive with this class of people, pursuing such as they deemed worthy of a residence there, and often the joke is carried so far, that some are conveyed miles out of town, and set down, and left to make their way back as they can. (*IWS* 2002, 253)

On February 8 Father Mathew invited Nicholson to join him at the jubilee of Mother Clare Callaghan at the South Presentation Convent on Douglas Street.[15] Nicholson watched the ceremony at which Father Mathew congratulated Mother Clare through the grating that separated the enclosed community from the people in the chapel. Mother Clare renewed her vows, and Father Mathew pronounced the benediction. His account of the jubilee in his papers concentrates on the liturgical celebration, listing the clergy who participated. Nicholson concentrated on Mother Clare: her humility in refusing the crowning ceremony and "her plump, placid face" untouched by the cares of the outside world as she lived her vocation of teaching the children of the poor. While Nicholson differed in faith from Mother Clare, she recognized a kindred soul in one who had lived a life of faith and service.

Father Mathew also arranged for Nicholson to visit another convent: the Ursuline Convent in Blackrock, the first of many doors he opened for Nicholson. Letters in the Father Mathew Papers indicate that he frequently asked the Ursulines to entertain his guests.[16] Although there is no letter of introduction for Asenath Nicholson, his brief, undated letter to the convent's Reverend Mother Mrs. DePassi Lynch is an example of such a request:

Dear Rev'd Mother,
　　With the pleasure of introducing my esteemed friend Mr. Robinson—please allow him to see the Convent. Your kind appreciation will be much obliged
　　With high respect,
　　　　　　　Dear Madam
　　　　　　　Yours devotedly, Theobald Mathew[17]

Of course, Nicholson was cordially received and shown the convent, the chapel, the garden, and the school. A piano player herself, she noticed that each room had at least one piano, and the music taught contributed to Nicholson's judgment that the Ursuline school offered a more "thorough" education than other Cork schools.

During her time in Cork, Nicholson also accompanied Father Mathew to a temperance meeting that included poor fish women who had taken the pledge, enjoyed five years of sobriety, and now were in charge of decorating the hall for temperance meetings. She attended another meeting the following night at the request of an old temperance priest and at the behest of Father Mathew. Reluctantly agreeing to speak at both meetings, she complained that the report of her mission in the local papers made her the subject of unwanted attention. "The notices made of me in their papers, brought me before the public so prominently, that I begged them to desist. I had wished to go through Ireland as unobservedly as possible, asking no honorary attention" (*IWS* 2002, 182).[18]

Nicholson had her last dinner and evening with Father Mathew on Friday, February 21. He left the next day for Tipperary, while she headed west toward Killarney. It may have been that evening that he gave Nicholson a gold locket as a token. It obviously was meaningful to her because two weeks later, she told an old woman carding wool in a cabin a few miles out of Bandon, who had noticed the locket, that it was "a memento of the kindness of Father Mathew" (*IWS* 2002, 199). The old lady blessed them both. As Nicholson took leave of Father Mathew that evening, she thought that it was a final good-bye. In fact, she would be back in Cork again in 1848. She marked their leave taking with an appreciation of his character, speaking to his "unceasing, unostentatious acts of goodness" (*IWS* 2002, 196): "His religion is truly catholic, dealing no anathemas to the dissention who may differ from his creed in either belief or practice; and his whole life, though one of daily self-denial, is an even tenor of chastened patience and cheerfulness" (*IWS* 2002, 197). When Nicholson mentioned Father Mathew in *Ireland's Welcome to the Stranger*, she talked most about his character: his mission to bring sobriety to Ireland and his compassion for the poor. Later, she would speak of his indefatigable efforts to those persons suffering from hunger and homelessness during the Great Irish Famine (*Annals* 1998, 174–75).

Nicholson does not mention that she was aware of the financial pressures under which he was operating his temperance mission, but she could not have helped but know Father Mathew's money troubles. A letter in James Haughton's *Memoir* speaks to his frustrated efforts to help the Capuchin in 1844. "There has been a good deal of money raised for Fr. Mathew, but owing to some difficulties which have been thrown in the way of the Dublin Committee by Fr. Mathew himself and some of his friends in Cork, I fear the large sum we hoped to obtain will not be raised" (Haughton 1877, 69). By 1845, however, there was a Father Mathew Fund to help address his liabilities; the lists of subscribers were published through February in the *Cork Examiner*. The March 8 issue of the *Nation* reminded readers of their debt to Father Mathew and urged them to help the man who "had wiped away a national stigma and a disgrace." Father Mathew's English friends stood by him. A letter from Joseph Sturge in the *Cork Examiner* on February 7 defended the Capuchin from criticism about his debt, and Samuel Hall became the honorary secretary of the London Committee to aid Father Mathew.[19]

His letters in the Capuchin Archives reveal the life of a man taken up with the practical matter of raising the resources to keep his temperance campaign going. There are letters scheduling sermons and pledge taking in parishes around the country. There are letters to his contributors and ones who would be likely to help; there are letters to the people who supplied certificates and medals to the individuals taking the pledge. A measure of his financial difficulties is that in 1843, he was arrested for his failure to honor a bill to his Birmingham supplier of temperance medals. While he was an urbane man, a member of the Catholic aristocracy who could approach the possible donors with confidence, nevertheless there were crippling debts, debts that would take a toll on his health and on his reputation.

While Nicholson said she left Cork on Saturday, February 24, she must have left for Bandon on Monday, February 26. The chief thing that she noticed about the town was the general mourning by "Romanists" and Protestants alike over the death of Father Daniel McSweeney, the beloved parish priest of the town.[20] Here again, Nicholson recorded her value of Christian charity over dogma. Father Mathew had advised her to go to Bantry. "If you wish to seek out the poor, go to Bantry, there you will see misery in all and every form" (*IWS* 2002, 201). Nicholson followed his advice and, perhaps, his point of view about the town, for she dismissed it as a dirty seaport and did not mention the White family's eighteenth-century Italianate mansion, Bantry House (1740), with its magnificent view from the head of Bantry Bay over the broad harbor that stood as a stark reminder of the earls of Bantry's failure of responsibility toward their tenants and their Bantry neighbors.

Instead, Nicholson called the workhouse "the most respectable-looking building," but it was not yet open because "the farmers stood and wouldn't pay the taxes" (*IWS* 2002, 202).[21] It was in Bantry that Nicholson began to notice that poverty was endemic in the rural Southwest. She found "haggard specters" living on straw with pigs in cabins in part of the town built on rocks that was called "Wigwam Row." The people suffered from want of employment, ate a diet of potatoes "when we can," and resigned themselves to live because they could not die (*IWS* 2002, 202). Nicholson pointed out that if the government had used the money to build the workhouse to create employment for the poor, they would have saved the cost of the building and its operation and would have provided immediate relief. She would repeat that advice all over the West of Ireland, but the government continued to favor the workhouse, which grew from 130 in 1845 to 163 in 1853, over other forms of poor relief.

She did not delay in Bantry but set off for Glengarriff, skirting the coves along the coast of Bantry Bay, balancing her basket, her carpetbag, and her large black bearskin muff that made her an object of curiosity to the staring country people and of terror to their children. John, her guide from Bantry to Glengarriff, suggested she go to the local hotel, but, as usual, Nicholson had her own way and opted for a private lodging, where she found all the things that she loathed: a low and dark den, ragged men drinking punch, and a slatternly woman serving mugs of black coffee who told Nicholson that she could have some boiling water when all the men were served. Leaving the she-been to wander in the glen, Nicholson saw the old Glengarriff Bridge, believed to have been built by Oliver Cromwell. She may have recognized it from seeing the engraving of the three-arch stone bridge that Hall and Hall used to illustrate the local story that Cromwell ordered the bridge built by the time he returned or he would hang a man for every hour it was delayed (1843, 1:154).[22]

While Nicholson was in Glengarriff, she tried to visit the thatched Glengarriff Lodge, where Richard White, First Lord Bantry, retired after his son Richard, Viscount Berehaven, was made the second earl (1835) and settled in Bantry House in 1842.[23] While Nicholson said attempting to describe "this valley of romantic wildness was a waste of time," other travelers, including the second earl of Bantry and Augusta, Lady Dunraven, left accounts of Bantry (Everett 2000, 141–42).[24] Lord Bantry did not receive Nicholson, but other travelers found him a genial host and discreetly left contributions to supplement his modest income after making over his estate.

Nicholson did not actually see Lord Bantry, but she was able to observe and to judge his stewardship of his tenants. She saw miserable housing, including a cabin made of two rocks, tenants living among stock in a cow house, and cabins in the "Eagle's Nest" that were dark and smoky where occupants shared their cabins with a calf and a pig and piles of manure.[25] She visited a Protestant school in the middle of mud and bog and praised the teacher, perhaps a Mrs. White, for working for little pay in a desolate place. She visited the national school and found the master and mistress bickering so loudly that she said she thought it was a place that every child should shun (*IWS* 2002, 212). While Lord Bantry was known to be generous to tenants in distress, Nicholson faulted his failure to encourage his tenants by visiting them or offering incentives to improve their holdings.

Her time in the glen reassured her that her practice of reading something interesting from the scriptures that spoke of Christian charity was the way to win the trust of her readers. When someone in the glen inquired whether she was a Protestant, a woman answered, "I don't care what she is. Nothing but the love of God could bring her across the ocean to see such a poor people as we, and stop in our cabins to discourse us, and give us good books. She's been well rair'd, the cratur, and that she has" (*IWS* 2002, 218). The local curate examined her testaments and tracts and reported to Father John O'Sullivan, the parish priest of Kenmare from 1839 until his death in 1874. A man known for his vigilance about proselytism, he thanked Nicholson when he met her on the road (Lyne 2001, 348; *IWS* 2002, 220).[26]

Traveling through western Cork and Kerry presented its own dangers for a widow of fifty-three with a history of chronic lumbago and arthritic feet. After Nicholson climbed up to the Eagle's Nest near Glengarriff, an old man helped her cross the rocks in a swollen river; returning to Glengarriff, she was able to scramble up a steep mountainside only with the help of Mary, a young companion who dragged her up the slope. A week later in Kenmare, she had a serious fall when she tried to climb the ivy-covered wall of Dunkerron Castle or, perhaps, the keep of the O'Sullivan Mór, but she carried on and started the next day for Killarney, riding over the wild track through Moll's Gap that brought her in sight of the Upper Lake. Her fall in Kenmare did not stop her, two weeks later, from throwing her muff and her parasol ahead of her and making a long leap across a stream.

Killarney was one of the places where Nicholson reported her impressions as a tourist. She had probably read Hall and Hall, and she may have reread the three volumes of their tour in Ireland while she was writing *Ireland's Welcome to the Stranger* because her observations seem almost to be a response to their impressions of places such as Muckross Abbey. Torc Cascade did not match the grandeur of Niagara Falls for her, a sight she must have seen when she traveled west along the Erie Canal in 1831; however, she admired its "unassuming modesty" (*IWS* 2002, 224). Although she visited the tourist sites, she saw them as part of local life. She watched a funeral party arrive in Muckross Abbey with its company of eight keening women, whom she described as howling and beating on the casket. Hall and Hall also described a funeral at Muckross Abbey; they also added a discussion about Irish funeral customs. Nicholson, as were Hall and Hall, was scandalized by the condition of the graveyard, with its bones of the previously buried thrown carelessly about to make room for the most recent dead.[27] Two days later Nicholson saw the funeral for a Presentation nun making its way to the graveyard at the Church of Aghadoe, Killarney's oldest burial grounds. Aware of the Irish custom of walking a few steps with a funeral procession, Nicholson joined the mourners.

Nicholson's Bible reading and gifts of books were prohibited in the Diocese of Kerry area because a previous Bible reader distributed anti-Catholic tracts. The local bishop, Dr. Cornelius Egan, required that his people take no book from a Protestant unless it had been vetted by the local clergy.[28] Nicholson's texts were judged to be acceptable. It was here too that she was quizzed about the Blessed Virgin by a woman who announced, "This will cut the garment. As ye think of the mother, so ye'd love the Son, and if yer tracts say nothin' of her, we would not read 'em" (*IWS* 2002, 230). As always, in the end it was charity, not orthodoxy, that won Nicholson's acceptance among the Irish poor.

She stayed in Killarney through St. Patrick's Day, observing the customs: a temperance band playing "St. Patrick's Day," the chapel bells calling people to Mass, the men wearing shamrocks on their hats, and the children wearing a ribbon called the "crass" on their left arm.[29] (Earlier in Glengarriff, children had begged "a penny for the crass" from her.) She thought of the Irish celebrating the day in New York and the homesick songs of Ireland sung by emigrants. She noted with approval that though the people gathered throughout the day, there was neither fighting nor drinking. Nicholson opted for a snooze on her muff in Lord Kenmare's deer park until she was summoned by the gate keeper, who was happy to hear Nicholson read from her testament, but she obeyed her bishop and declined a copy.

Making her way from Killarney to Cahirciveen, Nicholson meditated on elements of "common sense, observation and inquisitiveness" that distinguished the Kerry personality (*IWS* 2002, 235). She later added "cunning." For their part, that Nicholson was an

American was enough to make her welcome in even the most remote places in the country. Interested in why she had come from America, when they heard it was to read the Bible to the poor, they often concluded that her journey was penitential. "Here, as in many parts of the county, it was difficult to make them believe that I was not some holy St. Bridget going on penance" (*IWS* 2002, 240). Others thought she was on some kind of a pilgrimage. She came to realize that country people often explained her presence among them by turning to traditional saints' legends, generally medieval in origin and often linked to local parishes. Many of the legends told of the ways hospitality was rewarded. One of the earliest examples of this type of legend appears in the late-fourteenth-century *Leabhar Breacc* (*The Speckled Book of MacEgan*).

Along the thirty-mile journey, Nicholson again met the custom of washing the feet of strangers in mountain cabins, a custom she linked with John 13:14, "If I then, *your* Lord and Master, have washed your feet, ye also ought to wash one another's feet." She walked part of the road with girls, one of whom was carrying a heavy load of turf on her back. "What a sin, I thought, to take such a finished piece of God's workmanship, and convert it into a beast of burden! Weary and crippled as I was, my real condition called for fresh gratitude that I was not born in oppressed Ireland, where woman can never be woman if not born to an earthly inheritance" (*IWS* 2002, 242).

Nicholson spent the last part of Easter week in Cahirciveen, where she stayed with a woman flamboyant in her devotions. Nicholson scolded her, lecturing her from Matthew 6:5–6: "'And when thou prayest, thou shalt not be as the hypocrites are: for they love to pray standing in the synagogues and in the corner of the streets, that they may not be seen of men. But thou, when thou prayest, enter into thy closet, and when thou hast shut the door, pray to thy Father which seeth in secret and shall reward thee openly.' The woman responded by dragging her little girl into a corner to pray." She went to the fair that was held on Holy Saturday at the Fair Green behind Market Street, where she observed that the men in their blue-cloth panta-loons were better dressed than men she had seen at other fairs in the country.[30] Here, as in Killarney, Michael O'Leary, the local curate, a "stripling clerk of a parish priest," asked to examine her book to make sure that the Irish translation of the Bible was the true, presumably the Douay, translation (*IWS* 2002, 245).[31]

While the fair continued into the night, Nicholson herself had a very pleasant evening talking to a young woman who called at the house. She had returned from New York, where she had lived for ten years, caring for her mother. Nicholson observed the differences in dress, language, and manner that time in America made to Irish women. She noted with particular satisfaction, as she had when describing the young women who had worked for her and returned to Kilkenny, that such women confined themselves to work in their cabins. Although she was cheered by this example, the next day, walking to Valencia Island, she saw women gathering seaweed standing in water up to their chests for an entire day. Again, she objected to the exploitation of the women, who in this case were treated worse than beasts of burden, "because [they are] often made to do what the beast never does" (*IWS* 2002, 249).[32]

Nicholson's companion on her walk to Valentia was a man who had lived in her home state of Vermont and who had visited Chelsea, where he was treated with great hospitality. She inspected the slate quarry that employed two hundred men and praised the quarry owner, whom she called a resident Englishman, who invested in the island. The "resident Englishman" was one of the Blackburns, whose Valentia Flag Company leased the quarry from Maurice Fitzgerald (1772–1849), the Eighteenth Knight of Kerry, from 1839 to 1877.[33] Although she emphatically approved of the employment for men, when she visited the Valentia lighthouse at Cromwell Point and watched women gathering seaweed, she was again enraged to see women doing work regarded as degrading. And she would see more of it in Kerry.

Nicholson's Vermont friend escorted her to the boat and to the protection of a Kerryman, who promised to see her to Waterville. From there she planned to walk on to Derrynane, the home of Daniel O'Connell. She was assured that a welcome awaited her there, and she was confident that would be so. They both admired Father Mathew, though O'Connell kept his pledge for just over a year. All three of them were ardent abolitionists. O'Connell, who refused to shake the hand of any slave owner, was one of the most important and outspoken opponents of slavery of his time; however, Irish abolitionists such as Richard Davis Webb disliked O'Connell's political opportunism and utilitarianism and feared that his brand of nationalism would lead to a Roman Catholic national state.[34] Nicholson had doubts about what the repeal campaign had accomplished for the Irish poor, but she appreciated that O'Connell's calls for nonviolence and Father Mathew's temperance campaign kept peace in the Irish countryside. Although Nicholson found poverty among O'Connell's tenants, she also found that they paid a shilling an acre for rent, whereas tenants in other parts of rural Ireland paid as much as twenty or twenty-four shillings. Her positive impression of O'Connell as a landlord who did what he could for the poor of the area was corroborated by the Quaker W. E. Forster's visit to Derrynane the following year, in September 1846, after a season of famine.[35]

As she made her way toward Derrynane, Nicholson noted that from the top of a nearby mountain, it was possible to see the Skelligs Islands, seven miles off the Kerry coast. She had been in Cork on Shrove Tuesday, and she recalled, with some disapproval, the custom of sending bachelors and spinsters to the Skelligs to be married. Local wags produced comic "lists" that created unlikely couples from the local unmarried. These "lists" were known to produce threats of libel action.[36] While she gazed across Ballinskellig Bay, she mused about the influence of the Derrynane landscape on O'Connell and the matter of gender and politics. Although she acknowledged that women were expected to "walk softly," the gender imperative seldom silenced her: "Here were the principles, the agitations, of the ever-stirring mind nurtured and fed: as here wave after wave dashes against the rock, so has agitation after agitation dashed with impetuosity against Gibraltar of England, as yet impregnable. But hush! a woman must walk softly on political pavements" (*IWS* 2002, 254).[37]

Cheered by its welcoming approach, she made her way down the mountain road to Derrynane. Before her there was an old three-story farmhouse (now demolished) to which O'Connell added two wings after he inherited the property in 1825: the south wing, with its dining room and study, and a library in the crenellated east wing. In 1844 O'Connell added a chapel by way of thanksgiving for his release from Richmond Gaol.[38]

A courteous man opened the door; a waiter ushered her into the parlor, explaining that Daniel O'Connell himself was away from Derrynane. Had he been home, he certainly would have welcomed a fellow abolitionist and a friend of Father Mathew's, but he was in Dublin for the debate concerning the Irish University question, the proposal of the Peel government to establish a Queen's University with colleges in Belfast, in Cork, and in Galway. O'Connell shared the opposition of the Irish hierarchy, who regarded the bill as "a gigantic scheme of godless education," and he was determined to see it defeated. His presence did not matter; the bill passed (Macintyre 1965, 282). Sean O'Faolain described the enfeebled O'Connell after the college bill debate as "floundering about like a homeless Lear" (1938, 321).

Only O'Connell's son Maurice was at Derrynane, but he was not at home, so Nicholson met only the dour housekeeper.[39] Maurice O'Connell was his father's agent at Derrynane. He was popular with his tenants, and later, during the Great Irish Famine, he continued his father's policy of welcoming those individuals evicted from other estates to settle on the Derrynane estate. Maurice O'Connell too would have welcomed Nicholson, but the housekeeper, who no doubt was suspicious of the inquisitive American who had arrived without notice, showed Nicholson the library and the still unfinished chapel. Nicholson walked around the grounds and to the shore and returned to eat a solitary lunch of bread and cheese at the long dining room table where O'Connell hosted his guests. At twenty past four, she looked at the threatening sky and asked the housekeeper what she should do with a storm approaching and five miles of mountain road to walk on her blistered feet. There was no invitation forthcoming. The housekeeper said only, "It will be bad for you," as she showed Nicholson to the door. After six hours of walking through blinding rain and blasts of mountain wind, she arrived at Jerry Quirke's

Sportsman Hotel at Ballybrack, southwest of Lough Currane, where she found a copy of Lady Georgiana Chatterton's *Rambles in the South of Ireland during the Year 1838* (1839).[40]

The storm churned up the sea in Ballinskellig Bay, so the next day Nicholson observed a crowd of more than sixty women gathering wrack from the bay and carrying heavy baskets across the sand. Watching the women with more admiration for their spirit than pity for their circumstances, Nicholson was struck by one woman, a woman more than fifty years old, who danced spontaneously before Nicholson. "I do not believe that the daughter of Herodias herself was more graceful in her movements, more beautiful in complexion or symmetry, than was this 'dark-haired' matron of the mountains of Kerry" (*IWS* 2002, 257). Twentieth-century Kerry poet Brendan Kennelly later used that resonant image in his famine poem "My Dark Fathers":

> And yet upon the sandy Kerry shore
> The woman once had danced at ebbing tide
> Because she loved flute music—and still more
> Because a lady wondered at the pride
> Of one so humble.
>
> (Kennelly 1969, 15)

Nicholson had company for some of the road between Jerry Quirke's Sportsman Hotel and her next destination, Maurice Raheley's house, eleven miles away at Killoyra. Later, as she walked by herself, she heard a mournful sound that she learned was the keening for an old woman who had died alone in her mountain cabin and had to be brought "to lie with her kin in the valley" (*IWS* 2002, 259).[41] When she reached Raheley's, she found it was not a lodging house but a cabin with stock living with the family. She was welcomed with a dinner of potatoes, milk, and salt and an uncomfortable room with the suffocating smell of the resident cattle, but there were clean linen sheets. Glad to see the morning arrive, when Raheley said there would be no charge for her supper and bed, she pressed the usual sixpence on him.

She turned north from the Cahirciveen road and walked toward Killorglin through the Ballaghisheen Pass (Bealach Oisín), the hunting grounds of Fionn Mac Cumhail. She sat down to enjoy the spectacular view of the Macgillycuddy Reeks and began singing, probably one of her favorite hymns.[42] The moment would have added another Christian note to the lore of the pass, which was the site, in mythological tradition, of the meeting of Oisin and Saint Patrick in "Oisín i dTír na nÓg" where the two discussed Christianity.

Suddenly, a boy herding cattle responded with a piper's song, and the two began a duet across the Kerry mountains that continued until he disappeared with his song. As usual, children appeared to stare at the exotic American woman and to follow her along her way. They ran and screamed and laughed, having never seen a woman wearing a bonnet and thinking that it was part of her head.[43] Nicholson left the Killoglin road to walk through the much-visited Gap of Dunloe, where guides pestered her, telling her she could not go on alone. She persisted, saying that there was but one path. She tested the gap's echo by singing two hymns and took great satisfaction in hearing later in Killarney that two tourists hid among the rocks to listen to her and reported that they heard "the sweetest echoes imaginable" (*IWS* 2002, 265).

Near Hyde Cottage she found a hospitable family who, while they did not take lodgers, offered her a bed in a clean cabin and a meal of potatoes. Their frugal kindness brought her a nostalgic moment when she thought of the Vermont fireside of her girlhood. "'I thought of the days of other years, and my soul was sad.' Never in Ireland had an evening of such welcome sadness been mine" (*IWS* 2002, 267).[44] The family further endeared themselves to Nicholson by telling her about Rev. Arthur Hyde, the late Protestant rector of Hyde Church who was such an example of Christian charity that when he died, his Catholic neighbors insisted on carrying his body to the cemetery on their own shoulders. Charitable, ecumenical Protestant clergy would increasingly come to be valued by Nicholson's Christian exemplar. She regretted leaving the beauty of Killarney and the hospitality of her landlady and her daughters, but she had business in Dingle.

Although Nicholson herself practiced a certain ecumenism, even if she had her own reservations about the beliefs of the Catholics among whom she traveled, she looked forward to visiting the Protestant colonies in Dingle and in Achill that encouraged Catholic converts because she believed that only literacy and a thorough knowledge of scripture would convince Catholics to abandon their loyalty to Rome. Anticipating her visit to Dingle colony, she described it, in the words of Saint Matthew, as "a city on a hill," a place that would set an example to the rest of Ireland. First, she would have to take a car to Tralee to get the car to Kerry.[45]

The scenery from Killarney to Tralee was disappointing and the town itself hostile. She lodged in a house that turned out to be a whiskey den, where she was robbed of her gloves and her handkerchief. She lectured the woman of the house about selling drink and moved on to a second lodging house, where she was awakened by a drunk looking for his hat. Jonathan Walpole, the agent for the Limerick Coach and Dingle Car Proprietor, defrauded her out of her fare.[46] One of the Tralee magistrates tried to intervene, but Walpole would not refund her money.[47] Nicholson shamed Walpole by saying that she would walk to Dingle and set out covering eight miles on her blistered feet until she was overtaken by the car man, who begged Nicholson to take his offer of a lift. She did, and he found her lodging with his sister when they arrived in Dingle.

The Catholic woman who offered to show Nicholson Dingle took her first to Michael Devine, the parish priest. He may have heard news of her from Killarney. Nicholson understood that his reserve was based on the reputation of the local Protestant missionaries for "souperism," the practice of proselytizers offering food or work or housing to those converts from Roman Catholicism to Protestantism. The "soupers" had the reputation for using the Irish language to proselytize, and the language, as a result, suffered. Whereas Nicholson used only Irish translations of the Douay Version of the Bible, the soupers distributed translations of the Bible (1685) by the Protestant bishop William Bedell.[48]

Protestant missionary interest had begun in Dingle as early as 1829, when the Irish Home Mission sent Rev. Denis Browne and Rev. John Gregg, an Irish-speaking minister at the Bethesda Chapel in Dublin, on a tour of Dingle to bring the Bible to West Kerry.[49] Nothing further happened until Rev. Charles Gayer arrived in Dingle in 1831 and was appointed Lord Ventry's private chaplain in 1833 with the charge of establishing a Protestant colony on the estate. Dingle was meant to be the first of a chain of colonies that would go along the western seaboard from Kerry to Donegal. As superintendent of schools for West Kerry, Gayer imported Irish Society teachers for schools in Dingle and Ventry.[50] Initially, it was a success. By 1838 Gayer had 170 converts, and that number increased to 142 in Ventry and 245 in Dingle in 1846: however, by the time Nicholson arrived in 1845, there had been trouble about Catholics being evicted from Ventry so that the land could be assigned to Protestant converts. Unlike local Catholics, converts were paid wages of eight pence a day for their work.

The Catholic Church did not counter the missionary activity in kind directly, but the presence of Catholic teaching orders like the Presentation sisters in Ventry was an obvious response to the need for the Catholic hierarchy to take action. In addition to schools, the Catholic Church relied on their faith of their people, their loyalty to their priests, and their determination to resist evangelists' efforts. They also counted on the efficacy of certain forms of secular social control: boycotting, ridicule, or intimidation.[51] In her report about the Dingle Mission, Mrs. D. P. Thompson, wife of Lord Ventry's agent, complained that converts were boycotted by tradesmen, and the author of *Letters from the Kingdom of Kerry in the Year 1845* described the poor attendance at the funeral of a "turncoat," a Catholic priest who converted to Protestantism (1867, 167).[52] Complaints about bribery increased to an uproar when Father Brasbie, a Roman Catholic priest, converted in 1844. The Royal Irish Constabulary and the army were called out, and a man-of-war was anchored in the harbor to protect agents of the Irish Mission the day that the converts were to make their profession of their new faith at the Irish Society Church. Nicholson accepted the opinion of Thomas Jackson, the Dingle Methodist coastguardsman, that the whole episode was staged to discredit Catholics and to win support for the Dingle colony.

When Nicholson arrived in Dingle, the tension between Catholics and converts made Mrs. Gayer, however enthusiastic she was about the mission, suspicious of any visitor who had anything to do with Catholics. She invited Nicholson to call but received her coldly. She immediately cross-examined her:

> "Do you make a practice of going among the Catholics?"
>
> "I make it a practice of going among all the poor without distinction, but am sorry to say that 'my own' often reject me, and I should more than once have been without a shelter, if the Catholics had not received me when the Protestants would not." (*IWS* 2002, 272)

Nicholson was shown out.

Nicholson contrasted the lack of charity on the part of Rev. Charles and Mrs. Gayer and their colleagues with the warm welcome given her by Jackson and his family and the Christian spirit of their Sunday school. For Nicholson, Jackson was yet another example of the "redeeming zeal" of the Methodist clergy in Ireland.

Nicholson went on from Dingle to Ventry, where the Protestant colony was headed by Gayer's colleague the turncoat Catholic priest Thomas Moriarty, known locally as Tomás an Éithigh (Thomas the Liar). Moriarty would have exacerbated the already strained relationship between Kerry Catholics and converts. Nicholson does not speak of meeting Moriarty herself, but after a few visits to the cabin of converts, she was told that their clergy had forbidden them to receive the American lady. Nicholson understood that the restriction was simply a measure of the tension between Catholics and the Dingle Mission, but she was less tolerant when she applied her usual test of Christian charity to the school in Moriarty's care.

When she visited the Irish Mission School, Miss Rae, the teacher in charge of the sixty girls, told Nicholson that her pupils did not learn to read maps because "these are the daughters of the lower order, and we do not advance them" (*IWS* 2002, 274).[53] On the other hand, when Nicholson visited the Presentation school in the town, probably through her connection with Father Mathew, she registered her approval of the nuns' curriculum and the high standard of instruction given to their three hundred children. Again what Nicholson particularly noticed was the Presentations' attitude toward their charges. "Though they are the children of the poor, we do not know what station God may call them to fill. We advance them as far as possible while they are with us" (*IWS* 2002, 275).

Banned from further contact with Ventry clergy and converts, Nicholson used the rest of her time in the Corca Dhuibhne peninsula to see the Kerry sights with her Catholic and Methodist friends. A young Irish-speaking girl brought them to view a sublime seascape, prompting Nicholson to despair that such an intelligent and sensitive young woman did not have a chance to develop her obvious abilities. It was an indictment of British policy in Ireland and the class-based attitude of the Dingle and Ventry Missions toward their converts. "What a pity that government or aristocratic pride should place barriers to the improvement of the talented poor. In no civilized nation, probably, is there more waste of mind than in Ireland" (*IWS* 2002, 276).

Another wise child saved Nicholson from a bad fall when she prevented a mishap on the peak of Sybil Head. Alas for Nicholson, there was not time to visit Dunquin, a place she yearned to see, perhaps because Lady Chatterton had written so lyrically of the view from the summit of Mount Eagle:

> Halfway up the hill we paused to sketch the ragged islands and bleak cliffs of the bay, perching ourselves at the edge of a dizzy precipice. I commenced sketching and admiring the magnificent view of rocks and waves that was spread from right before me, but it was impossible to represent all that wild scene and it would also be vain to try to attempt a description of the broad Atlantic as I saw it rolling along before the south-west breeze and breaking against the bleak, sombre-coloured rocks along the rugged shore. (1839, 193–94)

Nicholson retraced her journey back to Tralee, where she left a note, no doubt a scorcher, for Mr. Walpole, the local agent for Limerick Coach and Dingle Car, and went on to Tarbert to take the steamer, possibly the Dublin Steam Company's paddle-wheel steamer

Garryowen that covered the Tarbert–Kilrush–Limerick run in three and a half hours. She traveled the cheapest way, on deck, in the company of many passengers bound for America (I. Murphy 1973–74, 70). She praised Limerick as a "busy and beauty" city, and she conversed with a working man about the Limerick workhouse that housed seventeen hundred inmates in 1844, one hundred over occupancy (J. O'Connor 1995, 262). Nicholson regretted that she could not stay longer, but she was bound for Connemara, another contested Catholic and convert site.

She paused in Ennis, "an ancient town going to decay," where she "heard a most solemn sermon" in the reroofed thirteenth-century Franciscan Friary. Founded by Donnachad Ciarbreach O'Brien in 1242, the friary was the property of the Church of Ireland until their new church was built in 1871.[54] Moving on to Gort, she heard people say that they had no bread to eat, but she finally found a few small loaves to sustain her on her fourteen-mile walk to Oranmore. The problem of a scant food supply was the same. The people had no work.

Nicholson stayed in the same place where she had lodged when she went through Oranmore in November 1844. She found the same hospitality but not the Connemara girl who was stricken when Nicholson laughed at her song. Although it was less than five miles to Galway, Nicholson's feet continued to trouble her, especially during the warm spring weather, so she accepted the offer to pay sixpence, to which she added a few extra pence, for a ride in an ass and cart. She returned to her Galway lodgings and went off to the Imperial Hotel to book her place on Bianconi's Royal Mail coach to Clifden, a trip that left Galway at 9:00 and arrived at Clifden at 5:00. The fare was seven shillings and sixpence. Once again she complained about her treatment. She found her carpetbag open and her things lying on the floor. Rudely treated by the agent, she vowed to have no more to do with Bianconi. She made her own way along the Clifden road to Oughterard, calling at a national school along the way where she remarked that Irish children's mastery of arithmetic was in advance of children in other places that she had visited (*IWS* 2002, 286).

While in Oughterard, Nicholson observed a schoolmaster who shared some of the characteristics of Matt Kavanagh, the schoolmaster in William Carleton's "The Hedge School," a story based on Carleton's own boyhood schoolmaster Pat Frayne. The Oughterard master conversed with his schoolboys in Latin and directed them to conjugate verbs for their American visitor, who made an appropriate speech praising the pupils and departed with an exchange of bows with the master for the road through Connemara to Clifden: "My journey lay through a wild mountainous country and the red petticoats scattered here and there upon hill and lake side gave a romantic touch to the strange scenery for many a mile" (*IWS* 2002, 287). Although Nicholson did not walk through Maam Valley, the subject of William Evans's watercolor *Cor, Maam Valley*, she passed near Lough Bofin, four miles from Maam Cross.

Having watched schoolboys demonstrate their mastery of Latin, it was Nicholson's turn to perform sometime later when she stopped, near Maam Cross, to read the Bible in a mountain cabin. She opened with what had become her favorite passage, John 14, "Let not your heart be troubled. In my father's house there are many mansions." She walked with an old man from the house for the first seven of the ten miles between Maam Cross and her Recess destination, with its barracks and lodging house where stormy weather forced her to stay an extra day reading, writing, and listening to local fiddlers. Before she left Maam, Nicholson visited the local Connemara marble quarry that promised employment "to thousands," but it was closed because the government and the quarry owner could not agree on a price for the stone. Nicholson observed yet another missed work opportunity for the poor of the West.

Clifden had its own proselytizing history. The Connaught Home Mission Society was founded in 1837 by the Protestant archbishop of Tuam, Power le Poer Trench.[55] Trench worked heroically and cooperatively with Catholic clergy for the poor of the West during the famine and cholera epidemics of 1816–17 and 1822; however, he joined the evangelical Christians' "Second Reformation" movement in the West. In her study of the Christian evangelical movement, Irene Whelan speculates that it was Trench's appeal to a "vanguard of evangelical curates" that influenced his decision to abandon his measure of ecumenism for the "Second Reformation" (2003, 245). The movement may have had a political rationale. Trench's experience of the rebellion of 1798, an insurrection that linked Romanism with republicanism for loyalists, emphasized the importance of maintaining a loyal Protestant yeomanry. It was an argument that appealed to the evangelical wing of the Church of Ireland.

As usual, Nicholson went straight to the schools, which revealed the sectarian tension in the area. She found that some Roman Catholic students attended the two-story school built by the Protestant Diocese of Tuam in 1824 because it offered a better education. The school served until 1956. She noted that students there studied more than the standard school curriculum; they added grammar and geography to the usual subjects. She observed too that the national school was neglected and nearly abandoned. She mentioned that John MacHale, the Catholic archbishop of Tuam, prohibited the reading of scripture in the national school; in fact, MacHale campaigned to keep the British government's national schools out of his diocese, arguing that there were private Roman Catholic schools available to children.[56] The Third Order of Franciscans opened a free school for boys at Ardbear, Moyrus parish, in December 1837 (Villiers-Tuthill 2000, 30–31). Nicholson passed, saying only that "its style and comfort are not like Mount Melleray," the Cistercian abbey near Cappoqiun, County Waterford (IWS 2002, 295).

On April 30, she visited the Gothic castle built by Clifden's founder, John D'Arcy.[57] By the time Nicholson visited, the property has passed to D'Arcy's oldest son, Hyacinth, one of the most zealous evangelists in the West (Whelan 2003, 250). Because D'Arcy was out of town, Nicholson did not meet him, nor did she speak of any knowledge of his efforts to evangelize the Irish poor. Instead, she described the exquisite gardens and the "fairy castle," which were as appealing for their accessibility to rich and poor as for their beauty: "Not a spot in Ireland has been to my liking so much as this, because it breathed such a republican air of liberty. Not a placard said, 'No trespass,' no surely porter followed to say, 'My master allows no one about the place without a written pass.' But here the visitor may sit, stand, or stroll fanned by breezes of summer with the sweet scent of every flower, and feel that all was made for his enjoyment" (*IWS* 2002, 294–95). The gardens would be lost to D'Arcy when his estate was sold for famine-related debt, and he became the rector of the Parish of Omey.[58]

Nicholson did not mention that rents usually fell due on the first of May. Instead, she took note of the May Day custom of welcoming summer by gathering flowers to decorate households in Clifden, and she reflected on the way that a holiday relaxed the usual landlord-tenant tensions and provided the opportunity for generosity and enjoyment. She considered those things as she walked out of Clifden on the road to Roundstone. A boy sharing the road with her through the low Roundstone blanket bog pointed out a pile of stones marking the grave of a robber who may have been Liam Dearg (Red William). According to tradition, Liam Dearg lived on an island in Loch an Ghadai (Lake of the Thief), near Dhoire Chunlaigh (Derry Cunlagh), until he was killed by his colleague Sean na gCannai (Robinson 1990, 56).[59] She noted with satisfaction that when she inquired in Roundstone about the robbers, she was told the story was true, but the district was safe for travelers since Father Mathew's visit to Clifden in the summer of 1840 brought temperance to the region (*IWS* 2002, 295).

An ejected tenant and a poor widow near Roundstone reminded Nicholson that tenant tenure was insecure and that there were no incentives for improving cabins and fields. Tenants were either penalized with higher rents for improvements or denigrated as lazy and improvident if they did not make changes. Landlords' failure to support tenant initiatives may explain the depiction of an untidy, chimneyless thatched cottage in the lea of the hill, the kind of dwelling Nicholson would have passed, in William Evans's watercolor *A Cabin Near the Shore with Figures, Connemara* (1838). Nicholson observed that here too, landless workers were equally without hope except for the possibility of emigrating to America.

In Roundstone as in Clifden, Catholic pupils attended a school supported by the Home Mission. The school manager, Presbyterian clergyman Mr. Crotty, explained its unprepossessing appearance by citing the endemic poverty that "sits brooding on everything here."[60] Crotty was unusual in two respects. He was a "turncoat priest," an individual usually despised and avoided; however, Nicholson reported that he was praised by his Roman Catholic neighbors as a "peacemaker" who "wished to do good to all" and was "given to hospitality," and "though a thorough adherent to those principles he once denied," he hired a Roman Catholic as schoolmaster (*IWS* 2002, 297). It may be that unlike the Christian evangelists in the region, Crotty did not try to proselytize his Catholic neighbors.

Roundstone also provided yet another example of how poor women and children were used to carry heavy loads of seaweed, a practice that continued well into the twentieth century.[61] She was as mystified by the uncomplaining young as she was indignant about the degrading work given them for which their compensation was limited to the potato. A young Roundstone man told her presciently, "The greatest curse that was sent on Ireland; and I never sit down, see, use or eat one, but I wish every divil of 'em was out of the island. The blackguard of a Raleigh who brought 'em here, entailed a curse upon the labourer that has broke his heart. Because the landholder sees we can live and work hard on 'em, he grinds up down in our wages, and then despises us because we are ignorant and ragged" (*IWS* 2002, 297).[62] Nicholson allowed that she had not ever heard the truth of the laborer's life expressed so concisely and with such gravity: his backbreaking work, his dependency on a single food crop, and the contempt of his landlord-employer.

On her way back from Roundstone, Nicholson met an old man walking across the bleak Roundstone moorland. She read the Bible to him as they sat in the lea of a wall, and he wept when she assured him that Christ was always with him. She promised him a Bible when she got a new supply of books. Back in Clifden on May 3, Nicholson found a letter with some money, a bundle of Bibles, and tracts from a clergyman friend who helped her get a grant from the Hibernian Bible Society. She wept with thanks for the generosity to a "stranger in a strange land" (Exod. 2:22), and then she went off to give a piece of her mind to the Bianconi agent in Clifden for imposing an additional eighteen pence for shipping. She paid the bill but made up her mind to have no further dealings with the enterprise. Before she distributed her tracts, she let a Roman Catholic woman lodging in her house examine them. Then Nicholson took her advice about not offering tracts on subjects that would be objectionable to Catholics: "'You have,' she said, 'done good here, by showing to the people that you did not come to quarrel with them about their religion, but to do them good, by giving such books as they might read; but if you circulate these, it will be said you are like the others, and the good you have done will be lost'" (*IWS* 2002, 300). Nicholson sensibly took the advice and maintained that course, a course that was difficult enough in the sectarian West of Ireland. Her position was not enviable. Catholics were suspicious of all Bible readers, and many Protestant evangelical missionaries suspected her broad tolerance and her democratic ideas.

Her Catholic friend joined Nicholson on an excursion to Diamond Mountain (Binn Ghuaire), a 420-meter hill located in the present Connemara National Park.[63] On the way they visited a miserable, impoverished school, probably in Letterfrack. Nicholson despaired of the dark and windowless cabin, the lack of books and benches, and the ragged children. Had she the gift of prophecy, she would have been cheered to known that English Quakers James and Mary Ellis would arrive in Letterfrack in 1849 and would be improving landlords who employed local people at fair wages and built houses for workers (Johnson 2000, 27).

They arrived at Diamond Mountain, set off on their climb, and, caught in the rain, took shelter under a rock and continued their ascent. A more cautious climber would have turned back, but not Nicholson, who described her Indian rubber boots slipping as she crawled up the trail, hanging onto tufts of heath.[64] She lost another pair of spectacles, her reading glasses, in the scramble, and they never succeeded in reaching the "diamonds."

When Nicholson and her companion walked on to Tully, they found conditions in the village as poor as the Halls found it when they passed through in 1842. Nicholson wrote with a reader familiar with the Great Irish Famine in mind, "Can you believe, who may read this, that in 1845, when there had been no failure of crops, an assize town with tasty-looking houses lived six weeks on nothing but potatoes!" (*IWS* 2002, 304). When she returned to Clifden, she met other kinds of distress: people who once were well off but who were struggling, another miserable school in the town, and a purse-snatching servant girl. She reported too about the things that moved her, such as the bedridden octogenarian whose room, filled with an attentive audience, listened to Nicholson read the Bible.

Nicholson left Clifden on May 15 for Galway, a stopping-off place on her way to Mayo. Pausing overnight in Oughterard, she was astonished when she was questioned by a local policeman, who suspected that she was a Lady Clare, a member of a rural agrarian organization who dressed in women's clothing and threatened householders, especially ones who bought land from which tenants had been evicted. There were reports of Lady Clare activities in Galway in the early spring of 1845, but the incidents occurred south and east of Oughterard.[65]

Nicholson did not delay in Galway but headed north to County Mayo. She stayed for just over three weeks in the county, but the experience informed her decision to return to Mayo for the terrible famine winter of 1847–48. She started in the market town of Westport by visiting the grounds of the marquess of Sligo, before she settled into her usual rounds of schools and local clergy.[66] Rev. Patrick Pounden, the Church of Ireland rector of Westport, was recommended to her as a man who worked to improve the conditions of the poor. She would praise him later for his famine relief, work that cost Pounden and his wife their lives. However, in her first visit to Westport, she reserved her praise for the "devoted, active, efficient Bible-reader" Presbyterian minister James Smith, who vetted her letter of introduction, perhaps from Joseph Sturge, by checking the handwriting against a previous letter of his own (*Annals* 1998, 116; *IWS* 2002, 317).

Not content with her perilous climb of Diamond Hill in driving rain, Nicholson decided to climb Croagh Patrick, Ireland's holy mountain, noting that it was the site of an annual pilgrimage.[67] When the girl who promised to accompany Nicholson failed to appear, she decided to make the trip by herself, even though a local schoolmaster begged her not to go alone. "You will be lost, and never find your way; and should any accident befall you, no one could know it, and you would perish alone" (*IWS* 2002, 314). As usual, Nicholson had her own way, though she admitted that she lived to regret her decision. "It was the height of folly, if not recklessness" (*IWS* 2002, 315).

Her report notes that she left at 2:00 for the ascent that takes about three hours. On May 28, 1845, the sun set at 8:11, giving Nicholson about six hours for the climb. She immediately went astray and spent two hours wandering around in the bog blanket that covers the land north and east of the mountain. As usual, she lost something—a beautiful testament. She finally found the Cosán Phadraig (Patrick's Path), the pilgrim's path that leads to the summit and to the spectacular view of Clew Bay below. She saw the remains of the old chapel and the stones believed to be marked by Saint Patrick's knee, and she recalled the legend of Saint Patrick banishing the serpents.[68] Then she began her descent. The safer path led down to Murrisk, but Nicholson did not know it and instead picked her way nearly three miles down the slippery Cosán Phadraig. While many traditionally ended their Croagh Patrick pilgrimages with prayers around the holy well at Kilgeever, she made her way meekly back to Westport. She learned her lesson; she would never be so "presumptuous" again. At the same time, she had the satisfaction of doing what, she was told, neither man nor woman had done alone. As her New York friends said, "She would always have her own way" (*IWS* 2002, 135).

Chastened, Nicholson heard one more sermon from Mr. Smith, who took his text from the Epistle of Peter 3:11, "Seeing then that all these things shall be dissolved, what manner of persons ought ye to be in all holy conversations and Godliness." She might have thought back on those words later and the ironic contrast they made with the nominal Bible Christians of the Dugort colony on Achill Island, the place Nicholson most wanted to see in Ireland. She traveled via Newport, where she called on the Independent Bible reader Mr. Gibbon on her way to Achill Sound, where she was welcomed by Susan Bole

Savage, the wife of R. R. Savage, the coastguardsman turned hotelier. Everyone had a good word for the Savages, who were later called on to distribute relief supplied for the Central Committee of the Society of Friends during the Great Irish Famine. Eager to get to Dugort, Nicholson left the hospitable Savages for the Achill Island ferry (McDonald 1992, 15).

Nicholson was well prepared for her Achill visit. Familiar with the story of Rev. Edward Nangle, who had established his mission at Dugort on August 1, 1834, she was prepared to admire him. However, there were some unsettling reports. Indefatigable traveler, antiquarian, and editor Rev. Caesar Otway visited Nangle's colony in the late 1830s. His picture of the prosperity of the Achill Mission was tempered by references to the economic difficulties that plagued the missionaries during what Otway described as "this uphill state of work."

Samuel Hall and Anna Hall visited Achill Island in the autumn of 1842. Favorably disposed to the Dugort colony because they "considered every conscientious accession to the Protestant faith as a contribution in aid of the well-being of the state" (3:398), they were troubled when they met an orphan boy by the name of Hart on the road to Achill. Nangle had expelled him from the colony and given him just three shillings to take him the sixty miles to relatives in Sligo. The Halls brought Hart with them to Achill and tried unsuccessfully to intercede with Nangle on his behalf. Later, a Newport clergyman introduced the Halls to five other boys who had been similarly turned out of the colony. The Halls' criticism threatened Nangle, who depended on English subscribers' support to keep the Achill colony solvent; thereafter, the Nangles were wary of outsiders.[69]

Still, Nicholson was prepared to endorse the Nangle experiment, and her initial impressions of the Achill colony were favorable. An 1833 lithograph of Dugort shows tidy two-story houses built around two sides of neat stone walls that enclosed a village green. Nicholson observed neatly dressed residents who appeared to be prosperous. Nearly one hundred orphan children were well fed and giving free schooling. The colony was served by the Royal Mail cart Achill and Nevin (Nephin).[70]

Nicholson's first surprise was her accommodations, or lack of accommodations. The hotel was not ready to receive guests; private homes did not accept visitors, so she was directed out of Dugort, through a cluster of windowless, thatched, stone-corbeled cabins that Nicholson called "kraals" and up a hill to Moll Vesey's shebeen.[71] She found a cow in the kitchen and a bed made up for her on a table in a room that Moll intended for her to share with a strange man. "What harrum, what harrum" (*IWS* 2002, 322).

The next morning an indignant Mrs. Nicholson met Dr. Neason Adams at his door. Having heard, before she arrived in Ireland, that Adams was a benevolent man, she asked him for a recommendation for better lodgings, but he was not helpful.[72] A woman who witnessed the conversation directed Nicholson to a Mrs. Barrett, who sold bread. Nicholson not got only a roll but also was offered a place to stay, without charge, while she visited island. Mr. Barrett carried Nicholson's letters of introduction to Mr. Nangle. One letter she described as "from a Protestant clergyman in New York to a gentleman of respectability in England, a friend of Mr. Nangle"; a second letter was from an editor of a Christian paper. She later identified "the gentleman of respectability" as Joseph Sturge; the editor may have been Joshua Leavitt.

Before Nicholson actually met the Nangles, she visited the Atlantic coast of the island along Keel Bay. She describes stopping en route at an ancient village, a cluster of mountain cabins where hungry people quizzed her eagerly about America. As always, in the most remote areas of the country, she was treated with courtesy and kindness. Her account is valuable because the settlement pattern that Nicholson described suggests that the village may have been the "Deserted Village," the village on the slope of Slievemore that was abandoned after the Great Irish Famine.

Because of the Nangles' suspicion about strangers' visits and Nicholson's own penchant for prowling around a community and making impromptu visits to houses, schools, prisons, and workhouses, their treatment, when she did meet them, should not have surprised her. When Nicholson returned to Dugort from her ramble in booleys in the Keel mountains and went to Nangle's weekly lecture, she was ignored.[73] When she arrived at the Nangles' house on the following Saturday for the appointment that she had arranged with Nangle, she was left waiting. The Nangles' daughters laughed at her through the window. When Nangle finally summoned her, he handed back her letters of introduction without comment. He responded tersely to her queries about the colony, saying that it had exceeded all expectations.

Trouble started when Nicholson inquired about the literacy of his adult converts. He responded that converts were not taught to read because it was deemed too difficult for them. Nicholson responded briskly that Irish immigrants as old as sixty were taught to read at a school for immigrants in New York. Although she earnestly explained that the purpose of her visit to the Achill colony was "to see the colony, and to hear from the founders of it, its progress and true condition, that I might tell to my own country what good work was going on in this remote island of the ocean" (*IWS* 2002, 327), the Nangles were unconvinced of her motives. While Mrs. Nangle accused her of coming on improper business and Rev. Nangle dismissed Nicholson as officious, he was sufficiently bothered to complain about her visit in the June 25, 1847, issue of the *Achill Herald and Western Witness.*

The interview concluded, Nicholson returned to the Barretts to reflect on the difference between the Nangles' smug attitude toward their converts and the Christian charity that she had found in Moll Vesey's cabin. While staying on Achill, Nicholson met the turncoat priest John Ródaigh. Had she known the Irish language, she would have been aware of the local stories about him, the trope of the turncoat priest. A local ballad that survived until the twentieth century called "Na Préachers" describes a cow who escaped from Dugort because she would rather drown than stay in a place where there was heresy. The ballad accuses Ródaigh of abandoning the true faith for "a piece of mountain with squinty Nangle."

Despite her treatment from the Nangles, Nicholson gave them their due for building a tidy community on a rocky island, for cleanliness, and for signs of economic prosperity however subsidized it was by outside supporters, but Nicholson predicted that such things would not make permanent converts. She believed that the Irish poor would abandon their Roman Catholic faith only if they were able to read the Bible. History confirmed her judgment; in nine years only 92 of the 6,392 Achill residents were converted by the Nangles.[74]

Nicholson considered staying in Achill long enough to hear Nangle preach once more, but when Susan Savage, who no doubt was familiar with the sort of hospitality the Nangles offered visitors, arrived and offered Nicholson a ride back to their Achill Sound Hotel, she accepted and spent a happy morning with one of the Savage daughters who had her own Sabbath school that provided bread and schooling to the mountain children. She left the Savages with regret and retraced her route to Westport via Newport, where she broke her journey with the Gibbonses and made a new friend, the widowed postmistress Margaret Arthur.[75] She praised the work of Sir Richard Annesley O'Donnell, Newport's resident improving landlord. When James Tuke visited O'Donnell, he found nearly 1,000 women employed at flax making.[76] Nicholson also praised the O'Donnells' school and noted that both O'Donnell and Lady O'Donnell taught in the school.

Nicholson had a speedy twenty-four hours in Sligo, enough time to see the town and the mile-long glen known locally as the Alt that is located southwest of Knocknarea (Kirby 1963, 27).[77] She spoke with local workmen about their conditions. When she heard them praise their landlord, she commented that Irish laborers, like American slaves, always spoke well of their situations to strangers for fear of reprisals should their comments get back to their landlord or master. As usual, the people she met on the road asked her about America.

Nicholson returned to her friends in Dublin on June 20 to spend seven weeks visiting more of Dublin's places of interest and social institutions. Her visit to the city's Mendacity, the city's institute for the poor and the elderly that operated with inadequate private funding, horrified her: the overcrowding, the filth, the degradation of the poor.[78] The Dublin Mendacity and its sister institutions, however, continued to keep the poor from actual starvation. All would be pressed beyond their capacities within the next year when the first reports of the potato-crop failure reached Dublin.

When Nicholson called at the premises shared by the Religious Tract and Book Society for Ireland and the Hibernian Bible Society at 15 Upper Sackville Street in July, she was shown a copy of Nangle's colony paper, the *Achill Herald and Western Witness: A Monthly Journal Exhibiting the Principles and Progress of Christ's Kingdom and Exposing the Errors and Abominations of That Section of the Rival Kingdom of the Anti-Christ Commonly Called the Papacy; Together with a Practical Exposure of the Civil, Social and Political Delinquencies Practiced by the Pope's Emissaries in Attempting to Re-establish His Wicked Usurpation throughout the World Generally and Especially in This Kingdom.* It described Nicholson's visit to the Dugort colony:

> During the last month this Settlement was visited by a female who is travelling through the country, (we have traced her from Dingle to this place.) She lodges with the peasantry, and alleges that her object is to become acquainted with Irish character; she states that she has come from America for this purpose; she produced a letter purporting to be addressed by a correspondent in America to a respectable person in Birmingham; but in answer to a communication addressed by the writer to that individual, he stated that he had no acquaintance with her either personally or by letter. This stranger is evidently a person of some talent and education; and although the singular course which she pursues is utterly at variance with the modesty and retiredness to which the Bible gives a prominent place in its delineation of a virtuous female, she professes to have no ordinary regard for that holy book. It appears to us that the principal object of this woman's mission is to create a spirit of discontent among the lower orders and dispose them to regard their superiors as so many unfeeling oppressors. There is nothing either in her conduct or conversation to justify the supposition of insanity, and we strongly suspect that she is the emissary of some democratic and revolutionary society. (June 25, 1845, 65)[79]

Nicholson made good on her threat in her letter to Mrs. Nangle to publish an account of her visit to the Nangles' colony. She promised that it "would make an interesting page in my published journal"

(*IWS* 2002, 337). Not only did Edward Nangle ignore Nicholson's letter, but he chose never to mention her by name. She does not even appear in his list of visitors to the colony in 1845. Nangle's treatment reinforced Nicholson's opinion that Ireland's darker shades included her reception by the middle and upper classes. Their treatment set into relief the Christian charity of the poor. Having gone to Ireland to try to better understand the poor who were coming to America, she appreciated that America, however flawed by slavery, welcomed the destitute Irish and offered the hope of America.

Believing she had observed "the remains of ancient grandeur trodden under foot," she was determined to investigate Irish history, including the *Annála Ríoghachta Éireann* (*Annals of the Four Masters*), the gathering of early chronicles and manuscripts edited by Franciscan friar Micheál ÓCléirigh, Farfassa Ó Maol Chonaire, Peregrinus Ó Duibhgeannain, and Cú Choigcríche Ó Cléirigh at a monastery near Drownes, County Donegal, between 1632 and 1636.[80] She copied some of the records from the collection in the Royal Irish Academy and from the Archaeological Society with the help of a friend, one of the O'Dowdas (*LS* 1850, 151).[81] She later used the information for the first section, "Early History," of *Lights and Shades of Ireland* (1850).

Nicholson tells in her "Unexpected Visit to Scotland" how she impulsively left Dublin for Belfast and Glasgow aboard a packet on August 8, 1845. She traveled happily in third class, remarking on the courtesy of her fellow travelers. Her interest in Scotland was informed by her reading of Sir Walter Scott's novels and Robert Burns's poetry and by the reputation of Scottish settlers in North America. "So much of the wealth, intelligence and piety of Glasgow I had heard in America, that my mind was free from any leanings toward prejudice and every opinion concerning it inclined to be favorable" (*Annals* 1998, 57). The Irish poor, however, were always on her mind, and as she walked through the Highlands, Nicholson frequently compared the Scottish and Irish characters. She found, for example, that her identity as an American did not ensure the same generous welcome from the Scottish crofters as she had received from their Irish counterparts.

She found Scottish thrift admirable, but she complained when an old lady charged her a penny for a thin slice of oatmeal bread, something that would have been given freely in Ireland. En route to a packet boat that would take her to Fort William, she found a lodging house that offered her a bed on the floor and then charged her a shilling, a price that was double the rate of hotels all over the country. Again, she thought of what her Irish hosts would have done. "An Irishman would have spurned at taking *any*thing" (*LP* 1853, 83).

At Dunbarton Castle on August 12, Nicholson did not speak of Scott's depiction of the castle in his collection of stories *The Chronicles of the Cannongate* (1827–28), but rhapsodized about "The Lady of the Lake." "Here at the age of sixteen, I had formed picture after picture of undying beauty in the graphic delineation of 'Lady of the Lake.'"[82] Nicholson's romantic ideas about the Highlands were spoiled by whiskey and a new horror, snuff. She attended temperance meetings in Glasgow and endured the usual response to her scolding: the citation of the Bible passages about Timothy's stomach and the marriage feast of Cana.[83] She would have been cheered, however, with the growth of the temperance movement in Scotland since John Dunlop, JJ, founded a temperance society near Glasgow in 1829.[84] Temperance received a boost from Father Mathew's visit to Glasgow in 1842, when some forty thousand Scottish workers took the pledge. The visit brought a cultural change to the city: coffee and tea shops replaced some public houses. Nicholson no doubt used some of her time in Glasgow to negotiate with William Brown about a Scottish edition of *Nature's Own Book* that Brown published in 1846.[85] This edition included Nicholson's observations about the Irish eating habits that she observed in 1844–45. An undated letter from Maria Waring to Lydia Shackleton refers to an untitled second book that she had received from Nicholson; it may have been the Scottish edition of *Nature's Own Book* (1846).

When Nicholson found that the price of the coach from the boat to Glasgow or Glencoe was thirty shillings instead of fifteen shillings, she set off resolutely with her parasol and basket to walk back in her Indian moccasins through the Highlands. She described the hospitality, a combination of canniness and kindness, that she met along the road as well as the frightening moment when she met a Highland shepherd near the Grampain Hills and worried about the safety of her gold locket from Father Mathew. She took another Scott route, the main tourist route to Fort William via Glencoe, and passed the site of the Glen Coe Massacre when thirty-two members of the MacDonald clan were murdered in 1692 by government soldiers. She would have probably known about the massacre from Scott's "On the Massacre of Glencoe."

Nicholson's impression as she headed to the Free Church of Scotland's revival meeting in Inverness (August 21–29, 1845) was that the Scots were "certainly a thinking, acting people; and besides, they are an independent people concerning *what* they think; they are not afraid, if tired of the Westminster Catechism, to change it for a less orthodox one." Her undated essay "The Highlands of Scotland" appears to have been written for William Goodell and her other American evangelical friends, readers who knew something of the Disruption of 1843, the schism within the Church of Scotland, that led to the founding of the Free Church and who were familiar with its leaders: first moderator Thomas Chalmers, William Cunningham, and Thomas Guthrie, a minister and philanthropist who was involved with the ragged schools. Her essay demonstrates Nicholson's extensive knowledge of Church of Scotland theology and policy and the way that the sermons by Cunningham and Guthrie and Chalmers's talk on the Church Sustentation Fund, a scheme like Daniel O'Connell's Catholic Rent, a penny-a-week contribution from church members to provide an income for ministers, informed her understanding of the contemporary Scottish church. As usual, Nicholson objected to the church's financial policies.

Nicholson appreciated the Free Church's benevolence to the poor and their zeal in building churches and schools, but "like all other precious ointment, there are a few dead flies in it" (*LP* 1853, 100). She questioned whether any church could call itself the Free Church if it continued to take money from the government, and she sharply criticized the church for accepting money from American slaveholders.

She described the practice as "building their walls with the price of blood" (*LP* 1853, 100). In his later speech "The Free Church of Scotland and American Slavery: An Address Delivered in Dundee, Scotland, on January 30, 1846," Frederick Douglass charged that Free Churchmen had blood on their hands.[86] Joseph Sturge also objected to the practice, saying simply, "Send the money back." These views recall parallels to the issue of slavery and the Free Church in the Evangelical Alliance founded in 1846 and Father Matthew, who was also criticized for taking money for the temperance cause from southern slaveholders.[87]

After the revival, Nicholson met the Inverness temperance community at a soirée hosted by the local agent, the Baptist minister Mr. Headley, whose zeal had compromised his health. Nicholson noticed the symptoms of tuberculosis. She was sympathetic about the "hard, hard battle" waged against whiskey and snuff in the Scottish countryside. Invited to a dinner party, she endured the criticism of another guest about American slavery with a "mortified" assent, but she defended her country against the charge that Americans loved money by charging that it was the Scotch, not the Americans, who were "proverbial the world over for their love of money" (*LP* 1853, 104).

Nicholson does not speak about news of the potato failure in Ireland in September 1845, nor does she refer to the arrival of Frederick Douglass, who was in Dublin that month when he stayed with their mutual friends Richard and Hannah Webb. Although Webb was delighted with Douglass at the beginning of his visit, in February 1846 he complained to Maria Weston (Chapman) about his guest. By then Douglass had moved on to Belfast and from there, on January 10, 1846, crossed the Irish Sea to Scotland. Nicholson could have met Douglass there because she was back in Glasgow in January 1846.

In February she went to visit the "Teetotal Tower" in Renfrew, near Paisley. Nicholson described the tower as a bricolage of jewels and junk that changed during the weeks between Nicholson's visits. Always one to commend and encourage every effort on the part of those individuals who worked in the temperance movement, even Nicholson was left speechless by the eccentric Mrs. C.'s testimonial to total abstinence. Her hostess wore an astonishing collection of temperance medals, buttons, seals, and rings. Hearing that Nicholson was a teetotaler, she greeted her guest with a matey slap on the back. Nicholson was so mesmerized by Mrs. C. that she went back for a second visit to make sure that she had captured every detail of the tower and its creator.

Who was she? Mrs. C. was Jean Caldwell, a woman just a year older than Nicholson, whose occupation was listed in the 1851 census as "Keeper of the Tee Tolar [*sic*] Tower." Robert Brown's note to William M'Nichol's poem "Viewing the Woods of Stanely" about his publisher, bookseller George Caldwell, provides some information:

> Mrs. Caldwell was a strong advocate for total abstinence from strong drink, and in this opinion her husband joined her in a moderate way. Besides being very *outré* in her manners, she was obstinate and self-willed which led her into many extravagances including the erection at considerable expense of a tower at Sandyford, on the road to Renfrew, where they dwelt, which was called "The Teetotal Tower." It was commenced in 1838, and finished two years thereafter, without any preconceived plan. It was constructed mostly of wood, in the Chinese style, and was five stories in height, with a room in each storey for the accommodation of refreshments. On the afternoon of Friday, May 1, 1840, a grand *soirée* took place in the tower, to celebrate its opening—the Rev. Patrick Brewster in the chair. Addresses were delivered by the Chairman, Mr. A. Wallace and other Gentlemen. Mrs. Caldwell herself also delivered an address to the ladies. The tickets for admission were two shillings each, and the free proceeds were given in aid of the Home Temperance Mission and the Total Abstinence Society. (R. Brown 1889–90, 371)

As we would expect, Nicholson investigated the success of temperance in Paisley. She visited Walter Stewart's temperance house with the predictable result that he invited her home to stay for the night with his wife, Mary, and their twelve-year-old daughter, Mary; they lived at 19 Old Smith Hills.[88] While she was in the region, Nicholson made a literary pilgrimage to Robert Burns's birthplace, a cottage in Alloway,

Ayrshire, and surveyed the Burns Monument and the sites associated with the poems she knew from childhood: "Tam O'Shanter" and the "Brig o' Doon."

Back in Ireland in 1846, Nicholson's 1848 essay "Malahide" described her summer visit to the village with the intention of seeing the castle. The owner was absent, so she made her way through the gloomy chambers, looking at pictures and pausing at the tomb of Sir Richard Talbot's wife, Maud, daughter of the baron of Killeen, who married Lord Galtrim in Malahide Abbey. They were no sooner married when Galtrim was summoned to battle, where his death made Maud "maid, wife and widow" in one day.[89] In addition to the castle legend, Nicholson may have been familiar with Gerard Griffin's ballad "The Bride of Malahide" (Griffin 1926, 17).[90]

On June 18, 1846, Nicholson wrote to Lewis Tappan about matters concerning American abolitionists. There is no trace of her letter; however, the reply was dated July 30, 1846, from her old friend William Goodell, whom Tappan deputized to respond for him. Writing from Honeoye, Ontario County, New York, Goodell began his letter by apologizing for not answering her letter sent care of Tappan because he was not sure whether she was in Ireland or in England.

Nicholson's correspondence with Goodell about the Free Church of Scotland suggests something of the depth of her knowledge about Protestantism; it would have reminded her of the conversation in her parlor in New York. Goodell used the metaphor of the Protestant Reformation to discuss the schism between the old American Anti-Slavery Society of Tappan's era and the current society, led by William Lloyd Garrison. Goodell acknowledged Garrison's "stirring style" and his imprisonment in Baltimore on the charge of criminal libel brought by a slave trader; "he introduced a new era."[91] Perhaps he was acknowledging Nicholson's independence when he told her that he himself differed in many respects from the leaders of both the old and the new American Anti-Slavery Societies.

Goodell's postscript addressed the matter of the Free Church of Scotland. He referred to Nicholson's letter to Tappan mentioning the good that Henry Clarke Wright, Frederick Douglass, and James

Buffrum were doing in England and in Ireland. She may have seen the men in London in the summer of 1846 when they attended the World Temperance Convention. Douglass addressed the convention at its last session at the Covent Garden Theatre (Haughton 1877, 73). Goodell shared Nicholson's views about the Free Church and slavery money; Scottish Free Churchmen should stay away from American slaveholders and return their tainted money. Her time in Scotland brought Nicholson back to the matters of evangelical churches and slavery, but she would soon be called to a new crisis in Ireland, a crisis that would test all of her strength and character in the crucible of the Great Irish Famine.

1. *A First Settlement*, W. H. Bartlett, 1843.

2. The Hatch homestead, Chelsea, Vermont. Courtesy of the author.

3. The common, Chelsea, Vermont.

4. Southwest view of Oneida Institute, Whitestown, New York. Courtesy of the Oneida County Historical Society.

5. Lewis Tappan. *Harper's Weekly*, July 12, 1873, 597. Courtesy of the Library of Congress.

6. William Lloyd Garrison. Courtesy of the Library of Congress.

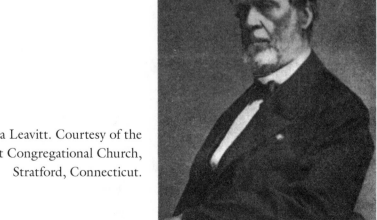

7. Joshua Leavitt. Courtesy of the First Congregational Church, Stratford, Connecticut.

8. Horace Greeley, *Harper's Weekly*. Courtesy of the Library of Congress.

9. Sylvester Graham. Courtesy of Oberlin College.

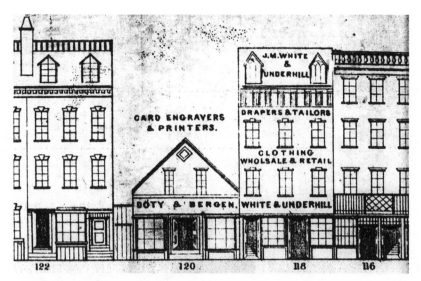

10. Nicholson's 118 Williams Street Boarding House, the East River water-front. Courtesy of the "Pictorial Business Directory of William-Street," F128.65.W5 P53 1849, Collection of the New-York Historical Society.

11. *The Early Days of American Shipping,* in *Valentine's Manual of Old New York,* 1921.

12. *The Five Points in 1859,* in *Valentine's Manual of Old New York,* 1860.

13. *Cor, Maam Valley,* by William Evans. Courtesy of the National Gallery of Ireland, 36.14.

14. The South Presentation Convent, Douglas Street, Cork. Courtesy of the author.

15. *Theobald Mathew*, by Daniel Leahy. © National Portrait Gallery, London.

16. *Father Mathew Receiving a Repentant Pledge-Breaker,* by Joseph Haverty. Courtesy of the National Gallery of Ireland.

17. *The Colony,* Dugort. Courtesy of the National Library of Ireland.

18. *Keel, Achill Island*, in Samuel and Anna Hall, *Ireland: Its Scenery, Character, &c., 1841*, 3:404.

19. A tall house overlooking the Liffey. Courtesy of the author.

20. *The Cork Society of Friends' Soup House, Illustrated London News,* January 16, 1847.

21. Charles Edward Trevelyan, assistant secretary of the Treasury. Courtesy of the Hulton Archive, Getty Images.

22. *The Day after the Ejectment, Illustrated London News,* December 16, 1848.

23. *The Irish Famine-Scene at the Gate of the Workhouse*, in Robert Wilson, *The Life and Times of Queen Victoria*. Courtesy of the Bridgeman Art Library, #XJF 105012.

24. Ruins of the home of Samuel Stock, Rosport, County Mayo. Courtesy of the author.

25. Richard Davis
Webb (1805–72).
Courtesy of the
Religious Society
of Friends, Dublin
Friends Historical
Library.

26. Famine graveyard, Belmullet, County Mayo. Courtesy of the author.

27. The Doolough Pass, County Mayo. Courtesy of the author.

28. *John Bunyan in Bedford Jail, 1667: The Blind Child Leaving Him for the Night*. Engraved by F. E. Jones from the original by T. G. Duvall.

29. *Departure of English Members of the Peace Congress for Frankfurt, 1850, Illustrated London News,* August 24, 1850.

30. *The Secret of England's Greatness (Queen Victoria Presenting a Bible in the Audience Chamber at Windsor),* by Thomas Jones Barker, ca. 1863. © National Portrait Gallery, London.

31. The Dairyman's Cottage, Hale
Cottage, Isle of Wight. Courtesy
of the author.

32. The grave of the dairyman's
daughter, St. George's Churchyard, Isle of Wight.

33. *The Inauguration of the Great Exhibition, May 1, 1851*, by David Roberts. Courtesy of the Royal Collection Trust © Her Majesty Queen Elizabeth II, 2013.

34. *Exeter Hall, the Great Anti-slavery Meeting, 1841*, by Thomas Shepherd, engraved by Henry Melville. The Strand, London. Courtesy of the Library of Congress.

35. Asenath Nicholson's unmarked grave, Green-Wood Cemetery, Brooklyn, New York. Courtesy of the author.

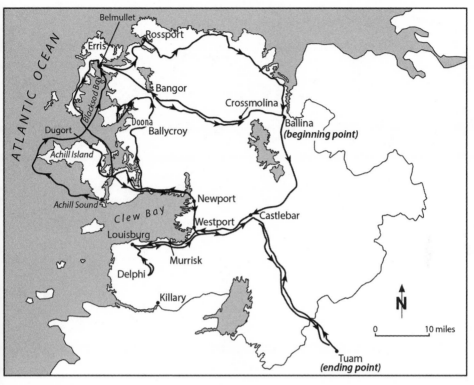

Map 2. Asenath Nicholson in County Mayo, 1847–49.

5

"If This Cup May Not Pass Away from Me"
Nicholson Begins Her Famine Mission

THERE IS NO RECORD of when Nicholson learned about famine conditions in Ireland. She would no doubt have been aware of the failure of the 1845 potato crop through the accounts of Ireland in British papers and through her correspondence with her friends and acquaintances in Ireland.[1] She knew the danger of a poor harvest to people who lived on a single food source. News of the second failure in the autumn of 1846 must have come as a call to action.[2] In the first pages of *Annals of the Famine* (1851), Nicholson tells her readers that she was aware of conditions in Ireland, that she could say "with the disciples returning from Emmaus, that 'my heart burned within me'" (1998, 32).[3] She returned to famine-stricken Ireland imbued with a sense that she was on a divinely appointed mission. Paraphrasing Luke 22:42, she said "Father, if you are willing, remove this cup from me, never the less, not my will but Yours be done," and she accepted her mission to minister to the hungry and to bring their story to others who could assist those persons who suffered. Her previous experiences in Ireland had given her a unique understanding of the poor, an understanding that informed *Ireland's Welcome to the Stranger*.

Her sense of mission involved bearing witness to their suffering and explaining not only how the Irish suffered but why. In *Annals of the Famine*, her account of the Irish in 1847–48, she challenged absentee landlords and the land system, as well as the government's and the churches' stewardship of resources entrusted to them for the starving, and she rebuked officials for their attitudes toward the poor. No hurler on the ditch, her own personal famine-relief efforts were marked equally by practical and sensible intervention and by her spirit of Christian charity.

Nicholson must have been in touch with the Webbs because when she landed in Kingstown on December 7, 1846, she was given the use of De Vesci Lodge, the Monkstown home of Richard Davis Webb's brother Quaker linen draper James Webb, who was out of town.[4] From her window at the back of the house on the second floor, she could see the old graveyard of Carrickbrennan.[5] Her first report of the famine described a poor widow brought into court by a local magistrate who had observed her cooking a half-starved dog in a pot with a few potatoes gleaned from a harvested field (*Annals* 1998, 36–37).[6] A kindly judge dismissed the charges and gave her money from his own pocket to purchase food for her children (*Annals* 1998, 37).

Nicholson went to work immediately, dispensing from the Webb kitchen a jellied gruel of Indian meal to twenty-five or thirty workmen every day until her supply was exhausted. A modest income from the sales of her Scottish edition of *Nature's Own Book* (1846) arrived providentially from her publisher, William Brown, during another crisis. She despaired that she did not have adequate resources and could do so little: "I would not say that I actually murmured but the question did arise, 'Why was I brought to see a famine and be the humble instrument of saving some few alive and then see these few die because I had no more to give them'" (*Annals* 1998, 40). What Nicholson did not know was that help was en route. A meeting was held at New York's Tammany Hall on December 26, 1846, to organize relief efforts for Ireland. Horace Greeley reported in the *New York Tribune* on the twenty-eighth that plans were made to collect money in time to send resources on the *Jamestown*, which would leave Boston on January 1, 1847, and arrive in Ireland sometime between the fifteenth and eighteenth. Greeley himself collected from the Fourth Ward; he told readers he would also receive contributions as editor of the *New York Tribune*. Mayor A. H. Mickle himself served as general treasurer. On January 1 Greeley told his readers that they had forwarded three thousand dollars to Ireland, "a sum smaller than it should have been, but still by no means despicable in view of this capacity to aid in warding off starvation." There was an additional sixteen hundred dollars from local merchants as well as a donation from Jersey City. Greeley called for Americans to raise at least one million dollars for Ireland.

By the time the New York funds arrived, the Central Relief Committee of the Society of Friends had established a soup kitchen in Charles Street, Upper Ormonde Quay, on January 23, 1847 (Society of Friends 1852, 53–54). Between January and July, when the Temporary Relief Act was passed and the soup kitchen was closed, the Quakers sold soup, an average of a thousand quarts each day for a penny a quart. They also sold soup tickets that could be distributed to the poor.

While the Quakers were feeding the Dublin poor, Nicholson continued to fret about her exhausted resources, so when James Webb arrived with a parcel from Greeley that included ten dollars and copies of the *New York Tribune*, Nicholson not only regarded it as intervention from a friend but also a sign of Divine Providence: "I adored that watchful Hand that had so strangely led and upheld me in Ireland and now, above all and over all, when my heart was sinking in in the deepest despondence, when no way of escaping appeared, this heavenly boon was sent" (*Annals* 1998, 40).

She lost no time writing to Greeley himself and to his *Tribune* readers, particularly its Irish readers. She also wrote to her abolitionist friend and old boarder Joshua Leavitt, who had become the editor of the American Anti-Slavery Society's *Emancipator* in 1847. Her letters to both papers thanked Americans readers for their generosity to the Irish, reported on the famine conditions in Ireland, and begged them for further help. Her February 1, 1847, letter to the *New York Tribune* appeared on February 27, 1847, under the headings:

STATE OF IRELAND

COMMISSIONED FOR *THE TRIBUNE*

LETTER FROM AN AMERICAN LADY

Dear Sir: I hasten with a grateful heart to acknowledge the receipt of your letter and the donations from yourself and those kind friends.—Tell them ten thousand times do I thank them for the blessed boon of having it in my power—yes of having the most humble part in relieving the dying suffering around me. I had just spent the last shilling had been obliged to lock the gate that leads to the domain where I am stopping a week or two with the servant, while the family [the James Webbs] are from home. The applications are so pressing the countenances so disconsolate, and the skin so shriveled and dried that no eye could see them but the oppressors that *would* or *could* be unaffected. I had sold the last of my books in my own possession and my means for *doing* exhausted and was asking, "Lord, what wilt thou have me to do!" and now allow me to tell you what I did this morning.

It was last evening when the parcel arrived which contained your letter and though it made me but ten dollars richer, yet had it been a thousand I could not have been happier, but I saw so much of a God in it that I could not doubt but when that should be distributed, He would send more.

There are two men cracking stones near the gate who are actually in a state of lingering starvation. One has a family of eight—had pawned all their choicest wearing apparel for food. He has seven and sixpence a week—pays two shillings weekly for rent which leaves him five and sixpence to warm and feed himself and family till the next Saturday night. *Judge ye.* In addition he had been sick for weeks before this temporary work was offered and fearing he should lose the opportunity, he undertook it when he was quite unable.

One child died last Monday night. The poor man came to me and said, "What can I do? I have nothing to wrap it in, no coffin, nor a candle in the house, not a farthing of money nor a mouthful of food but a little Indian meal."

A little money was given him. A carpenter went into the cabin and made a coffin. A few laboring men went before it was sunrise and carried the child to its happy rest—a child of four years. And this time was to be taken because the father must not lose an hour's labor. The other man is as destitute but has not so large family.

This morning I bought two large loaves of bread—made a portion of Indian meal stirabout—sent the servant to ask them in—and now, my friends, who had purchased this breakfast, had you seen these men, you would never wish to see the like again. They have subsisted about ten days on a breakfast of stirabout which I had made each morning, but the last six days I had no means to furnish it, and they had worked six days on four days scanty eating, twice a day, of this gruel—sometimes a little stirabout. The sick man has become so shriveled that his skin has dried, adhering to his cheek bones, his eyes are prominent and he was so weak that he appeared unable to walk, and finally said—"Last night I could scarcely reach home. I had not one mouthful to eat and had worked in a hard rain all day."

It was enough. I left the room and did just what any other weak woman would do—fell a weeping. Recovering a little, I took up *The New York Tribune* and met with the sentence—"Efforts for Ireland."[7] I read it, and wept again. I praised the Father of Lights that there are feeling hearts yet in my country. Cursed as she is with the besetting sin of slavery, yet her pulse can beat for poor, oppressed, neglected Ireland! I felt flying across the Ocean and falling on my knees before the audience in Tammany Hall in the name of the patient dying fathers and mothers, brothers and sisters of this abused People! Could angels weep, they would do it now. No wonder the Immaculate Son of God sweat drops of blood in that memorable garden if he had sins to bear like this—if the black guilt of the Rich Aristocracy of the Kingdom of Great Britain were upon him.

Do you ask who are the greatest sufferers? The Roman Catholics, of course, and to their honor be it said they bear this grievous burden with the most unheard of patience. Not one single reproach have I ever heard, from priest to peasant, upon the proud Protestant, though I have mingled with them in about every condition. The Priests are indefatigable by night and day—both doing and giving—not flinching from the most loathsome places of filth and putrefaction. And the Sisters of Charity need not be named—their self-denying, persevering labors may well put to the blush those who look upon them with contempt.

What more shall I say—but beg you to be instant in season and out of season—in keeping alive this subject. Flatter not yourselves that the Spring will make things more tolerable; it can only do this, help the starving suffer a few days longer by not adding cold to hunger—for though labor may be more plenty, yet this goddess of the world, this Kingly government, this Church and State combination are determined that the great gulf they have fixed happen, this "purple and fine linen" shall not be lessened and the price of labor shall not be increased. Why not set their hunting dogs upon them shoot them down in the field as slaveholders do?

A.N.

Nicholson's letter to Joshua Leavitt, editor of the American and Foreign Anti-Slavery Society's *Emancipator*, appeared on March 3, 1847, in the "Correspondence" column titled "Letter from Mrs. Nicholson" with an introductory note by Leavitt:

The *Cambria* brought us the following letter on the distresses of Ireland from Mrs. Asenath Nicholson, of New York, who has been in Ireland for the last two years. Mrs. Nicholson is extensively known as the author of the Life of John R. McDowall, and by her other literary labors. She is also extensively known as the keeper, for many years, of the Graham Boarding House in Williams Street, which used to be the resort of a great many abolitionists in the early days of the Anti-slavery movement, when every act of abolition attended with a certain loss or danger.

About two years ago she went to Ireland, prompted solely by the intense and benevolent interest she felt in behalf of the oppressed peasantry of that miserable country. She has been employed ever since traveling over the island—almost exclusively among the peasantry—going to their cabins, learning from actual inspection the gage and depth and dimension of their misery; and we have no doubt she has a more thorough and personal knowledge of their condition than any other Protestant person living. The letter, and the account she gives of her employment and manner of life, show the depth of her benevolence and self-denial. A perusal of it has suggested to us that she ought to have aid in her work of charity, and that she is a most suitable person to be the almoner of some liberal portion of the charity which our countrymen are pouring forth for the relief of poor Ireland. We assure our friends that any amount of provision, from a barrel of meal to a ship's cargo, that may be sent to Mrs. Nicholson, will be used and distributed with the most absolute fidelity, impartiality and economy. We venture to propose that her old boarders, throughout the country, unite in testifying their respect for her and their sympathy in her benevolence, by uniting to forward to her at Dublin, a liberal contribution of Indian Meal and other provisions, which she may have the pleasure of distributing to the perishing around her. And we take the liberty to request our friend, DANIEL FANSHAW, of New York City, to act as treasurer and agent of the Nicholson contribution, to receive the money, lay it out in food, and ship it to Mrs. N. in Dublin.[8] We know that no man will more cheerfully undertake the charge, and no one would do that business for international business, but he said that it was the charge, and no one would do the business more thoroughly. Now, friends, let us lose no time in this matter. Send money at once to Mr. Fanshaw.

Nicholson's second, unsigned, letter to the Irish in New York, "The Sufferings and Wrongs of Ireland: By an American Lady," written from Dublin on February 1, 1847, appeared in the *New York Tribune* of March 9, 1847:

For the *Tribune*:

It is to the Irishmen and Irishwomen of New York I would speak in behalf of your bleeding, dying country, where you drew your first breath, and spent your young laughing days. *Hear, hear,* for God's sake, for Christ's sake, and for your brethren's sake, *hear,* I pray. You have heard the sad wail across the Atlantic that her land is laid waste and that here *long, long* oppression has at length *filled up* the cup of her miseries. It is FULL—it is running over. Hundreds are dying by the highway, in the fields, and in their cabins. Yes, many who have begged for work in vain. Some who have obtained it have been so exhausted that they have died at their work, because the prudent would not pay them till Saturday—perhaps, till two weeks work was done.

You may know of Cork, Kerry, Galway, Mayo-Connaught, Conomore [Connemara?] and Donegal way across the Atlantic and see them lying on a pile of straw, the dead and the living together, some lying five days unburied, because they could not procure a coffin and sheet to wrap them in—because the living were in a state of dying, and could not go out and because no one went in to inquire for them. One poor man took the corpse of his wife on his shoulder, after she had been five days dead, and carried and laid her upon a tomb stone in the graveyard. A poor neighbor went in and alone dug her grave, and put her in without coffin or shroud. Surely the dogs of Prince Albert might look out from under his costly monument and yelp at such a burial as this.

I read in the *New York Tribune* the meeting at Tammany Hall for the relief of Ireland and had a portion of this letter previously prepared, and would now say that the hope of shaming the aristocracy of the country, by sending relief to the poor of Ireland, is as vain as to hope the Queen will lay aside her trappings and visit the cabins of Ireland, and eat, drink and sleep as they do. I know the aristocracy of Ireland: they are not capable of [illegible]. Could you hear them talk as I do *now*—yes, even now when the dead are about them, who have reaped[?] down their fields for nought," and have died because the petty wages they pay them cannot sustain life at the enormous price of food. *Shame* a Government that will give men ten pence a day for labor, when Indian meal is 2s 10d a stone, and often 3 s. English money.

Shame a noblemen with a pack of hunting hounds chasing some timid deer of mountain and glen while fifty or a hundred starving men are digging his ditches, draining his bogs, and laying out his pleasure grounds for the shameful reward of eight or ten pence a week. Shame the surpliced clergymen with a living of some thousands a year, and pays a trusty servant from four to six guineas a year! Talk not of shame to any such! You who have lived in Ireland under their despotism, may tell the Americans better.

I would not be understood that the aristocracy and the gentry are doing nothing in self-defense. They are blustering a little because now and then some starving group, grown desperate by positive starvation, have rushed upon a bread cart and carried away its contents and the delicate nervous ladies are thrown into spasms to think that American women go into the filthy garrets in Dublin to seek out the suffering. They should not dare do such a thing. Yet they will sometimes call at my lodgings and leave a bundle of old musty, cast off ragged garments to be given to the destitute.

The Quakers, too, are doing something and doing it quite efficiently, at least so far as investigation goes. The Presbyterians in Belfast have, many of them, done nobly, especially the females. But with all that *has* been done, with all that *will* be done, thousands—yes, thousands, will be neglected and die. And in conclusion, allow me to say, On-up this moment, and do what you can; wait not for Government, wait not for hard hearts to soften, but put on the whole armor, muster all your forces, call upon the servants who are getting £15, £20 and £25 a year to do a little, tell them to take the ribbons from their bonnets, the trimmings from their dresses, if they can do nothing else. Tell them here are servants who have worked for two and three pounds a year, now deprived of that, are going from door to door asking bread.[9]

One who has a home to visit has walked three miles every day to get a little stirabout and piece of bread to sustain life and every time she calls I can see an evident change for the worse. Tell your children that in the country where their fathers lived the children are crying for bread and cannot get it. And be sure if you send money be careful to whom you entrust it. Put it into no paid commissioner's hands. Give it to none who want pay for their time. Money is a tempting article and the man or woman who would not rejoice at being made the happy almoner of their gifts to the dying without reward is not to be trusted with it. Some of you entrust it.

Excuse the length, but I ask no excuse for the rest of this. Had I the tongue of an angel I should tell you things that my language cannot express. I had intended to let you off, but how can I. The condition of these poor laborers under my window, pining and starving, is sounding in my ears and the scenes are so dreadfully appalling in every quarter, you must bear a little more—for to whom shall I speak, for even the abolitionists here have so long breathed this corrupting atmosphere of aristocratic principles that though he blusters much on freedom and equal rights of "giving to all what is just and equal" he, like the slaveholder, has his salve at hand. When you talk of higher wages, he tells you this is not *his* fault. You must put it upon Queen Elizabeth and Cromwell who apportioned the lands to the drummers and soldiers as a reward for demolishing the temples of Popery, while he at the same time may keep his carriage with every attendant and every comfort if not luxury about him, and will not, does not pay a servant, comparatively speaking, anything; he sulks behind these plundering marauders as the slaveholder behind the piratical slavers who first brought the negro from Africa and entailed as a curse upon their fathers.

If you go to the religious, wealthy Protestant, who holds the "keys of this bottomless pit," he tells you—ah, it is just what might be expected. Their laziness and dirty religion have brought on the curse, and when you go to the poor starving laborer, he uncomplainingly says, "We must be content with what Almighty God gives us—he may send us something tomorrow." In truth I have heard this answer so much from lips that I knew must be soon silent forever, that its Christ-like patience and keen rebuke is something to my heart, and should you hear that they have arisen like hungry wolves to seize upon the snugly walled flocks and herds of the rich boasting shepherds would not call—call them not blood-thirsty and savage because this long century heated boiler has exploded at last.

Whoever has studied the character of the Irish must know that they have a quick perception of justice which is meted out with kindness, a ready response is given. "Keep them down," says Government, and their own aristocracy echo it. We must "*keep them* down," or they will deluge the island with blood. So says the slaveholder. If we give them their rights they will destroy us at once. And pray tell us the times when and the place where the Irish, as a people, ever had their rights. Tell me who can, what they might be if an equal standing were given them among the nations of the earth and every shackle broken?

But I must not preach but I will expostulate. I will plead for poor, abused Ireland so long as God gives me breath—mock and rant who may. Yes, did I know my county would shout me back should I ever reach its shores. Should they say, "Go back to the people you so love," I would say "Amen." Yes, I would cheerfully go back and in some humble mud-cabin, sit down and hear the hearty welcome and the "God love you kindly" with a cheerful heart. I know what I am saying. I have gone over every county of that beautiful island but one.[10] I have traveled in sunshine and storm—by night and day—*with* money and *without*—in company and alone and never was an unkind word or even an unkind look manifested by the laboring peasant expressed of any kind but "welcome, welcome, lady to our humble cabin and sure you're a stranger"—When I said I am an American stranger, "welcome, thrice welcome" was always the response. The poor laborer in Ireland looks to America as his only hope—his last hope.

When I have spoken to one who might be cracking stones by the wayside and asked him the price of his toil, he answered ten pence or a shilling as the case may be, seldom raising his head to answer, but as soon as I used my password "American stranger," his hammer instantly stopped, his head was raised, the welcome given, and the addition of, "Ah, America's the place. 'Tis there they give the mate. 'Tis there they give the wages," generally accompanied with an apology, "I thought by your tongue you were English." *This* told the story.

And shall I hold my peace when five millions of such a people are in a state of cruel pauperism—yes, starvation and *death*, many of them. No! may my tongue cleave to the roof of my mouth when it shall forget to plead for poor Ireland.[11] I will be more enthusiastic still, and say if there is a people on earth who preeminently and justly claim this sympathy, the admiration, and the love of mankind it is the Peasantry of Ireland. Give me three cheers for that across the Atlantic, ye brethren who hear me! Once more shall I add that I can never look into many of the cabins on the sea coast and in the mountains, where they have shared so heartily with me the potato, and can see them dying by starvation—yes, dead, and lying days without burial and now and now again awake and keep awake.

Nicholson also wrote a second letter to Leavitt on February 1, 1847, from Ethelinda Warren's house at 5 Hardwich (Hardwicke) Street in Dublin. This letter reflected her desperation for help for the Irish. Her letter was a cry from the heart.

Mr. Leavitt—

Sir:—From the land of desolation, of double distilled horror and sufferings, I write, and I write because your heart is open to the cry of the needy and those who have no helper. I send you a picture which is no caricature—of daily scenes witnessed in burying the poor, starved peasantry of this long-oppressed people. No people ever suffered so much and suffered so patiently—the poor creatures creep about the streets, shriveled and black because of the famine— asking for a morsel, and often die while it is in their mouth. Ah, what can I say, to give an American, in that land of plenty, the faintest idea of a famine. Yes, a famine and pestilence![12]

Have I lived to see it? And was this my sad errand to Ireland to witness scenes like these? Yet, I am glad I am here—I am glad that God gives me strength to do a little—to save now and then one from the jaws of death by hunger. As my means are quite limited, I have confined myself to a few families—buying Indian meal, (which is at the shameful price of six shilling, York money, for fourteen pounds), and going to habitations, showing them how to cook it, and also in giving it out at the door as the poor, emaciated creatures call. My own living is Indian meal gruel and two pennies worth of bread in a day—vegetables are out of the question, and fruit is scarcely named among us. I go seven miles weekly to feed two men, whom I found starving upon the road at work—not receiving any pay till they had toiled a week, and then but seven and sixpence, is all their reward; out of this they must pay rent, and feed six and eight in a family.

The bare-faced, heaven-daring oppression of the peasantry of Ireland can only find a parallel in American slavery; and even in that, there are some loop-holes which a poor Irishman has not. The slave, if he can run, has not an ocean to cross, before he has some hope of safety; but the poor Irishman, fly where he may, unless he swim the ocean, meets nothing but oppression still. England and Scotland are no hiding places for him—here he is hated and hunted like a hare upon the mountains.

You probably read much, and hear much, but be assured the half cannot be told you. And the scenes are daily becoming more formidable, thousands and thousands must die in the mountains and on the islands who will never be looked after. Their carcasses are a prey to the dogs and fowls of the air. Everything has been eaten but human flesh, and then pestilence follows. Sleep departs from my eyes, while the imploring supplicants haunt my imagination like specters; and what is quite remarkable, not a word of reproach or fretfulness falls from their lips. They suffer in patience and die in silence. The mirth of the land has ceased—the merry joke and ready wit which are so much the characteristics of the Irish have ceased, and gloom seems depicted in every countenance.

Read Lamentations II: 11th and 12th verses, and in Ireland you have it literally fulfilled.[13] The sight of a starving person is unlike any death scene, whatever; the prominent eye—the shriveled, black skin, and the imploring silence would melt any heart but that of the (shall I say it?) British Parliament and Irish landholders. I do not mean that they do not any of them feel, or any of them care, but their acting is wrung from them by sheer necessity—in most cases when they have power.

The Quakers have done nobly in Ireland, and all are in self-defense mustering a little, but they have so few efficient women to go into the garrets and cellars, the cabins and desolate places; that those little things which none but a woman can do are all neglected. They are astonished at my temerity, and wonder I dare put my head into such places. I was glad, yea I was proud when I read what my country had done in sending relief. But shame on a government— a proud monarchy, that will starve her subjects, so that a young republic must go to her relief.

But stir them up to greater diligence—leave not a stone unturned; if you cannot shame England, save what of poor Ireland you can. It will be a star in your crown of glory. Show this picture— put it in your paper. Again I tell you, it is no caricature, but every day's occurrence,

If you have any patience left, do send me a line and let me know the state of things with you, and may my God have you all in his kind care and keeping—and never doom you to feel or see the miseries that are before my eyes.

Sincerely and kindly,
Asenath Nicholson

Apart from private efforts like Nicholson's, the Central Relief Committee was alone in providing relief to the poor. The government had decided to abandon its public works relief scheme in favor of direct distribution of food to the poor, but there was a gap between programs in the spring of 1847. Christine Kinealy has traced the close of the Public Works Act in the spring of 1847 and its effect on the poor, and Mary Daly has observed that this break in relief programs "during one of the most difficult periods of all—one marked by extremely high death rates—was one of the most serious inadequacies in the whole government. But for the Central Relief Committee, the mortality in the city would have been still higher" (1986, 88).

Quaker women were essential to the work of their Dublin soup shop. While the women in the engraving of the Cork soup shop that appeared in the *Illustrated London News* on January 16, 1847, portrayed women as middle-class visitors to the soup shop, Jonathan Pim's letter of July 2, 1847, to Jacob Harvey in New York mentions that it was "generally ladies" who were distributing cooked rice to the sick and to the children, but it is Nicholson who provides the description of the Quaker women at work. "Quaker matrons and their daughters with their white sleeves drawn over their tidy-clad arms—their white aprons and caps, all moving in that quiet harmony so peculiar to that people" (*Annals* 1998, 43).

Although Nicholson admired the Quaker women working together in their soup shop, she went her own way in establishing her own modus operandi in the spring of 1847. She described her decision to "operate individually . . . as woman is wont to do when at her own option." She kept no books, so the people who came to her were spared the delay and the danger of having to wait for their names to be entered officially into the relieving officers' books. She describes herself in *Annals* living in third-floor rooms in "a tall house over-looking the Liffey" (1998, 53).[14] Her room was furnished with a bed that was really "a short sofa, or an apology for one, placed in the middle of barrels of meal, spread upon blankets on the floor, and one crazy old chair, which served to make out my lodging at night and provide a seat while copying manuscripts; an old deal table with a *New York Tribune* for a table cloth" (*Annals* 1998, 53). She removed the carpet to create storage space for the sacks of meal that had arrived from Daniel Fanshaw in New York.[15]

Nicholson's daily schedule was as ascetic as her lodging and her diet. Living among the poor, she limited her own food budget to less than two shillings a week: two pence ha'penny for cocoa, three pence ha'penny for milk, three pence for sugar, and fourteen pence for bread (*Annals* 1998, 45). She reduced that mite when her families needed something more. She rose at four to copy the manuscript and correct the proofs for *Ireland's Welcome to the Stranger* until seven, when she ate her penny roll of bread and began to organize food for distribution each morning at eight o'clock at her lodgings.[16] She then set off with a large basket of three loaves of bread that she distributed as she made her way to Cook Street, also known as Coffin Street, a street bordering St. Audoen's Arch and the remains of the city wall.[17] In 1847 it was a street of derelict houses, tenements, and sixteen coffin makers or undertakers (*Thom's Dublin Directory* 1848, 672). Crowds of hungry people followed Nicholson; she felt safe enough, but the pleading and cries for help of the hungry were heart-scalding.

Unlike the Quakers, Nicholson did not sell her food; she distributed it gratis. She realized that given her limited resources, it would be better to concentrate her relief efforts on a small number of families in her Cook Street neighborhood. She could not save everyone, but she could save some by making porridge of Indian corn and teaching her families to prepare their own meals. She rescued a poor family who lived in an alley of the Liberties who supplied her with kindling. A daughter became Nicholson's seamstress. In his autobiography Alfred Webb speaks of Nicholson occasionally bringing him or his brother Richard on her visits around the city.[18] The experience may have informed his decision, in 1847, to urge the Dublin Society of Friends to establish a Famine Relief Fund (Legg 2009, 817).

Nicholson's friendship with Richard Davis Webb gave her access to the Central Relief Committee and to Quakers and other philanthropists who visited Ireland to see Irish famine conditions for themselves.[19] It was at the Webbs' home, during the first week in April 1847, that Nicholson met English Quaker philanthropist William Bennett. It was the beginning of an important friendship for her. He would provide material and moral support; he would be a valued confidant, and he and his wife, Elizabeth Trusted Bennett (1798–1891), would host her at their St. John's Wood home when she went to live in London in the fall of 1848. Bennett left his first impression of Nicholson in his account of his 1847 visit to Ireland, *Narrative of a Recent Journey of Six Weeks in Ireland: In Connection with the Subject of Supplying Small Seed to Some of the Remoter Districts*:

> At the house of my earliest friend in Ireland—to whose kindness and assistance we were almost wholly indebted for the success of our first enterprise many years ago in the west, and which have been continued to the present time—we met an American lady, of singular and strong character, whose first acquaintance with the Irish peasantry, in the garrets and cellars of New York, had ripened into a feeling of sympathy and commiseration, which had induced—I believe I may

say compelled—her to come over on a mission of philanthropy, in order to visit the people she had so much pitied and admired, in their own homes; and to learn what soil had nurtured such a hardy and impetuous,—such an intelligent yet down-trod,—such a poor but generous race. She came almost without scrip or purse, and has now spent upwards of two years in walking over nearly every part of Ireland, going from cabin to cabin wherever she found access, that is, almost everywhere among the poor, administering according to her measure and ability, both to their physical and spiritual destitution. I found her with limited and precarious means, still persevering from morning to night in visiting the most desolate abodes of the poor and making food—especially of Indian meal—for those who did not know how to do it properly, with her own hands. She was under much painful discouragement, but a better hope still held her up. Having considerable quantity of arrow-root with me, at my own disposal, I left some of it with her, and five pounds for general purposes. (Bennett 1847, 96)

Nicholson must have told Bennett that she was writing *Ireland's Welcome to the Stranger* and shown him some of the text, because after his visit to the homes of the poor of Arranmore, he referred to the manuscript in his *Narrative*: "The dwellings, upon the whole, were perhaps, externally, a shade better than the mere turf-hovels of Erris; but all within exhibiting the truth of the words (still I believe in MS) of a vigorous and acute observer from another land, who went by herself 'to see the poor peasant by way-side and in bog, in the field, and by his peat-fire, and read to him the story of Calvary'" (1847, 71).

Apart from the Quakers, Nicholson reported that the rest of middle-class Dubliners took little interest in the poor around them. They paid rates to support Dublin's Union workhouses and contributed to charitable societies, but they showed no interest in visiting the poor themselves. She gave Dubliners their due for charity, but she distinguished between *giving* and *doing*, the "antipodes in her who has never been trained to domestic duties" (*Annals* 1998, 57). They listened to Nicholson's accounts of her relief work in the spring of 1847 and were often prompted to offer her a meal when she finished her reports. She always accepted because it meant more money for her families.

By the following winter, her criticism of the Dublin middle class was sharper. She rejected the belief that Irish poor were lazy. The Irish problem was lack of opportunity, not indolence. When she returned to famine-stricken Ireland in December 1846, she criticized the attitude of the middle class toward the poor: "Ye withhold from them labour and then call them 'idle.'" According to Nicholson, it was not the poor who were lazy; no one hired them. But the rich were idle too, and their idleness came from "pride and a long habit of indulgence" (*Annals* 1998, 33). Middle-class Dublin women rose late, paid little attention to domestic economy, and gave their daughters a genteel but not a practical education; therefore, when the Great Irish Famine came, they had no idea how to respond.

She indicted the middle and upper classes for their indifference to the famine, pointing out that "the winters of 1847 and 1848 in Dublin were winters of great hilarity among the gentry" (*Annals* 1998, 106). F. J. Davis's "The State Ballroom, St. Patrick's Hall, Dublin Castle" (1845) documents an evening ball hosted by Lord Lieutenant and Lady Clarendon and their official entourage and featuring beautifully dressed women and their escorts (Kennedy 2000, 30–31).[20] She pointed out to readers that it was the English people who "felt more deeply, and acted more consistently" than the Irish about famine suffering, and she listed by name the English Quakers who traveled to Ireland to bear witness and to bring relief, including Joseph Crosfield, William Forster, and James Tuke (*Annals* 1998, 106, 54).[21]

Nicholson rejected the opinion of people who called the famine a Divine judgment. First, there was the potato itself. She recognized in her earlier visit to Ireland that the potato was a mixed blessing. She heard it from the poor themselves, and she observed the degradation that came with the dependence on the potato. Among others who damned the potato, she would have recalled the young man she met in Roundstone in May 1845 who told her it was "the greatest curse that was ever sent on Ireland" (*IWS* 2002, 297). When the food source of the single-crop economy failed, the blighted potato harvest became a famine because the government mismanaged the crisis. There was excess food in other places; there was food in Ireland that left the country that would have made it possible to feed the Irish poor. Nicholson's judgment? It was not a crop failure; it was a failure of stewardship that created the Great Irish Famine.

Nicholson greatly admired the Central Relief Committee and their work; however, her admiration was not uncritical. When food supplies arrived for her and for Maria Edgeworth aboard the frigate *Macedonia*, Nicholson objected to the Quakers' compliance with the government policy that the Indian meal that arrived in barrels be transferred into sacks purchased from the CRC for a half crown each.[22] She objected on two grounds: that the meal survived better and for a longer period in barrels and that the money spent on sacks meant less money for food for the poor. The note to her letter of July 2, 1847, written from 45 Hardwicke Street to the Central Relief Committee registered her objection to being charged for the sacks:

> Allow me to say I am quite sorry that the Americans have made you so much trouble through me—in the simplicity of my heart. I wrote them when you first commenced your work of benevolence to send their contributions through your channel not *then* supposing any would be sent to me. They have done so and have done it without my request but be assured if there is more upon the ocean *now* for me to come through your hands. There will be none hereafter as I have written them begging they will make you no more trouble.
>
> The ship *Macedonia* has some five barrels of meal, flour and biscuit for me directed, as I am told, to 45 Hardwicke St. and hope you will have no inconvenience on account when I am gone to the Coast.
>
> Respectfully, A. Nicholson

> Note: Your clerk told me when I received your order that I must pay for the sacks, but if they are returned in good order, this money would be refunded. When this was refused, he denied the engagement saying that I should pay freight if not pay for the sacks. This I am willing to do if it is just, but the donor in New York sent me

notice that all they sent me was freight free and sent in barrels, and I quite prefer them because sacks will not keep the meal so well and much that I had was seriously injured.

As usual, Nicholson had the last word. A July 5 notation from the committee on her letter said, "The Committee recommends that this party should not be put to the expense of sacks."[23]

The end of Nicholson's letter to the CRC indicated that she was planning to leave the city, but first she arranged that the meal and biscuit sent her by poor schoolchildren in New York that arrived aboard the *Macedonia* go to Mrs. Phepoe, the mother superior of the Presentation school at George's Hill, the site of the first Presentation Convent (1794).[24]

During the spring of 1847, while Nicholson was working among Dublin's poor, the circumstances of the split between the factions of the Anti-Slavery Society surfaced again. Richard Davis Webb's sister-in-law Maria Waring wrote to Lewis Tappan on April 4 to ask him about the transfer of the *Emancipator* from the auspices of the American Anti-Slavery Society to the American and Foreign Anti-Slavery Society. Waring, whom Webb described as an "impartial minded, scrupulous truth loving person," was apparently trying to verify whether Nicholson's remarks about the schism in the American Anti-Slavery Society were accurate.[25]

Four months later, on August 14, 1847, Tappan answered Waring's letter from Kingston; the letter was postmarked Liverpool. Though he believed Waring to be a Garrisonian, he said he felt "quite disposed to answer your enquiries trusting that you are a candid person desirous of truth."[26] Nicholson apparently told Maria Waring that the Garrison-Tappan split had to do with the seating of women delegates at the 1840 meeting of the American Anti-Slavery Society. Tappan acknowledged that he and others on the old American Anti-Slavery Executive Committee did not approve of women taking part in their public meetings, but he assured Waring that seating the women would not have precipitated the schism. He spoke instead of what he called the "bad spirit," the "trickery," on the part of Garrison, leading a contingent of one hundred or more people from one vicinity (Boston) to outvote the members of the society who "converged from various states in the usual manner."

Tappan's references to Nicholson are telling. He begins his letter to Waring by describing Nicholson as an "intelligent and excellent woman" who did not have accurate information to answer Waring's question. At the end of his letter, Tappan returns to Nicholson again, calling her "a plain woman of good sense, of devoted philanthropy and highly esteemed." Although Tappan does not dismiss Nicholson, he distances himself from her. He does not mention their associations: the Graham Boarding House, Rev. John M'Dowall, and the old American Anti-Slavery Society in New York in the 1830s. Webb forwarded Tappan's letter to Maria Waring Chapman with the comment that Tappan's "denial of women's rights as having much to do with that affair is news to me. It seems to me to take a pretty plain story and one that does not redound to his own credit."[27] The exchange of letters demonstrates that Nicholson was well informed about issues. That she continued to side with the Tappanites did not mean that she was unaware of the women's rights issue that caused the division in the American abolitionist movement.

During this exchange about the American Anti-Slavery Society, Nicholson finished *Ireland's Welcome to the Stranger*. In her concluding pages, Nicholson mentioned her plan to urge Americans to come to Ireland's aid; it was her reason for writing the book. She reaffirmed her commitment to do what she could to provide relief to the poor and pledged herself to do any good that was in her power. She dated her preface June 10, 1847, Dublin. Richard Davis Webb himself published the book. Charles Gilpin (5 Bishopsgate Street Without) was her London publisher; Webb and Chapman printed the English edition. Her manuscript delivered to Webb, Nicholson left Dublin for Belfast on Tuesday, July 6, 1847, aboard *The City of Dublin* steam packet. She had spent a few weeks in Belfast in 1845 and found a congenial society among the Northern Irish Presbyterians who made her feel "as if I were by a New England fireside" (*IWS* 2002, 339). She would have recognized a kindred spirit between the Boston women abolitionists who raised money working together to hold their antislavery bazaars and the 150 women members of the Belfast Ladies' Association for Connaught, an organization founded on January 1, 1847, by members of the First and Second Presbyterian Congregations. The association supported the work of Dr. John Edgar for the maintenance of his industrial schools in the West of Ireland (*Annals* 1998, 58).[28]

Nicholson praised the Belfast women for their active ministry, citing the "indefatigable" Mary Ann McCracken. She was the younger sister of Henry Joy McCracken (1767–98), the United Irishman who was hanged for his part in the '98 Rebellion. McCracken worked at her philanthropies until her death at the age of ninety-six on July 26, 1866.[29] When Nicholson met her in 1847, McCracken was president of the Ladies Industrial School; the school's annual report documents her active participation at their weekly meetings, "as long as she was able to attend" (McNeill 1960, 293). Gordon Bigelow has observed that Nicholson, like Mary Ann McCracken, believed that the industrial schools provided the opportunity for their pupils to develop the habit of industry, a habit that would transform them and then Irish society (1999, 137). Such an industrial school system, Bigelow argues, was built on the "disciplined heart" of the "rational mother," which would foster a model of industrial economy and efficiency that would be heightened by love.[30]

Nicholson certainly would have approved of schools that developed character, but in her visits to Irish schools, she was equally interested in the skills and knowledge taught to the children: practical skills as well as basic literacies. She saved her criticism for the schools, like the ones in the Dingle and Achill Missions, that limited children's education based on misperceptions or prejudicial attitudes about their character.

Nicholson mentioned that Maria Webb (1804–73), Richard Davis Webb's cousin by marriage, was also active in the Belfast Ladies' Association; she also worked for the Central Relief Committee, particularly after she moved with her husband to Dublin in 1848.[31] Many of the association were also members of the Belfast Ladies Antislavery Association, and they were in close touch with the American women abolitionists and supported their fund-raising efforts. Maria Webb apologized to Maria Chapman for their rather smaller 1847 box for the annual Boston Anti-Slavery Bazaar. She explained that the distressed state of the country had "engrossed the attention" of the women who ordinarily would have contributed to the American bazaar.[32]

It was no doubt through Mary Ann McCracken that Nicholson met the Grimshaw family, who invited her to stay with them at White-house, near Belfast, where Nicholas Grimshaw had built a cotton mill in 1784.[33] While there, Nicholson met Susan Hewitson, a woman who had family in Rossgarrow, County Donegal. Susan or her mother, also a Susan, successfully applied to the Central Relief Committee for a grant for a women's employment scheme.[34] When Nicholson left Whitehouse, she took a coach to Londonderry, where the Hewitsons met her and took her to their home at Rossgarrow, near Ramelton, County Donegal. The visit to the Hewitsons rather eased her way into the famine-stricken West.

Both Hewitsons were involved in local famine relief. Mr. Hewitson, a pensioned British army officer, was an overseer of Board of Works projects during the first year of the famine; Mrs. Hewitson conscientiously weighed out sacks of meals that she dispensed each morning from her kitchen, where the lower windowpane was replaced with a board when it was broken by the poor pressing their faces against the glass. The image of starving people staring through the windows of the homes of local gentry haunted Nicholson. Another striking image was her account of a boy who presented the clinical signs of one literally dying of starvation. It is just an image. She does not linger. Sensitive to the despair Nicholson felt facing the suffering around her, the Hewitsons tried to distract her with the natural beauty of the Donegal coast, but the pleasure of the sightseeing was diminished for Nicholson. She remembered fondly the engaging children she met in 1844–45 who were always present during her first visit to Ireland to point out local sites to the American. She found their absence and the silence of the countryside chilling.

Nicholson used a cordial meeting with Rt. Rev. Patrick McGettigan, bishop of Raphoe, at his home in Letterkenny as a moment

to reflect on the relationship between priests and the poor in rural
Ireland.[35] She pointed out that the great majority of Roman Catholic
clergy were poor themselves. They were also victims of sectarianism
in the awarding of grants during the first years of the famine. She
argued that it made no sense to send people out to *look for* the suffering when local priests knew exactly the needs of their parishioners
and the conditions in each cabin in the district. She mentioned the
case of the Protestant clergyman who shared as much of his grant
as he could with his Catholic counterpart. She continued to observe
and to report about the cooperation between Protestant and Catholic
clergy working among the poor to offset the accounts of the efforts
of some Protestant clergy who exploited famine conditions to realize
their proselytizing goals.

Nicholson used her visit to the estate of George Augustus, Lord
Hill (1801–79), as an opportunity to observe the difference an improving and Irish-speaking resident landlord could make to his tenants.[36]
Even in the worst year of the famine, Nicholson found that conditions
among Hill's tenants were more comfortable than the circumstances
on the neighboring Conyngham estate.[37] To demonstrate the quality
of life in the district before Lord Hill, Nicholson reprinted the full
text of the description of the district, an area of appalling destitution,
written in 1837 by Patrick M'Kye, the teacher in the local national
school and published in *Facts from Gweedore* (1846, 12).[38]

Nicholson described in detail the changes Hill made in reallocat-
ing land from the old rundale system of tiny parcels of lands of different quality to a system of consolidated holding to which he added
additional parcels of land that he purchased for tenants on his estate.
He curbed distilling; introduced other foods; built a corn barn, a kiln,
a new school, a store, and a quay; and offered premiums for improvements to cottages, for agricultural diversity, for husbandry, and for
cottage-made textiles and clothes. These changes and his encouragement of industry and employment were a model of what could be
done in a poor and desolate area, but Nicholson recognized there was
a price for the economic improvements. "The Rundale system, when
disturbed, brought new difficulties to these people; it broke up their

clusters of huts, and the facilities of assembling nights, to tell and hear long stories" (*Annals* 1998, 70).[39] She ended her account of her visit by saying that Hill wrote in 1850 that although there were premature deaths in the area, "*no person*" died of famine in Gweedore (*Annals* 1998, 72).

Nicholson left Hill's model Gweedore estate to go deeper into the poverty of West Donegal through the Rosses to Roshine Lodge, the home of Lord Hill's "able and intelligent" agent Francis Forster near Dungloe (Bennett 1847, 82).[40] A horror awaited her on the next day when she crossed Rosses Bay to visit Arranmore with Valentine Pole Griffith and a party of six men. It was a sunny day, but the island seemed deserted except for an occasional well-nourished, sleek dog. Nicholson asked innocently why the dogs seemed so fat before she realized that their food source was the island dead. Later on Achill she would hear the story of the body of an orphaned girl who was devoured by dogs, but the Arranmore moment was one of arresting horror.[41]

The sight of a field of barley growing from seeds given earlier in the year by William Bennett when he visited Arranmore in March prompted Nicholson to muse that if those fields could flourish, then other plots supplied with free barley and turnip seed could have fed the poor.

Here, as elsewhere, what relief came to the island was supplied by subscriptions raised by English churches. She had a brief respite from the unrelieved misery she witnessed when she heard the laughter of children, a sound she had not heard since she arrived in Ireland on her famine mission.[42]

Nicholson wrote to her friend English Quaker William Bennett from Templecrone, County Donegal, on August 3, 1847. It was a cri de coeur to one who understood the magnitude of Nicholson's mission. He had suggested to the London Friends that they distribute seed for green crops, not for potatoes, to the poor. The London Friends felt they could not take on an additional project, but a private donor, probably Joseph Sturge, sent Bennett the funds with which to purchase turnip, carrot, mangel-wurzel (beet), cabbage, flax, and parsnip seeds. Bennett's account of his visit, *Narrative of a Recent Journey of Six Weeks in Ireland*, supplements Nicholson's record of famine conditions. He had been in Templecrone five months earlier, March 21–23, 1847. The parish of ten thousand on the western coast of Donegal included the bleak and rugged wildness of the Rosses; even in better times, there was frequently a scarcity of food (Lewis 1832, 2:603). Bennett knew and admired people such as Valentine Pole Griffith and his wife, Elizabeth, and their counterparts in Mayo Samuel Bourne and Samuel Stock.

Bennett passed Nicholson's letter along to his St. John's Woods (Regent Park) neighbors William and Mary Howitt, who published it in their *Howitt's Journal*.[43] The Howitts' headnote to Nicholson's letter mentioned their admiration for her work among the poor and that she would be using the profits from *Ireland's Welcome to the Stranger* to finance her work in the West of Ireland:

> We hear, that having printed her book, and probably having procured some pecuniary funds on its account, she has gone away again into the west, to minister any relief she can to the wretched and dying, or at least to make known their misery to the public.
>
> By thus drawing attention to her work and her labour, we hope to promote her benevolent object; and to show that the need of help and sympathy will remain great for the poor of Ireland, we give a copy of a letter from this lady to a friends of ours, which opens up a lamentable view of their suffering at this moment.

TEMPLECRONE, DONEGAL

AUGUST 3, 1847

> I must trouble you with another letter, though no response had been made to a former one. But a visit to Donegal, to Gweedore, Arranmore, and Templecrone has completely stirred my inner soul that I cannot conscientiously withstand the call to talk a little with you on the subject, knowing you will understand what I say.
>
> I must not spend time to dwell on the labours of Forster, Griffith and Hewitson. You well know they have been untiring, and I am prepared to say, almost unparalleled, and they need not only

supernatural wisdom, but supernatural strength, to withstand the mighty torrent that is pouring upon them. What they can do, I cannot devise, if something more efficient be not done, and that immediately. Yes, now the people are fainting and dying in the most heart-rending manner in Arranmore and Templecrone, and none come to the relief. The boilers have ceased operation, and the poor famished creatures are gathering chicken-grass and turnip tops, boiling them, and letting them stand still till they get cold, and eating them for almost their only support. They cannot fish, but by sitting upon a rock, and taking a solitary crab, or their like, for they cannot man a boat.

I went on Monday to the island of Arranmore, the kind Mr. Griffith for my guide, and what shall I tell you what I saw? One of the boatmen was sent forward to say, that an American lady was coming to look at them but would give them nothing that day and that they must not trouble her by begging. We entered their dark abodes; there, in groups, were they sitting or lying with the emaciated, desponding, lifeless look of inanity, that nothing else but long starvation could give, and without uttering a syllable, they gave us looks which *never, never* can be effaced from my memory. I gave a little boy, whose shriveled face and looks altogether had the appearance of a monkey's more than a child's. I gave him a biscuit, and the ghastly smile, which followed, to say the least, was horrid. I cannot now get away from the sight. We went to the grave-yard, saw a new-made grave, a straw rope lying by the side, and was told by a man who accompanied us that this was the grave of three children, whose father had carried them, lashed to his back, by the rope, and being unable, for want of strength, to bury the last, *he* put it into the dust for him.

I went over to the island and saw here and there a little barley and oats waving in the breeze which was the product of a little seed given them last spring, and now and them a small patch of potatoes, but the whole on the island would not feed them, as all say, more than six weeks, if all were in the most economical readiness for use. Mr. Griffith took me over hill and dale of that romantic island, and he showed me immense tracts of mountain land, good for grazing and much of it good for grain, and not a cow, horse or sheep upon it, nor a patch of anything eatable to be seen.

Now, my friend, you with me will say, "What ought to be—can be done?" And while in Britain or America there are means sufficient to put such a machinery as would relieve them into operation, blood-guiltiness will be upon the hands of such as neglect it. Mr. Griffith showed me his road and pier, which the poor, famished creatures have finished with so much taste, and he testifies that it was done with the greatest cheerfulness and patience; though they worked in hunger and in nakedness, not one, he said, complained. This little piece of work does honor to the laborers, as well as to Mr. Griffith who contrived it.

I need not multiply facts. You have seen all these places, and your name is mentioned with much respect.

I am now at Mr. Forster's, and in an hour start for Gweedore, to meet Mr. Hewitson, and go to Dublin, where I hope to find some supplies from America, for the poor, for further distribution and expect soon to visit the county of Mayo. Do not be angry with my long letter; I have not said half I have on hand about my poor Donegal. And who will arise for her help, and those good men who are spending time and strength to mitigate her suffering? The women are beyond all praise. Mrs. Hewitson, Mrs. Forster and Mrs. Griffith have a twofold if not a tenfold share; more much more than any female should be called to suffer, especially those who are mothers.

I must stop and may the God of all grace, give us a disposition to act as we should act, so that when we meet Him at last, and receive his approbation when these poor creatures shall stand with us at his dreadful tribunal.

Respectfully and thankfully,
A. Nicholson[44]

Nicholson left the desolation of West Donegal to meet Mrs. Hewitson in Gweedore to travel on to Belfast. They stopped for an afternoon to attend and admire the flower and cattle show in Londonderry. The some three thousand women dressed in their best caused Nicholson to remark once again that the famine took the measure of Irish women. Women like Mrs. Hewitson and members of the Belfast Ladies' Association rose to meet the crisis.

Ireland's Welcome to the Stranger was published in the fall. The book was reviewed under the title "Ireland and the Irish" in *Tait's Edinburgh Magazine.* Elizabeth Grant of Rothiemurchus, Scotland, who married Colonel H. Smith in 1830 and moved to Baltinboys, County Wicklow, recorded her impression of Nicholson's book in her journal entry for November 14, 1847. When she had called on Lady Milltown during a visit to Dublin, she was introduced to Nicholson, whom she described as an oddity who was too quick to judge:

> She [Lady Milltown] gave me a curious book to read which has much diverted us all. An "American Stranger," a woman of fifty, educated, used to decent habits, comes to Ireland to judge of its condition. She drinks no fermented liquors, no tea, no milk, eats no flesh, walks her tour for the most part, sleeps in the cabin lodging houses in dirty beds, sometimes with dirty bedfellows often in a crowded room, dressed in mud boots, a polka coat of the newest fashion, a velvet bonnet, a parasol, carries a basket on her arm with a change of linen, wears a belt underneath the polka attached to which are two bags full of testaments, and in her gown she has pockets filled with tracts. She reads wherever she goes and attracts large crowds by singing hymns. She is not quite mad—only an enthusiast, and too imaginative, too quick, to be quite correct in her facts or her inferences. (1999, 354–55)

Nicholson returned briefly to Dublin to check on her pensioners in Cook Street, the ones she left with their rents paid and with wool to earn money from selling their knitting. She forwarded a grant to Mrs. Hewitson and arranged to take a box of clothing with her west to Mayo to her old friend Margaret Arthur, the widowed postmistress of Newport, where she found "misery without mask" (*Annals* 1998, 83).

Nicholson knew Mayo from Westport to Achill from her earlier visit, in May and June 1845, but she was unfamiliar with the area of greatest destitution from Ballina west to the Erris peninsula. She followed the route of Quakers William Forster, James Tuke (1819–96), William Bennett, and Richard Webb. Webb was probably the most helpful to her. She does not mention his tours to the West in May 1847 and in February 1848, but his letters to the Central Relief Committee identify the people and places that Nicholson describes in the *Annals*.[45]

Through her Quaker contacts and her friends from her earlier visits, Nicholson was able to stay with many of the people who were administering local relief: the Savages of Achill Sound who acted for the Quakers, Margaret Arthur, and Samuel Bourne (ca. 1790–1864), a landlord with a small estate of about seventy tenant families. Located in the midst of suffering, she set about to witness, first in letters and then in the *Annals*, the famine and then the heroic efforts to bring comfort to the hungry and the dying.

6

"Misery without Mask"

Mayo in the Winter of 1847–48

WHILE NICHOLSON visited her friends the Savages at Achill Sound, she met the Honorable William Butler, who had served as the inspecting officer of Belmullet and Binghamstown from May 1846 until September 1847. Although Nicholson was usually critical of government relief officers for putting regulations before relief, she admired Butler. "He acted kindly as an inspector, and devised the best means which he could, and I was informed, when making the inquiry respecting his distinguished humanity, that he accepted his appointment from principle, not from necessity, that he might see that justice was better administered" (*Annals* 1998, 61).[1] Butler urged Nicholson to visit the barony of Erris and offered to pay her fare, so the two traveled together by boat from Achill Sound to Belmullet, where she found a treeless plain and dunes of blown sand.[2]

She stayed in Belmullet with William Paul Dawson, rector of the parish of Kilmore and a member of the Erris Relief Committee, who distributed aid to the poor from the Dublin Central Relief Committee (*Thom's Dublin Directory* 1848, 300). The committee was chaired by Samuel Stock, rector of Belmullet, which was then known as Kilcommon-Erris; he had lived in the parish since 1816. Stock's wife established a soup depot in her rectory kitchen and set up a clothing industry with local women until an outbreak of fever interrupted the work (Bowen 1970, 192).[3]

From Belmullet Nicholson traveled the twelve miles along Broad Haven Bay to Rossport to Samuel Bourne and his family at Rossport

House.[4] William Bennett sent Nicholson's description of Rossport to the London Society of Friends, which published part of it under the title "Ireland" in the November 1, 1847, number of the *Friend* (London). The letter described famine conditions that she found around Rossport:

> The crop of flax looks well; but the country is in a three-fold worse state than when you were in it. For myself, I am wholly outdone. I have struggled and struggled on, clinging to every straw of hope for poor Ireland, but now Erris and Arranmore have put me in a state of petrification, now that I can only look on in silent despair. . . .
>
> —— took me to see his parsnips, turnips and carrots yesterday, and, to say the least, they were a joyous sight, thrifty, abundant and delightful to the taste.
>
> From a window I have a novel sight presented; men, women, and children, with enormous loads of flax upon their backs, bringing from boats which have wafted it ashore; and the loads upon the shoulders of women and children to me look hideous as well as degrading.

Samuel Bourne's household was one of "comparative comfort," but they had a "burden like an incubus with the mass of starving creatures" (*Annals* 1998, 96).[5] Nicholson described Bourne's household, the people living nearby whom they visited, and the relief efforts made by Bourne, and by members of his family, to help the poor of the region.

The Bourne family acquired land in the Rossport area at the beginning of the eighteenth century, a result of the Cromwellian land confiscations; however, Samuel Bourne did not settle in Rossport until the 1830s. Michael Corduff, a Rossport native who collected the folklore of the district in the 1960s, reported that Bourne provided employment to his tenants constructing Rossport House, reclaiming land and building a pier for shipping. Although all of his tenants, some seventy families, were required to give twelve *laethantaí dulgais* (duty days) free, workers were paid eight pence per day for their other labor (Póirtéir 1995, 205–6).

The stories collected a century after Nicholson's visit corroborate her account of Bourne's stewardship during the Great Irish Famine. "It has been conceded on all sides that Samuel Bournes [*sic*] was a generous and charitable man. Whatever his motives, he was indeed a philanthropist. He preserved the people of a large area, not merely his own tenants but those of adjoining estates also, from the rigors and starvation caused by Famine in other parts of the country" (Póirtéir 1995, 205–6). The local attitude toward Bourne can be found in the proverbial expression "Bíodh foighid agat agus tiocfaidh do chiud ón Teach Mór chugat" (Have patience and your share of food will come from the Big House). The saying alludes to Bourne's reputation as the provider of food from the "Big House" to tenants and neighbors during the hungry times (Póirtéir 1995, 206).

Bourne invited Dr. John Edgar, who had established the Connaught Industrial Schools with funds from the Belfast Ladies' Association for Connaught, to establish a school on his estate. Nicholson, of course, visited the school and found that the students were instructed in knitting and sewing. She would have preferred that students also learned to read. Nicholson also visited the little school supported by the Dublin Central Relief Committee that was started in a remote corner of the parish by a Miss Carey, the daughter of the coastguardsman Captain Frederick Carey. Nicholson described the sight of "the pale, emaciated children walking barefoot to school to study and work till three o'clock for the scanty meal of stirabout or a piece of bread" (*Annals* 1998, 98). When her meager resources were exhausted, Miss Carey had to close her school and leave her children to a precarious life in their mountain cabins.

Another Nicholson Rossport heroine was a Miss Wilson, a well-traveled idealist who came to live with the Bournes and committed to living the rest of her life doing acts of Christian charity.[6] In addition to her praise of Bourne for his care of the poor, Nicholson also names other generous landlords and relief workers in the Erris area. Her Belmullet letter mentioned Samuel Stock and James O'Donnell's parlors (*Annals* 1998, 100). James O'Donnell was a local landlord who received aid from the CRC: forty pounds for relief expenses and four bushels of Indian meal (Central Relief Committee 1865, 58).

Nicholson's friend Richard Davis Webb, who was traveling for the Central Relief Committee in Erris at the same time Nicholson was in the West, praised Bourne and other indefatigable Erris landlords and relief workers. "The poor people in the district round Rossport say they would be lost if it were not for the persons to whom you have given grants. From strict enquiries and close observations, I am satisfied that the lives of hundreds have been saved by the efforts of these men as their families" (Society of Friends 1852, 200).

In addition to her description of the Erris landlords, Nicholson's account preserves stories of minority groups—submerged populations such as local women gentry and tenantry—whose stories do not feature in the conventional histories of the Great Irish Famine. Her story of a Rossport woman, one of the "faded respectable," is a cautionary tale of one who was too proud to accept relief. Another detail of famine life is Nicholson's account of the extreme efforts of the poor of Erris to get food. "Everything that could be eaten was sought out and devoured, and the most hazardous attempts were made to appease hunger by the people" (*Annals* 1998, 96). She described men and women walking along the cliffs to gather seagulls' eggs and edible seaweed such as sloke.[7] While she was in Erris, two women in search of sloke along the cliffs near Dunkeehan were washed out to sea, and two men in search of eggs were swept from a cliff and died of their injuries (*Annals* 1998, 97).[8]

During the Great Irish Famine, the Erris people not only had the sea as a food source, however meager and however dangerous to obtain, but also had the possibility of piracy, raiding shipping for their food cargo. Nicholson does not mention instances of such attacks while she was Erris, but Richard Davis Webb reported a thwarted attempt to seize Indian corn when he visited Rossport later in the spring of 1847 after Nicholson's visit. He wrote to the Central Relief Committee from Belmullet on May 13, 1847:

> While I was in Rossport in the northern part of Mayo, a vessel, lying
> ten miles from shore, was thus plundered of thirty sacks of Indian

corn, by thirty-four men in eleven *corraghs*, the fishing boats or canoes of this county.

These men with their boats and plunder, were taken prisoners by five of the coast-guards in a four-oared galley, and conducted twenty miles to Belmullet, where I saw them in prison. With two or three exceptions, they were stout healthy-looking young men, apparently well clad and well fed. This robbery took place in Broadhaven. Some weeks before, a similar circumstance occurred in Blacksod Bay, south of the Mullet. (Society of Friends 1852, 200)

Although Nicholson did not observe any instances of attempted piracy while she was in Erris, her single recorded instance of resistance took place in Erris, three miles from Belmullet, where she witnessed a young boy of about fourteen foil the attempt of drivers, protected by armed gentry, who were rounding up the stock of tenants who had defaulted on their rents. As the drivers herded the cattle and sheep, the boy ran shouting between them, scattering herd and flock. The astonished drivers just rode away (*Annals* 1998, 99–100). Nicholson may have been reminded of Genesis 32, the story of Jacob, who divided his flock and his people so that if Esau attacked one group, the other could escape.[9]

When the English Quaker James Hack Tuke made a second tour of the West in the autumn of 1847, he visited the Bournes at Rossport, where he met Nicholson. They traveled together to Ballina, and Nicholson went on from there to Belmullet and west to the peninsula, known locally as the Mullet, where, in Irish mythology, the Children of Lir were doomed to spend their severe last three hundred years of exile off the coast on the bleak little islet of Inishglora in Erris Bay. Nicholson found the flat, treeless, long, narrow Mullet peninsula bleak. Her accounts from the Mullet, the locale she identified as Erris, demonstrate the way that her famine writing differed from the correspondence of her male counterparts. William Bennett, Richard Davis Webb, and James Hack Tuke wrote of the horrific conditions they found in Erris; Richard Davis Webb spoke for all when he wrote from Belmullet on May 8, 1847, "Such wretchedness, starvation, filth and degradation I never saw before" (Society of Friends 1852, 199). The men were concerned with famine conditions and the logistics of relief. Nicholson focused on human suffering.

She began her October 5, 1847, letter to William Bennett with the horrific conditions she found in the Mullet. She spoke first of Castle Bingham, where the "Famine Earl," Sir George Charles Bingham, Third Earl of Lucan, was as notorious for his evictions of tenants as he was later for his disastrous order at Balaclava that was immortalized in Alfred Lord Tennyson's poem "The Charge of the Light Brigade."[10]

> I walked from Belmullet to the Castle (Bingham), and such pictures of desolation never, never, met my eyes. Almost the entire country lies waste; houses tumbled down, or with padlocks on the door; scarcely a sign of cultivation, but now and then a patch of turnips, and these the poor starved creatures have nearly destroyed in many places by cutting so closely. Mr. S. says, "Tell Mr. B. that his turnip seed has done more good than £300 would have done, laid out upon meal. The ignorant creatures had sown the seed too thick; never having cultivated the root, they did not understand it: still it is spinning out a wretched existence, a few weeks more; and had the whole country been covered with them, they might have struggled through, but now die, they must."[11]

A measure of Nicholson's growing despair was a second letter to Bennett from Belmullet on October 30, 1847, a letter that Bennett passed along to his neighbors William and Mary Howitt, who published it in *Howitt's Journal* on November 27, 1847, with this note from the editors: "Let us lay before our readers some revelations from Ireland of its conditions at the present moment. The first is a letter to a philanthropic friend of ours [Bennett], who has laboured personally and zealously for the relief of the poor Irish, from that extraordinary American lady, Asenath Nicholson, the author of 'Ireland's Welcome to the Stranger,' who has for many months been going among the Irish peasantry examining their condition and endeavoring to attract the notice of the wealthy and powerful to it" (340). Nicholson's letter that followed reflected her despair at the scene of the "heart-sickening" suffering she witnessed and her utter despair of being able to do anything to rouse the interests and efforts of others to aid the Irish poor. She called for a militant radical such as abolitionist George Thompson to speak for Ireland; she suggested new initiatives such as American intervention.[12] Nicholson believed that only employment schemes would solve the problems of the poor, and she predicted that six more months of demoralizing indolence and hunger that had made the poor prey to "every immorality" would materialize.

My Dear Sir, Please prepare yourself—I am about applying some of those "offensive points" in my character, which you say I possess, and which may require not only your "true charity," but untiring patience, to plod through. I have been riding and walking through desolate Erris, and in worse than despair, if possible, have sat down asking what *am* I to do? What *can* I do? And what *should* I do? Every effort of the friends of Ireland is baffled by the demoralizing effects that feeding a starving peasantry without labour has produced. And now the sound again is echoing and re-echoing, that on the 1st of November, the boilers up the mountain and in the Glen, are to be foaming and splashing with Indian meal—while the various idlers shall have nothing to do but fight their way over necks of old women, and starved children, missiles of police-men, elbows fists of aspirants, to secure the lucky hodge-podge into can and noggin, pot and bucket, and trail over ditch, and through bog from a quarter of a mile to five, as hap may be; then to sit down in his mud-built cabin, sup and gulp down the boon, lie down upon his straw till the hour of 9 or 10 will again summon him to the next warlike encounter. Indeed, sir, your friend who was last here, said that he could think of nothing better than to take up a turf cabin with its inmates and appurtenances, and set it down in England. I can outdo him in invention—I would take some half dozen of your George Thompsons, if so many truly independent members of Parliament you have, and would transport them through the waste lands of Erris, and seat them snugly around a boiler under full play. They should sit unobserved and see the whole working of the machinery. The array of rags, each one equipped with his canteen to hold his precious gift, should approach; the ghastly features, staring eyes, bony fingers, slender legs, in fact ghosts and hob-goblins, hags and imps, should draw near; the fighting and tearing, tumbling and scratching, should commence and go on till the boiler was emptied, and these *facsimiles* of fighting dogs, tigers and wolves, had well cleared the premises. I then would invite them to a seat in Samuel Stock's, Samuel Bourne's and James O'Donnell's parlours.[13] Then let them patiently watch from ten to twelve, from twelve to two, and perchance from two to four, and witness the intensity of action in making out lines, and diagrams and figures to show in plain black and white to government that Pat Flanagan, Samuel Murphy, Biddy Aigin and Molly Sullivan had each his and her pound of meal made into stirabout on the 3rd of November Anno Domini 1847. And let it be understood that these Pat Flannagans, Aigins, and Murphys had only to spend the day in the terrific contests before described to earn this pound of meal, and then betake themselves to the mountains and dens, turf hovels, to crawl in and then and there sup up this life-giving, life-inspiring stimulus. They should further be told that the Stocks, Bournes O'Donnells, & had the privilege of handing over these nightly made-out documents to officers, paid from six to ten, from ten to twenty shillings per day, that they might have the promise of a six month's nightly campaign, should papers be found to be true and legible, as aforetime.

This is but a short preface to the story. My heart sickens at looking over the utter wasting of all that was once cheerful, interesting, and kind in these peasantry. Hunger and idleness have left them a prey to every immorality; and if they do not soon practice every vice attendant on such a state of things, it will be because they have not the power. Many are now maniacs, some desperate and some idiots. Human nature is coming forth in every deformity that she can put, while in the flesh; and should I stay in Ireland six month longer, I shall not be astonished at seeing any deeds of wickedness performed, even by those who one year ago might apparently have been as free from guilt as any among us. I have not been able yet, with all my republican training, to lose the old-school principle of man's total lost state.[14] I have never yet seen him without the restraints of custom or religion anything but a demon in embryo, if not in full maturity; doing not only what he can, but sighing and longing to do more. The floodgates in Ireland are certainly set open, and the torrent has already made fearful ravages.

From Clare and Tipperary what do we hear? One post after another runs to tell that not only deeds of darkness are done, but deeds of daylight desperation, sufficient to startle the firmest.[15] What Moses shall stand up to plead with God? What Phineas shall rush in to stay the plague?[16] Where are your men of moral, yes, of spiritual might? You have them; bring them out! I look across that narrow channel. I see the graves of martyrs. I see the graves of men whose daring minds stood forth in a majesty of greatness to speak for truth and justice; and though they may long since have taken flight, where are their mantles? Where is your George Thompson? He who shook the United States from Maine to Georgia in leading long and loud for the down-trodden black man? Can he not, will he not lift his voice for poor Ireland? She who stands shivering, sinking on the Isthmus, between two worlds, apparently not fit for either. Will he not reach forth a kindly hand and try to snatch this once interesting and lovely, though now forlorn and forsaken creature, from her fearful position? Must she, shall she die? Will proud England lose so bright a gem as Ireland might have been in her crown? Will she lose her, when the distaff and the spade, the plow and the fishing net, might again make her mountains and her valleys rejoice; when the song of her husbandman, and the laugh of the milkmaid might make her green isle the home of thousands, who are now sinking and dying in wasting despair?

Do you say she is intriguing, she is indolent and treacherous? Try her once more. Put instruments of working warfare into her hands; hold up the soul—stirring stimulation of remuneration to her; give her no time for mediating plunder and bloodshed; give her no inducement to be reckless of a life that exists only to suffer. Feed her not in idleness nor taunt her with her nakedness and poverty, till her wasted, palsied limbs have been washed and clothed, till her empty stomach has been filled, and filled too with food of her own earning, when she shall have strength to do it. Give her a little spot on the loved isle she can call her own, where she can 'sit under her own vine and fig-tree, and none to make her afraid and force her not to flee to a distant clime to purchase that bread that would be sweeter on her own native soil."

Do you say you cannot feed and pay four million of these your subjects? Then call on your transatlantic sister to give you food for them. The earth is the Lord's and the fullness thereof; and though she has a right to say she will not send Ireland food to keep them strong in idleness, she has no right to say she will not send them food to give them strength for labour. She has not a heart to say it; foul as her hands may be with slavery, yet she will feed the hungry with a cheerful hand. If she has not done her duty there is room for repentance. Her fields, the past season, have been waving with rich corn, and her storehouses are filling with the golden harvest. You have given her gold in profusion for the produce of her soil. The blast of the potato has been to her the blossoming and ripening of her pastures—her waving fields of pulse and corn. The husbandman has been stimulated to plow up fresh lands so that he might fill his granaries abundantly with the rich harvest, because free trade has opened your ports and you will demand more corn; and why should he not send over a few sheaves as a thank—offering to God for all this bounty? American will do it if required; but an inquiry has come across the ocean. Is it right to feed a country to encourage idleness? Will not the evil be much greater than the good? Answer, you who are statesmen—you who are Christians; answer, you who can. Look at the peasantry of Ireland three years ago, and look at them now! Even their enemies must acknowledge that they are a tractable race, to have developed so much intrigue and cunning under the training of the last two years. Shall I scold, shall I preach, shall I entreat any more? What is woman's legislating amid the din of so many wise magicians, soothsayers and astrologers as have set up for Ireland the last two years. Prophets and priests have so far failed; but certainly there must be a true chord to strike somewhere; for what is now wrong, when traced to its source, may disclose the hidden cause of the evil, and put the willing investigator into a position to work an amendment.

You who know Erris, tell, if you can, how the landlords can support the poor by taxation, to give them food, when the few resident landlords are nothing, and worse than nothing, for they are paupers in the full sense of the word. When can Samuel Bourne, James O'Donnell and such like men to in their present position? If they have done wrong, and do it not more, the torrent is so strong that they cannot withstand it. I must and will plead, though I plead in vain, that something may be done to give them work. I have just received a letter from the curate of Bingham's Town saying that he could set all his poor parish, both the women and children, to work, and find a market for their knitting and cloth if he could command a few pounds to purchase the materials. He is young and indefatigable, kind-hearted and poor and no proselyte.[17] Mrs. Stock has done well in her industrial department. The Hon. William Butler has purchased cloth of her for a coat to wear himself, which poor women spun, and gave a good price for it.

I pray you, sir, if this malignant letter does not terrify you, you will write and say what must be done.

A. Nicholson (344)

Following Nicholson's letter, the Howitts printed a copy of a letter from Samuel Stock to Lord John Russell dated Belmullet, October 28, two days before Nicholson's letter. Stock painted a stark picture of suffering for Russell, reminding the prime minister of his letter of a year ago: "I expressed my conviction that unless immediate relief was afforded, *hundreds*, must perish under that visitation; that warning was overlooked till too late, the timely relief we sought for was delayed, and the fearful results were, that not alone hundreds, but thousands, perished from want and consequent disease."

Stock continued with alarm about the desperation of the starving people of Erris: "I forbear to particularize any of those scenes of woe.

I am daily doomed to behold; they are too shocking, too disgusting; but as an instance of the pressing want of a hitherto most patient people, permit me to state that, while in the act of writing this, my hall door has been burst open by a starving multitude, unable from hunger to endure the regular distribution of a small quantity of rice confided to me by the Society of Friends, for the sick and convalescent in my neighborhood." Stock ended his letter by asking, "My Lord, should such things be suffered to exist in a country profoundly Christian?" (Stock 1847, 341).

Stock forwarded Russell's prompt response to the Howitts:

> DOWNING-STREET,
> NOVEMBER 2ND, 1847
> Sir,—I am desired by Lord John Russell, to inform you, that he has no funds at his disposal to apply in the manner pointed out in your letter of the 28th ultimo.
> I am, Sir,
>> Your obedient servant,
>> George Keppel (341)

William Howitt followed the Nicholson, Stock, and Keppel letters with a comment that called for action, lest the government "stand before the world in the humiliating and culpable position of the conjuror's apprentice who raised the devil and did not know how to lay him again." The metaphor was drawn, perhaps, from Nicholson's anguished, "What is woman's legislating amid the din of so many wise magicians, soothsayers and astrologers as have set up for Ireland?" (342).

The synergy created by the Nicholson and Stock letters and the Russell response invites speculation. Did Nicholson and Stock discuss their letters? Did she see Stock's letter before she wrote her letter to Bennett? She sent a copy of her Bennett letter to the *Tyrawly Herald and Sligo Intelligencer* (Ballina), which published it a month later on December 2, 1847, with the following editorial note: "The following letter from that philanthropic lady Asenath Nicholson addressed to a friend will give a frightful picture of the conditions in poor Erris."

Having written her call for action, Nicholson made a stormy crossing of Blacksod Bay from the Mullet to Achill Sound on November
9. When she arrived the sea calmed, and the fishermen set out in the
curraghs. Suddenly, there was a violent storm, and by the next morning nineteen men were lost. Nicholson's November 18 letter to the
Tyrawly Herald described the loss.[18] Ten days later, on November 28,
Nicholson described a fisherman's widow who traveled twenty miles
to "prove" her husband, who had washed ashore and was buried without a coffin. "She bought a white coffin and took it to the spot where
he was buried. With her own hands, she dug him from his grave,
'proved' him by a leather button she had sewed upon some part of his
clothes, and buried him in the white coffin that she had brought with
her" (*Annals* 1998, 104).[19] John Millington Synge's biographer W. J.
McCormack also finds echoes of Nicholson's *Annals* in *The Playboy of
the Western World* and concludes that Synge must have read Nicholson
in what would have been part 3, "The Famine of 1847, '48 and '49,"
of *Lights and Shades of Ireland* (1850) and argues that details appear in
Riders to the Sea: Cathleen's use of the number of stitches in Michael's
stocking to identify her drowned brother and her request to an old
man to make a coffin for Michael out of the "fine white boards" that
she bought are based not on Aran Island tradition but on Nicholson's
text describing the famine in Mayo, a famine that claimed Synge's
own grandfather Robert Traill (McCormack 2006, 246–47, 249).

Their rags soaking wet, the poor crowded into the Savages' hotel.
Without consulting anyone, Nicholson rose, made pails of Indian
meal gruel, and moved quietly among the destitute, feeding them
from tin cups and dippers. She continued to feed the people until they
quieted. Having executed her "loaves and fishes" exercise, Nicholson
regarded the wretchedness about her, the degraded poor. "On what a
slender thread hangs all our standing here!" (*LP* 1853, 52). Why did
Nicholson choose not to include this vignette in *Annals of the Famine*? She leaves no clue except her reticence to portray herself as doing
anything heroic. For Nicholson, her deeds spoke for her. Her time at
the Dugort colony did not lead to any sort of rapprochement with
Rev. Edward Nangle, who ignored her presence in the colony. When

the superintendent of his eleven schools on the island told Nangle that Nicholson had given clothing to the poorest children, he commented only, "If she can do any good I am glad of it" (*Annals* 1998, 105).

Nicholson went from Achill Sound back to Newport in January 1848, where she stayed with the widow of Rev. Charles A. M. Wilson, Sir Richard O'Donnell's tenant, who was the rector of Achill, Newport-Pratt, who died in 1847.[20] She noted sadly that Mrs. Wilson had so beggared herself for the poor that the house and effects of their generous hostess were to be at auction for taxes and rent and Mrs. Wilson was to be imprisoned for debt (*Annals* 1998, 115). Her troubles led Nicholson to meditate on the terrible evictions of the poor in Erris.

The evictions of the tenants of Dublin solicitor and land speculator John Walshe right before Christmas 1847 were fresh in Nicholson's mind when she visited one of the hamlets cleared by Walshe's agent.[21] When she asked about the people evicted, if they all died, she was told, "Worse than died. For if they are alive, they are in sandbanks on the bleak sea-shore, or crowded into some miserable cabin for a night or two, waiting for death; they are lingering out the last hours of suffering" (*Annals* 1998, 116).[22] When Richard Davis Webb visited the Mullet the following month, in February 1848, he wrote to the Central Relief Committee that there were probably two hundred cabins destroyed, leaving four hundred homeless (Society of Friends 1852, 208; see also Tuke 1848, 61).[23]

Nicholson used two considerations, evictions and employment, to evaluate the behavior of landlords. When James Hack Tuke exposed Sir Richard Annesley O'Donnell as an evicting landlord, O'Donnell argued that he was not aware of the evictions and that his driver was responsible. Nicholson dismissed O'Donnell's defense, saying that ignorance was no excuse; landlords were responsible for their employees. Although Nicholson and Tuke condemned the evictions, both gave O'Donnell his due for his employment schemes for his tenants. Tuke reported that O'Donnell employed nearly a thousand tenants, primarily women, at flax making. "Even at this miserable rate of wages (four pence a day for women and eight pence a day for men), I have seldom seem more cheerful or industrious laborers" (1848, 9).

When Nicholson left Erris, Mrs. Wilson's son took Nicholson in a pony and trap from Newport to Ballina via Ballycroy. Traveling north, along a path in the lee of Nephin, Nicholson noticed that conditions were marginally better in that part of the country. The *Tyrawly Herald* for December 16, 1847, reported that Thomas Martin, "the practical [agricultural] inspector" in Erris, identified large tracts of land around Ballycroy that could be reclaimed, and Richard Davis Webb, who visited Ballycroy just after Nicholson, observed that "the people were exerting themselves with much energy and there was a prospect of large tracts of land around Ballycroy being sown" (Society of Friends 1852, 210). While she thought the countryside looked more promising, the local national school fell below Nicholson's standards. She found some hundred pale, barefoot children squatting in a cold, crowded room waiting for their ration of ten ounces of bread and an occasional turnip (*Annals* 1998, 121).

Nicholson's destination was Ballycroy Lodge, the hunting lodge that had been associated with William Hamilton Maxwell, author of *Wild Sports of the West* (1832).[24] Along the way she met a mother and a hungry child. Nicholson gave the child a biscuit, swept her up onto the car, and tucked the little girl under her cloak until they arrived near the child's cabin and the child ran off with a parting, "Bless you, lady." Nicholson regarded her visit to Ballycroy as an opportunity to observe the habitat of the sportsman, and she used the opportunity to describe the hunt as a "kind of enchantment, a witchery," with excoriating irony. She was particularly critical of the bright four-year-old daughter of the household, who was rapturous about hunting timid, defenseless hares.

Wilson brought Nicholson finally to Doona, where she noticed stumps of large water-logged tree trunks submerged along the shore near the home of the Daly family that was situated near Doona Castle, another castle associated with Granuaile.[25] Nicholson took a car from Doona to Bangor and the mail coach to Crossmolina and to

Ballina, the home of her friend Peter Kelly. Kelly was an attorney with an office in Castle Road who had married the daughter of Thaddeus O'Dowda (*Slater's* 1846, 105). When she provided a short history of the O'Dowdas, in *Lights and Shades* (1850, 178–82), Nicholson said that her knowledge of the family came from information she found at the Archaeological Society in Dublin.[26] Nicholson may have been acquainted with the family through John T. O'Dowda, who was listed at 42 Lower Ormonde Quay, not far from the premises of the Central Relief Committee and perhaps close to Nicholson's Dublin residence, the "tall house over-looking the Liffey" (*Annals* 1998, 53).

Nicholson became friendly with James O'Dowda's son Thaddeus, who in 1848 was living at O'Dowda's-town, where he was active in local relief.[27] A note from John Lees, the Church of Ireland curate in Ballina, to Bewley and Pim, members of the Central Relief Committee, enclosed "a list of the distribution of the past grant of meal and rice your Society made through me to Mr. O'Dowda. . . . I should feel obliged by your giving another grant, say of 2½ cwt [hundredweight] of meal rye and 2 cwt of rice."

When Nicholson met O'Dowda in 1848, she described him as "a man of the real amiable Irish stamp, conciliating in his manners, kind in disposition, cheerful without vulgarity, and dignified without austerity or hauteur, maintaining a mild dignity, which emanates entirely from instinct" (*LS* 1850, 180). O'Dowda had married the daughter of Charles White, a Dublin merchant, and they had five sons and four daughters. Nicholson was friendly with two of his daughters, Mrs. Peter Kelly and Miss O'Dowda (*LS* 1850, 178).

Her time in Ballina in February 1848 appears to have been a happy interlude. The seaport and market town, situated at the estuary of the river Moy, was on the main road between Castlebar and Sligo. She would have been aware of conditions in the Ballina workhouse. It was designed to accommodate twelve hundred residents when it opened for admission on November 3, 1843; by 1847 a fever shed for thirty was added (J. O'Connor 1995, 259, 239). The Ballina workhouse served the entire northwestern coast of Mayo; additional workhouses at Belmullet, Claremorris, Killala, and Newport were not added until the 1850s. Starving skeletons begged for admission to the overcrowded facility.

In February 1847 people were dying of fever at the rate of almost ninety persons a week (Bowen 1970, 219). In February 1848 Nicholson found suffering in Ballina, but nothing compared with what she had experienced in Erris. The heroic efforts of local voluntary relief workers were heartening.[28] One of Nicholson's Ballina heroes was Francis Kinkead, the Church of Ireland curate in Ballina, who came to Ballina in 1837 and died on January 27, 1847. The large marble memorial tablet to Kinkead on the wall of the Church of Ireland in Ballina reads:

To the Memory of
Rev d Francis Kinkead
This Tablet
Erected by his sorrowing friends and the parishioners
    of Kilmoremoy
Here for almost 10 years he labored with
Faithfulness, patience and untiring zeal:
Exemplary as a minister, he was in his daily walk
A consistent servant of his heavenly master
Gifted with high intellectual endowments
He consecrated them all to his Redeemer's service,
For the excellency of the knowledge of whom
He counted all things but loss.
His work of faith and labor of love were terminated by
Typhus fever, contracted in his
Unwearing efforts to relieve the wants of the poor,
During the season of grievous famine.

Nicholson admired two things about Kinkead: his concern for all the poor, Roman Catholics as well as Protestants, and his efforts to provide employment opportunities. The *Tyrawly Herald*'s obituary called Kinkead "the mild, the gentle, the humane, the charitable." A measure of his esteem in the town was that Catholics as well as Protestants contributed to the memorial tablet. Just two weeks before he died, on January 11, Kinkead founded the Ballina Ladies Institution (Bowen 1970, 221). A year later Nicholson reported that the industry was still in operation, but there was not enough work for the women, who were desperate to get work as spinners (*Annals* 1998, 125).

In Ballina Nicholson was among friends. One was the widow of Kinkead's devoted friend Captain Short, whom she had met previously in Erris. She certainly would have met Richard Davis Webb, who wrote the Central Relief Committee from Ballina on February 18, on March 2, and again on May 8 (Society of Friends 1852, 208, 210, 199). Nicholson wept when she left Ballina on February 28 to return to the suffering of western Mayo. Her friends Miss O'Dowda and two of the O'Kelly girls waved her off to Castlebar, where she found a crowded workhouse and the poor begging on the streets. While in the town, Nicholson went along to the courthouse for the trial of a man charged with murder. She noted, with approval, that Bourke, the defense attorney, made a "most able defense."[29] It was an opportunity for Nicholson to consider the fallibility of the human justice system; she concluded that we can expect impartial judgment only at the "last grand Assize" (*Annals* 1998, 128).

Nicholson spent St. Patrick's Day in Castlebar; she must have thought at some point during the day about the St. Patrick's Day she had spent in Killarney in 1845, a holiday for Mass and for wearing a sprig of shamrock, or the "crass." Nicholson observed a few shamrocks but a subdued spirit. In 1848 the day was political rather than traditional. The Parisian revolution three weeks before on February 24 led to the downfall of Louis Philippe's reactionary government; Alphonse de Lamartine declared a republic that lasted from 1848 until 1852.[30] The French success inspired O'Connell's followers to use the day to call for new agitation for the repeal of the Act of Union. Although she was sympathetic to the grievances of the Irish—the indifference of the government and the loss of confidence in landlords—Nicholson's own experience with abolitionism precipitating violent opposition caused her to be apprehensive. While the boys lit tar barrels and shouted, "Hurrah for the Republic," the crowd was dispirited. "The spirit is broken" (*Annals* 1998, 129).

Shortly after St. Patrick's Day, nationalist leaders, including William Smith O'Brien and Thomas Francis Meagher, went to Paris to secure support from the new French Republic. On April 3, 1848, they presented Lamartine, minister for foreign affairs, with an address of support for the new government and a request for their help to realize their own Irish nationalist aspirations. Lamartine, who did not want to jeopardize French relations with Britain, gave only an equivocal response that fell short of the assurances that the Irish delegation sought (R. Davis 1998, 244).

Nicholson would see Lamartine's Second Republic for herself in 1849, but in the spring of 1847 she continued her mission to serve the poor. While she was in Castlebar, Nicholson accepted an invitation from Peter Conway, the Partry Roman Catholic curate, to visit his impoverished parish, a place she described as being without parallel even in Skibbereen. (While Nicholson herself had not visited Skibbereen, by the spring of 1848 James Mahoney's engravings of the suffering in the Cork market town in the *Illustrated London News* made Skibbereen a vivid metaphor for the Great Irish Famine.) Nicholson noted, as she had done elsewhere, the names of people who were working to alleviate suffering: Rev. W. B. Stoney, rector of Castlebar, who provided employment, and Peter Conway. Invited to witness a baptism in a miserable cabin, she dismissed the sacrament as nonsense, but she praised the work of Father Conway among his suffering parishioners. "To do these poor priests justice, they have labored long and hard since the Famine, and have suffered intensely" (*Annals* 1998, 129). She was moved by the compassion of Father Conway, who said, "Sure, as I can give them no money, I should give them kind words," and she shared his despair about the suffering that he had no power to relieve, a despair with which she was only too familiar (*Annals* 1998, 132).

Nicholson made her way west to Louisburgh to reconnect with the Kelly family: Peter Kelly's sister Julia who had married Edmund Francis Garvey, of Fallduff, Old Head. She visited the estate pauper school where the schoolmaster, Anthony Egan, did his best to appear respectable in desolate West Mayo by wearing "a white vest and linen pantaloons" (*Annals* 1998, 136). Even the cooperative efforts of Father Thomas McCaffrey and the Protestant curate Patrick James Callanan were insufficient to meet the needs of the poor. Callanan had replaced the former curate Robert Potter, who, with his wife, died of typhus fever ministering to the poor in 1847.[31]

Before she left Louisburgh, Nicholson traveled with a party that included Jane Jordan Garvey of Tully, widow of William (1769–1840), and her sons James and John. The Tully Garveys held land in the valley between Louisburgh and Delphi, and Jane Garvey, like all of the Garveys, was generous to her tenants, forgiving rents and providing meal as long as she was able. Nicholson's lighthearted account of the trip through the Doolough Pass to Delphi described the discomfort of her companions and the sight of the chubby Jane Garvey tumbling down the rocks and emerging, shrieking, from under her crumpled bonnet. Nicholson confessed that she suppressed her laughter only by assuming a grave expression and a deadly silence.

A trip through the same Doolough Pass a year later was the site of a tragic famine episode. Four hundred starving people set off from Louisburgh to walk to Delphi, where the Poor Law Board of Guardians was meeting. The guardians said they could do nothing to relieve the suffering of the petitioners, who had no recourse then except to begin the return journey to Louisburgh. Weakened by hunger, exhaustion, and despair, the walkers were no match for the storm conditions that overtook them. Some were blown into Doolough; others died of exposure. A contemporary letter written in Louisburgh on April 5, 1849, reported that the poor had been ordered to Delphi or be dropped from the relief rolls. Five people were found dead along the road. A second letter (April 13, 1849) noted that two more bodies were discovered, and nine or ten more people failed to reach home and that "several of those who did, were so fatigued with cold and hunger that they in a short time ceased to live" (Lyons n.d., 63).[32]

Nicholson left her own mark on the grounds of Mrs. Garvey's home: a rockery with spring flowers that she created on an April morning in Tully. Her reported leave taking of her garden was her valediction to Mayo and a thanksgiving to the vigilant God who brought her safely through her Mayo ministry. "Stand there, when the hand that raised you shall be among the dead; and say to the inquiring traveler who may visit this spot, that Asenath Nicholson, of New York, raised these stones as a memento of the suffering country she so much pitied and loved, and as a monument of gratitude to the God who conducted her safely through all the dangerous scenes encountered while passing over it" (*Annals* 1998, 142). She paused to visit the John Christopher Garveys, who lived near Murrisk Abbey, before she left Mayo forever.[33]

As she boarded the coach that would take her to Westport and on through Castlebar to Tuam, Nicholson must have reflected on what she had accomplished during her mission to Mayo. She had visited the poor, bringing with her what resources she could—money, food, clothing—to relieve the poor. She bore witness to the suffering and wrote about what she observed to journals whose readers could provide additional funds and supplies to local relief workers. She also left an eyewitness account that documented the people who suffered, the ones whose work among the poor was informed by the Christian charity, not by sectarian sensibilities. She believed that she was sustained by Divine Providence and that she brought to the people she met the generous spirit she recognized among those individuals who loved the poor.

7

Back to Cork

"Ireland, I Love Thee Still," 1848

HAVING SPENT MONTHS among the destitute and dying, it was not surprising that Nicholson headed for Cork and for Father Mathew, the one person who would most understand what she had witnessed in the West and who would have shared her utter frustration that she could not do more for the poor. Her visit had a special urgency because she had no doubt heard that the Capuchin had suffered a stroke in early April, a condition that had been brought on by exhaustion and his rigorous Lenten fasting (Kerrigan 1992, 172). When his health stabilized, Father Mathew left Cork at the beginning of May to spend two months convalescing at Lehenagh, his brother Charles's home near the city.

During the weeks Father Mathew was at Lehenagh, Nicholson made her way south from Westport to Cork. She stopped first in Castlebar to visit her friends the independent Bible readers Murry and Jordan, who had established an independent church for the Irish Evangelical Society in the town. Nicholson reported that the men preached without opposition; she surmised that they were successful because they neither proselytized nor limited their relief to members of their own congregation.

She went from Mayo south to Cork via Tuam, Galway, and Limerick. In Tuam she found the condition of the idle inmates in the workhouse infuriating; however, she gave the institution credit for sending those inmates eligible to leave the institution back into the world with clothes made from recycled bedclothes rather than the rags they wore when they arrived. She looked, as always, to the local school to take the measure of the real condition of the local people, and, no doubt, using the name Father Mathew as a shibboleth, she visited the Presentation Convent in Tuam.[1] The dozen nuns who cared for some four hundred children were "hiding from the world, and yet completely overwhelmed with it" (*Annals* 1998, 145).

Accustomed to children suffering from hunger, disease, and deprivation, for the first time in nearly two years, Nicholson saw children with healthy coloring and normal affect. The nuns told Nicholson that the children had been saved by the "good Quakers'" gift of Indian meal, which they learned how to prepare properly for the children. There were also gifts of clothing. Adequately fed and clothed, the four hundred or so children were producing fine samples of knotting, interlaced cords, or ribbons.

The Tuam children were the one bright spot in Galway for Nicholson. When she reached the workhouse in Galway town, she found the inmates silent and despairing.[2] The Claddagh was no better. The women sat listlessly in their cottages, waiting to die. Glimmers of hope were provided by the Jesuits' school for the Claddagh boys, where they were taught and fed, and by the efforts made by the Quakers to revive the town's fishing industry.[3] The year before, in 1847, the Quakers decided that reviving the fishing industry in the country was a better use of their limited resources than a program dedicated entirely to providing food aid. By the summer of 1847, the British government's Soup Kitchen Act was implemented, freeing the Quakers to concentrate on aiding fishermen (Society of Friends 1852, 391–92).[4]

The rainy morning she arrived in Limerick, Nicholson tried to visit the workhouse, but she found the facility so crowded and the staff so harried that she got little information about conditions. Had she talked about the census with the master or matron, she would have learned that by May 1847, their 1,600 capacity has risen by 912 additional residents, many of whom lived in sheds around the workhouse. The crowding continued into 1848. In Limerick she would have heard that some in the city had violated their temperance pledges, another consequence of the despair brought on by famine that destroyed the self-confidence and hopefulness built by Father Mathew's temperance crusade.

The rest of Nicholson's journey to Cork was marked by the chronic problems that she experienced traveling by Bianconi car. She was prepared to reconsider the complaints she had lodged against the system in *Ireland's Welcome to the Stranger*, but the constant overcrowding, an insolent cabman, and a lost trunk convinced Nicholson that her initial judgment about Bianconi and his drivers was accurate and fair. She certainly would have mentioned her friendship with Father Mathew, Bianconi's schoolboy friend, in at least one of her complaints, but she got no satisfaction.

Bianconi notwithstanding, Nicholson finally arrived in Cork in early June 1848, and she stayed fifteen weeks (*Annals* 1998, 146). Although rural Cork continued to suffer, Nicholson found the city rallying a little from the worst of the Great Irish Famine. Conditions in the Cork workhouse had improved, and the mortality rate had abated, but the South Presentation nuns, from their convent on Douglas Street near Father Mathew's house at 10 Cove Street, were still feeding hungry children, and the streets of the city were filled with orphaned children who explained the loss of their parents by saying, "They died in the stirabout times" (*Annals* 1998, 150).[5]

Nicholson would have been relieved to have seen the amount of local support for famine victims: the Cork Committee of the Society of Friends under Abraham Beale, who died of typhus at age fifty-four in the summer of 1847; the nuns of the Presentation and Ursuline Convents; the British Relief Association; and, above all, the work of Father Mathew. He was the first to alert the government to the emergency; he opened a soup kitchen in Cork in the summer of 1846 and kept it open even after the Central Relief Committee closed its kitchens at the end of May 1847. He also negotiated with the city for a cemetery, the first for Catholics, located on the site of the old Botanical Gardens (Augustine 1947, 108; C. Lincoln 1981, 90; McNamara 1981, 108). Between September 1, 1846, and June 1, 1847, ten thousand bodies were buried in St. Joseph's Cemetery (Augustine 1947, 432).

The Presentation nuns whose work with the children of Cork was so critical described the famine as an act of Divine judgment. They said only of their indefatigable efforts, "During the years of 1846–7 when God visited this Cork City by Famine, Father Mathew spent nearly every half-penny of which he was possessed in relieving the poor starving children. He had a host of friends who gladly opened their purses to him. By this means he was able to keep the spark of life in them. We experienced his generosity more than others. Flour and meal came to us from America which we dispensed for a lengthened period among the poor children until God sent brighter times and removed the Scourge."[6]

Nicholson would have been most relieved to meet Father Mathew again, apparently recovered, when he returned to his Cork home and his parish in July. He went back to parish work and to his temperance crusade with a new worry added to his cares: the fate of the nationalist leaders, including his personal friends Charles Gavan Duffy and William Smith O'Brien, who were involved in planning a strike for Irish freedom in 1848, the heady year of European nationalism.[7]

Nicholson felt things were stable enough in the city for her to enjoy an excursion to Blarney, a place she had visited on her earlier trip to Cork with her friend Mrs. Danker and her young son. This time the party included the young Beale sisters from 7 Myrtle Hill Terrace and an English friend. Although the break from famine suffering was a temporary one for Nicholson, it illustrates the proximity of comfort and want in cities such as Dublin or Cork.

Walking along Blarney Lane on their way back into Cork, Nicholson noticed some signs of small comforts provided by women's hands that were "more valuable because diffused insensibly where most needed" (*Annals* 1998, 151). Nicholson's American sensibility credited Cork's improvement not only with its effective leadership of men such as Quakers Abraham Beale and Father Mathew and the work of lay and religious "active useful women" but also with a Cork society that was the least class-bound or caste-bound city that Nicholson met in Ireland (*Annals* 1998, 150).

Father Mathew had put off his planned temperance crusade to America because he was concerned about the members of the Young Ireland movement and a possible rising in Munster. Nicholson must have had frequent contact with him during those weeks. On July 29 the Young Irelander rising did occur, on the grounds of the widow McCormick's house near Ballingarry, County Tipperary. Hardly more than a skirmish, the rising was a dismal failure, and the leaders were charged with high treason. In August, while he waited for the trial of the leaders in Clonmel, Father Mathew ministered to the poor: victims of famine and eviction and emigrants who were making their way to Queenstown to board ships.

Another excursion out of the city gave Nicholson the opportunity to revisit Dr. Richard Barter's spa at St. Anne's Hydro. By its sixth year, Dr. Barter had relaxed his regime sufficiently to permit his patients meat more than once a day, though Nicholson assured readers that he himself knew that meat and gravies were not suitable to his patients' health. She observed that only the wealthy could afford St. Anne's and that there were no provisions for offering the spa's therapeutic facilities to the poor. Nevertheless, Nicholson spent a week at the spa, and, true to her Graham principles, she no doubt did her share of plunging and dipping in and out of the bathing tubs.

Her views about bathing were part of her Graham regime. She wrote in *Nature's Own Book* that she directed her boarders to sponge off with cold water every morning and to immerse their bodies in water once a week, three times a week in warm weather (1835, 19–20). In her later *A Treatise on Vegetable Diet, with Practical Results; or, A Leaf from Nature's Own Book* (1848), she gave additional brief instructions about bathing. Like Graham, she followed the advice of Dr. John Bell (1796–1872), a Philadelphia physician and temperance advocate, who advocated tepid baths and cold baths with caution. Her own usual practice was a sponging with cold water followed by brisk toweling.

Nicholson admired Dr. Barker's knowledge as an agronomist. She predicted that were local lands left to his discretion, "famine if not pestilence would banish from that rich soil" (*Annals* 1998, 167). Although she enjoyed her excursions from Cork, the famine was never far from her mind. On another trip out of the city to Castlemartyr, the village associated with the Boyle family, the earl of Shannon, Nicholson observed fields of wheat, barley, and oats ripening; however, the potato crop was again blighted, and she remarked that the people treated the blasted crop as they did any phenomenon beyond their control, with anxiety, silence, and secrecy.[8] Although there was some recovery in Castlemartyr, the village, like much of rural Ireland, would experience the long-term effects of the Great Irish Famine: the decline in population from death and emigration continued until the end of the century.

Before she left the area, Nicholson wanted to see the convicts in the prison at Spike Island in Cork Harbor. Although unrest in the country caused visitors to be prohibited from the island in 1848, Nicholson's friend Dr. Maurice Power was able to arrange permission for her to accompany the Power family to inspect it. By 1848 Maurice Power had attained some local importance. He chaired the public dinner in honor of Captain Bennett Forbes and the officers of the *Jamestown*, the American relief ship that came to Cork in March 1847. Power's speech on that occasion was described as "floridly eloquent" (J. Coleman 1904, 30; Forbes 1847, appx., 15). Later that year Power, the Repeal candidate, was elected MP from Cork to fill the seat of Daniel O'Connell, who had died in May. Power served from July 29, 1847, until March 22, 1852, when he was offered and accepted the position of governor of the West Indian island of St. Lucia (R. Davis 1998, 224).

During their visit to the prison, Nicholson discovered that many of the convicts were incarcerated for minor offenses. Poet Edward Walsh, the prison schoolteacher, told Nicholson that he believed that his three hundred pupils' only crime was stealing food when starving (*Annals* 1998, 153).[9] Although Nicholson pointed out this injustice, she judged the prisoners to be better off than inmates in the country's workhouses. Nicholson was shown the large cell assigned to John Mitchel while he waited on Spike Island from May 28 until June 1 to be transported to Bermuda aboard the *Scourge* and from there to Van Diemen's Land.

While visiting the Powers, Nicholson heard Catherine Power playing the "Soldier's Grave," an air to Charles Wolfe's "The Burial of John Moore," a song that Nicholson heard shortly before leaving New York for Ireland.[10] Struck by the coincidence that Rev. Charles Wolfe, the author of "The Burial of John Moore," was buried within two miles of the Powers' cottage, Nicholson and Mrs. Power set off to visit Wolfe's grave in the cemetery of the ruined church of Clonmel.[11] Because the sexton was not there to let the women into the site, Nicholson looked through the keyhole of the gate and noticed that the weeds and stones from a crumbling wall had covered the gravestone. The extended information that Nicholson included in a rather lengthy biographical note probably came from the appreciation of Wolfe in the *Dublin University Magazine* (1847) that was the basis for a later (1847) short biography of the poet (J. Russell 1842, 618–34; 1836). Certainly, Nicholson would have commended Wolfe for his Christian charity. He worked tirelessly among the poor of his Tyrone parish until his health broke. Wolfe's burial in a neglected graveyard seemed to stir a special sense of dread for Nicholson. Did she think at that moment that she too could die abroad and be buried, unknown and unmourned, in an untidy, forgotten grave?

Nicholson's elegiac mood may have been exacerbated by the reports that were beginning to circulate about another failed potato crop in 1848. She reported that Father Mathew's brother Charles had planted twenty-seven acres of potatoes in Lehenagh that seemed to have thrived until the blight appeared in August. On August 13 Father Mathew wrote to his friend and patron William Rathbone: "I regret that the melancholy task of announcing the *total destruction* of the potato crop has devolved upon me. The blight appeared three weeks back, but it seemed confined to particular places and affected only the stalks. Since then wet weather has been so constant the blight has become general, and the tubers are rotting with frightful rapidity" (Augustine 1947, 473). While Nicholson faced the news of yet another famine year, there was a respite, certainly the happiest occasion during her visit to Cork. In late August Nicholson and some friends traveled out along the Lee to Mount Patrick where William O'Connor, a modest tailor, had built a tower in honor of Father Mathew. Dedicated on October 30, 1843, a story about the tower, including an engraving of the structure, appeared in the *Illustrated London News* (November 18, 1843). Officially opened on November 10, 1846, the tower was really two towers: a squat crenellated Martello-type tower and a tall, narrow, round tower also with a crenellated roof.[12]

The occasion for the tower was Father Mathew's visit to London for the week beginning July 28, 1843, when he gave the pledge to thousands at the grounds of the Catholic cemetery on Commercial Road. While Father Mathew took pains during his English mission to disassociate himself from O'Connell's repeal agitation, the same year a cartoon titled "The Temperance Pledge, a Rare Gathering" portrays Father Mathew administering the pledge to a group that includes a devout Queen Victoria, Prince Albert, and her court, but lurking behind the Capuchin is a lightly sketched, mischievous O'Connell wearing a bag marked "RINT" and carrying a miter-topped walking stick (National Portrait Gallery, D33590).

Nicholson described her visit to the tower and her gift of books to the tower cottage in great detail.[13] Her gift was memorialized in an exchange of letters in the *Cork Examiner* ("The Mathew Tower: Mrs. Nicholson," August 30, 1848, 3.) that started with an account of Nicholson's visit and a letter of thanks from William O'Connor that was published on August 30, 1848:

THE MATHEW TOWER—MRS. NICHOLSON

Last week, Mrs. Nicholson, now well-known by her tour on foot through Ireland, and the very interesting book which she has written descriptive of her wanderings, paid a visit to Mountpatrick. She was accompanied by some friends. She was met by the Very Rev. Mr. Mathew, Mr. O'Connor, the hospitable proprietor, and some other gentlemen. After visiting the Tower, which is now superbly finished, and promises to stand, in firmness and durability, for the next five hundred years, and perambulating the grounds which are laid out in a highly ornamental style, the parties partook of lunch which consisted principally of fruits and coffee. Mrs. Nicholson, and the friend who accompanied her, are, besides being strict total abstainers, are also vegetarians, disciples of a strict dietetic school, in which no animal food is permitted. The object of her visit was then announced; it was to present to Mr. O'Connor, a small but beautifully selected library, in testimony of her ardent respect for the cause and the Apostle of Temperance, and in kindly appreciation of the services and worth of Mr. O'Connor, who not only built a testimonial unexampled in the history of such memorials created by private individuals but with a hospitality that cannot be overestimated, throws open his grounds daily to the public. Mrs. Nicholson presented the following short address:

To William O'Connor

These volumes are presented by a few friends of Temperance, in grateful acknowledgement of his generosity in throwing open his tasteful and beautiful place to the public, and for the purpose of affording a profitable recreation for its numerous visitors: with a desire that this lovely spot may be ever sacred to that glorious cause, to whose most successful and untiring advocate has been dedicated, and to the advancement of universal philanthropy.

William O'Connor's polite response to Nicholson's gift of books is valuable for his note that Nicholson was planning to return to the United States because she could not endure another visitation of the famine to the poor she loved. This remark is the only instance that suggests Nicholson suffered a kind of famine fatigue as she contemplated another failed harvest. O'Connor urged her to remember that she would travel with the gratitude of all among whom she had worked. In fact, Nicholson did not return immediately to the United States. She stayed abroad until 1852. By then that charitable O'Connor had died of cholera.

CORK, AUGUST 28, 1848

Madam:—I receive the books with pride and pleasure. The subject of each volume and the names of the authors remarkable in our literature for their genius or scientific knowledge, are the best tests of your own pure taste and judgment.

Ten years have elapsed since I found this spot a wilderness—for such a monument, I hope an enduring one, has been erected, to perpetuate, in a small degree, the true greatness and glory of the Christian benefactor of Ireland. As that monument belongs to him and the public, and as those grounds, which you and others have been pleased to eulogize, and but the abiding place of the Tower of Temperance, so my gates have never been closed and never shall be, against visitors, whether they be residents of our own favored but unfortunate land, or citizens of Europe or of your own great country.

It is a singular spectacle to witness—a lady, gently nurtured and brought up, giving up, for a time, home and country and kindred—visiting a land stricken with famine—traversing on foot that land from boundary to boundary—making her way over solitary mountains and treading through remote glens, where scarcely the steps of civilization have reached, sharing the scanty potato of the poor but hospitable people, and lying down after a day of toil, in the miserable but secure cabin of a Kerry or Connaught peasant. All this is unusual, but above it shines, with a steady light, your sympathy, your benevolence, your gentleness of heart and your warm appreciation of the virtues, rude but sincere, of a people whose condition it is necessary to improve in order to make them contented and happy.

The first step to raise them socially, is to create in them self-respect, and elevating their shrewdness into the wisdom of morality, has been taken by the MAN whom you revered so much, and to whom and not to me, you have this day paid a grateful and graceful tribute. May he live forever in the memories of his country.

You are about to depart for your own great country, because you could not witness again the desolation of another famine. But you will carry back from Ireland the heartfelt sense of her people for past kindness to your Christian countrymen. To them, to the generous people of England, and to the Society of Friends in England, Ireland and America, we are indebted, but utterly unable to discharge the debt.

Again, Madam, expressing my deepest sense of your kindness and personal worth, and wishing you many happy years in your beloved America,

> I beg to subscribe myself
> your grateful servant,
> William O'Connor
> Mount Patrick, August 1848

The following week, on September 4, Nicholson wrote a letter of thanks to William O'Connor that was published in the *Cork Examiner* on September 6 with the note that "this amiable lady had forwarded the following note to Mr. O'Connor":

To William O'Connor

Sir—The unmerited compliment you publicly bestowed on a stranger, in the last week's *Examiner*, deserves public acknowledgement, and the more cheerfully given, because it affords an opportunity of saying that not to me alone is the honor due of the small bestowment of books upon your table. It says, "There are hearts in Cork that do immeasurably appreciate the Mathew Testimonial, as well as the noble generosity of the man who designed it, and though small the offering, it may be a prelude to more liberal demonstrations of a people's gratitude.

These few volumes, it is hoped, are but the alphabet to a well chosen library that shall one day grace a room in the Tower, affording the citizen and the stranger a profitable as well as a pleasant recreation.

And now, Sir, allow me to say, that in four years tour[ing] through this beautiful island—from the mountains of Wicklow to the Killery Peaks, I have never seen from the top of mansion or castle a flag so gracefully waving—a flag on which is inscribed so much love of country—so much just appreciation of worth and so much that deserves the appellation of "Well done," as that which is flying in the breeze from the Tower of Mt. Patrick, and should my eyes ever again look out upon the proud mountains and waters of my own native land when memory should revert to the summer of '48, the brightest and happiest associations will be—the hours passed in the cottage and tower, the gardens and walks, dedicated to the man, who lives for humanity. And though I return to my people with a sorrowing heart that the tear is still on the long wasted cheek of Erin, yet this shall be my joy, that there live among her country-loving sons' hearts that can feel and hands that can act when work and virtue make the demand and to the proud monument of Mt. Patrick will I point as a witness to all who may sail upon the green banks of the sweet-flowing Lee.

When the hand of Theobald Matthew shall cease to rest on the head of the pledge-taking postulant and when he shall have gathered to the dust of his fathers—when the generous heart that devised the lasting memorial shall have stopped its pulsation forever—every health-blowing breeze that fans the flag of Mount Patrick, shall whisper, "Peace to the Apostle of Temperance, who said to the wine-maddened brain of the maniac, "Peace, be still, who wiped the tear from the face of the weary-stricken woman, and who "lifted up him that was ready to fall."

And then from heaven's high battlement his gentle spirit shall look down on this Tower, future generations shall rise in succession and call him "blessed."

And let their long sounding echo reverberate over mountain and glen, "honor and gratitude to William O'Connor."

Asenath Nicholson

Ireland, "I love thee still" (*Annals* 1998, 158–60).[14]

As she prepared to leave Cork, Nicholson happened to observe a funeral passing the premises of William Martin on Patrick Street and noticed that women were walking in the procession. Painfully conscious of her friends in America who had died one by one while she was in Ireland, she thought, "Why should she not go in company now to the house appointed for all living, and where, she shall, in her own due time, be transported?" (*Annals* 1998, 168). She joined the funeral procession to the graveyard and stayed for the obsequies. She was deeply moved by the experience. In some way, in bearing witness to that unknown person, Nicholson mourned all of the Irish famine dead.

After that funeral Nicholson did not delay further in Cork. She took leave of her friend and landlady Mrs. Fisher, who would not take any money for Nicholson's stay of fifteen weeks. Father Mathew and the Beale sisters waved her off from Cork. She stoically turned away from the waves of friends and from a last view of the city, but her last glimpse of Father Mathew left a memory of his "grief and blasted hope" (*Annals* 1998, 174). To leave Cork was to leave Ireland.

Dublin was an anticlimax and a disappointment. Nicholson had left her trunk with Bridget, the serving woman in the house where she had lodged the previous winter. Nicholson had no reason to doubt Bridget's honesty, but when her husband took to drink, she broke into Nicholson's trunk and pawned her clothes, books, and other possessions. Bridget challenged Nicholson with her words that expressed the importance of life over property, and Nicholson acknowledged that she was thrown back on her own principles. She recovered some clothes, but grieved over the loss of a silver spoon of some fifty years, a relic of her marriage with "indenture made by an agonized child [perhaps little Henry Nicholson], taking medicine" that she had brought from America and had been her companion in her travels. She did recover it, and she reported in 1850 that it was safely stored in her room in London. Nicholson said she would have trusted Bridget again, but her landlady fired Bridget. Nicholson found the woman living in a hovel without means of support.

She stayed with Richard and Hanna Webb while she prepared to leave for London; she continued to agonize over whether she had done enough and to catechize herself about whether she had allowed herself a measure of comfort that could have gone to the poor or whether she had lived Christ's Gospel. She thought too about the difference between the government relief, the relief offered by clergy of the established church, and the private relief measures supported by churches and relief organizations in England and America, concluding that only those groups who gave freely and in the spirit of Christian charity deserved mention (*Annals* 1998, 30).[15]

While Nicholson was in Dublin she received her last donation from American friends of famine relief. There was no reason to stay on. She planned to spend some time in London, but before she departed she reflected on her ministry. She began by saying that her work was not without its faults and that she continued to ask herself if she had done enough to relieve suffering (*Annals* 1998, 173). Although she believed that she acted "entirely as a passive instrument; moving because moved upon," there was nothing passive about her indictment of the government and the established church's stewardship of famine relief programs and their self-serving appointees. She contrasted them with the clergy of all denominations who themselves or with their families ministered to the poor, often at risk of their own lives. She told her reader that only the Irish language could do justice to the proselytizers, and she predicted accurately, as it turned out, that their gains would be short-lived.

As Nicholson was leaving Dublin, she saw two of the people she had helped. She met Mary, her seamstress from the Liberties, who appeared well dressed and reported that she was selling fruits and vegetables. One of her workmen who had heard that Nicholson was leaving walked seven miles to say good-bye. They missed each other, but Nicholson recorded his gesture of thanks as the most meaningful testimony to her work in famine Ireland. Richard Davis Webb was certainly the "lone Quaker" who saw her to the packet waiting on the Liffey quay. A few of her dearest Dublin friends had gone to the quay to bid her good-bye, but the crowd and darkness prevented their meeting, and Nicholson left Dublin as she had arrived—alone. She described herself looking back on Ireland with words from the 137th Psalm: "And when my heart shall cease to feel for their sufferings may my tongue cleave to the roof of my mouth."[16] Another psalm, 126, "They that sow in tears shall reap in joy," provides the title for the poem that ends *Lights and Shades of Ireland*, a poem urging the husbandman, despite sorrow, to "sow thy seed" in hopes of reaping a new harvest, a poem that may have been written by Nicholson herself.

8

Peace and Progress, 1848–52

Nicholson in the UK and on the Continent

WHEN NICHOLSON left Ireland on October 22, 1848, she said that she intended to spend some months recovering from the fatigue of famine relief work and to see something more of England before returning to New York in the spring of 1849.[1] She accepted an invitation from William and Elizabeth Bennett to stay with them in their home in Park Village, Regent's Park. A notice in the *Vegetarian Advocate* in late 1848 reported that Nicholson "kindly promised her active cooperation in getting up" a vegetarian supper "in an efficient style," probably with the Bennetts, who were involved in the London vegetarian movement (51).[2] In 1849 Bennett wrote an anonymous pamphlet, *A Letter to a Friend in Reply to the Question, What Is Vegetarianism?*[3]

The Bennetts were friendly with their neighbors William and Mary Howitt, the Victorian husband-and-wife team of writers and editors who lived near them at 28 Upper Avenue Road, St. John's Wood. For years they tried without success to convert the Howitts to vegetarianism (Woodring 1952, 205). The Howitts had known of Nicholson through William Bennett and had published Nicholson's October 1847 letter to Bennett in *Howitt's Journal* in 1847 (340–41).

Nicholson did some literary and spiritual sightseeing from London in the fall of 1848. She was eager to visit John Bunyan's grave in Bunhill Fields, on the City Road.[4] Opened in 1665, for the overflow from St. Paul's, Bunhill (Bone Hill) was a city cemetery for Nonconformists until it was closed in 1852.[5] Bunyan was not buried at his home in Elstow near Bedford when he died on August 31, 1688. He was on a trip to London, caught a chill, died of fever in the home of his friend John Strudwick, and was buried in the Strudwick family vault at Bunhill. When Nicholson visited Bunyan's grave in 1848, she said that the gravestone was barely legible, but, by the time she wrote "John Bunyan," she reported that the stone had been "revived."[6]

On a cold, late afternoon in 1849, Nicholson followed her Bunhill visit with a pilgrimage to Bunyan's cottage in Elstow, near Bedford. She must have taken the train from King's Cross to Bedford and walked the mile and a half to Elstow. At the cottage where Bunyan was born, she had a moment of nostalgia.[7] Noticing the seat built into the cottage fireplace, she wrote, "In the opposite corner was a little niche under the long mantelpiece, evidently intended for a seat, where, in olden time, the contending urchins of a farmer's log cabin in New England struggling to secure a warm seat for the winter's evening" (*LP* 1853, 196).

Nicholson tells her reader that she saw the place in front of the seventeenth-century market house Mote or Moot Hall, where Bunyan preached. While Nicholson described Bunyan's sermons as coming from lips "touched with a live coal from off the altar" (Psalm 18:5–7), she was concerned that the anonymous woman who offered Bunyan a refuge for a few hours between his sermons be acknowledged. Stopping at the ruins of the woman's cottage in a woody dell, Nicholson compared the woman with Abishag, King David's young Shunamite wife, who ministered to him in his old age (1 Kings 15). Nicholson thought too of the Shunamite woman, the heroine of Kings 4:8–37, who offered hospitality and accommodation, but judged the Elstow woman more deserving because she "won Christ at a dearer price than did the Shunamite, whose 'chamber, candlestick, and bed' were given with the concurrence of her husband and when no threats of imprisonment or confiscation tried her faith and hospitality" (*LP* 1853, 195). Although Nicholson was not able to name Bunyan's "Shunamite," she assured her reader that the woman of Elstow, "like many women of old," is recorded in the "Book of Life." Just the telling of her story puts the "Elstow Shunamite" into the gallery of heroines, unknown but for Nicholson.

Nicholson's metaphor for Bunyan was a flame from the altar of Divine Truth, the flame that informed Bunyan's vocation. When Bunyan was arrested for preaching without a license, he refused to guarantee that he would not continue to do so because he believed that he should be able to worship without state or ecclesiastical interference. As a consequence, he spent the better part of twelve years in prison. Nicholson avoided commenting, as others have, on the question of whether Bunyan made a wise decision to subject his family to impoverishment for the sake of his principles. For Nicholson, Bunyan's actions were what was required of a "chosen instrument" who accomplished "great things with small means" (*Annals* 1998, 198). She had used similar words to describe the challenges she faced with the same faith just a year earlier in Ireland.

While traveling from London to Ramsgate early in 1849, Nicholson heard about a two-week excursion to France for five pounds. When an unnamed friend sent her the money and encouraged her to join the party, Nicholson set off with the group of some 350 under the leadership of Henry, Lord Brougham. They left on Holy Thursday, April 5, from London Bridge to see Louis Napoléon's Second Republic for themselves (*LP* 1853, 204).[8] Nicholson's account of the trip is part travelogue, part appreciation of French hospitality, and part appreciation of the two Frenchwomen, whom she admired.

The English travelers were charmed by the welcome given them by their French hosts. As the steamers arrived at the pier at Boulogne-sur-Mer, on April 6, Colonel Sansot and his National Guards played "God Save the Queen" and "La Marseillaise," which, according to Nicholson, carried "neither Wellington nor Waterloo in their notes."[9] The mayor, civic authorities, and thousands of Boulogniers greeted their guests with banners, speeches, bouquets of flowers, and breakfast laid out in the city's custom house. A Mr. L. Lloyd responded in French on behalf of the English guests, who then hurried on their way to Paris. Along the way, the English were greeted by French waving their caps and handkerchiefs. At Amiens the mayor and an honor guard were waiting with a meal and speech that ended, "The agreement of France and England secures the peace of the world," a sentiment that Nicholson believed, "if true, should be written in capital over the entrance of every door in the kingdom" (*LP* 1853, 209). The French reception given the British delegation, which included Nicholson, was part of the efforts to establish friendly relations between the Second Republic and their cross-Channel visitors.

From their first morning in Paris, Good Friday, and through the next eight days, the French extended the hospitality of the city to their visitors so as to show the Republic in its best light. Nicholson and her companions responded with enthusiasm; "every tower was ascended; every picture gallery explored." Having come to investigate the Second Republic, Nicholson declared herself satisfied with its egalitarianism, the courtesy to all regardless of class, the apparent lack of caste, and the neatly dressed workers. At the same time, she sensed "a subdued waiting, as though something momentous was in reserve" (*LP* 1853, 209). She may have observed the tension between the conservatives and the democratic socialist radicals that surrounded the upcoming August elections for the National Assembly of the Second Republic.

When the travelers were offered excursions from Paris, Nicholson, as we might have expected, chose to inspect an institution providing social welfare. She visited the Hospice de Bicètre, the famous asylum for male lunatics and indigent old men founded by Cardinal Richelieu in 1634, on the site of the Château de Wincestre, which was built by John, bishop of Winchester, in 1204. The hospice was located just outside the Porte d'Italie on the road to Fontainbleau.[10] Having witnessed the treatment of the Irish poor, she was impressed with the generosity and respect with which the poor and infirm were treated. Their quarters were large and comfortable; they had a garden for walks, and they were given ample amounts of nourishing food. Unlike the Irish poor for whom there was no employment in the workhouses, the French provided employment for their able-bodied poor, and those poor who worked were paid. She added that French welfare was even extended to animals, which were properly looked after at the "Hospice des Animaux" where owners were charged for their care according to their means.

With her concern for women in the places she traveled, Nicholson celebrated the two she most admired: Empress Josephine and Madame Lamartine, the mother of the romantic poet and politician Alphonse de Lamartine. Moved by the simple inscription "A Josephine, Eugène et Hortense, 1825" on Josephine's tomb in the Church of St. Pierre and Paul at Reuil, Nicholson wrote that it was "a graphic epitaph, speaking in three words the affection of those lovely children to a mother whose eventful life had been marked with unheard of sorrows, and had, amid them all, been the kind and prudent mother, the faithful and affectionate wife, even when the cruel separation rent her heart. The *true* woman was there, in all the magnanimous greatness of her soul, which few of her sex possessed" (*LP* 1853, 217). Nicholson's view of Josephine was a romantic one. If she were not popular in Paris for her service as empress to the First Empire, in 1849 she was the maternal grandmother of Louis Napoléon, president of the Second Republic.

What would Nicholson have read at the time that romanticized Josephine? While she was a devoted mother and grandmother, twentieth-century scholarship demonstrates that Josephine was hardly a faithful wife. She was a woman whose morals and behavior reflected someone of her society and the turbulence of the age. During her first unhappy marriage to Alexandre, vicomte de Beauharnais, both partners sought other lovers.

Beauharnais was arrested during the Reign of Terror and sentenced to the guillotine in 1794. Josephine also was imprisoned for months, and she lived uncertain whether she would survive. Released after Robespierre's trial, she met Napoléon in 1795. They married the following year, but, again, neither was faithful. While Napoléon crowned her as his empress at Notre Dame in 1804, Josephine knew that the marriage would not last because she was not able to provide him with an heir.[11] He married Austria's Marie Louise in 1810, and Josephine retreated to her garden at Malmaison, where she spent the last four years of her life.[12]

Nicholson defended Josephine with unusual passion as the virtuous woman scorned and exiled. What did Josephine represent for Nicholson? She considered the suggestion urged by many that Josephine be moved to Les Invalides with Napoléon when he was interred there in 1840, but Nicholson sided with people who regarded his treatment of Josephine as unforgivable. She was content to see Josephine remain at Reuil.

> The place where her dust now rests is quite in character with all belonging to her, simple, unostentatious, yet possessing innate beauties which can never be lost; a place where reflecting minds can pause with profitable satisfaction, and where the more frivolous will meet a check; where they find the one so much loved and so refined, sleeping here as unpretending as she had lived. France, in different ages, has had women of whose talents they made be proud, and some whose goodness as well as greatness has been an honor to God who sent them to glorify him in body and in spirit. (*LP* 1853, 218–19)

Nicholson's admiration for D'Alix des Roys de Lamartine is easier to understand. By the time Nicholson arrived in Paris in April 1849, Lamartine's son poet and politician Aphonse de Lamartine's brief career as head of the 1848 provisional government and minister of foreign affairs was over.[13] During his period as minister, a delegation of Young Irelanders, including Thomas Francis Meagher and William Smith O'Brien, presented a formal address to Lamartine on April 3, 1848, asking for the French Republic's support of Irish nationalist aspirations; however, Lamartine realized that such recognition would jeopardize the relationship that the French Republic was trying to forge with the United Kingdom.

Nicholson concluded "The Mother of Lamartine" with a reference to Lamartine's political fall: "Though France, in her ignorance and folly, rejected him, yet *there* he stands, the same untarnished friend of his country, the same love of that freedom for which *they* have professed to have uprooted the throne. Whether in peace or war, evil or good report, prosperity or adversity, he *has* been, and still is, the *son of his mother*" (*LP* 1853, 222).

Nicholson found much to admire about Lamartine's mother. After her husband was imprisoned during the French Revolution for his Royalist sympathies, Madame Lamartine took her family to Milly, near Mâcon (Burgundy), where she educated her young son. He was greatly affected by her ardent Catholicism and her affectionate and sensitive nature. Nicholson envisaged Madame de Lamartine's childhood in the gardens of the royal castle of St. Cloud, playing with the young Louis Philippe. (Her mother was an undergoverness for the Orleans family.) Nicholson admired Madame de Lamartine's brave efforts to aid her husband and her charity to the sick and poor of the village.

Needless to say, Nicholson approved of Madame de Lamartine's vegetarianism that her son described in *Les Confidences* (1849): "My mother was convinced, a conviction I share, that killing animals in order to feed on their flesh and blood is one of the weaknesses of the human condition, that is one of those curses inflicted on mankind, either by his fall from grace, or by the hardening of the heart through his own perversity" (1857, 60). Nicholson would have recognized the Grahamite principle in Madame de Lamartine's conviction that eating meat was linked to the fall from grace. Perhaps more than anything, Nicholson admired M. de Lamartine's piety and her faith, and she urged the example of her life as a mother as a model for others to imitate. She might have left the last word on mothers to Lamartine himself: "There is a woman at the beginning of all great things" (1857, 60).

Nicholson did not meet Lamartine during her visit to Paris, but she certainly would have identified with his support of Elihu Burritt's Second Peace Congress that met in Paris on August 22–24, 1849. Indeed, she would participate in Burritt's 1850 Frankfurt Peace Conference. Lamartine's contemporary Alexis de Tocqueville, the minister of foreign affairs of the Republic from 1849 to 1852, admired Lamartine's courage and eloquence and had written of him in *Recollections of the French Revolution of 1848*, "I do not think I ever met in the world of ambitious egoists in which I lived, any mind so untroubled by thought of the public good as his" (2003, 108). Burritt's May 19, 1848, letter to his friend Gerrit Smith, urging him to attend the Paris meeting, spoke of his hopes for the congress. Lamartine's name at the head of Burritt's list of notables who lent their names to the meeting demonstrates his support for world peace as a public good.[14]

Nicholson and her party left Paris for London, returning on Saturday, April 14, to Boulogne, where they found that the city had enlarged and renovated its public theater for an elaborate farewell reception attended by nearly two thousand people. The trip appeared to have met its goal of promoting Franco-British friendship. Nicholson mentioned her "most pleasant" trip to France when she wrote to her friend William Goodell from 9 Elizabeth Terrace, Liverpool Road, London, on May 8, 1849. It was her first letter to Goodell since before she left Ireland in 1848. He had moved to Honeoye Lake in upstate New York in 1843, founded the Liberty League in 1847, and ran unsuccessfully on the Liberty ticket as a candidate for governor of New York in 1848.[15] He continued to argue the case for abolitionism. His latest book, *The Democracy of Christianity* (1849), argued not only that slavery was undemocratic but that it was also anti-Christian.

Because Nicholson told Goodell that she was sending her letter to him with Father Mathew, it is likely that she visited the Capuchin between May 17 and May 23 while he was staying at Greenbank, the home of William Rathbone.[16] In 1849 Rathbone paid the friar's insurance debt of five hundred pounds so that he could travel to America. If Nicholson went to Liverpool, she certainly would have joined Father Mathew and Rathbone at the meeting to support the Irish poor. Rathbone, who was the liberal mayor of Liverpool, had been responsible for distributing the funds and food provided by the New England Relief Society that had arrived with Captain Robert Bennett Forbes aboard the *Jamestown*.[17] On May 23 Father Mathew left for America aboard the *Ashburton* (Augustine 1947, 486). In her letter Nicholson asked Goodell to befriend Father Mathew. "He is a friend to his country, friend to man and been a friend indeed to me. God bless him and induce America to treat him kindly."

Her request suggests she may have anticipated that Father Mathew's American trip would be controversial. It was. When she met Father Mathew, she may have warned him about being co-opted by the Garrisonians. He did resist their overtures. When the Garrisonians wanted him to attend a meeting in Boston marking the abolition of slavery in the West Indies, he did not respond to their invitation. He also made it a point not to speak about slavery. When Father Mathew took his temperance campaign to the South and accepted the hospitality of southern slave owners, the abolitionists repudiated him. Unrepentant, he wrote Mrs. Rathbone on March 8, 1850, from Mobile, Alabama, "Had I done anything to prevent my journey through the Southern States, I should never have forgiven myself. There are tens of thousands of my beloved countrymen scattered over the South" (Augustine 1947, 507).

In her letter to Goodell, Nicholson wrote about their shared interest in Christian evangelism and abolitionism. She credited the Bible with the English success on the battlefield and with administering their empire. "They are armed with the word of God which a missionary on the Thames said in the Military and Evangelical Bible Society meeting was as necessary an accompaniment for the soldier or sailor as the musket of any weapon of destruction to kill his enemies."[18] Nicholson's remark anticipated Thomas Jones Barker's 1863 painting *The Secret of England's Greatness*, which depicts Queen Victoria presenting a Bible to an African chieftain in the audience chamber at Windsor Castle.[19] The painting hangs in the Expansion and Empire Room of the National Portrait Gallery, where a note explaining the anecdote that informs the scene suggests that Nicholson heard the story and put her own version of it in her letter to Goodell: "The scene depicted is based on a popular but unfounded anecdote current in 1850. When asked by a diplomatic delegation how Britain became so powerful in the world, our beloved Queen sent them, not the number of her fleet, not the number of her armies, not the account of her boundless merchandise, nor the details of her inexhaustible wealth, but handed him a beautifully bound copy of the Bible, she said, 'Tell the Prince, that *this is the secret* of England's greatness.'"

Nicholson wrote candidly to Goodell about the British and the causes they espoused: evangelism, abolitionism, and the disestablishment of the Church of England. Having experienced antislavery riots in New York, she told Goodell she thought that the frank speech of the English that she heard at their antichurch state meetings would have led to violence in America. "They use great liberty of speech, indeed the abolitionists of the States, would be in danger of a *mobbing*—if not a lynching should they venture on such high ground."

She knew Goodell would be interested to hear about the sensational "coming out" of the Church of England clergyman Baptist Wriothesley Noel, who had published his controversial argument for church reform, "Essay on the Union of Church and State," in December 1848, the month after he had announced to his St. John's Chapel, Holborn, congregation that he was resigning from the established church.[20] Nicholson had gone along to hear Noel on May 7, 1849. She reported to Goodell that Noel challenged the Church of England to address the spiritual needs of the urban poor.

> I last evening heard Baptist Noel preach in an independent chapel from these words, "Let this mind be in you that was in Christ etc." and surely he has that mind in a most eminent degree, his whole Christian life has evinced and thus *now evinces* that he has been with Jesus and learned of him, connected as he is with the highest aristocracy of the kingdom, possessing wealth and influence to a great extent, his concession to win for the *lowest* estate, his regard for the poor and oppressed . . . whoever calls him "Beelzebub" must *do* so because they hate his Master. He appears ready to go both to prison and to death.

In the end neither happened; however, within three months Noel left the Church of England and was publicly baptized into the Baptist Church on August 9, 1849. He became a Baptist minister in September 1849.

Nicholson's comments on Victoria and Albert suggest that she thought their powers to do any good were limited by the government. "They are mere *tools*." Though an ardent Republican, Nicholson believed it would be to England's advantage were the monarch to have more power. "If he and the Queen had as much *power* and *ability* as some of our Presidents possessed, the kingdom as a whole would be in a much better condition than it now is."

Having heard that Goodell had moved to western New York, she playfully inquired whether it was true that he was living among "rude and uncultivated men and women." She also reported that she had met people ignorant about America in her English travels: "A lady asked me if my parents were not blacks as she supposed that all natives were and a second inquired if N. York was not situated a great distance in the country surrounded with woods and wild beasts. Now these are not the daughters of Wilberforce nor Elizabeth Fry, but they are women who *should* be informed and who moved in respectable society and such ladies are not *rare*."[21] Nicholson confessed that she sometimes felt that she had "lost all nationality," but she was eager to hear news from Goodell about the progress of the abolition movement under the presidency of Millard Fillmore.[22]

The end of Nicholson's May 8 letter to Goodell revealed that her mind was still on Ireland. Nicholson told Goodell that she had news that prompted her to consider returning to Ireland.[23] She was devastated to hear that the little school she had started, perhaps the little school in Kilcommon parish, had been closed.[24]

I have said nothing of Ireland and my reasons are that my heart is so full had I begun the letter on *that* question, else would have been said, for be assured, use does not harden my heart to sights and sounds of misery and for the last two days the letters I have received from that country have so fully verified what my fears were inducing me to believe that I am half resolved to return and die with them if needs be. I have lived on that altar and whatever my Heavenly Father places before me must be done and done *willingly*. I was enabled last year to get up a school in one of the most desolate parts where a hundred or more assembled in a cabin from the mountains, instructed and fed once a day. This school prospered. The children so improved in work that they could earn a little and I was about collecting something more for it, when a letter arrived from the faithful benevolent teacher saying that the house was taken from her. The children sent in agony again into the mountains there to die if something be not done. "Lord, what wilt Thus have me do" is not the inquiry. Whether to go partly by sea partly by land over bog and mountain where no public conveyance can be had, and try to gather them into some dark cabin or let them die is the distracted inquiry. *O God, direct and lead me.*

It is unlikely that Nicholson returned to Ireland. If she did, there is no record of her visit. What we do know is that she set off for Southampton by train from London on July 29, 1849, to visit the Isle of Wight. She had long yearned to visit the places associated with Leigh Richmond's pious tales of village life, "The Dairyman's Daughter," "The Young Cottager," and "The Negro Servant," that had enthralled her as a girl in Vermont.[25]

Nicholson's account of her journey is part travelogue and part spiritual pilgrimage. She landed at West Cowes, admired the pretty cottages on the hillsides, and reported she had no trouble securing comfortable lodgings with a mechanic and his family. The town had all the amenities that Nicholson valued: churches of different denominations, two excellent libraries, and warm sea baths. She paid her ha'penny to take the ferry to East Cowes to see Osborne House, Queen Victoria's country home that she purchased in 1845 and rebuilt on a grand scale according to Prince Albert's design.

While Nicholson's landlord encouraged her to think that she might get a glimpse of the queen, who would return her salute, "as any plain people would do," she did not see the royals, but the porter let her have a peep at one corner of the palace. An elderly man invited her into his ancient cottage; they talked of salvation, and she mused about how little we require for us to be comfortable.

Leaving East Cowes, Nicholson took a circuitous route through Newport, Carisbrooke, and Ventnor to reach her *Annals of the Poor* sites of Brading and Arreton. In Newport, the capital of the island, she stayed with the family of the Baptist minister who was employed during the week as a blond lace weaver, work Nicholson, usually a great respecter of honest labor, dismissed as "trifling." She surveyed the town and its public institutions: school, library, museum, and the House of Industry. She visited the twelfth-century Church of St. Thomas of Canterbury, the chapel of ease to the village of Carisbrooke. Built in 1172 by Henry II, architectural elements and memorials from the medieval church were preserved in the rebuilt Victorian parish church. Given her penchant for sermons, Nicholson took special note of the 1676 pulpit.

She went on to Carisbrooke village, stopping to visit the old church of St. Mary the Virgin, a Benedictine priory founded in the twelfth century by William Fitz Osbern, the first Norman lord of the island (Winter and Winter 1987, 53). The priory was dissolved by Henry V in 1415, and the buildings fell into disrepair and were demolished. Some architectural elements have been preserved in the later restorations of the church. As we would have expected, Nicholson noticed the monuments that celebrated the role of women: the sixteenth-century tomb of Lady Wadham, wife of the governor of the island and aunt of Lady Jane Seymour, who founded the Hospital for Cripples (Farrow 1993, 6). She quoted the entire verse composed by the wife of seventeenth-century sailor William Keeling, who discovered the Cocos Islands (*LP* 1853, 158–59), but, surprisingly, she did not mention the tablet that marked the death of Mary Stephens, who was praised for her humility and chastity (Winter 1987, 60).

So eager was Nicholson to get to the Dairyman's Cottage that she was reluctant to stop at Carisbrooke Castle, the Norman castle where Charles I was imprisoned in 1648–49. She was critical of the condition of the castle chapel ("more suitable for a stable") and urged its proper preservation as a historical site. She found herself caught up with the story of Charles I, and she added something of her own experience to the traditional account. She said that while she was in the West of Ireland, she had a drink of water from the silver cup reputed to have been the cup from which Charles had his last sup of wine as he stood on the gallows (*LP* 1853, 161).[26] After describing the castle and its lore, Nicholson urged her readers to use such sites to cultivate the love of history in children.[27]

Walking south to Ventnor, Nicholson was delighted to discover island flora she knew from her childhood in Vermont: hollyhock, wild weeds, mint, and thistle, a coincidence that complemented her island association with the *Annals of the Poor* stories. Nicholson described how the undercliff scenery at Ventnor with its southern exposure had created a microclimate that supported a wide variety of plants. By the time Nicholson visited Ventnor, the town had developed as a spa. She used Ventnor as a base to explore Black Gong (Blackgang), Chine, a natural fissure in the cliff formed by water cutting through the sandstone to the sea. The Chine and a cliffside garden had opened as a park in 1843.[28] One evening Nicholson attended services at the twelfth-century St. Lawrence's Old Church, the island's smallest. She was charmed by the church and the music and pronounced the lay preacher's sermon "quite a tolerable one," until she learned he was a brewer. She huffed that if she had known his occupation, she could not have listened to him (*LP* 1853, 193).

From Ventnor Nicholson turned north to Shanklin and Braiding. She took the coastal footpath, passing the cascade that turned the old Ventnor mill wheel and passed through the Shanklin Chine along a fisherman's path. She found that the clay soil of a dark path called Landslip made walking difficult; the land had actually slid into the sea in 1810.[29] Her journey from Shanklin to Braiding was lightened by the offer of a ride from a man in a carriage, who spoke about the Irish with a sympathy she found unusual in an Englishman. His kindness and compassion seemed an appropriate introduction to Braiding, where Leigh Richmond had come after his ordination in 1799 to be curate of Braiding and Yaverland.

When Nicholson caught a glimpse of the squat tower of St. Mary the Virgin Church at Braiding, she realized her dream to visit the place associated with Richmond. Richard's stories evidently spoke to a young woman's developing spirituality. "I thanked God and took courage. The impression made on my youthful mind by reading 'The Dairyman's Daughter' was entirely beyond any fact I had ever read; and often have I said, 'Oh that God would let me see the spot'" (*LP* 1853, 172).

Richmond met Elizabeth Wallbridge, the dairyman's daughter, in 1800. Having heard him preach at St. George's Church in the neighboring village of Arreton, Elizabeth wrote Richmond, asking him to bury her sister Hannah. Richmond agreed, and it was the start of a remarkable friendship. Elizabeth had worked in service, but she returned home to take care of her parents and their little dairy. Impressed with Elizabeth's simple, sincere spirituality, Richmond became a regular visitor to the Dairyman's Cottage. When Elizabeth developed consumption, Richmond visited frequently, and his own faith was strengthened by her acceptance of death and her trust in God.

After he left Braiding for Turvey in Bedfordshire in 1805, Richmond told her story in "The Dairyman's Daughter" (1809), which he published with "The Young Cottager" and "The Negro Servant," two other tales based on Richmond's Isle of Wight experience, in the *Christian Guardian* (1809–14). The Religious Tract Society reprinted the stories under the title *The Annals of the Poor* in 1814. Richmond revised and expanded "The Dairyman's Daughter" in subsequent editions. It was immensely popular in its day, selling some two million copies during Richmond's lifetime. It is still in print.[30]

The appearance of the village reminded Nicholson of a "miserable Irish hamlet in the bogs of Connaught," but Richmond's church did not disappoint her. She visited the church at twilight and felt a "holy calm" resting on the hillside graves. She was directed to the grave of "Little Jane," Jane Squibb, the saintly heroine of "The Young Cottager." She did not quote the inscription on Jane's gravestone, "the rustic verse, like most others found in country churchyards among the poor":

Ye who the power of God delight to trace
And mark with joy each monument of Grace
Tread lightly o'er this grave as ye explore
"The short and simple annals of the poor"
A child reposes underneath the sod
A child to memory dear, and dear to God.
Rejoice! Yet shed the sympathetic tear
Jane "the Young Cottager" lies buried here.
(*LP* 1853, 172)

Nicholson also visited the cottage where Jane died of consumption in her fifteenth year on January 30, 1799. A nineteenth-century engraving indicates that a porch was added to the cottage. Now a preserved building in Braiding, the cottage and Jane's grave continue to attract visitors.

Nicholson visited Richmond's vicarage. As she stood gazing at the old house in a stand of trees that stood at the foot of the cemetery opposite the church, she imagined Richmond walking, praying, and working in the garden. Nicholson questioned Braiding villagers about their memories of Richmond. Although very few of them had actually seen him, they were eager to share their elders' memories of him. The brass memorial to Richmond on the south wall of the church dated 1898 supports Nicholson's pronouncement, quoting Henry Wadsworth Longfellow's "A Psalm of Life," that Richmond had definitely left his "footprints on the sands of time."

Leaving Braiding the following day, Nicholson got a lift on a carrier's cart to St. George's Churchyard, the grave site of the dairyman's daughter. As they traveled over the downs and the treeless hills, the cart man pointed out sites with Richmond associations. Nicholson became nearly overwhelmed with the anticipation that she would finally see the Dairyman's Cottage:

> I found myself on the very path, looking at the same landscape, and going to the identical Dairyman's cottage where this good man slowly bent his way to the sick girl, produced emotions which, if not peculiar to myself, never occurred before. The lane shaded with trees, the gate, and the old Dairyman leaning over it, had become as familiar as the door-yard before the dwelling of my father; and, alighting from the carriage, I walked up the hill, the better to enjoy when I never had in reality seen, and should never see again. The trees which shaded the cottage now appeared; the carrier pointed me to the churchyard, nearer the cottage, and bade me adieu. (*LP* 1853, 174)

Elizabeth Walbridge's grave stands next to her sister Hannah's outside the north wall of the thirteenth-century chancel. She met other pilgrims there. While Nicholson says, "The slab at the head of Elizabeth simply records her age and death" (*LP* 1853, 177), now there is a rather long inscription that reads in part:

She being dead, yet speaketh
Stranger, if e'er by feeling led
Upon this hallowed turf thy footstep tread
Turn from contemplation of this sod
And think of her whose spirit rests with God,
Lowly her lot on earth but He who bore
Tidings of grace and blessings to the poor
Gave her His strength and faithfulness to prove,
The choicest treasure of His boundless love.[31]

Leaving the graveyard, Nicholson walked to Hale Commons, the site of the Dairyman's Cottage. She felt that she was entering sacred ground.[32] The cottage owner, a grandson or grandnephew of the old dairyman, invited Nicholson to visit Elizabeth's room. It was an emotional moment: "When I had looked about the room and collected myself a little; when the first sensation of entering the walls where stood the arm-chair and where sat the humble Elizabeth and the chamber door with its wooden latch, which conducted to the room where died the sainted girl" (*LP* 1853, 177). When Nicholson identified herself as an American, her hosts brought out their guest book for her to sign. Nicholson recognized the names of some Americans:

E. Weston, Boston, 1 October 1840
Samuel Walley and 2 daughters, Boston, 25 May 1841
Rev. Benjamin Chase, Natchez, Tennessee, 2 September 1841[33]

Nicholson's own entry in the guest book is dated Saturday, July 21, 1849:

A memorable day. A stranger in a strange land. I find myself in the cottage where the Dairyman's Daughter died and the associations with youth again rekindle that which then so vividly awakened on reading the touching sketch of her humble yet exalted life written by Leigh Richmond. And which the writer and the subject are doubtless together in the paradise above. May all who read that sketch and visit the spot *say from the heart*, "Let me so live that I may die the death of the righteous." May the descendents of this pious family who once honored the memory of the departed by following them as they followed Christ at last make up our happy family above whom their dust shall mingle with that of their fathers is the sincere desire of one who has been *much* gratified by the visit and the kind hospitality of the family. May the work of the Lord ever shine in this tabernacle.

Asenath Nicholson
New York, U.S. July 21, 1849[34]

Nicholson spent three hours in the cottage examining family artifacts: Elizabeth's churn, silver teaspoons, china teacups, and pewter plates. Although she had often thought that writing for posterity was "a vain and foolish ambition," the story of the dairyman's daughter had been an encouragement to so many of the Christian poor.

She did not see the room where Elizabeth died because it had been altered. Elizabeth's armchair had been taken to New York and not returned. Nicholson told the householder that she understood that the chair was taken by a member of the American Tract Society and that she had seen the chairman of the society sitting in Elizabeth's armchair at the society's meeting in 1843 (*LP* 1853, 181).[35] Theodore Frelinghuysen was chairman of the American Tract Society between 1842 and 1846.[36]

Nicholson left the Dairyman's Cottage reluctantly. She stopped several times to look back on the rose-covered chimney and then made her way back over the downs to Rye. Invited into a cottage for a cup of tea and a piece of homemade bread, Nicholson noted that it was the first such invitation that she had received from anyone in England, and she thought of the hospitality of the Irish poor, who felt that a lone stranger was sent by God.[37]

Rye hospitality was repeated on Sunday when Nicholson met a shoemaker and his family at the Baptist church. Invited to supper, Nicholson stayed on with them for the rest of her Rye visit. She went away refreshed and restored. The shoemaker repaired her shoes; the eldest daughter mended Nicholson's clothes, and the younger daughters cut and styled her hair.

A visit to St. Thomas's chapel with its galleries designated for charity children prompted Nicholson to think about the difference between the English, who dressed the poor in clothes that identified them as poor, and the Catholic French, who did not so designate the dress of the people who received charity. She concluded that the English practice made the poor feel poor, and it drew the attention of others to the charity given them.

One morning during her time in Rye, Nicholson walked to Needles Point, a Victorian fort built on the cliffs above the sea at the westernmost part of the island at Alum Bay. The Needles Park now offers a chairlift ride to see the sand cliffs and the spectacular view of the Needles Rock, but in Nicholson's day one approached the point from the road through the downs. When Nicholson walked out on to the chalk cliffs, she confronted a "terrific wall, hanging over the sea." The precariousness of the location brought her back to her walk up Croagh Patrick when she ignored local advice and climbed the reek without leaving sufficient daylight to return. Tempted to make her way down the cliffs to the sea, she dismissed the gathering rain clouds and went down steps cut into the side of the cliffs by workmen. It poured; she got drenched and found herself hanging onto the cliffs and wondering whether she would survive. When the storm cleared, she clambered back up the slippery path, leaving her veil behind, "a memento of that fearful hour" (*LP* 1853, 189).

Soaking wet, Nicholson began her sixteen-mile return walk to Rye via Newport. Although it was not her longest walk on the Isle of Wight, it was the hardest. Her Needles ordeal was more dangerous than anything she faced in Ireland, but once safely in the home of the Baptist minister at Newport, she did not, for one moment, regret her adventure. Nicholson returned to Rye one last time before leaving from the pier for Portsmouth. Her friend from Rye, the Baptist shoemaker, walked her to the pier and waited with her for the packet, "to convey me forever from that sweet isle" (*LP* 1853, 187).

9

Peace and Progress, 1850–51
Lights and Shades of Ireland

IN AUGUST 1850 Nicholson had another opportunity to travel to the Continent as part of a peace delegation. American Elihu Burritt, who had organized a successful international peace meeting in Paris in 1849, started planning an 1850 congress in Frankfurt by traveling around the United States to educate people about the purpose and importance of the meeting in Germany. He succeeded in recruiting forty American delegates (Curti 1937, 39). This time Nicholson was part of the official party.

Burritt (1810–79), known as the "Learned Blacksmith," was another New England reformer from New Britain, Connecticut, who shared a number of causes with Nicholson. Burritt's intense gaze from under a broad forehead dominates the contemporary daguerreotypes of him. He had a prominent nose and a thin, set mouth in the convention of the day. Although his expression is serious, there is a suggestion of a smile. He appears to be too slight for his work as a blacksmith. A largely self-taught linguist, he mastered languages as diverse as Breton, Arabic, and Sanskrit.[1] When he visited Northampton, Massachusetts, Burritt met Sylvester Graham. Like Nicholson, Burritt admired Graham; he called him "an original genius." At Graham's invitation, Burritt gave a lecture to the people of Northampton on February 15, 1843 (Curti 1929, 19). Before turning to world peace, Burritt's other causes were temperance and abolitionism. He spent the remaining three decades of his spartan, bachelor life campaigning for peace (Curti 1937, 24).[2]

He spoke of that decision in his journal entry for January 1, 1845: "I find my mind is setting with all its sympathies toward the subject of Peace. I am persuaded that is reserved to crown the destiny of America, that she shall be the great peace maker in the brotherhood of nations. And I think that I cannot better employ that talents and time that God may give me, than to devote a year or two to this cause" (Curti 1937, 42).

He had already joined the American Peace Society in 1843 and promoted the cause of peace in his humanitarian weekly, *Christian Citizen* (1844–51), which he edited in Worcester, Massachusetts. His own innovation was the series of "Friendly Addresses" exchanged by American and British correspondents and published in newspapers in 1845–46 during the Anglo-American Oregon border dispute.[3] Discouraged by the American Peace Society's reaction to the Mexican War, Burritt concentrated on his own work for peace. Building on the success of his "Friendly Addresses," in June 1846 Burritt went to England, where he organized the League of Universal Brotherhood and founded its journal, the *Bond of Universal Brotherhood* (1846–56).

Like Nicholson, Burritt was moved by the suffering of the poor during the Great Irish Famine. He traveled to Ireland in 1847, "to fathom the cause, extent & cure of its misery."[4] He was no doubt prompted to go to Skibbereen by the series of articles with arresting engravings by Cork artist James Mahony in the *Illustrated London News* that captured the harrowing conditions in the town and the surrounding region. Nicholson was in Ballina, County Mayo, in February, so she did not meet Burritt in Ireland; however, she would have been cheered by his interest in and on behalf of the Irish poor. The parish priest took Burritt through the town on February 20; Dr. O'Donovan, the dispensary physician, gave him a tour of the surrounding countryside, where people lay dying in hovels.

Before Burritt left Cork on February 28, he appealed to New Englanders to send aid to Ireland through the auspices of the Boston Relief Committee. That request and his short pamphlet *Four Months in Skibbereen* (1847) brought in some one hundred thousand dollars. When he returned to England, Burritt met with Lord John Russell to discuss the cost of transporting the relief supplies to Ireland (Hatton 1993, 116). His efforts resulted in the *Jamestown* expedition to Cork in March 1847 (see Curti 1937, 31n3; and Hughes 1899, 120–21).

When tension developed between England and France, in 1847 and again in 1852, Burritt started *Olive Leaves*, another kind of "Friendly Address" that took the form of short antiwar messages published in papers on both sides of the Channel (Curti 1929, 33). These initiatives prompted Burritt to organize a series of peace congresses with the purpose of promoting an international organization of nations to prevent war. Liberal intellectuals, free traders, and Quakers such as Joseph Sturge and John Bright supported Burritt's work. The peace congresses would have engaged Nicholson's reforming spirit. Welsh minister and reformer Henry Richard (1812–88), head of the English Peace Society, became Burritt's deputy in organizing the congresses that met in the early 1850s until the Crimean War and the American Civil War discouraged further meetings.

Burritt planned the first 1848 meeting for Paris, but the city was embroiled in the Revolution following the abdication of Louis Philippe on February 24, 1848, so he took the congress to Brussels, where Richard and Burritt added disarmament as a provision for universal peace. They planned the 1849 Paris Peace Congress with the advice of Richard Cobden. Before the second congress began in Paris, Burritt met with Alexis de Tocqueville, minister of foreign affairs. He described their conversation in his journal, written in Paris on July 15, 1849. De Tocqueville was for world peace, but he was concerned that the Paris meeting not be an occasion to "broach political and questionable subjects" (Curti 1929, 60).[5] In fact, it was Victor Hugo (1802–85) who, in his role as president of the congress, made the most radical contribution to the congress: a speech with a vision of an alliance between a United States of America and a United States of Europe.[6]

Determined to increase participation in the Frankfurt congress, Burritt traveled the United States to promote the idea of his peace congresses and their importance. He succeeded in convincing forty people to join the American party to Germany. Who joined Burritt's delegation? There were people who shared Burritt's aspirations for universal brotherhood and peace, and there were some who went to promote other reforms. Women promoting abolitionism went prepared to present an address promulgating equal rights. "The Creator has established an equality in the human family, perfect and beautiful as it is beneficent, without limitation to sex or complexion or national peculiarities" (N. Hewitt 2001, 20). Abolitionist Henry Highland Garnet (1815–82), who studied at the Oneida Theological Institute and became pastor of the African American Presbyterian Church in Troy, New York, traveled to Frankfurt, as did George Copway (1818–63), an Ojibwa from eastern Ontario who became a Methodist missionary. He appeared in his tribal dress (Vecsay 1983, 168; Curti 1929, 182). Harriet Beecher Stowe's sister-in-law Anne Tuttle Jones Bullard (1808–96) accompanied her husband, Artemas, who was an official delegate. Her letters to a St. Louis newspaper were published in book form as *Sights and Scenes in Europe* (1852).[7]

Nicholson's reforming spirit would have prompted her to join the British delegation to the Frankfurt congress. "Departure of English Members of the Peace Conference for Frankfurt," the cover story of the *Illustrated London News* for the week ending Saturday, August 24, 1850, was featured with an illustration portraying the delegation setting off from London:

> The friends of peace, from various countries in Europe, and from the United States of America, are about to hold their third Congress at Frankfurt-on-the-Main. A large part of the delegates and visitors, upwards of 500 in number, proceeded from this country, special trains and steamers having been engaged to convey the company directly from London to Frankfurt, *via* Dover, Calais, Malines and Cologne. Of this number 420 left the London bridge station in a train of twenty-four carriages, specially engaged, at half-past ten o'clock on Tuesday morning.
>
> A large number of delegates have arrived from the United States, including men of high influence, both in the literary and political world; and not the least interesting among the American delegates

are two ministers, one of whom is a Red Indian, who, twelve years ago, was a hunter in the forests of the

Far West; the other a coloured man, of pure negro descent; they are both gentlemanly and well-educated men, and are highly esteemed as ministers in America. The sittings of the Congress commenced in St. Paul's Church on the morning of the 22nd and continued on the 23rd and 24th. Resolutions were submitted to the Congress, and fully discussed, affirmed the impolicy and immorality of all war, and suggesting certain practical measures tending to establish the peaceful relations of nations and to provide efficient substitutes for war in the settlements of international disputes. (166)

The engraving depicts groups of travelers on the railroad platform at London Bridge Station. Two railway cars are ready for departure; one woman is seated by a window. Although there is no woman who matches Nicholson's description precisely, she could be any one of the five women wearing shawls and bonnets. In his journal (14), Burritt says he and a company of 350 English delegates reached Frankfurt on the twenty-first. Burritt had negotiated a three-shilling fare each way between Cologne and Frankfurt. He described his arrival in his journal (July 29): "Reached Frankfurt about 10 and found ourselves again at our old quarters at the Hotel de Russie."

Nicholson says she was to have traveled with a couple from Edinburgh, but the wife got sick and the husband was detained, so she arrived at 2:00 a.m., alone. Leaning against a lamppost and unable to communicate with anyone, there was an intervention that Nicholson considered providential. It was Burritt. "Who appears but 'an old acquaintance from the land of my birth'" (LP 1853, 223). Burritt meant New England as well as America for Nicholson.

Burritt himself described the encounter with Nicholson on Wednesday, August 21, in his journal (14): "Asenath Nicholson standing alone about 1 with no one to accompany her, so I hunted up a cab and drove with her to a private dwelling in a distant part of the city where she had a ticket for lodging. After ringing and rapping nearly half an hour, we aroused one of the inmates who opened the door and showed her a room. Not one of them can speak a word of English nor she German but they seemed to interpret her wants. It was 2 AM when I retired to bed with a terrible headache."[8]

Nicholson stayed with a family called Riebling, a trader father, his wife, and their seventeen-year-old daughter and eleven-year-old son, Frederic (*LP* 1853, 238). Nicholson describes the Rieblings as living about two miles from the terminus but a mile from the church where the meetings were held. In his journal (14), Burritt wrote that he had hoped to have the meetings at the neoclassical Paulskirche because it was the site, in 1848, of the first freely elected German parliament. Burritt and Joseph Sturge stayed at the Hotel de Russie. Nicholson visited the hotel and met the Englishman who had found her glasses that she had lost when she had put them down to read a bill. She called it another sign of Divine Providence.

Burritt did not face the difficulties of Paris's uncertain politics. There had been another unsuccessful rising in Paris on June 13, 1848, about ten weeks before his Paris meeting; however, a peace conference in a military nation brought other challenges.[9] There was the matter of recruiting delegates, and there was the poor timing: the failure of the 1848 liberal government to create a united Germany. In the end five hundred gathered in Frankfurt. Eighty German delegates pledged to attend.

Nicholson says nothing about the meetings themselves. She did not speak of the arguments against standing armies or the burden of war payments, Burritt's address to the congress, or his plan to convene a body to formulate a code of international law (Greeley 1851, 285). Later, when Henry Richmond was MP for Merthy Tudful, the House of Commons accepted his motion "to command the home secretary to contact foreign powers in order to try and introduce further improvements to the international law and establish a permanent arbitration system."[10]

In addition to the peace meetings, there were excursions. There was an outing to Heidelberg on an "uncommonly fine" day with a great spirit of fellowship among the party. (On her return to the Main-Neckar-Eisenbahn, Nicholson lost her spectacles yet again.)[11] She was less sanguine about the excursion to Wiesbaden. Perhaps she chose to go on the tour to inspect the thermal baths that date to Roman times, but she and her companions drifted, possibly through the Kurhaus Kolonnade (1827), into the famous Spiekbank, Wiesbaden's casino. Horrified, Nicholson described the Kurhaus as "a hideous deformity" in "a garden of delight" in her essay "Gamblers of West Baden, Germany." Watching the patrons placing bets around a roulette wheel, Nicholson took particular exception to a young woman who arrived to play and "to barter away the morning of her days, the principles of honesty, and the loveliness of female simplicity, in these damp, deep meshes of deceit and intrigue" (*LP* 1853, 237).[12]

Nicholson disapproved of gambling for its own sake and for what she regarded as either a first step to a state that would "give the depraved heart license to riot in sin unchecked" or the "finishing step on the ladder of sin" (*LP* 1853, 238). Nicholson was not the only member of the British delegation to be horrified by the gambling parlor. In his study of Joseph Sturge, Alex Tyrrell describes Sturge and his peace colleagues "stumbling across the gambling rooms of Wiesbaden" during an excursion and recoiling with horror (1987, 170).

Had Nicholson been in the city a decade or so later, she would have heard that Fyodor Dostoyevsky, a compulsive gambler, made three trips to the Wiesbaden tables (1863, 1865, and 1867), where he lost his money and pawned his watch and his wife's wedding ring (Simmons 1940, 115, 128, 183). He turned the experience into his novel *The Gambler* (1866), which in turn furnished the inspiration for Robert Siodmak's film *The Great Sinner* (1948), a melodrama set in Wiesbaden in the 1860s that shares Nicholson's moralistic view of gambling. She and her Quaker companions would have been relieved to know that the casinos were closed by imperial decree in 1872 and gambling did not return until 1949.[13]

On the third evening of Nicholson's stay in Frankfurt, Frau Riebling took her through dark alleys to what sounds like a temple: a man in white reading from an enormous book and people upstairs responding. From there they went to a "better street" to visit a Jewish family called Sterne who had English-speaking daughters.[14] Frau Sterne asked Nicholson to spend the winter with them. Nicholson declined the invitation, but she spent time between sessions of the conference with the family and learned from Theresa Sterne, the family's oldest daughter, that Herr Sterne, who had come from a rabbinical family, trained for the rabbinate, and been in charge of a Jewish school, became a Christian convert. Disowned by his own family, another Christian convert, a Londoner, gave Sterne a job as a missionary to the Jews in Frankfurt. Nicholson was impressed with all of the Sternes, but she was particularly taken with the filial honor and affection that the daughters had for their parents.

Later in 1850 Nicholson met Theresa Sterne in Halifax, where she was working as a governess for the children of Jeremiah and Hannah Brown, a Scotch family living at West Field House. The English 1851 census listed Theresa as a twenty-one-year-old servant from Frankfurt-on-the-Main who was employed as a governess, probably to Ann (thirteen) and Isabella (twelve). Nicholson noted that Theresa was willing to endure the separation from her family, a separation she described tearfully, in order to earn the money to see her parents through their old age (*LP* 1853, 234).

While Nicholson admired the Sterne daughters, she was especially fond of the eleven-year-old son of her hosts, Frederic Riebling. They could not converse, but Frederic became her self-appointed guide during her stay in Frankfurt. He walked her to the Paulskirche each morning, returning to see her safely home. He showed her the sights of the city, including the market, a local square where two sides had stalls and goods covered by a portico. At the end of Nicholson's stay, he escorted her to dinner with the Sternes where Theresa told her that Frederic was determined to go back with her to America. His mother said she had given Frederic her permission to humor him, but he was serious, and when he was told that it would not be possible, Nicholson said that she did not see him again; however, she did not forget him.

She ended her story of his kindness to a stranger with a charge to any of her younger readers. "And now to the boys and girls of America allow me to say, should Frederic Riebling, from Frankfurt-on-the-Main, ever come to your country, when I shall be sleeping in the dust, be careful to treat him kindly, and with the greatest courtesy" (*LP* 1853, 244). It is tempting, then, to wonder about a Frederic E. Riebling listed in the 1910 US Census living in Queens, Ward 4, with his wife, Anna. Born in Germany about 1845, Riebling arrived in New York in 1860. Could he have been Nicholson's Frederic?[15]

Nicholson's participation in the Frankfurt Peace Conference was a diversion from her main activity of 1850, her book *Lights and Shades of Ireland*, which was published in London that year by Houlston and Stoneman at 65 Paternoster Row.[16] The book had three parts: "Early History," "Saints, Kings and Poets of the Early Ages," and "The Famine of 1847, '48 & '49"; however, from the two epigraphs on the title page, the book is, in fact, dominated by Nicholson's famine narrative, the most important and valuable part of the book. She chose first a passage from Lamentations 2:12, "When their soul was poured out into their mother's bosom," scripture that speaks to the scarcity of food. Her second quote, from Hezehiah Niles, "Not e'en in the hour when my heart is most gay, / Will I lose the remembrances of thee and thy wrongs," was, perhaps, selected for its resonance to the line from Psalm 137, "If I forget thee, O Jerusalem, let my right hand forget her cunning."[17]

The impulse for *Lights and Shades* may have come from her desire to revisit Ireland. She had decided to write *Ireland's Welcome to the Stranger* as she observed conditions in Ireland in 1844 and 1845; she called her book "a simple narration of facts that passed under observation" (*IWS* 2002, 1). *Welcome* was not a jeremiad; she did not project the famine on the text, though while she wrote the book in Dublin in the spring of 1847, the famine raged around her. She may have decided to write *Lights and Shades* to contextualize her earlier experiences in the historical evidence of elements of early Irish history: physical remains, printed and manuscript sources, and individuals who represented the transition from the Gaelic world to Ireland after the Union.

The opening words to the preface to *Lights and Shades* prepare the reader for the part 3 account of Nicholson's famine ministry by explaining that the events she had witnessed had produced an extraordinary narrative: "The readers of these pages should be told that, if strange things are recorded, it was because strange things were seen, and if strange things were seen which no other writer has written, it was because no other writer had visited the same places, under the same circumstances" (*LS* 1850, iv).

Although readers tend to dismiss parts 1 and 2 and move straight to the famine, the earlier sections are worth revisiting to study Nicholson's writing of history and her use of sources. She believed that readers had to be prepared for her account of the famine, and she was assured that she could provide an impartial history. "It has never been my lot to meet with a straight-forward, impartial real matter-of-fact work, written on that devoted country, till the famine commenced. It has been suggested that an Irishman *could* not write an impartial book on his country, and an Englishman or Scotchman *would not*" (*LS* 1850, 7). Then she explained that she would provide an outline of Irish history and add her views about what brought Ireland to its present state in 1850. In doing so she would, as Margaret Kelleher demonstrated in *The Feminization of Famine*, find a way to "express the inexpressible." Like Kelleher, she described the famine, but she had also witnessed Ireland at a moment of transition from the eve of the Great Irish Famine to 1850 and reported on its effects on the suffering poor: their patient suffering and their generosity to one another until they could give no more.

Nicholson had arrived in Ireland on her mission "to investigate the condition of the poor," having been told stories that she assumed had elements of fantasy about them; however, her mining of evidence demonstrated to her that stories of Ireland as a home to kings and poets had elements of truth to them. Nicholson was moved by the physical remains of Ireland's past, remains of sacred and secular structures that spoke to Ireland's past glory. Readers of *Ireland's Welcome to the Stranger* will recall that moment at Holy Cross Abbey near Thurles, County Tipperary, when Nicholson had a glimpse of "the grandeur of the Romish church in Ireland's early history" (*IWS* 2002, 76).

She referred to artifacts she saw in the Archaeological Museum in Dublin such as the petrified shoes, found in a bog, that the king stood in during his inauguration and the gold ornaments that are now housed in the Treasury, the permanent gallery of pre-Christian and early Christian art at the National Museum. The library and archives of the Archaeological Society in Dublin and the Royal Irish Academy provided Nicholson with printed and manuscript sources, including *The Annals of the Four Masters*, and records about Cormac from the Records of Tara. Although she appears not to have seen the Book of Kells or the Cathach, the Psalter of St. Columba traditionally ascribed to Saint Columcille, Nicholson quotes the passage from James Wills's six-volume *Lives of Illustrious and Distinguished Irishmen from the Earliest Times to the Present Period . . . Embodying a History of Ireland* (1840–47) that mentions a copy of Gospels believed to have been written in Columcille's own hand and said to be housed in the Library of Trinity College (the Book of Kells).[18]

Nicholson's access to the sources was facilitated by her friends the O'Dowdas, "one of the princely families nestled among the mountains of Connacht" (*LS* 1850, 175, 178). She made a special study of the family: their records in the Archaeological Society and in the Royal Irish Academy, O'Dowda lore in bardic poems, the remains of the O'Dowda family in the Abbey of Moyne, and especially the O'Dowdas themselves, who remained "a specimen of an ancient noble race, which had retained the lineaments of a stock once existing among these mountains, and whole last glimmering of light I longed to behold before the fading rays should be extinguished forever" (*LS* 1850, 176).

Nicholson not only used the present to study the Irish past, but also looked to the Irish past to find metaphors for the present. For her, slavery was a metaphor for Ireland, a subtext of Nicholson's account of the early history of Ireland. While Nicholson would have come down on the side of the Reformation in Ireland, she began her section on Oliver Cromwell by referring to the studies of Cromwell by Thomas Carlyle and particularly by Jean-Henri Merle d'Aubigné, the Swiss evangelical Protestant best known for his *Histoire de la Reformation au XVIie siècle* (Paris, 1835–53), who wrote *The Protector: A Vindication* (1847), a sympathetic study of Cromwell. Nicholson, however, did not admire Cromwell; she compared the cruelty of Cromwellians to American slave owners and the Irish to so many cringing slaves (*LS* 1850, 76, 140). When praising O'Connell as one who repudiated slaveholders, telling them they could keep their money, Nicholson could not resist a swipe at her Scottish brethren, saying, "Let the Free Church of Scotland blush when she reads this" (*LS* 1850, 146).

Anticipating doubters about the abusive treatment of the Irish poor, Nicholson referred the reader to the sentence of exile passed on William Smith O'Brien "in the enlightened Bible age of 1848" (*LS* 1850, iv). If readers need further proof for present cruelties, Nicholson invites the reader to "come with me in the year 1850 and see the houseless wanderer dying in the mountains and bogs without *food*, without *clothes*, driven there by merciless landowners who have fattened on soil wrest from the fathers of those exiles" (*LS* 1850, v). "The year 1850" suggests that Nicholson might have returned to Ireland for a brief visit during that year.

In "Saints, Kings and Poets of the Early Ages," the second section of *Lights and Shades*, Nicholson tells her reader that along with the resources of the Archaeology Society of Dublin and the Royal Irish Academy for her discussion of saints and kings, she relied on biographies. It is interesting that Nicholson devoted attention to Irish saints, because as an evangelical Protestant she considered the Catholic veneration of saints a form of idolatry, but she researched the saints' lore with the same careful attention that she gave to early Irish secular history. Perhaps she overcame her scruples about saints by comparing some of them to the figures from the Old Testament. For example, she likens Bridget to Deborah. Again James Wills's biographies in his *Lives of Illustrious and Distinguished Irishmen* were her chief source for her survey of saints. She said simply about her account of Saint Patrick that she used Wills because his was such a simple account of the saint (*LS* 1850, 156).

The details of Nicholson's famine narrative in part 3 have informed the account of her life in Ireland during the years 1846–48. It remains to examine the way that Nicholson told the story of those harrowing years. Nicholson combined her eyewitness account with other forms of discourse to describe the horrors she witnessed: parables, dramatic scenes, and dialogues written in the cadences of the Old Testament. She drew on the Bible, lines from hymns, and literary allusions to record scenes that were beyond the experience of the reader. Discussing the challenges of finding appropriate language to describe the Great Irish Famine in his introduction to *The Hungry Voice*, Christopher Morash observes that "images from the prophetic books of the Bible provided a central means of comprehending the accelerated change brought on by the Famine" (1989, 21).

In evoking images from the prophets, Nicholson made it clear that she believed that the famine's devastation was not a Divine judgment, but the failure of man to use God's gifts responsibly.[19] Nicholson considered herself as "acting entirely as a passive instrument; moving because moved upon," but there was nothing passive about her indictment of those groups in power, the government and the established church, for failing in their stewardship of their relief resources. She distinguished between hired relief officials, whom she dismissed as bureaucratic, hierarchical, and self-serving, and local volunteer workers, including clergy of all denominations and coastguardsmen and their families.

From the start, reviewers of *Lights and Shades* focused on the famine section of the book. An appreciative notice in the *Northern Star and National Trade Journal* (Leeds) in October 1852 began: "Mrs. Nicholson is an American lady, who, with praiseworthy benevolence has devoted herself to the task of alleviating the miseries of the Irish people, in the terrible year of the famine. She was living in Ireland during the whole of that awful period, pursuing her own course of honorable benevolence; and she has stories to tell of physical suffering in point of mere fact to anything Mr. Osborne's work, which we recently noticed."[20] The reviewer picked up Nicholson's criticism of the failure of Irish middle-class women, with the notable exception of the Ladies' Committee, to devote themselves to famine relief, and some resident landlords, whom she praised as egalitarian and selfless. The reviewer's judgment of Nicholson's famine account would be repeated over the next 150 years.

A measure of the success of *Lights and Shades* was an American edition of part 3 published as *Annals of the Famine in Ireland in 1847, 1848 and 1849* by E. French at 135 Nassau Street in 1851 with an introduction by J. L. (Joshua Leavitt), editor of the *Emancipator*, who published Nicholson's letters from Ireland in 1847. Leavitt's characterization of Nicholson became the standard tribute to her intelligence and character that would inform the descriptions of later reviewers and historians. "She is a woman of great acuteness of intellect, and of the most self-sacrificing benevolence, with great independence of mind and force of character" (*Annals* 1998, 23).

With *Lights and Shades* published in England and in America, Nicholson took advantage of an opportunity to travel outside of London. She appeared on the English census for 1851 as "Elizabeth" Nicholson, a fifty-six-year-old widow from New York who was a visitor in the home of Thomas Elgie, a fifty-seven-year-old master painter who resided with his wife, Sarah (fifty-four); a son, Thomas (twenty-two), who worked locally as an apprentice; a daughter, Isabella (thirteen); and a grandson, Edward (one). The Elgies lived at 119 Westgate in the town of Thirsk in northern Yorkshire, a region known to contemporary readers of James Herriott's *All Things Bright and Beautiful*. Whatever brought Nicholson to Yorkshire, she was back in London by May.

The highlight of 1851 for Nicholson was certainly the Great Exhibition of the Works of Industry of All Nations that opened at Hyde Park's Crystal Palace. Nicholson devoted a long essay to it: "The World's Fair," in *Loose Papers* (1853, 244–60). She noted that there was some controversy about the idea of a world's fair. There was the matter of financing the exhibition; there was the philosophical and political issue of whether the exhibition should be a national one or a more representative international one. Even Prince Albert, president of the Society of Arts (later the Royal Society of Arts), and a man known for his keen interests in industry and design, was a reluctant player in the preparations, though Nicholson, like most people, gave credit for the success of the fair to the consort (Auerbach 1999, 39).

Prince Albert proposed that the exhibition venue, the Crystal Palace, an iron and glass building designed by Joseph Paxton, be located in Hyde Park.[21] The building was completed in seven months, in time for the official opening by Queen Victoria at 10:00 a.m. on May 1, 1851. Admission to the opening was limited to season ticket holders like Nicholson.[22] Her commentary on the opening explains the ceremony that was the subject of H. C. Selous's painting *The Opening of the Great Exhibition* (Auerbach 1999, 179).[23] As was her wont, Nicholson focused on a single detail from the event, a Chinese man in mandarin dress who walked back and forth in front of the platform until, overcome by the moment, he prostrated himself before the queen. In the Selous painting, he stands, as Nicholson described him, to the right of the platform (*LP* 1853, 247–48). Nicholson imagined what the effect of the opening would have had on the Chinese man.[24]

Nicholson did not actually see Queen Victoria making later visits to the exhibition, because the queen visited before the Crystal Palace was opened to the public, but Nicholson noted with approval that she understood that the queen dressed simply, behaved unpretentiously, and focused on learning more about the artifacts on display. As Nicholson had asked her friends to purchase clothing made by poor Irish women by way of encouraging them in their cottage industries, the queen purchased items on display to encourage local manufacturers.[25]

Nicholson purchased an exhibition catalog and visited all of the four major areas of the Crystal Palace: raw materials of manufacture, British, colonial, and foreign; machinery and mechanical inventions; decorative manufactures and sculpture; and architecture and fine arts. Though she does not mention the Irish stands, Nicholson certainly would have taken an interest in the Irish displays and may have noticed the difference in iconography between the Belfast and Dublin entries. Belfast's Mr. Andrew's damask tablecloth was decorated with the arms of the earl of Clarendon, whereas brooches made by the Dublin jewelers Waterhouse and West were replicas of early Irish brooches, including the Tara brooch, that Nicholson would have observed in the Royal Irish Academy. Perhaps she did not mention the Irish displays because she was more interested in local employment and not in industrialization.

What Nicholson did notice with approval was that the exhibition cut across class lines, with special excursion fares offered depending on the day of the week one attended and some philanthropists offering to pay for trips for the poor. As the exhibition continued, there were two general fare reductions. Even the location of the exhibition in Hyde Park was a nod to the poor, who traveled to an area once thought to be the exclusive preserve of the rich. Even though the Chartist threat had greatly diminished, the location was a gamble, because two years before they had selected Hyde Park as the "symbolic location" for their march (Auerbach 1999, 46–47).

Nicholson took a great interest in visitors to the exhibition and liked to guess the occupation of parties of working-class visitors based on the exhibitions that they chose to visit after first being dazzled by the "sky of glass" (*LP* 1853, 251). She created a cast of different characters and described their response to the exhibition—a tradesman, a laborer, a literary man, an aristocratic lady, a mustached dandy, a little old lady, and a countryman—and imagined them arriving at the Crystal Palace and choosing how to manage their visits to the exhibition.[26] Nicholson took a particular interest in a group of miners from Cornwall who made the day their own and ignored the signs telling visitors not to touch the objects. Nicholson found them exotic, a race apart from people who worked above the ground (*LP* 1853, 255–56).

There was no religious presence at the exhibition; the official tone of the exhibition was "pacifist internationalism"; however, there were prayer meetings and sermons organized during the period at Old Exeter Hall, the large public auditorium that stood in the Strand from 1831 to 1907. It was a place associated with temperance, evangelism, and, especially, abolitionism.[27] The morning that the exhibition opened and the day that it closed, a group of prayerful people, no doubt including Nicholson, spent an hour at Exeter Hall, asking for blessings for the stranger and for the host. Nicholson spent much of her time there listening to visiting clergy preaching sermons to the faithful.[28] She would have enjoyed especially the hymn singing from *Psalms and Hymns Selected for the Congregations Assembling in Exeter*

Hall, during the Great Exhibition of 1851, the pamphlet of hymns prepared especially for the exhibition.

An Exeter Hall highlight for Nicholson was the gathering, at Exeter Hall, for a "feast day," part of the First International and General Conference of the Evangelical Alliance, eight hundred Christians representing fifty denominations, which was founded at Freemason's Hall in London in 1846 to unite Christians of different churches "to enable Christians to realize in themselves and to exhibit to others that a living and everlasting union binds all true believers together in the fellowship of the Church."[29] The activities at Exeter Hall would have been congenial to the exhibition organizers, who had among their goals the promotion of universal peace. The peace initiative was designed to divert attention from the free-trade debate (Auerbach 1999, 634).

When the exhibition closed to the public, there was a sorrowful singing of "God Save the Queen." Many wept. Nicholson said nobody moved until the police cleared the building. The exhibitors were invited to bring their own guests to the exhibition for two days, but the spirit of the place had departed. Prince Albert presided over the formal closing ceremony. There was a prayer, the commissioners read their report, and there was a melancholy requiem. For Nicholson, herself, the opening and closing days began with prayer meetings at Exeter Hall, praying that good would come of an exhibition that brought English and foreign visitors together. She quoted one speaker as saying, "We Englishmen are not noted for our abundance of modesty. We have been prone to believe that *we* were the people; but this summer has taught us that there are in the world with others with whom we *cannot* compete at present—*others*—who can teach us lessons we might do well to learn, and we hope it may check our boasting and humble us" (*LP* 1853, 249).

Nicholson wrote extensively about the exhibition, but she did not mention meeting her old friend Horace Greeley, who traveled to London to visit the Crystal Palace and arrived in time to attend the opening. As one of the few American visitors who was not an exhibitor, Greeley was asked by the American commissioner to serve on a jury of hardware judges. He was rewarded for his efforts by an invitation to a banquet, where he was asked to propose the toast to Joseph Paxton. He responded with his usual ebullience: "When people were skeptical about the properties of the M'Cormick Reaping Machine, Greeley jumped on the reaper, started the team and demonstrated how the reaper could get the grain ready for binding" (Parton 1855, 371–72). While Nicholson left an account of the exhibition in *Loose Papers* and Greeley published his *Glances at Europe: In a Series of Letters from Great Britain, France, Italy, Switzerland during the Summer of 1851* (1851), neither mentioned the other. If Greeley was in the Crystal Palace every day and if Nicholson was at the exhibition as often as she claimed, they could hardly have failed to meet.[30]

After the exhibition closed, Nicholson was on the road again. She spent the winter of 1851–52 in Bristol, where Elihu Burritt had served as the American consul in 1847. Nicholson went to the city to visit sites associated with the evangelical educator, author, abolitionist, and philanthropist Hannah More (1745–1833), another Nicholson hero.[31] After successful pilgrimages to More's Bristol schoolroom and Barley Wood, the home that More built and occupied for some twenty-five years, the place Nicholson called "the *great* attraction," Nicholson described her unsuccessful efforts to find the cottage where More was born in the parish of Stapleton.[32] She left, on a sunny day in early March, with her friend Mrs. C. driving a horse and carriage to visit the More homestead. They were certain that villagers would know exactly where Hannah More was born, but they were met with only bewilderment from locals. Exasperated, but with her usual persistence, Nicholson met people who identified More variously as a dressmaker, a traveling writer, or perhaps a woman whose brother lived nearby (*LP* 1853, 262, 264). When Nicholson scolded the Stapleton postmistress for not knowing anything about its most famous citizen, the old lady responded, "The women of England, ma'am, mind their own business and have no time to be running after great things, them that work for a living" (*LP* 1853, 265). Nicholson gave up when even the parson knew nothing about More. With the coming of spring, she returned to London with thoughts of home.

10

Last Years

WHEN NICHOLSON returned to London from her winter in Bristol, she decided to finally return to New York. She had planned to spend only a few months in Britain; however, she stayed four years, about the same amount of time that she had spent in Ireland. She sensibly chose a spring crossing rather than a stormy winter sea voyage, and she chose to travel on the *Cornelius Grinnell*, an American Line ship described as "by all odds, . . . the strongest ship of her size ever built in that vicinity [Boston] which, when it arrived in London . . . excited much curiosity among persons interested in ship building."[1] She did not leave from Bristol or Liverpool; she returned, instead, to London, no doubt to say good-bye to her friends there, certainly the Bennetts and the Howitts. She would have visited the office of Baring Brothers at 3 Bishopsgate Street or of Grinnell Tinker, and Morgan, the ship's broker at 113 Fenchurch Street; both firms handled bookings for the American Line. She paid between twenty and thirty guineas for her passage.[2] She departed from the London Docks on a day in mid-April.[3] One of eight cabin passengers, she is listed in the ship's manifest as "Acinith" Nicholson, a fifty-eight-year-old widow. She arrived back in New York on April 30, 1852.

She no doubt gave serious thought to where she would settle when she returned to the city. Roswell Goss's Graham Boarding House was gone; Goss himself had died on August 24, 1847. Sylvester Graham died in 1851, the year before Nicholson returned to New York. The initial impulse for her mission to Ireland was to "personally investigate the condition of the poor." Now with her knowledge of the Irish before and during the Great Irish Famine, she would have been eager to seek out the poor of New York and apply that information and understanding to improve the conditions for the immigrant Irish. Henry S. Clubb provides a clue as to her whereabouts in "The Late Asenath Nicholson," his appreciation published in the *Water-Cure Journal* in August 1855. He wrote that in her last years, she "never seemed more happy than when visiting the poor sons and daughters of Erin in the shanties in the suburbs of Brooklyn, where we have sometimes had the pleasure to accompany her on her missions of charity and Christian philanthropy" (1855, 30). In the 1850s the Irish poor lived south of the Brooklyn Navy Yard in the area below Brooklyn Heights along the waterfront, where Irish laborers had built the Atlantic dock and basin in the 1840s (Brasher 1970, 129; Snyder-Grenier 1996, 32).

Nicholson would have found an important advocate for the Irish poor in Brooklyn in Walt Whitman, editor of the *Brooklyn Daily Eagle*. On May 22, 1846, he called on his readers to welcome the Irish who were fleeing from the Great Irish Famine: "Shall we not welcome them? Shall they starve in their pent up and misgoverned island, while we have millions on millions of unoccupied and fertile acres, created by the same God who rules over them and us—and destined for the use of all his creatures who need it?" (Brasher 1970, 128). The article suggests that Whitman was arguing for the Irish to settle on the land, but the reality was that the Irish settled in port cities, including Brooklyn.

The following year, the worst year of the Great Irish Famine, Whitman supported the initiative that dispatched American-financed relief ships with supplies to the Irish, in an article in the *Brooklyn Daily Eagle* on March 4, 1847: "In the history of the selfish and dark and gloomy things of nations, this act of congress dispatching the U.S. frigates *Jamestown* and *Macedonia* at the public expense with food for starving Ireland appears like a beaming star" (Brasher 1970, 242).

Finally, there is Whitman's undated manuscript titled "Wants," a sympathetic description of Irish women applying for positions as domestic servants in the city's Intelligence Office. "They are stout, square shouldered. Not a few of them are really good looking;

although, as a general thing, the best part of their countenances is an expression of patience, honesty and good nature" (Brasher 1970, 89).

Joann P. Krieg traced Whitman's sympathy with the Irish in Brooklyn to his family's early financial straits: "Brooklyn's 'Irish Town' was located near the navy yard, not far from where the Whitmans lived in the 1820s and where Walt's brother Jesse worked for a time. The family was still in Brooklyn in 1855 when the Irish made up Brooklyn's largest foreign-born element, numbering 56,753 out of a population of 205,250" (2000, 19). By the 1860s Irish communities were concentrated in the area just south of the Navy Yard and between city hall and Red Hook, as well as in Sunset Park and Flatbush. Whitman described one of the worst areas, a shantytown near Clinton Avenue, in the August 16, 1847, issue of the *Brooklyn Daily Eagle*: "Descending from Fort Greene, one comes amid a colony of squatters . . . They are permitted by the owners here, until the ground shall be wanted, to live free, as far as the land is concerned" (Snyder-Grenier 1996, 33).[4]

Did Nicholson herself initially settle in Brooklyn? If so, did she live near the abolitionists who were members of her old friend Simeon Jocelyn's Brooklyn congregation? In the Brooklyn census for 1850, Simeon Jocelyn was listed as a Connecticut-born engraver living with his wife, Harriet, and their six children in Williamsburgh; in the 1870 census, he is listed as a minister of the Gospel living in Brooklyn's Thirteenth Ward in central Williamsburgh. When William Goodell and his family left the little town of Honeoye in western New York in 1854, they moved to Brooklyn, where they were members of a Congregational church that was committed to the principles of abolitionism and temperance. Perhaps it was Simeon Jocelyn's church.

While Nicholson was settling herself in New York, did she try to reestablish a connection with her Hatch family relatives in Vermont? Her brother David had died the year before, in 1851, at the age of seventy-five, but if she had wished, she could have contacted David's wife, Olive, who lived until 1862, or their children. The family lived on in Chelsea for generations. Did Nicholson see her stepchildren Pluma and George Sidney Nicholson, who had returned to Elizabethtown and who survived her? By 1850 George Sidney had followed in his father's footsteps and been elected county clerk for Essex County. He lived with his wife, Louisa, and their six children on Water Street, perhaps in the family home. An 1855 Elizabethtown census lists Pluma as a servant, possibly a child minder, in the household of George's business partner, George S. Root.

The streetscape of Nicholson's New York had changed in the eight years that she had been gone. The American Bible Society was still at its premises at 72 Nassau Street, but it had purchased a city block between Third and Fourth Avenues and Astor Place and Ninth Street and built a six-story building. The Anti-Slavery Society office, publisher of Nicholson's last book, *Loose Papers*, was located in her old neighborhood, at 48 Beekman Street.

What else changed in the eight years between 1844 and 1852? Nicholson would have disapproved of the Mexican War (1848), but she probably would have sympathized with the Irishmen who joined the Mexicans as the San Patricios to protest their treatment by the army's noncommissioned officers. Millard Fillmore, president of the United States (1850–53), supported Henry Clay's Compromise of 1850 that protected the balance between free states and slave states; however, Nicholson's uncompromising attitude toward slavery meant that she would have scorned Clay's compromise, even to save the Union.[5]

She would have actively opposed the Fugitive Slave Law of 1850 that required citizens to capture runaway slaves.[6] The year Democrat Franklin Pierce succeed the Whig Fillmore, Harriet Beecher Stowe published *Uncle Tom's Cabin* (1852). An immediate best seller, the book was widely translated so that international as well as national attention focused on the issue of slavery. Although Nicholson does not mention the novel, she certainly would have read it and have concluded that Stowe had raised support for the abolitionist cause, as she had raised American awareness of Irish suffering during the Great Irish Famine with her books and letters.

Like all abolitionists and most northerners, Nicholson would have considered President Franklin Pierce's support of the divisive Kansas Nebraska Act (1854) a betrayal of the civil rights of those individuals protected by the Missouri Compromise. She could have been present with members of the New York Anti-Slavery Society at the Broadway Tabernacle on March 7, 1854, to hear Ralph Waldo Emerson's "Second Address on the Fugitive Slave Law," his speech that argued that southern slaveholders should free their slaves and be compensated for their value. Whether she attended or not, it is likely that she had mixed feelings about Emerson's solution. Although she would have supported a plan to end slavery, she certainly would have objected to the recognition of slaves as chattel and, therefore, eligible for owners to be compensated for their worth. Despite efforts to contain the violence, skirmishes between pro- and antislavery forces erupted in Kansas, but by that time Nicholson was dead.

During her absence, members of Nicholson's abolitionist circle had continued to advocate for the end of slavery. The year Nicholson returned to New York, William Goodell published *Slavery and Anti-Slavery: A History of the Great Struggle in Both Hemispheres* (1852). He followed with *The American Slave Code, in Theory and Practice* in 1853. When he settled back in Brooklyn in 1854, he was appointed editor of the weekly *American Jubilee*, later the *Radical Abolitionist*, and finally *Principia* for the Abolitionist Society.[7] Goodell's 1854 letter to Lysander Spooner from 48 Beekman Street suggests that he worked out of the American and Foreign Anti-Slavery office that shared the 48 Beekman Street premises with the Abolitionist Society. It is also likely Goodell met Nicholson when she called at his Beekman Street office, near Nicholson's old Graham Boarding House.

Although there are many questions about Nicholson's activities between her return to New York on April 30, 1852, and her death on May 15, 1855, what we do know is that she turned again to her writing. It is likely that Goodell may have been helpful to Nicholson when she was looking for a publisher for her last book, *Loose Papers; or, Facts Gathered during Eight Years' Residence in Ireland, Scotland, England, France and Germany* (1853). The book was printed by John A. Gray of 95 and 97 Cliff Street, New York, and sold at 48 Beekman Street.

Loose Papers is a miscellany of unpublished travel writing. Perhaps she published these uncollected pieces to earn some money, or should we consider her epitaph from John 6:12, "Gather up the fragments that nothing be lost," at face value? Unlike *Ireland's Welcome to the Stranger* and *Annals of the Famine*, Nicholson had no single earnest message to her reader. Instead, her purpose was largely aesthetic, the telling use of detail. In her preface to *Loose Papers*, she remarks that the virtue of the thirty-two pieces is that they are short, but then she speaks, as an experienced traveler, about the way that small things, often overlooked, can provide the real insight into a people or culture: "But long experience in traveling has shown me that the *little things*, the *common* things, and the *every-day* things, are the *under*-currents, which throw *up* and throw *out* all that is *great*, all that is *needful*, all that is to be *valued*; and whoever, when traveling, would gather the richest material for *thinking*, and for knowing the *true* character and conditions of a people would do well to spend a part of his time among the trifles with which every country can furnish a considerable amount" (*LP* 1853, i–ii).[8]

The essays provide details about her travels in Britain and on the Continent that are not included in her other books, information this writer has used in earlier sections of this book. "Kerry Mountains" could only have been written about, or at least inspired by, her walk through those mountains in March 1845. From a height on the road to Derrynane, she glimpsed the Skellig Rocks and mentioned the Shrove-eve Skellig lists. She began "Skellig's Isles" by saying that she never actually visited the islands and that her essay was based on information from a "well-known" but unnamed authority. She ended the essay, as she often did with accounts of visits to pilgrim sites, saying that the Skelligs were associated with superstitions that, she was happy to report, had "nearly died away" (*LP* 1853, 15–16).[9]

"A Night's Adventure" is no doubt a description of Nicholson's walk from Galway to Urlingford on November 19, 1844, when, almost penniless, she trudged through the winter mud from Birr to Roscrea. The point of the piece is to affirm, with an example, what she believed was the Divine Providence that saw her safely through her travels in Ireland. She must have cut the piece from *Ireland's Welcome to the Stranger* and, instead, left a shorter, more general expression of her confidence: "The protecting kindness of God must be recorded in particular, as I never had been in the habit of being out alone after nightfall in city or country, and should have shrunk from it as improper, if not dangerous. Here, the peace of mind, the unwavering trust which I ever felt in the arm that sustained me, kept me not only from fear, but kept me joyful" (*IWS* 2002, 154).

Nicholson varied the usual tourist trope of beggars as pests in her "Beggars of Ireland." Based on the beggars she met in her travels, she constructed a typology of beggars, concluding that all beggars suffer not just from physical want, but also from the damage that begging, a form of oppression, inflicts on their self-respect. She confronts those individuals who despise the beggar by saying, "What virtue of yours has left you on this vantage-ground, and what decree of the Almighty has determined that he shall always be tormented, and you always comforted? And how know you when you pass such with scorn, but that a few kind inquiries might lead to results which would place the poor outcast beyond the world's scorn, and restore to society a useful member among the working class?" (*LP* 1853, 44). Her position on beggars, like her advocacy for the Irish poor, irritated the middle and upper classes, who resented her outspoken criticism of the social and economic system.

Nicholson ended part 2, the "Lights" of *Lights and Shades of Ireland,* with a sketch of the Connacht pirate queen Granuaile (Gráinne Ní Mháille), whose character she dismissed as "masculine and revolting" (*LS* 1850, 213). She revisited Granuaile (spelled "Grana-Uille") and revised her assessment in her essay "Grana-Uille and her Castles" in *Loose Papers.* It is possible that Nicholson made notes about Granuaile while she was in Mayo in the winter of 1847–48, but she may have declined to publish it because it would have diverted readers of *Annals of the Famine* from her message of famine suffering.[10]

She began her essay with a reference to the storied 1593 meeting between Granuaile and Elizabeth, a main feature of Granuaile folklore. Chances are that Nicholson saw the engraving *Grana Uile Introduced to Queen Elizabeth* in *Anthologia Hibernica* (1793).[11] Instead of leaving her reader with her *Lights and Shades* judgment that Granuaile was a coarse-looking, rough-mannered woman, she followed her usual practice of distinguishing between the perception of the Irish and the Irish character by contrasting Granuaile's appearance with her capacity for bold action and firm decisions. She repeated the local legend of the abduction of Lord Howth's grandson before she described the Mayo castles associated with Granuaile.[12]

Nicholson herself visited Granuaile's castle, located near Newport, County Mayo, when she stayed with her friend Mrs. Arthur, the postmistress, before the Great Irish famine in June 1845 (*LS 1850*, 214). The castle, on the shore of Clew Bay, is the only castle that can be positively associated with Granuaile (Killanin 1967, 391). Nicholson climbed to the first floor on a ladder and looked out through a defensive "loop-hole" to the sea. She located Granuaile's grave in the ruins of the Cistercian Abbey on Clare Island and mentioned the small Kildawnet Castle associated with Granuaile that had a reputation for frightening children who misbehaved with abduction by the pirate queen. She did not repeat the story she used to end part 2 of *Lights and Shades*, her meeting with children who pointed to Granuaile's castle, saying, "And that's the lady marm that kept the country in dread and would frighten the life of ye" (*LS* 1850, 215).

The unnamed author of Nicholson's obituary in the *New York Tribune* on May 16, 1855, reported that Nicholson left unpublished manuscripts "chiefly of a religious character" and was working on her memoir at the time of her death. None of Nicholson's unpublished manuscripts have been found. The remark indicated that Nicholson continued to write to the end of her life. She may have considered new reforms based on her years in Ireland; she may have had something to say about the Irish in New York, or she may have needed the money for her modest needs or to fund yet another cause.

Nicholson's friendship with Henry S. Clubb suggests that she may have attended the New York Vegetarian Society's first annual banquet at Metropolitan Hall on September 3, 1853. She may have even taken part in planning for the event, as she had done in London in 1848. Clubb, who had emigrated from England in the summer of 1853, would have arrived in time for the banquet. Their mutual friend William Bennett would have been the bond between them. Clubb described Bennett as Nicholson's best friend in England. He added that it was Bennett, who knew Nicholson and her foibles well, who said that he "often reconciled to her those who had been offended by her style of address" (1855, 31). Nicholson knew her reputation for plain speaking because she warned Bennett in the opening sentence of her letter of October 30, 1847, "Please prepare yourself. I am about applying some of those 'offensive points' in my character which I so eminently possess and which may require not only your true charity, but untiring patience, to plod through" (*Annals* 1998, 100). Nicholson may have been the one who introduced Horace Greeley to Clubb, whom Greeley hired as a *Tribune* reporter.

Nicholson may have attended the Whole World's Temperance Convention in New York in November 1853. Had she done so, she would have met Rev. John Pierpont once more. Like Nicholson herself and many of her friends, Pierpont's life changed course over the years. In 1845, the year after Nicholson left for Ireland, Pierpont resigned as pastor of the Hollis Street Church after wrangling with his congregation over Pierpont's ardent support of abolitionism. By 1853 he was the pastor of the Unitarian First Parish Church in Medford, Massachusetts.

Having been an enthusiastic season ticket holder for the Crystal Palace Exhibition in London, Nicholson certainly would have been curious about New York's American Crystal Palace Exhibition of the Industry of All Nations at Reservoir Square, Sixth Avenue, between Fortieth and Forty-Second Streets, which opened on November 1, 1853, and ran through 1854.[13] Its design, borrowed from London's Crystal Palace, included the addition of the 350-foot Latting Observatory, a structure that anticipated the Eiffel Tower, which until its destruction by fire in 1856 was New York's tallest landmark (Symmes 2005, 100–101). The space continued as an exhibition space until it was destroyed by fire in 1858.[14]

Nicholson's final address, 95 Erie Street, Jersey City, is a puzzle. Her earlier work situated her in Manhattan, and we know that she worked among the Irish poor of Williamsburgh in Brooklyn. What would have brought her to a Jersey City neighborhood of tradesmen (carters, machinists, and carpenters) and office workers (bookkeepers and clerks) not too far from the ferry to New York? Is there any reason that Nicholson moved to 95 Erie Street? According to the *Directory of Jersey City for 1855–6*, Elias Winter, a bookkeeper, was the head of the house at 95 Erie, which was located near the northeast corner of Erie and Sixth Streets.[15] Based on information in the 1860 census, the English-born Winter would have been a fifty-nine-year-old widower with four young sons, the youngest of whom would have been three in 1855. That his oldest son was born in England and his younger sons in Canada suggests that Winter emigrated from England to Canada before settling in Jersey City.

Winter is listed in the 1855 directory as a bookkeeper, but in the 1860 census he appears as the sexton of the First Dutch Reformed Church in Jersey City. It is probable, then, that the Dutch Reformed Church was the bond between Winter and Nicholson, and indeed the church may have drawn Nicholson to Jersey City. Winter and Nicholson were probably congregants of the Third Reformed Dutch Church at the southeast corner of Erie and Third Streets.[16] Although the Dutch Reformed Church was not a feature of Nicholson's life, she would have been attracted to the preeminence the church gave to scripture. This church had recently been founded in April 1852, and it had a membership of sixty-three families in 1856 (Taylor 1857, 420–27). She may have found a home worshipping with that small congregation.

The church's first pastor, Rev. Joseph Paschal Strong, who was installed on January 21, 1853, and served until 1856, was a neighbor who lived at 150 Erie Street, at the southeast corner of Erie and Pavonia Streets.[17] He had a Brooklyn connection: his father, Rev. Thomas M. Strong, ministered in Flatbush for forty years at the Flatbush Dutch Reformed Church (1796), which is still located at 890 Flatbush Avenue. Joseph Strong was the kind of minister Nicholson admired: an earnest preacher with "remarkable powers of description" and a man known for his kind and gentle manner with his congregation (Corwin 1902, 756). That he was "of nervous organization and never enjoyed robust health" may have reminded her of John M'Dowall. In any case, he was the clergyman who attended her in her last illness.

Nicholson's death certificate designates her as a "housekeeper." Was that designation simply the conventional way to indicate the occupation of a woman who was not otherwise employed or married to the owner of the house, or was Nicholson actually employed by Winter as a housekeeper to look after his motherless boys? She may have needed to find work to support herself. Clubb's notice about Nicholson suggests that her financial condition was precarious enough in her last years, a situation that may have been exacerbated by her philanthropy to the Irish poor in New York. It would have been the final realization of her initial impulse to visit Ireland to "investigate the condition of the poor." Her investigation complete, she may have spent her last years trying to help the Irish immigrant in New York. We do not know for sure, but Clubb suggests it may have been the case: "Although incessantly diligent, she never remained in possession of any property she may have acquired; her feelings were too frequently excited by objects of distress and misery to think of retaining anything which could minister to the alleviation of suffering. Indeed, she seemed to regard her own privation as of less consequence than the privation of the Irish exile" (1855, 31). Clubb also identified J. T. Sanger as Nicholson's benefactor in her last years whose "private benevolence" provided for "many comforts of her old age." J. T. Sanger probably was Joseph T. Sanger, whom Nicholson could have met in 1839–40 when she was operating her boardinghouse at 21 Beekman Street. He owned a fancy-goods business nearby at 186 Pearl Street, near the Tappan brothers' premises. Sanger is listed on the 1850 census as living with his family in Brooklyn's Tenth Ward.[18]

According to Nicholson's obituary in the *New York Tribune*, Nicholson's chronic and debilitating spinal complaint returned in the winter of 1854–55. She probably suffered from inflammatory lumbago or acute traumatic myofascitis, the most common cause of lower back pain (Merck 1997, 917). She mentioned a disease of the spine in *Ireland of the Welcomes* when she described the fall she took in March 1845 climbing a wall near Dunkerron Castle, the old keep of the O'Sullivan Mór, outside of Kenmare. Having experienced months of suffering with back pain in New York, she was pleasantly surprised when she quickly recovered; however, when she recovered from her back-pain episode in the spring of 1855, the author of her obituary surmised that she got up too soon and walked too far. Her condition was complicated by bleeding in the lungs. Although her doctors got her hemorrhage under control, her health quickly declined. Her death certificate listed the cause of her death as typhoid fever, so it is possible that this infection caused her back complaint.[19]

As Nicholson fought her last illness, on April 4, 1855, William Goodell and the old abolitionists—Frederick Douglass, Simeon Jocelyn, James McClure Smith, Gerrit Smith, Lewis Tappan, George Whipple, and W. E. Whiting—announced a meeting of the radical abolitionist party, the Liberty Party, in Syracuse, New York. They described the Liberty Party as "the only political party in the land, that insists on the right and duty to wield the political power of the nation for the overthrow of every part and parcel of American slavery."[20]

Clubb's account of Nicholson's death draws on his reading of the *Tribune* account, but he includes important additional details of her last months. He tells his reader that during her suffering of nearly two months, she was "attended with much assiduity and care by her adopted sister, Miss Warren and her numerous friends." Unfortunately, there is no record of a Miss Warren, nor has she been identified.

The end itself must have come quickly because on May 13, Rev. Joseph Strong traveled to East New York to attend the dedication of a new Reformed church where he served as pastor, his first appointment, from 1850 to 1854. Had Nicholson been close to death, it is doubtful that he would have left her bedside; however, her other clergy friends may have joined the vigil and excused Strong to assist his father in Flatbush. Nicholson died two days later, on Tuesday, May 15, 1855, the day that Louis Baker, who murdered Bill Poole, the notorious "Bill the Butcher," leader of the Bowery Boys, arrived aboard the clipper ship the *Grapeshot* while Poole's Know-Nothing pals were holding their convention in Philadelphia.

The notice of Nicholson's death was carried in the obituary section of the May 16 edition of the *New York Herald* and the *New York Tribune*. The notice was also carried in the *Brooklyn Eagle*.

In Jersey City, on Tuesday, May 15, ASENATH NICHOLSON, late of this city, well known as the keeper for fifteen years of the Graham Boarding House and author of "Travels in Ireland during the late Famine" and other work of merit.

Her funeral will take place from the Dutch Reformed Church, Erie Street, Jersey City, at two o'clock this afternoon and her remains taken to Greenwood.

At her funeral, Strong described her last days, which she bore with the stoicism with which she faced her other adversities. On May 18 the *Tribune* reported that she endured her last painful days with patient suffering. "She had long been inured to *do* the will of her Heavenly Father. She now learned the harder lesson of sweet and passive *submission* to that will." The account added that when a clergyman, probably Strong, started to pray with her, she asked, "Pray not for any alleviation of my pain, but only for 'grace to endure it.'"

During the service Joseph Strong read from scripture, perhaps the passage from John 14 that Nicholson often chose to read to her Irish listeners. Her old friends who had shared her work for abolitionism were there. William Goodell described her character and her work in his eulogy, and Rev. Simeon Jocelyn offered the funeral prayer.

Later that day, under the direction of an undertaker aptly named Henry Stiff, Nicholson was brought across the river to Brooklyn's Green-Wood Cemetery, the city's most eminent graveyard, where fellow abolitionists Horace Greeley and Henry Ward Beecher repose. Thomas Hastings (1794–1872), who wrote the music for Nicholson's favorite hymn, "Majestic Sweetness Sits Enthroned," is also buried in Green-Wood (Richman 1988, 206). Nicholson was first buried in J. T. Sanger's family plot, located along Battle Avenue in lot 2247, section 111. Green-Wood historian Jeffrey Richman provides an explanation for why Nicholson was buried in Green-Wood: "You didn't have to be wealthy to be buried at Greenwood—It helped, though, particularly if you wanted a prime location, or if you wanted to have a plot for you and your family. But public lots were available, where single graves could be purchased at relatively modest prices. And if you had good friends or comrades, they might even pay for your final resting place at Green-Wood Cemetery" (1988, 51). There is a final Nicholson mystery. On June 3, 1862, her remains were removed to unmarked grave 645 in lot 8999, one of the cemetery's public lots.[21] There are no Green-Wood records about the transfer, but there are plans to mark the plot with an appropriate memorial stone.

On Friday, May 18, 1855, the *New York Tribune* published Nicholson's obituary (7). It is tempting to think that Horace Greeley was its author; he certainly would have provided information about her life and work. The notice is an attempt to record the life of a remarkable woman who accepted her call to help the Irish poor and who lived her life as a model of Christian charity. The notice is reprinted in its entirety because it demonstrates the unusual coverage of Nicholson's life in New York's most powerful and influential newspaper:

> The decease of Mrs. Nicholson was announced in *The Tribune*, on May 16th, with a brief allusion to her labors, travels and writings. Some further account of her may be expected by the public, and will interest her numerous friends in both hemispheres. She was born in Vermont. Her family name was Hatch. For several years she was a very successful teacher. Some of the best educated men in the country were her pupils and still cherish a grateful remembrance of her teachings, and a high appreciation of her learning and talents. Her life was beclouded with many sorrows, and for many years she lived a lone widow without any children of her own, though her husband left some by a previous marriage to comfort her.
>
> She was long known as a vigorous and chaste writer in a number of public journals to which she was a constant contributor. In this way she assisted to introduce and inaugurate the principal reformatory enterprises of the day, in their incipient stages, when the most needed help, and encountered strong opposition.
>
> It was *her* pen chiefly that made Solomon Southwick's paper the dread of the Masonic fraternity, and she became, as she believed, the object of long-continued and secretly conducted espionage and persecution on that account.

She became a regular contributor to *The New York Genius of Temperance*, as early as 1830–1; and afterward the principal writer in *The Female Advocate*, issued by the same publisher. She was a warm friend of the late Rev. J. R. McDowall, and became his biographer. For fifteen years she kept the Temperance or Graham Boarding House in New York, which was the home and resort of radical friends of Temperance and kindred reforms, both in the city and country.

It was under her roof and sometimes threatened with mobs, that a consultation of friends of the enslaved from different States matured and the preliminary measures for forming the American Anti-Slavery Society in 1833. And it was from her house that a large portion of the Eastern Delegation to the first National Anti-Slavery Convention started for Philadelphia, in December, to complete their organization. In her boarding-house it was, that Mr. Greeley, now of *The New York Tribune*, then a young man and a new adventurer in New York, became first deeply interested in the Anti-Slavery cause, as he was afterward accustomed to mention.

After this, Mrs. N. went to Ireland, and travelled on foot, from cabin to cabin through the country, just before and during the famine. Her letters and appeals to the people of America through Mr. Greeley, Mr. Leavitt and other editors were instrumental in procuring large supplies of food from this country, some of which she received and distributed with her own hands.

In Ireland, she became revered as the American Mrs. Fry, the idol of the peasantry, the admiration of the wealthy, the almoner of the philanthropic, the wonder of all. O'Connell and Father Mathew were among her warm friends. From Ireland she passed over to England, and thence to the Continent. At the World's Peace Convention at Frankfurt, she assisted, with Elihu Burritt and others, to represent the philanthropists in America.

She spent some time in Paris. Returning to Great Britain, she scrutinized society in England and Scotland, made many friends, acquired rare information, and accomplished great good. In London, she was kindly received by all classes, she found a wide field for the exercise of her peculiar gift of personal labor, conversing with the rich and poor, on the highest topics of interest to rational and immortal beings.

After an absence of about eight years, she returned home about three years ago. Some years previous to her going to Europe, she had visited the West Indies and the Southern States for her health where she gained much information respecting slavery.

She wrote several pamphlets on various subjects. Among her published volumes are her *Memoirs of the Rev. J. R. McDowall, Ireland's Welcome to the Stranger, Lights and Shades of Ireland,* and *Loose Papers,* or incidents of travel in France, England and elsewhere. Whoever would become truly acquainted with the Irish and with Ireland must possess themselves of the writings of Mrs. Nicholson. Her *Loose Papers* are a rich magazine of miscellaneous sketches of scenery, character and biographical anecdote. She had commenced writing her own memoirs. How far she proceeded, we are unable to say. It is much to be hoped that her attempts in that direction will not have been wholly lost. She has left other valuable manuscripts, chiefly of a religious character, which we trust, will be published.

As a writer, she possesses rare talents and though she unfolded a rich vein of thought, peculiarly her own, was remarkable for neatness and naturalness of style, a chastened imagination and correct taste. She was preeminently a Christian philanthropist, and a Christian reformer. Abounding in good works, she was a hearty believer in the primitive Protestant doctrine of "justification by faith." *Her* dying motto and testimony, like that of John Howard, was: "*My hope is in Christ.*" When someone at her bedside sought to comfort her with the quotation of "blessed are the dead," &, "for their works do follow them," she returned an answer, disclaiming all dependence on the merit of her good works. She rested in Christ as her Saviour.

Early in the winter, she was visited with a return of an old spinal complaint, which confined and weakened her. On getting better, she went out on some business, and probably walked too far. She was attacked soon after with a bleeding at the lungs. This too, by medical assistance was checked. But both these attacks reduced her strength, and she declined rapidly. She suffered much pain but bore it with great patience. She had long been inured to *do* the will of her Heavenly Father. She now bore the harder lesson of sweet and passive *submission* to that will. When a clergyman was about to pray with her, she said, "Pray not for any alleviation of my pain, but only for the grace to endure it."

She was attended by kind friends. Her funeral was held at the Reformed Dutch Church, in Erie Street, Jersey City, whose pastor Mr. Strong, had been much with her in her last sickness, and on this occasion, read selections of appropriate Scriptures, and gave an interesting account of her last hours. He was followed by William Goodell, in some statements of her general character and labors. The Rev. S. S. Jocelyn offered the funeral prayer. The remains were followed by her friends to the Greenwood Cemetery, where they were interred in the grounds of her friend J. T. Sanger, Esq.

By unusual diligence, self-denial, benevolence and frugality, she has been enabled to accomplish great good, but has left little behind her but the rich legacy of her Christian example and valuable writings. "Precious in the sight of the Lord, is the death of his saints."

The *Friend* (London) for the "Seventh Month" of 1855, carried the full text of the notice of Nicholson's death from the *New York Tribune* because the notice of her death would be of interest "to many of our readers who knew her when in this country on her mission of benevolence."[22] In August Henry Clubb wrote his own appreciation of Nicholson in the *Water-Cure Journal*. After that, the memory of Nicholson disappeared.

Afterword

ASENATH NICHOLSON was rediscovered when English novelist
Alfred Tresidder Sheppard (1871–1947) published an abridged edi-
tion of *Ireland's Welcome to the Stranger*, which he titled *The Bible in
Ireland* (1926).[1] In his introduction Sheppard compared Nicholson
to George Borrow (1803–81), an agent of the British and Foreign
Bible Society who spent five years in Spain bringing Spanish and
Basque translations of the New Testament to the Spanish. His expe-
riences were the subject of his book *The Bible in Spain* (1843).

Sheppard was delighted with the response from readers, who recognized the historical value of Nicholson's account. Its review in the
Times Literary Supplement brought a response from Margaret Howitt, the younger daughter of William and Mary Howitt, who clearly
remembered Nicholson, who called herself Asen'ath, not the more
usual As'-e-nath, visiting the Howitts' home on Avenue Road in
Regent's Park. She also shared her vivid recollection of the American
passing insouciantly through Piccadilly, dressed in her green polka
coat and wearing Indian moccasins. As unconventional in manner as
Nicholson was in appearance, Margaret Howitt also recalled Nicholson visiting the house when Mary Howitt was preoccupied with
domestic duties. Nicholson was having none of it. "You talk about
stockings and such things when I came expecting to hear something
improving." She may have been an oddity, but Margaret Howitt concluded, "yet there withal she remains a most heroic figure in the long
list of noble women" (Sheppard 1926, 105).

Margaret Howitt also mentioned that her older sister Anna Maria Howitt had made a pencil portrait, "an exact likeness," of Nicholson that Nicholson left with Howitt's friend Mary Elizabeth Bennett. In 1926 Bennett still had the portrait and coverlet that Nicholson had made for the Bennetts. Sheppard published a reproduction of the portrait with his article about Nicholson and the Howitts in the *Bookman*. In the drawing a robust-looking Nicholson gazes placidly at the writing in her lap. Her hair, still dark, is parted in the middle and curls around her face and out from under her bonnet. She wears a scarf over her full-cut jacket. When Sheppard talked with Bennett, an alert ninety-two-year-old lady living in Hammersmith, she too had clear memories of Nicholson, who had met William Bennett in Ireland. Bennett invited Nicholson to stay with his family in Park Village, Regent's Park, when she came to London.

The Bible in Ireland brought a fresh appreciation of Nicholson and her work. "Inis Cealtra's" review of *The Bible in Ireland* in the *Catholic Bulletin* in November 1926 dismissed Sheppard's "rather useless" introduction that robbed the reader of more of Nicholson herself.[2] Like Margaret Howitt, a Catholic convert, "Inis Cealtra" objected to Sheppard's change of title from *Ireland's Welcome to the Stranger* to *The Bible in Ireland*. While Nicholson had been scrupulous about her choice of scripture when reading to the Irish poor, Borrow was a proselyte. There was no question that the reviewer was taken with Nicholson as a reliable reporter of conditions in the Irish countryside in 1844–45. "Inis Cealtra" was so taken by Nicholson that a second Nicholson article, "A Puritan Writer on the Famine," appeared in December 1926 to introduce the reader to *Lights and Shades of Ireland*.

Stephen Gwynn too read *The Bible in Ireland* and devoted a chapter to Nicholson that quoted liberally from *The Bible in Ireland* in his *Saints and Scholars* (1926). (She would have been pleased that Father Mathew was the subject of another chapter.) Gwynn was the first to write a modern appreciation of Nicholson, and he set the pattern for his contemporaries, who praised her reliability as an observer. Praising her diction as worthy of Dr. Johnson (1926, 186), Gwynn called her account "probably the most enlightening document before the Great

Irish Famine" (1926, 187). He described Nicholson's determined character, her generosity and charity, and her love for the Irish poor, who "understood the reality of a religion which was not hers" (1926, 186). Gwynn knew that Nicholson labored among the poor during the famine, but he had no knowledge of how she accomplished her mission.

Joseph Hone followed with an article in the *Dublin Magazine* in 1934, praising Nicholson's similar qualities, and there was a sympathetic appreciation of Nicholson in the *Irish Rosary* in 1933 by the distinguished Dominican historian Ambrose Coleman. Seán O'Faoláin further established Nicholson's credibility in his biography of Daniel O'Connell, *King of the Beggars* (1938), where he called her "one of the most intelligent of all observers" of Ireland before the famine. O'Faoláin's Cork contemporary Frank O'Connor, who would have read *King of the Beggars*, included passages from *The Bible in Ireland* in his Irish anthology *A Book of Ireland* (1959). When he wrote *The Backward Look: A Survey of Irish Literature*, he called Nicholson's *The Bible in Ireland* "one of the two best descriptions of the [prefamine] period" (1966, 134).[3] Her reputation established, Nicholson began to appear regularly in anthologies of Irish travel and in scholarly accounts of nineteenth-century travelers to Ireland.[4] She was so well established that in 1991, Seamus Deane, the general editor of *The Field Day Anthology of Irish Writing*, included sections of Nicholson's *Annals of the Famine* in an anthology that was criticized for not giving sufficient attention to women. When Patricia Craig, who reviewed *Ireland's Welcome to the Stranger* in the *Times Literary Supplement* (October 9, 1998, 36), published *The Oxford Book of Ireland*, she included six short passages from *The Bible in Ireland* and *Annals of the Famine*.

The 150th observance of 1847, the worst year of the Great Irish Famine, prompted a renaissance in famine scholarship and, regardless of historical, political, or theoretical approach, situated Nicholson's accounts of Ireland before and during the Great Irish Famine as a preeminent, contemporary document.

A new edition of *Annals of the Famine in Ireland* (1998), published by the Lilliput Press, made Nicholson's narrative widely available. The new paperback edition meant that Nicholson is taught in schools and is on the reading list for university famine courses. New York State's Great Irish Famine Curriculum (2001) includes a lesson titled "Asenath Nicholson: Shaper of History" that asks students to read excerpts from *Annals of the Famine* to consider how she worked by herself and with others to provide relief for the suffering poor. In 2010, Irish students taking the History Higher Level examination at Leaving Certificate Level were offered the opportunity to answer the question, "What was the contribution to Irish Affairs of Asenath Nicholson and/or Mother Mary Aikenhead?"

Contemporary scholars continue to appreciate Nicholson as a reliable reporter. Cormac Ó Gráda is one of the few contemporary historians who offered a qualitative comment on her revealing observations (1999, 178). Other scholars have brought new theoretical approaches such as gender analysis to their discussion of Nicholson's contribution to famine literature. In her seminal study of literary and visual famine literature, Margaret Kelleher described Nicholson's ability to "cross the thresholds of class and gender" to provide a narrative rich with literary and visual images of famine suffering. Kelleher also admired a woman who went beyond bearing witness. She was not simply "a woman at the keyhole gazing at the spectacle of famine suffering"; she played a part, her own part, in relieving famine suffering.

Building on Kelleher's analysis of Nicholson, in his "The Indigent Sublime: Specters of Irish Hunger," David Lloyd called Nicholson "possibly the most sympathetic and *participatory* of observers of the Famine, and—as Margaret Kelleher has insightfully shown—one of the few who constantly crosses thresholds, repeatedly registers the unbearable, haunting nature of the spectacle of the starving." He used Nicholson's observations and responses to construct his argument that the Great Irish Famine was a crisis of representation and memory and the way those processes have haunted modern Ireland.

Mary Gilmartin examined Nicholson's representation of space in *Ireland's Welcome to the Stranger*, and her analysis of Nicholson's text is the framework of the four voices that Benedicte Monicat identified in women's travel literature. Gordon Bigelow identified Nicholson's transformative, domestic economy as a "model of economic efficiency" that critiqued both the British laissez-faire economic policy and their delayed and inadequate response to famine suffering. For Nicholson, "'industry' is first of all a quality of human behavior, a value best taught at home, which will itself radiate through the public arena of the market and transform it" (Bigelow 2003, 137). The 2012 *Atlas of the Great Irish Famine* includes Lorraine Chadwick's account of Nicholson's Irish journeys (Crowley 2012, 476–81).

No doubt Nicholson would have objected to the designation of the 1998 Afri human rights walk through the Doolough Pass as the *Ireland's Welcome to the Stranger* Walk. She preferred to avoid such attention, but the walk's purposes—to fight poverty and racism—would have spoken to the causes that informed Nicholson's life of service, and the walk was led by Bishop Desmond Tutu in 1991, shortly before the abolition of apartheid in South Africa. Nicholson was modest, but she had one vanity—her singing voice—so she would have taken pleasure in her text having inspired Donnacha Dennehy, one of Ireland's young composers, who was commissioned by the St. Paul Chamber Orchestra to write a piece for the American soprano Dawn Upshaw. Dennehy wrote "If He Died, What Then?" a song cycle based on an episode in *Annals of the Famine*. The episode comes near the end of *Annals*, when Nicholson tells the story of an old man who had traveled seven miles with a child on his back. He was refused meal by the relief officer because he had not had time to enter the name of the man on the relief roll (*Annals* 1998, 197–99). Nicholson gave the man a little money. When Nicholson saw the man again, he was in the advanced stage of starvation, and again he was denied food and told to return. Nicholson gave him the money to purchase seven pounds of meal. Nicholson's last sight of the man was of him making his way back toward home on his knees. Later, when the relief officer was asked whether the dying man returned, he responded, "If he died, what then?" Dennehy's restrained, lyric work ends with that question. For Nicholson, the episode was a metaphor for the government programs' failure to relieve the suffering poor. For the reader, the image of Nicholson acting in the face of institutional indifference is the model of compassionate courage.

Notes

References

Index

Notes

Prologue

1. Robert Dudley Persse (1800–1854) was the third son of Henry Stratford Persse, Augusta, Lady Gregory's great-uncle. They were both born at Roxborough House, which was destroyed during the Irish War of Independence in 1922. While James Pethica and James Roy describe Persse as a minor official in the Galway Post Office (1998, 57), the *Thom's Dublin Directory* (1845) lists him as the postmaster of the Galway Post Office.

1. Puritan Beginnings on the Vermont Frontier

1. William Lloyd Garrison (1805–79), radical abolitionist, was born in New-buryport, Massachusetts, and joined the abolitionist movement in 1830. His manifesto in the first number of his abolitionist journal, the *Liberator* (1831–65), "I do not wish to think, or speak or write, with moderation," promised that he would be heard in his campaign for the "immediate and complete emancipation of all slaves." He founded the New England Anti-Slavery Society in 1832; the following year he helped organize the American Anti-Slavery Society. He supported John Brown's actions. He also supported Lincoln during the Civil War, but criticized the president for putting the preservation of the Union above the emancipation of slaves. After emancipation, Garrison spent the rest of his life promoting women's suffrage and pacifism.

Arthur Tappan (1786–1865), philanthropist, reformer, and abolitionist, was born in Northampton, Massachusetts; he was the eighth son of a pious New England family. His apprenticeship with a textile dealer prepared him for a successful silk-jobbing business in New York's Pearl Street. A strict Sabbatarian who supported a number of Christian causes and organizations, Tappan was an ardent abolitionist who lived with threats against his life. He died in New Haven in 1865.

Louis Tappan (1788–1873), Arthur Tappan's business partner until 1841, founded a successful credit-rating business that later became Dun and Bradstreet.

271

The brothers shared many philanthropic and reform interests. Louis Tappan published a biography of his brother in 1870, the year that he suffered the first of the strokes that led to his death in Brooklyn in 1873.

2. *Tappan Journal,* June 6, 1839, Lewis Tappan Papers, MSS42317, Library of Congress.

3. William Goodell, like Nicholson, had a rural background. He was born in Coventry, New York, in upstate Chenango County, but he was raised by his evangelical grandmother in Pomfret, Connecticut. He spent two years at sea, returned, and worked, unsuccessfully, in the shipping business before he devoted himself to publishing journals of reform such as the *Investigator and General Intelligencer* in Providence (1827). Renaming the journal *Genius of Temperance* when he moved to New York in 1830, Goodell's other reforming passion was abolitionism. He worked with Arthur Tappan and William Lloyd Garrison to form the American Anti-Slavery Society in 1833 and edited the society's paper, the *Emancipator,* from 1835 to 1837. He moved to Utica, New York, in 1836 to edit, for six years, the abolitionist paper *Friend of Man.* He later edited the *Anti-Slavery Lecturer* (1840) and the *Christian Investigator* (1842). Goodell helped organize the Liberty Party in 1840 and later the Liberty League. Although Goodell was never officially ordained, in 1843 he found a church organized along his social principles of abolitionism and temperance in Honeoye, New York. He was back in New York by 1854, where he edited the radical New York weekly *American Jubilee,* which became the *Radical Abolitionist* and then *Principia.* The Goodells moved to Janesville, Wisconsin, to be closer to their children. Goodell died there on February 14, 1878. William Goodell Family Papers, Record Group 30/029, Oberlin College Archives, Oberlin, OH, http://www.oberlin libstaff.com/archon/index.php?p=collections/controlcard&id=33&q=william+goo dell+family+papers. See also Strong 1928.

Joshua Leavitt (1794–1873), a Yale-educated Congregational minister, lawyer, and abolitionist, edited the *New York Evangelist* from 1830 until December 1831. He helped to organize the New York Anti-Slavery Society in 1833 and was involved with raising funds for and defending the African slaves on the *Amistad* in 1839. Leavitt edited the *Emancipator* from 1837 to 1847; he ended his connection with the publication in March 1848. In November 1847 Leavitt became the interim minister of the Second Congregational Churches in South Weymouth, Massachusetts. He left after seven stormy months of fighting with his conservative congregation.

4. Ernest Russell, Founder's File (1789–1858), Typescript, Records, Town of Chelsea, VT. Although the author has a copy of this document, its original has disappeared from the town records. The information is included with that caveat.

5. Conversation with the late Jean Hatch Farnham and Kay Hatch Campbell, Apr. 21, 1997.

6. In 1867 the Honorable Barnes Frisbie of Poultney, Vermont, described the town's first settlers (including his grandfather) with these details (Dodge 1987, 8–9).

7. "Jacob Hatch," last modified Sept. 8, 2002, http://home.comcast.net/~kaeh/Histories/jacob1.htm.

8. Family History Library, Salt Lake City, film no. 0496902.

9. Vital records of Sturbridge, MA, Ancestry.com.

10. Information from http://www.MyAncestry.com about Martha Rice and her children.

11. An Asenath born in 1775 married Aetemus Loomis; an Asenath born in 1792 had a daughter Asenath by her second husband, William Brewer, in 1815; an Asenath born in 1794 married Charles Eldridge Avery, and an Asenath born in 1798 or 1799 married David Blackman.

12. In the Genesis text, Asenath is also the heroine of an apocryphal story, a narrative that tells the story of her conversion from the worship of idols to the worship of Joseph's God. When the famine came to Egypt, Joseph prudently managed the grain supply to avert starvation; he had enough corn to sell it when others starved. When the Great Irish Famine came to Ireland (1845–52), Asenath Hatch Nicholson would devise her own relief program for the Irish poor, and she too used corn prudently as famine food. Despite the fact that she was a devoted Bible reader, Nicholson herself never mentioned the coincidence between her name, her work among the Irish during the Great Irish Famine, and the Asenath who was associated with the Egyptian famine of the Old Testament.

13. Generally, the writer will use Nicholson, Asenath Hatch's married name, as the term of reference in the text.

14. A wood-framed, shingled-roof cabin in Williamstown, Massachusetts, dated to 1753 is constructed with contemporary tools and materials and is built on a foundation made of two or three courses of flat stones. The cabin has a door, a window in the front and in the gable end of the house, and a fireplace but no chimney. A Bartlett engraving of New England titled *A First Settlement* (London, 1842) depicts a pioneering couple with two children and a dog. They stand outside a partially built log cabin; a cooking pot hangs from a tripod over an open fire. In the background two men are cutting and clearing the forest around the cabin.

15. Martin Chittenden served as a Vermont representative in Congress from 1799 to 1803; he was governor of Vermont in 1814–15.

16. The recipient of the letter, London-born Quaker reformer and philanthropist William Bennett (1804–73), was a tea dealer, educator, and author of books on religious topics. He was a keen botanist who corresponded with Charles Darwin and sent him specimens from his own collection. Bennett shared Nicholson's commitments to abolitionism, temperance, and the Peace Society. Bennett's botanical interests informed his visit to Ireland to distribute seeds to the impoverished Irish. He

published *Narrative of a Recent Journey of Six Weeks in Ireland: In Connection with the Subject of Supplying Small Seed to Some of the Remoter Districts* (1847). During his six-week visit to Ireland in 1847, he met Nicholson at the home of their mutual friend Richard Davis Webb. He subsequently sent Nicholson funds to help her relief efforts. When Nicholson went to London in 1848, she stayed with Bennett and his wife, Elizabeth Trusted Bennett (1798–1891), who taught the children of the poor before she married. In 1851 the Bennetts retired to Brookham Lodge, Betchworth, near Reigate, Surrey.

17. The Rev. Henry Clubb (1827–1922), a pioneering vegetarian, was born in Colchester, England, where he was raised in a family who followed the principles of Swedenborg. Like Nicholson, Clubb was a fervent Bible Christian who found scriptural authority for his vegetarianism. He later joined the Concordium sect in London for a short time. Trained as a teacher of shorthand before he joined the vegetarian movement, Clubb emigrated to the United States in 1853, where he worked as a journalist in New York. He went west to Kansas to establish a vegetarian colony; it was not successful. Clubb became a journalist for Horace Greeley and published his abolitionist reports of slavery that put his life in danger. Clubb fought in the Union army, saw action at the Battle of Bull Run, and was wounded at the siege of Vicksburg. After the Civil War, when Clubb settled in Michigan, he was elected to the state legislature. Clubb was the founding president of the American Vegetarian Society and edited their journal *Food, Home and Garden.* "History of Vegetarianism—USA: 19th Century," last modified June 10, 2010, http://www.ivu.org/history/usa 19/clubb.html.

18. Olive Wright, the daughter of Samuel Wright and Mary Coburn, was born August 8, 1777, in Winchester, Cheshire County, New Hampshire.

19. In 1997 Jean Hatch Farnham, a sixth-generation descendant of Michael Hatch and David's great-great-great-granddaughter, was Chelsea's only resident who was a descendant of an original town settler. Her collection of David's carpentry tools is a tangible link with Chelsea at the end of the eighteenth century.

20. Christopher Hatch gave his grandfather's paper to the Vermont Historical Society in 1999 (MS acc. no. 99.6). David Hatch's house was built about 1830; it was the first house in Chelsea to have electricity. It now houses the Chelsea Historical Society.

21. The Chelsea Historical Society cites John M. Comstock's *The History of Chelsea* (1944) for this information.

22. *Adirondack Record and Elizabethtown (NY) Post*, July 23, 1925. I am deeply grateful to Elizabethtown historian Dr. Margaret Bartley for providing me with information about the Nicholsons of Elizabethtown and Asenath Hatch's period teaching school in the village. Janet Cross supplied information about Norman Nicholson's enlistment in Calkins's company.

23. Despite the fact that the Chelsea Congregational Church website does not list Michael Hatch and his immediate family among its members, Comstock notes that David Hatch sold his pew in the church to John Stearns in 1817 (1944, 59).

24. Comstock says that Thompson left the congregation, but the church records say that Thompson was dismissed (Chelsea Historical Society 1984, 17).

25. Hal Barron's analysis of Chelsea's out-migration demonstrates that there was a high level of persistence, but younger Chelsea men tended to leave the area; therefore, the population of Chelsea aged (1984, 81). The town has changed very little in terms of its population or appearance in the past one hundred years. Its population was 1,250 in 2000.

26. Like Nicholson, Connecticut-born Emma Willard (1787–1870) attended her local school and went on to teach there. In 1807 she was offered a teaching position in a female seminary in Middlebury, Vermont. Concerned with educational opportunities for girls, she opened the Troy Female Seminary in 1821; it was later renamed the Emma Willard School (1895).

27. Leigh Richmond (1772–1827) was born in Liverpool and educated at Trinity College, Cambridge. After his ordination, Richmond was appointed to two curacies on the Isle of Wight. Known best for his religious writing, his best-known stories, "The Dairyman's Daughter," "The Young Cottager," and "The Negro Servant," were published in a collection titled *Annals of the Poor* (1814) by the Religious Tract Society.

28. Unpublished manuscript in the care of Carisbrooke Castle, Isle of Wight. The writer saw John T. Cooper's copy of the guest book on her visit to the Dairyman's Cottage. Quoted here with permission, courtesy of Carisbrooke Castle Museum.

29. Hannah More (1745–1833), teacher, playwright, novelist, essayist, and social reformer, was associated with the Religious Tract Society. Her best-known tract was "The Shepherd of Salisbury Plain."

30. "The whole country rang with the praises of the poet crowds dashed off to view the scenery of Loch Katrine, till then comparatively unknown" (Jenkinson 1873, 103).

31. Nicholson appropriated a stanza of Scott's "The Vision of Don Roderick" for her first chapter of *Annals of the Famine* (1998, 27).

32. Maria Edgeworth (1767–1849) was the daughter of Richard L. Edgeworth, MP for County Longford. *Castle Rackrent* (1800) was published anonymously. She visited Scott at Abbotsford in 1823; he visited Edgeworthstown two years later. She was a model landowner during the Great Irish Famine—indefatigable in her efforts to get relief for her tenants. In an often-quoted passage from the general preface to the 1829 edition of *The Waverly Novels*, Scott wrote that he "felt that something might be attempted for [his] own country, of the same kind with that which Miss Edgeworth so fortunately achieved for Ireland" (1870, 9).

33. Felicia Dorothea Browne Hemans (1793–1835), the Anglo-Irish poet and dramatist, published *Poems* (1808). She married Captain Alfred Hemans in 1812, the year she published *The Domestic Affections*. After the marriage failed, Hemans supported her five sons with her writing.

34. Born into rural poverty in Amherst, New Hampshire, Horace Greeley (1811–72) apprenticed with the printer of the *Northern Spectator*. The awkward, lanky Greeley came to New York in 1831, where he started as a journalist with the *New Yorker*. In 1841 he founded the *New York Tribune*. Greeley shared Nicholson's interest in social causes: temperance, vegetarianism, and especially abolitionism. Greeley also interested himself in socialism and feminism. During the Great Irish Famine, Greeley used the pages of the *Tribune* to make readers aware of conditions in Ireland and to solicit and collect relief funds. He opposed the Fugitive Slave Law (1850). Although he supported Abraham Lincoln in 1860, he criticized Lincoln's making abolitionism secondary to the cause of the Union. Greeley was the Liberal Party candidate for president in the 1872 election, a candidacy savagely ridiculed by Thomas Nast in his political cartoons. The cartoons were so vicious that friends thought Nast's mockery contributed to Greeley's death on November 29, 1872. There are two statues of Greeley in New York: John Quincy Adams Ward's 1890 seated statue in City Hall Park and Alexander Doyle's bronze sculpture of the seated Greeley in Greeley Square that was dedicated in 1894.

35. Frances Milton Trollope (1779–1863), mother of Anthony Trollope, moved with her family to North America in 1827 to establish a department store in Cincinnati, Ohio. When that enterprise failed, her nearly four years in America gave her the observations and experiences to write *Domestic Manners of the Americans* (1832), the first of the more than one hundred books, mostly fiction, that she would produce during the last thirty-four years of her life. Although Nicholson would not bother with her *Domestic Manners*, she may have found Trollope's fiction with its sympathy with the oppressed more attractive.

36. Thomas Hastings (1784–1872) started as village choir leader in Clinton, New York. He wrote the music for "Rock of Ages" and for "Majestic Sweetness Sits Enthroned" (Richman 1998, 206).

37. Letter from Asenath Nicholson to Sylvester Graham, Apr. 20, 1833, no. 3 of the *Asculapian Tablets*, 17–20, Amherst College Library Special Collections, Amherst, MA.

38. "A boarding-school was established here as early as 1823 which was kept by Miss Asenath Hatch who became the wife of Norman Nicholson" (H. Smith 1885, 471).

39. H. P. Smith identified the former schoolhouse as the old brick building just back of Williams's store (1885, 490). Water Street is County Road 10A.

40. I am grateful to Rachel Arciniega, a descendant of Nicholson's brother John, for information about Norman Nicholson. In the 1880 census, George S. Nicholson lists the birthplace of his father, Norman Nicholson, as Connecticut. Village of Elizabethtown, 22, Supervisor's District 7, Enumeration District 45.

41. Although it is not clear whether Norman Nicholson's family came to Elizabethtown from Connecticut, his sister Mary, known as Polly, came to Essex County, where she married Dr. Alexander Morse. Her mother may have lived with them because "Widow Nicholson" is listed among those who attended the church organization meeting at Morse's home on June 12, 1812 (H. Smith 1885, 491). See Morse monument, Riverside Cemetery, Block 1, Elizabethtown, New York. The location of Nicholson's post office is not certain, but Brown speculated that it may have been near the site of the present Elizabethtown Post Office, where Nicholson's grandson John D. Nicholson served as postmaster (G. Brown 1905, 104). The present post office is on Ware Street. There is a Nicholson-Hatch connection here. Nicholson's grandnephew Willard S. Hatch was Chelsea's postmaster for fourteen years.

42. See also the *Adirondack Record and Elizabethtown (NY) Post*, July 23, 1925.

43. Two "Insolvent Notices" that appeared in the *Plattsburgh Republican* newspaper in 1813 and 1816 indicate that the insolvent clients were represented by Gross and Nicholson. Ezra Carter Gross (1787–1829), an 1806 graduate of the University of Vermont, held a captain's commission in the War of 1812. A rising young lawyer in 1811, he was the supervisor of Elizabethtown in 1818. He served as a representative in Congress in 1819 and in 1821, when he made a memorable speech opposing slavery during the debate about the Missouri Compromise. He died on April 9, 1829, while serving as a member of the New York State Assembly.

44. Records of appointments for school inspectors and highway supervisors between 1822 and 1827 were made by Norman Nicholson, serving as one of Elizabethtown's justices of the peace. The records for the appointments are preserved in the Essex County Clerk's Office, Elizabethtown, New York.

45. The inscription on her gravestone in Elizabethtown's Old Post Cemetery reads, "Sacred to the Memory of Harriett, the wife of Norman Nicholson Esq. who died February 11, 1824 aged 26 years, 10 months and 28 days." Her death is also listed as 1825. I am grateful to Margaret Bartley for this information. The Frisbies were a Westport, New York, family.

46. Pluma, who is listed, appears on the 1855 Elizabethtown census as a servant in the household of George Sidney's business partner, George S. Root. The men owned a building in what was called the Nichols/Prime Block (1850–61). The notice of Pluma's death was listed in the *Elizabethtown Post* on March 10, 1860. Birth, Marriages, Obituaries extracted from Essex County, New York, Newspapers,

1831–1864, compiled by Joyce Rainieri, http://www.rootsweb.ancestry.com/-nyess ex/extract.htm.

47. Van Buren's Bucktails and Albany Regency were associated with the Masons (Niven 1983, 82–83).

48. In 1866 when the Adirondack Lodge no. 602 was chartered, George S. Nicholson became an active member, serving for three years as master of the lodge (H. Smith 1855, 320).

49. H. P. Smith said that a new Baptist church was founded in 1834 in Elizabethtown.

50. When the Masons regained control, Calkins was "run out of town" (G. Brown 1905, 320).

51. Nicholson to Graham, Apr. 20, 1833, no. 3 of the *Asculapian Tablets*, 18.

2. Social Gospels, Garrets, and Cellars

1. The Ninth Ward is presently bounded by Carmine Street, North River, West Fourteenth Street, as far east as Sixth Avenue and as far south as the East Village and the Lower East Side.

2. US Census for 1830, New York City, Ninth Ward, Roll 97, 393.

3. In 1831 Prudence Crandall opened the Canterbury Female Boarding School with her sister Anna. The following year she offered a place to Sarah Harris, an African American student; parents of her white students withdrew their daughters. She proposed in 1832 to open a school for only African American girls, and that school was boycotted by the community. The state passed a Black Law prohibiting Crandall's school. The case went to court, with the cost of defense provided by Arthur Tappan. The case was eventually dismissed. While the case was being tried, local people resorted to violence. Fearful for her students' safety, Crandall closed the school in 1834.

4. The *Genius of Temperance* was founded in January 1830 by William Goodell; Prudence Crandall was listed as its editor and proprietor. In her article "Reform Periodicals and Female Reformers 1830–1860," Bertha-Monica Stearns identified some scattered copies of the *Female Advocate* for October–December 1833, in the library of the American Antiquarian Society.

5. Charles Wheeler Denison (1809–81) was born in New London, Connecticut. An Episcopalian clergyman, Denison edited the *Emancipator*. In 1846 he married Thomas Jefferson's daughter Mary. In 1853 Denison was appointed US consul to British Guinea. During the Civil War, Denison served as chaplain to the Northern army. A prolific author as well as clergyman and journalist, Denison published a series of biographies for young readers, poems (*The American Village, and Other Poems*), and prose tales such as "Paul St. Clair: A Temperance Story."

Sylvester Graham (1794–1851) was born in Suffield, Massachusetts, the seventeenth child of the Rev. John Graham and Ruth Smith. Graham's father, who was seventy-two when Sylvester was born, died when Sylvester was two. His mother appeared to be unable to cope with her young family, so Sylvester was boarded out and spent an unsettled life in different households, working odd jobs. The instability of his early life was a poor preparation for the ministry. He was dismissed from Amherst Academy after only one term. When his health broke down, he was nursed by the Earl sisters, one of whom, Sarah Manchester Earl (1802–68), he later married. He completed his studies and was ordained in 1826; he was affiliated with the Presbytery of Newark from 1826 to 1828 (Nissenbaum 1980, 12, 13, 86).

Engraver and reformer Simeon Jocelyn (1799–1879) was born in New Haven, Connecticut. He studied for the ministry at Yale but left before ordination. He was the founding pastor of the Temple Street "Congregational Society of People of Color," the first African American Congregational Church in America. It later became the Dixwell Congregational Church. Jocelyn is credited with converting Lewis Tappan to abolitionism. He was less successful in trying to establish a college for African Americans in New Haven. In 1839 Jocelyn became prominent for his role in defending the slaves on the *Amistad*. He died in Tarrytown, New York, in 1870. There is a monument to the *Amistad* defenders in New Haven.

John Robert M'Dowall (1801–36), born in Fredericksburgh, Upper Canada, was the son of a clergyman who went as a missionary from Albany to Canada about 1797. An 1828 graduate of Union College, John M'Dowall went on to the Princeton Seminary in July 1830. After his ordination in late April 1832, he was licensed by the evangelical Third Presbytery of the Presbyterian Church.

Henry Clarke Wright (1797–1870) was the son of Seth Wright and Miriam Clarke Wright. The family moved in 1801 from Connecticut to Cooperstown, New York, where Miriam Clarke died of apoplexy in 1803. Wright reported that he was deeply affected by seeing a total eclipse of the sun in 1806. Ten years later he experienced a religious conversion at a revival meeting in Norwich, New York. He joined the Presbyterian Church and prepared for the ministry at Andover Theological Seminary. He served as minister in West Newbury from 1826 to July 1833, when he resigned to become a missionary for the Home Missionary Society. In 1835 Wright met William Lloyd Garrison and became an ardent abolitionist. That year he became one of Theodore Weld's agents until he was removed by the society because of his strong opinions. He traveled as an antislavery agent from 1837 until he went abroad in 1842 to lecture on abolitionism and nonresistance. In 1870 he died of a "fit" while staying with friends in Rhode Island.

6. M'Dowall met William Goodell in Providence (M'Dowall 1838, 414).

7. Leavitt later recruited M'Dowall in 1832 to serve as a correspondent for the *Evangelist*. The *Evangelist*'s alarmist rhetoric anticipated the alliterative hyperbole of Amanda McKittrick Ros (1860–1939), the County Antrim writer who often appears on the short list of the world's worst writers. It is not surprising that Edwin G. Burrows and Mike Wallace found the phrase irresistible to use as the title for their chapter on the nineteenth-century evangelists in their magisterial *Gotham: A History of New York City to 1898* (1999, 529).

8. The author of Nicholson's obituary in Horace Greeley's *New York Tribune* (May 18, 1855) identified Nicholson as the anonymous "compiler" of M'Dowall's *Memoir and Select Remains of the Late Rev. John R. M'Dowall, the Martyr of the Seventh Commandment in the Nineteenth Century*. The book was published by Joshua Leavitt on January 5, 1838.

9. *Genius of Temperance*, n.s., 1 (June 15, 1831): 49.

10. Whitney R. Cross (1950) coined the term *Burned-Over District* in his study of the evangelical revival in upstate New York.

11. George Gale (1789–1861) was born and reared in Stanford, New York. His parents died when he was a boy. He entered Union College, but his poor health and finances did not permit him to finish his degree until 1814. He became a traveling teacher in upstate New York. When he finished at Union, he enrolled in the Princeton Theological Seminary; he was ordained in 1816. He became the minister of the Presbyterian Church in Adams, New York, where he met his protégé, Charles Grandison Finney. In the spring of 1826, Gale began to experiment with a work-study program for young men who were eager for education but lacked the means. He founded the Oneida Institute in 1827. After he left the Oneida Institute in 1833, he founded similar institutions, including Knox College in Galesburg, Illinois. He was a teacher and administrator at Knox College until his death in 1861.

Charles Grandison Finney (1792–1875) was born in Warren, Connecticut. He was educated at Hamilton Oneida Academy in Clinton, New York, and taught in New Jersey before taking up an apprenticeship in the law office of Benjamin Wright in Adams. While working in Adams, he experienced a religious conversion and began to study with George Gale, pastor of the Adams Presbyterian Church, in 1823. He was ordained in 1824. Finney became a fervent revivalist who preached a modification of Calvinist theology.

12. The institute was closely connected with the Presbyterian Church of Whitesboro until David Ogden was called to the church in 1836. Within the year, Ogden began to challenge Green and the institute's abolitionism. The Presbyterians split, with Ogden keeping control; the dissidents formed their own abolitionist Congregational church.

13. In his "Rules and Regulations," Graham dates the publication of *Nature's Own Book* as May 30, 1832. The second "enlarged and improved" edition of *Nature's*

Own Book was published in New York by Wilbur and Whipple, 4–6 Green Street. Nicholson filed for copyright with the Southern District on February 13, 1835.

14. Philip Hone (1780–1851), businessman and diarist, served as mayor of New York from 1825 to 1827. The diary that he kept between 1828 and 1851 is a valuable record of New York life.

The *Carrick* arrived in Quebec City on June 8, 1832, from Dublin; it reached Montreal the following day. It lost 40 of its 170 passengers. Marianna O'Gallagher's note indicates that the *Carrick* lost 42 passengers, a carpenter, and a boy, but the ship's reputation for being the first to carry cholera to Canada is not proven (1984, 24).

15. Graham later published the talk under the title *A Lecture on Epidemic Diseases Generally, and Particularly the Spasmodic Cholera*, delivered in New York in 1832 (1833).

16. In Boston a Graham Boarding House was opened at 23 Brattle Street.

17. The Nicholsons' boardinghouse was not the only Graham Boarding House in the city, but it was the first. An advertisement in the *New York Commercial Advertiser* for June 12, 1849, described it as "the Graham Boarding House in Barclay Street kept by a Mr. Gose where Mr. Greeley of the *New Yorker* lodges and where Governor Seward is a guest." It was called a vegetarian boardinghouse.

Longworth's American Almanac, New York Register and City Directory, 1839–40 (1841) lists Roswell Goss's boardinghouse at 62 Barclay Street. Possibly Nicholson herself boarded at Goss's when she gave up her own establishment; she is listed as living at 65 Barclay Street in 1843.

18. William Beaumont (1785–1853), a Congregationalist schoolteacher, studied medicine and became an army surgeon during the War of 1812. His reputation rests on a study he made of the digestion system of Alexis St. Martin, a French Canadian man who received a musket shot to the abdomen in 1822. Beaumont attended him, and his study of St. Martin became a classic.

19. Alfred Webb (1834–1908) was the son of Richard Davis Webb and Hannah Waring Webb. The manuscript of his diary is in the Religious Society of Friends Historical Library, Dublin (Diary 126), and was reprinted by Cork University Press. Extracts from *Alfred Webb: The Autobiography of a Quaker Nationalist* (1999) are reprinted with the kind permission of Cork University Press, Youngline Industrial Estate, Pouladuff, Togher, Cork.

20. M'Dowall also believed in the efficacy of phrenology. "There is something in phrenology that may be happily adapted to man's best interest" (1838, 264). Orson and Lorenzo Fowler, with their brother-in-law Samuel Wells, became publishers of nineteenth-century periodicals, including the *Water-Cure Journal*, the journal where Henry Clubb's appreciation of Nicholson was published in 1855.

21. Arthur Tappan's family lived in New Haven. Tappan spent his weekends there. He kept his New York home, but in the summer of 1834 he lodged in Cedar Street. The Nicholsons' boardinghouse was at 79 Cedar Street.

22. Daniel Fanshaw (1788–1860), "the greatest printer of his day," produced the work of the American Bible Society and the American Tract Society from his shop at the corner of Ann and Nassau Streets. He may have known Nicholson while she lived on Williams Street. He moved his family from Williams Street to Yorkville. In his obituary in the *New York Times* (Mar. 1, 1860), he was described as "affable in his manner and ever ready to assist the poor and unfortunates of his craft." He left one-quarter of his considerable estate to the Dutch Reformed Church in Yorkville. He is buried in New York's Marble Cemetery, Vault 28.

23. Benjamin Bussey Thatcher (1809–1840), born in Warren, Maine, was an 1826 graduate of Bowdoin College. He established a law office in Boston but preferred to pursue his avocation as a historian. His works include a study of Native Americans, *Indian Biography* (1832); an early biography of the African American poet Phillis Wheatley (1834); and *Traits of the Boston Tea Party and Being a Memoir of George R. T. Hewes, One of the Last of Its Survivors* (1835). Thatcher died in Boston in 1840.

24. In December 1833 Lewis Tappan helped found the American Anti-Slavery Society in Philadelphia; Arthur Tappan was elected its first president.

25. The New-York Historical Society owns a lithograph based on the engraving.

26. Elihu Parsons Ingersoll (1804–87), a graduate of Yale (1832) and the Yale Seminary (1835), joined the faculty of Oberlin Collegiate Institute in 1835, when he was appointed professor of sacred music, the first such appointment in the United States. He stayed only one year (1835–36) and went on to join his brother, who was trying (unsuccessfully) to establish a Christian colony in Grand Rapids, Michigan. He died in Kansas in 1887.

27. Alarmed by their students' antislavery activities, the Lane Board of Trustees voted to disband the student society in October 1834. By the end of the month, thirty-nine students had resigned from Lane, claiming that banning their society was an infringement of student free speech. Zealous abolitionist the Rev. John Jay Shipperd, who started Oberlin in 1833, invited the dissident Lane students to transfer to his institution. The students accepted, provided that abolitionist Asa Mahan be appointed president, that Charles Grandison Finney be appointed professor of theology, and that black applicants be admitted on the same basis as white students (Fletcher 1971, 169). Arthur Tappan agreed to give ten thousand dollars if the students' conditions were met. The Oberlin Board of Trustees voted to leave the matter of admissions to the faculty; it was a signal that the board would leave internal matters to the faculty and would uphold the students' right to free speech. In addition to its pioneering role in offering college education to black students, Oberlin was the first college to grant a degree to women in a coeducational setting.

28. That Tappan issued arms to his clerks is important. He became a member of the Board of Directors of the American Peace Society in 1828. The Radicals' wing of the American Peace Society led by William Lloyd Garrison was committed to non-violence; Tappan's decision to arm his clerks demonstrated his belief that violence in self-defense was permissible (Ziegler 1992, 61, 184n8).

29. John Jay Shipherd (1802–44) also founded Olivet College in Olivet, Michigan. Funded by the Tappans with the understanding that Oberlin would welcome African American students, the college adopted the Oneida Institute's work-study program. For a while Oberlin also embraced Grahamism. Shipherd died of malaria at Olivet on September 16, 1844.

30. Asenath Nicholson to John J. Shipherd, July 15, 1834, Nicholson 1, Oberlin College Archives, Oberlin, OH.

31. George Donisthorpe Thompson (1804–78) joined the antislavery movement in London in 1831. An immediatist, he called for immediate abolition of slavery. He met William Lloyd Garrison in Scotland in 1832 and American and Irish abolitionists in London at the Anti-Slavery Convention in 1840. He converted Richard Davis Webb to the cause of abolitionism (Harrison 1993, 23). He was elected to Parliament in 1847.

32. An article in the *Sentinel and Ticonderogian* (Nov. 28, 1884) that describes how George Sidney Nicholson and Albert A. Durand were successful in inviting Horace Greeley to appear in Elizabethtown to address the annual fair sponsored by the Essex County Agricultural Society mentions that Nicholson had worked for Greeley in New York.

33. Fanshaw moved his family from William Street to Yorkville in 1840.

34. Two years later, in October 1768, the John Street Methodist Church was dedicated.

35. Born in Connecticut, Theodore Weld (1803–95) started his education at Hamilton College in Clinton in 1823, but, in 1825, he transferred to the nearby Oneida Institute in Whitesboro to prepare for the ministry. While at Oneida, be became an ardent abolitionist. Weld went on to the Lane Seminary, where he was expelled for his part in starting a student antislavery society. He led the students who transferred from Lane to Oberlin. He married abolitionist Angelina Grimke in 1838. He died in Boston in 1895.

36. Pierpont was the financier J. Pierpont Morgan's paternal grandfather. In 1829 a young William Lloyd Garrison began his public abolitionist mission with his speech "Dangers to the Nation" at Pierpont's Park Street Church.

37. MS A.9.2.9, vol. 14, courtesy of the Trustees of the Boston Public Library/ Rare Books. Anne W. Weston (1812–90) was one of the six Weston sisters prominent in the abolitionist movement in Boston. In 1834 she was one of the founders of the Boston Female Anti-Slavery Society. Anne and her older sister Maria Weston

Chapman (1806–85), the best known of the sisters, were the driving force behind the popular Boston antislavery fairs.

38. F. Jackson wrote to Maria Weston Chapman, offering to send sixty or seventy copies of Pierpont's defense of his action if Maria thought they would be suitable for sale at the Anti-Slavery Fair. MS A.9.2.12, vol. 68, courtesy of the Trustees of the Boston Public Library/Rare Books.

39. New Yorkers were anticipating the appearance of Halley's Comet in the summer of 1835. Prompted, perhaps, by Edgar Allan Poe's "Hans Phaal: A Tale," a story of a balloon journey to the moon, Richard Adams Locke wrote his "moon series" for the *New York Sun* that resulted in readers believing that the moon was inhabited (Goodman 2008, 12).

40. The panic of 1837 affected the Oneida Institute, which received significant support from the Tappans, including part of Beriah Green's salary (Sennett 1986, 94).

41. Herbert Asbury's *The Gangs of New York*, the book that inspired the Martin Scorsese film, is responsible for the popular view that the area was full of drunks and felons, mainly Irish. Current scholarship has demonstrated that although the area was overcrowded and its inhabitants lived on the edge of poverty, it was a working-class neighborhood of hardworking immigrants. See the lithograph *The Old Brewery at the Five Points* in Symmes 2005, 95.

42. It is interesting to consider Nicholson's place in the phenomenon of the wider attraction of women, particularly rural and small-town antebellum Northern women, who were a force of some fifty thousand in 616 local reform organizations. See Wright and Sklar 1999.

43. Margaret Fuller was born in Cambridgeport, Massachusetts, on May 23, 1810. Her father, Timothy Fuller, a congressman and the Speaker of the Massachusetts legislature, supervised his daughter's rigorous education in the classics. Like Nicholson, she taught school. Both suffered from headaches and nervous complaints, but whereas Nicholson pronounced herself cured by the Graham regime, Fuller's health problems were lifelong. A Transcendentalist, she edited the *Dial* from 1840 to 1842, before she turned to her feminism. She completed *Women in the Nineteenth Century* in 1844; it was published by Greeley the following year.

44. Like Asenath Nicholson, Mary Cheney Greeley (1811–72), an independent New Englander who became a schoolteacher and settled in New York City, was a follower of the Graham regime. She met Greeley not at the Nicholson Graham Boarding House but at Roswell Gross's Graham Boarding House on Barclay Street.

45. "The Irish Character," *New York Tribune*, June 28, 1845. See also Fuller 1855, 321–25; and Chevigny 1976, 344–46.

46. The Garrison-Goodell feud continued at least through 1842, when Garrison went to western New York to attend meetings of the American Anti-Slavery Society to answer Goodell's attack on the society.

47. In a letter to the Tappans, William Lloyd Garrison mentioned that Roswell Goss was opening a Graham Boarding House at 63 Barclay Street. Garrison wrote his wife on May 15, 1849, that Goss's boardinghouse was attacked by a mob. There were too many delegates who arrived to attend the 1840 American Anti-Slavery Society Convention to all stay at Goss's, who was identified as "a friend of the cause." See the ad for Goss's in the *Graham Journal of Health and Longevity* 5, nos. 1–25 (1839): 264.

3. An Errand in the Wilderness

1. Nicholson always used the King James Version of the Bible. Although it is difficult to identify with certainly the source(s) of Nicholson's quotation, playwright Elizabeth Kuti used Nicholson's words in *The Sugar Wife* (2005), a play set in Dublin in 1850. Former Quaker Yorkshire philanthropist Alfred Darby tells Hannah, the wife of the Dublin tea merchant Samuel Tewkley, "Remember Rachel. I have made you desolate. I want you for other purposes. Go work in my vineyard" (2005, 55).

2. See the "Funeral Service for a Christian Worker" that takes as its text "As the Father sent me into the world, so have I sent you," says Jesus. "Work today in My Vineyard." The comments draw the reader's attention to the imperative mood, the Divine commission, the awful need, and the constraining love ("Funeral Service" 1889, 382).

3. For a bibliography of Irish travel writing, see McVeagh 1996. The nineteenth-century travelers in Constantia Maxwell's *The Stranger in Ireland* include Charles Bianconi (1802–75), Sir John Carr (1805), Sir Walter Scott (1825), Herman Ludwig Heinrich von Pückler-Muskau (1828), Johannes Kohl (1842), and William Makepeace Thackeray (1842). Maxwell does not include a chapter on Nicholson; however, she mentions her as "an American lady, a kind of female Borrow, who had been impressed with the misery of the Irish emigrants in New York and crossed the Atlantic to see the country for herself" (1954, 212). She includes Nicholson's description of the people who danced for her in Kilkenny and who predicted that the patience of the poor had its limit. "'There must needs be,' she adds, "an explosion of some kind or other'" (1954, 213).

4. Alan J. Singer has challenged Bradford's biography of Tubman in his article "We May Never Know the Real Harriet Tubman," Read Periodicals.com, Jan. 1, 2012, http://www.readperiodicals.com/201201/2599645561.html#ixzz20KfJHwYz.

5. Samuel Carter Hall (1800–1889) was born in County Waterford. He went to London in 1821 to begin to study law at the Inner Bar in 1824. He abandoned law for journalism. Starting as a parliamentary reporter, he began to edit the *Art Union Monthly Journal* in 1839. In her introduction to the Oxford World Classic edition of Charles Dickens's *Martin Chuzzlewit*, Margaret Cardwell identifies the rather pompous Hall as the book's model for Pecksniff. Hall married Anna Maria Fielding

(1800–1881) in 1824. She wrote a number of novels and sketches of Irish life, and her plays *The French Refugee* (1837) and *The Groves of Blarney* (1838) were popular successes in London. The Halls collaborated on *Ireland: Its Scenery and Character* in 1843.

Charlotte Elizabeth was the pseudonym of Charlotte Browne Tonna (1790–1846). She wrote pamphlets for the Dublin Tract Society, Orange songs, and some thirty novels, including the Irish historical novels *The Rockite* (1832) and *Derry: A Tale of the Revolution* (1839). She regarded Catholicism as a "system of idolatrous delusion" and "a crafty piece of masked atheism" (Elizabeth 1838, 36, 59). Elizabeth detested Daniel O'Connell and actively opposed Catholic Emancipation, referring to the legislation as "national apostasy" (1838, 122). Nicholson also read Elizabeth's reforming novel of a young factory worker, *Helen Fleetwood: A Tale of Factories* (*LP* 1853, 288). It is tempting to think that Nicholson might have read the two-volume 1844 edition of Elizabeth with an introduction by Harriet Beecher Stowe, who described Charlotte Elizabeth in terms that could have been used for Nicholson. "That the author is a woman of strong mind, powerful feeling and on no inconsiderable share of tact in influencing the popular mind, will be, we suppose, very generally conceded" (1844, 1:5). The *Achill Herald and Western Witness* announced Elizabeth's death in a black-bordered box in the July 1846 issue of the paper (109).

6. Elizabeth also said, "The Irish are a most affectionate people; win their hearts, and they are wholly yours" (*LP* 1853, 45).

7. Richard Davis Webb (1805–72), son of James and Deborah Sparrow Webb, was born in Dublin. He chose to be educated in Ballintore, County Kildare, at the famous Quaker school that numbered Edmund Burke (1729–97) and, a century later, Paul Cardinal Cullen (1803–78) among its past pupils. Whereas Richard Webb's brother James H. Webb (ca. 1796–1878) joined their father in the linen business, Richard opted for printing. In addition to his successful printing business, Richard Davis Webb was known for his energetic work on behalf of a number of social causes: temperance, abolitionism, and famine relief. Webb met William Lloyd Garrison at the great Anti-Slavery Convention in London in 1840; it was the beginning of a lifelong friendship. Garrison corresponded with Richard and Hannah Webb for the rest of their lives.

8. Robert Hawell's *Panoramic View of New York from the East River, 1844* captures the last view of New York that Nicholson would have observed from the deck of the *Brooklyn* (1980, 28–29). See also Symmes 2005, 65.

9. The *Brooklyn* was built of oak, pine, and black birch in Newcastle, Maine, in 1834 for New Yorkers Abel W. Richardson, Edward Richardson, and Stephen C. Burdette.

10. I am grateful to Karen Millhouse, assistant curator of maritime archives, National Maritime Museum, Liverpool, for information from *Lloyd's Register, 1844*

for information about the *Brooklyn*, which led to Mormon resources about a party of their people traveling on the ship (Sonne 1987, 32–34). The voyage of the *Brooklyn* from New York to San Francisco was the subject of the award-winning documentary *Forgotten Voyage.*

11. Nicholson changed Cowper's word "son" in the last line to "child."

12. Architect Francis Johnston (1760/61–1829) designed Academy House and contributed substantially to the expense of the building project. Completed in 1824, Academy House and its two exhibition galleries were destroyed in the 1916 Rising.

13. Father Theobald Mathew (1790–1856), the "Apostle of Temperance," was born in Thomastown Castle, near Cashel, County Tipperary. He entered the Maynooth Seminary in 1807. He joined the Capuchin Order the following year and was ordained in 1814. His second parish assignment was one of Cork's poorest parishes, where he established a number of programs to address social problems in the city. In 1830 he purchased the old Botanical Gardens to use as a cemetery for Catholics. On April 10, 1838, Father Mathew began his total abstinence campaign that was to dominate the rest of his life. His work for temperance was interrupted by the catastrophic Great Irish Famine (1845–52) when Mathew worked tirelessly to help the poor. He took his crusade to the United States from 1849 to 1851. He returned to financial worries and poor health, and he died in Queenstown, County Cork, in 1856.

14. Built on the site of the House of Industry (1773), the North Dublin Union was opened in 1841 as one of the workhouses built according to George Wilkinson's design. Wilkinson (1814–90) came to Ireland in 1825. The Poor Law Commission's architect, he built 160 workhouses between 1845 and 1855. In 1927 the North Dublin Union was given to the Legion of Mary for a men's residence called Morning Star Hostel (Casey 2005, 261). Nicholson may have seen the notice advertising the position of assistant schoolmistress at the North Dublin Union at an annual salary of twenty-four pounds, with a furnished apartment and "rations." *Freeman's Journal,* June 15, 1844, 1.

15. In a letter to Maria Chapman Weston, Hannah Webb mentioned a visit from Dr. Madden, "a good Catholic and regular Irish rebel as rebels were counted 40 years ago." MS A.9.2, vol. 22, p. 26A&B, courtesy of the Trustees of the Boston Public Library/Rare Books. When Madden published his book *United Irishmen: Their Lives and Times* in 1842, his sympathetic account of the Irish resulted in his dismissal from the Colonial Office (Ó Broin 1961, 88–89).

16. The *Dublin Post Office and Annual Directory and Calendar* lists Richard Wilson as a rope and sail manufacturer whose sail loft and canvas and rope warehouse were at 17–18 Sir John's Quay. His rope walk was at Ringsend (1844, 382). Still in business in 2009, Wilson's makes sails for, among other class boats, the Mermaids who race in Dun Laoghaire Harbor.

17. Gordon Bigelow's "Asenath Nicholson's New Domestic Economy" considers the way that her critique of Irish social and economic conditions corresponded to the critique of British society by political economists such as John Stuart Mill. Bigelow describes Nicholson's "transformative domestic economy" that involved bringing the model of the well-run household: thrifty, temperate, efficient, and compassionate (2003, 135).

18. Nicholson's boat was slower; they reached Tullamore in eight hours (*IWS* 2002, 338). Tullamore was located three-quarters of a mile from the twenty-sixth lock of the Grand Canal. Gerard D'Arcy's *Portrait of the Grand Canal* includes a map of the Grand Canal System (1969, 24).

19. Nicholson also noted that like the American slaves who praised their master to strangers, the Irish poor praised their landlords to the inquiring traveler (*IWS* 2002, 331–32).

20. Frederick Douglass (1817–95), born Frederick Washington Bailey, was the son of a white man and a black woman who was a slave. In 1838 he escaped from slavery from his native Maryland and made his way north to New York, where he changed his name to Frederick Douglass. He worked with John Brown, but broke with him when Brown planned to attack the arsenal at Harpers Ferry. Indicted for treason, Douglass fled the country and took refuge with his British and Irish abolitionist friends. He arrived in Dublin in September 1845 just as the city received the news of the failure of the potato crop. When he returned to the United States, he served as marshal of the District of Columbia (1877–81) and the US ambassador to Haiti (1889–91). He died in Rochester, New York, in 1895.

21. Michael Byrne tried to identify Nicholson's host family in Tullamore. Working through Catholic parish registers, Byrne found three or four sets of twins born in 1833, so it was not possible to identify Nicholson's friends.

22. An Elizabeth Horner lived at 7 Dorset Street; her brother Frances was a linen draper who probably would have known James Webb (*Thom's Dublin Directory* 1846, 776, 334).

23. Margaret Sherwood erected the memorial in memory of her husband, John Sherwood, who died at the age of forty-eight on January 9, 1825, and of Joseph, their son, who died at the age of sixteen on August 21, 1822.

24. William Howard (1788–1869), the Fourth Earl of Wicklow, married Cecil Francis Hamilton (1795–1860), daughter of the 1st Marquess of Abercorn. Lady Harriet Howard (1820–46), the Howards' second daughter, wrote *The Birthday: A Tale for the Young* (1848). She also collaborated with Cecil (Fanny) Alexander on a number of religious tracts. Another Howard daughter, the Hon. Catherine Howard (Lady Petre), converted to Catholicism and published religious poetry under the pseudonym "Lady—, a convert from Anglicism to Christianity" (O'Donoghue 1912, 205; Loeber and Loeber 2006, 619–20).

25. Thomas Moore (1779–1852) was born in Dublin to an Irish-speaking father from the Kerry Gaeltacht and a mother from Wexford. He was educated at Trinity College with Robert Emmet, who was expelled from Trinity for his politics and was executed in 1803 for his part in the unsuccessful insurrection that he led. Moore studied law in London before his series of ten numbers of *Irish Melodies* (1808–34) brought him popular success as a poet and musician. The early numbers of the *Melodies* evoke the leaders of the 1798 Rebellion, and his *The Life of Lord Edward FitzGerald* (1831) was an argument for the Catholic nationalist position. Although he was a public success, his personal life was marked by tragedy, as all of his five children predeceased him.

26. Christine Kinealy has pointed out that there were exceptions to the 1833 act, notably in India, where the East India Company, the oldest of the British trading companies, virtually ruled India until the middle of the nineteenth century.

27. Even the austere Ulster Protestant John Hewitt responded to the haunting note of national and spiritual aspiration sounded in Moore's "Song of Fionnuala" in his "An Irishman in Coventry": "Yet like Lir's children banished to the waters / Our hearts still listen for the landward bells" (Ormsby 1991, 112).

28. Nicholson would have paid three shillings, four pence, for her second cabin ticket; first cabin passengers paid five shillings (Fraser 1844, 676). The distance along the Grand Canal from Dublin to Athyis is 54.5 miles.

29. There was a Johnstown doctor named John Joseph Delany who had a dispensary in White Gate; however, it is likely that the unidentified man practiced folk medicine. Lady Wilde lists a number of traditional folk remedies for warts in *Cures, Charms and Usages of Ancient Ireland* (1890, 24).

30. Nicholson's servant girls were probably from the parish of Johnstown. The earlier name for Johnstown was Fertagh (Fertagh na gCaorach, the tombs or graves of the sheep). It is mentioned in the *Annals of the Four Masters*, 861. The town was merged with Galmoy in 1861. In the *Ordnance Survey Letters*, John O'Donovan translates Urlingford as "the ford of the sledgings, the ford at which the Old Irish and the thieving Danes did sledge each other's heads long ago" (1839, 39, #120).

31. Griffith's Valuation lists an Edmund and Mary Hackett and a Michael Healey in Mountfinn.

32. Nicholson uses her visit to another household of a former servant girl in the Urlingford area as her typical example of culture and generous hospitality (*IWS* 2002, 67–69).

33. See the mention of crossroads dancing in P. Dowling 1968, 35; and Elizabeth 1838, 36–37.

34. See the similar language in the descriptions of the American wakes in Maurice O'Sullivan's *Twenty Years a-Growing* (1933) and Liam O'Flaherty's short story "Going into Exile" (1927).

35. Nicholson returned to Urlingford on October 1–15 and December 1–4 (*IWS* 2002, xxi–xxii). Nicholson identified Dr. White by name (*IWS* 2002, 98, 118–19, 158). She also identified a Catholic Mr. C. in Urlingford who was a friend (*IWS* 2002, 98, 102).

36. Barker succeeded his father, Chambré Brabazon Ponsonby, in 1834; Ponsonby supported his stepsister Sarah Ponsonby, one of the ladies of Llangollen. The Tithe War had fostered unrest to which Sir William contributed when he established Orange Lodge 808 on his estate. On the other hand, Barker sold the family jewelry in 1847 to finance an employment scheme for the poor on his estate (Neeley 1983, 96, 108).

37. There is a drawing of the home Barker planned in Neely (1983, 105).

38. See Nicholson's account of holy wells in Wexford (*IWS* 2002, 170) and in Mayo (*Annals* 1998, 137).

39. Lewis said that Urlingford was the center of fabric manufacturing—coarse stuffs, flannels, and worsteds—and there was extensive trade with the district (Lewis 1837, 2:670). Dublin linen draper James Webb may have provided Nicholson with the introduction to his Urlingford counterpart.

40. Nicholson stayed in the Urlingford area on August 2–17, October 1–15, and December 1–4, 1844.

41. The *Oxford English Dictionary*'s three-column entry for "faction" describes its use. "In Ireland applied to certain mutually hostile associations among the peasantry consisting usually of the members of one particular family (which gives the name to the faction) and of their relatives and friends." William Carleton's stories of faction fighting have been collected in John W. Hurley's *Irish Gangs and Stick Fighting in the Works of William Carleton* (2010).

42. Lewis reports that there were two national schools in Urlingford in 1837: one supported by the Earl of Kilkenny and one by a Mr. Fitzpatrick for seventy boys and seventy girls. There was also a private school.

43. Lewis notes Ballyspellin's reputation for curing obstructions and dropsy (1837, 2:31). Thomas Sheridan praised Ballyspellin with this verse:

All you who would refine your blood
As fair as famed Llewellin
waters clear come every year
To drink at Ballyspellin

Jonathan Swift replied with a fifteen-stanza ballad, including these lines:

Dare you dispute
You saucy brute
And think there's no refilling
You scurvy lays

And senseless praise
You give to Ballyspellan
(A. Dowling 1978, 15)

Barter's Cold Water Establishment, also called St. Ann's Hydropathic Studio, was established in 1842 by Richard Barter (1820–70). There is a bust of Dr. Barter in the Crawford Municipal Art Gallery in Cork. See the photographs in C. Lincoln 1981, 88, 89. Nicholson's gentrified Roman Catholic Ballyspellin priest was Father Robert Power, the parish priest of Galmoy (Ó Macháin 2004, 200).

44. Nicholson's hostess was possibly a Mrs. James Walsh (*Slater's* 1846, 316).

45. A medieval Gaelic poem describes the abbey as "the true church of the Lord's cross, with its stone monuments and coffins and hosts of angels in reverence, a fort, a sanctuary for the soul" (Carville 1973, 20).

46. Joachim Carlos Bianconi (1786–1875) immigrated to Ireland from Italy. In Ireland he changed his name to Charles and started life in Ireland selling religious good and prints, but he made his fortune with his Bianconi car service that he started in 1815. By the time Nicholson arrived in Ireland in 1845, Bianconi was transporting passengers, goods, and post in his 100 "Bian" cars. When the railroad came to Ireland in the same decade, Bianconi simply adjusted his routes to serve those areas where there was no railroad service. He was mayor of Clonmel in 1845 and 1846. He was a lifelong friend of fellow Clonmel man Father Theobald Mathew, a friend from Mr. Flynn's school in Market House, Thurles. His second daughter, Mary Anne, married the nephew of his friend Daniel O'Connell, and his son married O'Connell's granddaughter.

47. Mount Melleray was founded in 1832 by Irish Cistercians under the leadership of Father Vincent Ryan, on land located on the slope of the Knockmealdown Mountains provided by Sir Richard Keane of Cappoquin. "Cistercian History," Mount Melleray Abbey, http://www.mountmellerayabbey.org/index.php/history/story/history-of-the-abbey.

48. Father Vincent, O. Cist., a member of the Melleray community, said that Nicholson's account was accurate, if exaggerated. He thought her description of corn sheaves lying in the field was unlikely, as there was very little tillage land. Conversation with Father Vincent at Mount Melleray Abbey, 1998. Nicholson described an organ donated by a Dublin man who joined the community. A Mr. Jones donated an organ valued at seven hundred guineas. He joined the community but left because of poor health. He may have been a novice when Nicholson visited (Moloney n.d., 35).

49. Sharman Crawford (1781–1861), the radical MP from Dundalk (1835–37), supported Catholic Emancipation and tenants' rights (Macintyre 1965, 210–11).

50. The anonymous writer of a very favorable review of *Ireland's Welcome to the Stranger* cautions readers that Nicholson shared the fault of her countrymen,

"reporting private conversations with public individuals." The reviewer supposed that Nicholson failed to appreciate that her eccentric appearance and uninvited and unexpected appearance at Musgrave's door would have elicited his chilly reception ("Ireland and the Irish" 1847, 640).

51. After the cancellation of his October 8, 1843, monster meeting at Clontarf, O'Connell was sentenced to twelve months in the Richmond Bridewell and a fine of two thousand pounds on November 3. The House of Lords reversed the sentence on September 4, 1844.

52. W. B. Yeats's two-line poem "Parnell" expressed the same sentiments about a later politician who worked for Home Rule, a later form of repeal: "Parnell came down the road, he said to a cheering man: / Ireland shall get freedom and you still break stone" (1996, 312).

53. The Roman Catholic doctrine of the Immaculate Conception was not proclaimed until ten years later, in 1854.

54. Nicholson transcribed the word that she said was an Irish word as "confete"; it may have, in fact, been the Irish word "confach," which means "sharp," as in "speaking sharply."

55. Robert Persse was the third son of Henry Stratford Persse, Augusta, Lady Gregory's great-uncle. Robert's father did not think much of Robert's ambition. He wrote in a letter, "[Robert] is only fit to be a driver over slaves. He would not for £500 a year spoil the shape of his nails by any unfashionable occupation" (Pethica and Roy 1998, 122). When Robert finally settled into the Galway Post Office, Henry Stratford Persse wrote, "Robert goes on correct and regular at the Post Office. It is a poor thing, but he will not overrun the emolument and thus he will be happy and respectable" (Pethica and Roy 1998, 151). His father's opinion suggests that Robert would not have gone out of his way for the stranded American.

56. Nicholson noted, "The docks have been built at immense expense, and the unfortunate man who pledged himself to do the work died with grief at his misfortune" (*IWS* 2002, 127). The commercial dock was built in 1832 for thirty-one thousand pounds. In his essay "Aspects of Nineteenth Century Galway," Gearóid Ó Tuathaigh says the Galway fishing industry in prefamine Ireland was extensive but underdeveloped. It was a center for emigrant traffic (1984, 140, 194).

57. Nicholson mentioned that in the spring of 1844, during the state trial of Daniel O'Connell on the charge of conspiracy, she heard that "England was taking the liberty to break the seals of letters going from Ireland to America and to retain such as did not suit her views of matters relative to the country" (*IWS* 2002, 84).

4. "A City on a Hill," 1845

1. "Grants to Individuals: Mrs. Nicholson for distribution in the South and West of Ireland: 12 Testaments, 5 shillings, 4 pence." In 1846 she received one

Bible and fourteen Testaments, eight shillings and sixpence ("Grants to Individuals" 1849, 1845).

2. The three-quarter-length polka coat was designed for greater mobility. *Godey's Magazine* 52–53 (1856): 259. See also Camilla Toulmin, "Miss Brightington's Polka Jacket; or, Susan Bennett's Christmas Day," in *Stray Leaves from Shady Places,* by Mrs. Newton Crosland (1845). Nicholson would have approved of the changes that were developing in women's clothing that allowed more freedom of movement.

3. Because the rural Irish often associated Bible readers with proselytism, Nicholson was very careful to give Roman Catholics the Douay Bible, the first Bible in English to be translated from the Latin Vulgate by Catholics at the University at Douay.

4. Although playwright Brian Friel does not acknowledge William Carleton as the source for his Hugh Mór O'Donnell, the hedge schoolmaster in *Translations* (1981), Friel would have known Carleton's autobiographical account of Pat Frayne's hedge school. Friel does mention P. J. Dowling's *The Hedge Schools of Ireland* (B. Friel 1999, 74, 75, 116).

5. Lady Neville has not been identified. Perhaps she was one of the Nevilles of Ballinaboola who owned 150 acres, much of it bog.

6. A Mrs. Fisher lived at 40 Terrace in 1844 and was Nicholson's hostess in Cork. Was she also the Ellen Fisher who owned a hotel and livery stable at 1 Caroline Avenue? There may have been two women named Ellen Fisher in Cork in 1845 (Aldwell 1846, 174).

7. Maurice Power (1811–70), born in Ringacoltig, married Catherine Louise Livingston (1815–90), daughter of Judge Henry Brockholst Livingston, in New York in 1832. They had three daughters: Eliza (1839–97), Mary (1841–1921), and Lucinde Frances (1850–1919). On July 2, 1847, Power was elected to Parliament from County Kerry to fill Daniel O'Connell's seat. In February 1852, Queen Victoria appointed Power lieutenant governor of the island of St. Lucia in the British Antilles (1852–57). He was the last to be appointed to that office. During his administration, he was responsible for the "Ordinance to provide for the importation of coolies into the colonie at public expense," legislation about which Nicholson would have disapproved. *Parliamentary Papers* 16 (1854): 499.

8. William Martin (1772–1853), Quaker baker and Irish temperance pioneer, founded with others the nondenominational Cork Total Abstinence Society in 1831 (Harrison 1997, 153–55).

9. William Makepeace Thackeray (1811–63) was born in Calcutta and educated in English at Charterhouse and at Trinity College, Cambridge, where he left without taking a degree. Talented as an artist as well as a writer, he lost his family money in the Indian bank failure of 1833; three years later he married Isabelle Shawe, who turned out to be mentally unstable. Although Thackeray's reputation rests on his

novels, he made his living as a journalist, reviewer, and travel writer who illustrated his books with sketches. His *The Irish Sketchbook* (1843) was based on his visit to Ireland between July 4 and November 1, 1842. In her article "Thackeray in Ireland," B. G. McCarthy criticized Thackeray's critical ability as well as his superficial knowledge of Ireland (1951, 55–68).

10. Johannes G. Kohl (1808–78) was born in Bremen, but settled in Dresden in 1838. He traveled extensively in Europe and in America and published accounts of his travels (1842–51). A cartographer, Kohl became the city librarian of Bremen (Maxwell 1954, 278). Kohl visited Ireland from September 22 until October 25, 1842.

11. Father Mathew appears in his Capuchin habit in the rather ordinary statue by Mary Redmond (1892) that is on O'Connell Street, Dublin. A statue of Father Mathew in his Franciscan habit was started in Cork by John Hogan, who died before completing the project. The monument was finished by John Henry Foley and unveiled to a crowd of one hundred thousand in 1864 (M. Lysaght 1983, 5).

12. When the Trustees of the National Portrait Gallery considered purchasing the Leahy portrait, in 1865, Thomas Carlyle, in his capacity as a trustee, wrote to the board, objecting that the "author merely of a temporary row against whisky in various quarters, can have solid claim to a place among the great men of the British nation." The Trustees purchased the painting. Fintan Cullan found the letter in the National Portrait Gallery Archive, Register Packet 199 (46).

13. Letter from John Greenleaf Whittier to Richard Davis Webb, Portfolio 3b, no. 69, courtesy of the Religious Society of Friends Historical Library, Dublin. Whitman shared his strong commitment to abolitionism with Irish Quakers like Webb.

14. James Beale (1798–1879), a Cork entrepreneur who was a pioneer in transatlantic steam travel, worked for a while in partnership with Abraham Beale and was also a painter. *Skellig Night*, one of Beale's best-known paintings, was on loan from Dominic Daly, Esq., for many years at Cork's Crawford Municipal Gallery. The painting was sold at auction by Lynes & Lynes on May 24, 2005. *Skellig Night* is reproduced in Crowley 2012, 22, fig. 9.

15. Nicholson dates the jubilee as February 2, but the South Presentation Convent Archives, Cork, lists the date of the jubilee as February 8, 1845.

16. Another guest Father Mathew sent to the Ursulines was Captain R. B. Forbes, who brought the American relief ship the *Jamestown* to Cork in the spring of 1847. Forbes and Father Mathew's Liverpool friends and patrons, the Rathbones of Liverpool, visited the Ursulines on April 19, 1847 (J. Coleman 1904, 26).

17. Father Mathew Papers, Capuchin Archives, Dublin, Letter 853. I am grateful to V. Rev. Donal Sweeney, OFM Cap of the Capuchin Friary, St. Mary of the Angels, for his kindness in making this source available. The Correspondence of Fr. Theobald Mathew OFM Cap., Irish Capuchin Provincial Archives, CA/FM/COR.

18. Nicholson appeared to have endorsed Thucydides when he said, "The greatest achievement for a woman is to be as seldom as possible spoken of." Although Nicholson reported that her name appeared in local papers during the first week of February 1845, there is no mention of Nicholson in the *Cork Examiner*, the *Cork Commercial Courier*, or the *Southern Reporter* for February 1–7, 1845.

19. Joseph Sturge (1793–1859), English Quaker corn factor, philanthropist, and reformer, shared Nicholson's commitments to the causes of temperance, abolitionism, and world peace. He was a generous contributor to Nicholson's famine relief efforts.

20. The *Cork Examiner* reported the death of Father McSweeney on Monday, February 26, 1845, and that his funeral was held on Wednesday, February 28.

21. The Bantry Workhouse opened in April 1845 (J. O'Connor 1995, 259).

22. Although the bridge is called Cromwell's Foot Bridge (1627–87), one of Cromwell's lieutenants built it. The "mustached shape" of the bridge may have provided the name. In the Irish language, a mustache is a *croimeal* (Lucy 2010, 7). There is an engraving of the bridge in Hall and Hall, *A Week in Killarney* (1865, 70).

23. Richard White (1767–1851) was from a landowning family with roots on Whiddy Island. He became wealthy and was rewarded with successive Irish peerages: Baron (1797), Viscount (1880), and Earl of Bantry and Viscount Bearhaven (1816) for his part in the defense of Bantry Bay during the unsuccessful French invasion of 1796 and for his continued support of the government after the Act of Union.

24. Although Everett does not mention Nicholson by name, he refers to her account of Lord Bantry's hunchback servant girl. He also mentions other visitors to Glengarriff Lodge: Lady Chatterton, Samuel and Anna Hall, Herman, Fürst von Pückler Muskau, and W. M. Thackeray.

25. Hall and Hall described the family living in the rocks in the summer and working or begging in the neighboring town, probably Glengarriff, in the winter (1843, 1:140). Sharing living quarters with a cow was an old practice that survived through the nineteenth century. People believed that a cow kept the house warm and that she yielded more milk. There was also a belief that the fire protected the cow from evil spirits, and the household fire provided that safeguard (Evans 1957, 43).

26. Father O'Sullivan (1804–74) held a house and land rent free from Lord Lansdowne while he was parish priest in Kenmare. The Landsowne Estate was founded by Sir William Petty, a Cromwellian surveyor. That he was also a loyalist influenced his decision not to support local tenants' agitation. He could be considered a "political opportunist"; however, during the Great Irish Famine, O'Sullivan worked to get relief from his Kenmare parishioners (Lyne 2001, 348–52). Father O'Sullivan's diaries were a valuable source for Gerard Lyne when he wrote his history of the Lansdowne Estate during the agency of W. S. Trench (Lyne 2001, ix). Lyne

includes a photograph of O'Sullivan, who appears as a tall, heavy-set, balding man with a full, dark beard.

27. Hall and Hall described the Muckross graveyard as being in a "very revolting state," saying that it was "often necessary to remove the remains of one inmate before room can be found for another" (1843, 1:200–201). Their account of the keeners in *A Week in Killarney* includes engravings of keeners and the musical notation of the *caoine* (1865, 95–97).

28. Cornelius Egan (1780–1856) was appointed to the See of Kerry in 1824; he served until his death in 1856.

29. Erskine Nichol's painting *The 16th, 17th (St. Patrick's Day) and 18th March, 1856* depicts children selling shamrocks to a well-dressed couple and a man with shamrocks in his hatband. The chapel bells Nicholson heard were from the chapel in Chapel Lane. While the foundation stone had been set in 1842 for the cathedral designed by Augustus Welby Pugin, the building was delayed by the Great Irish Famine (Ó Caoimhe 1990, n.p.).

30. Daniel O'Connell gave the Fair Green to Cahirciveen as a way to promote the commercial growth of the village as an agricultural market (O'Farrell 2009, 214).

31. The parish priest of Cahirciveen in 1844 was Edward Fitzgerald.

32. Watercolors in the collection of the National Gallery of Ireland by William Evans of Eton (1798–1877) include images of women carrying burdens in their arms, on their backs, and on their heads.

33. The slate mines employed a hundred men in 1839; "however, the evidence suggests significantly more worked there prior to the Great Irish Famine" (Crowley 2009, 263; Ó Cléirigh 1992, 62). See also Fisher 1847, 21–24.

34. Paul Townsend has argued the point in his chapter "The Confluence of Temperance and Repeal" (2002, 192–234). See also Riach 1976, 3–25.

35. In his chapter "Daniel O'Connell and Iveragh," Fergus O'Farrell traces the attacks made on the reputation of O'Connell as landlord that were made by T. C. Foster in 1845–46. Later, in the *Letters on the Condition of the People of Ireland*, Foster charged that O'Connell's rents were unjustly high, that tenants lived in squalor, and that he permitted excessive subdivision of plots (1846, x). O'Connell refuted the charges in the *Times*, and they sent a second reporter, William Howard Russell, to Derrynane. He corroborated Foster's account. In September 1846 Foster visited Derrynane, where he found that poverty on the O'Connell estate was the result of allowing tenants evicted from other estates to settle on Derrynane land for modest rents (Reid 1888, 178–81).

36. The custom continued until at least 1903 (Foley 1903, 27–28).

37. Nicholson's use of the phrase "walk softly" might be an allusion to Judges 4:21, which describes Jael "walking softly" as she went to Sisera's tent to drive a nail into his head. The irony would not have been lost on Nicholson.

38. Robert Havell the Younger's aquatint *Derrynane Abbey, Co. Kerry, Home of Daniel O'Connell, MP (1775–1847), with O'Connell and Friends in the Foreground,* based on John Fogarty's *Derrynane Abbey, 1831,* is a contemporary, rather idealistic, view of Derrynane and is in the collection of the National Gallery of Ireland (NGI 11842).

39. Maurice O'Connell (1803–52), Daniel O'Connell's eldest son, was a native speaker of Irish brought up at Derrynane. He was educated by the Jesuits at Clongowes Woods College and at Trinity College. He was admitted to the Irish Bar in 1827. He helped his father with Catholic Emancipation and then with the Repeal campaign. He died in London in 1853.

40. Lady Chatterton described Jerry Quirke's Sportsman Hotel as being southwest of Lough Currane, which suggests that Nicholson retraced her steps toward Cahirciveen when she left Derrynane. Born in London, Henrietta, Lady Chatterton (1806–76), settled in Cork when she married William Chatterton of Castle Mahon (F. Clarke 2009, 2:479). Like Nicholson, Lady Chatterton said in the "Advertisement" to *Rambles* that her object was "to remove some of the prejudices which render so many people afraid to reside in Ireland." Lady Chatterton's name appears in the 1847 List of Patrons of the Cork Ladies' Relief Society for the South of Ireland (Luddy 1995, 53).

41. Frank O'Connor's short story "The Long Road to Umera" (1940) is based on the longing of an old woman who dies in Cork to be buried with her family in Umera.

42. Nicholson mentions that she was walking on a new road through the Ballaghisheen Pass that connected Waterville and Killorglin. There is a photograph of the Ballaghisheen Pass in Lyne's history of the Landsdowne Estate (2001, 391). In 1868 Lansdowne tenants, escorted by Father O'Sullivan on horseback, greeted the Fifth Marquess of Lansdowne (2001, 39). Lyne notes that choreographed welcomes of the gentry by their tenants were a feature of nineteenth-century Irish estate life.

43. A legend about 1798 in the Ballinamuck, County Longford, area describes local people thinking that the tall hats worn by Hessian soldiers were a part of their heads. The expression "Mahussin" was used locally to describe a large person.

44. This quotation has been traced to the 1845 Diocese of New York *Proceedings of the Annual Convention of the Episcopal Church*; it has not been otherwise identified. Nicholson used the phrase again in *Lights and Shades of Ireland* (1850, 176).

45. "Ye are the light of the world. A city that is set on a hill cannot be hid" (Matt. 5:14).

46. Walpole appears on a list of Limerick "Protestants and Dissenters" in de Brún 1986, 143–48. During their confrontation, Nicholson, who had learned Walpole was a Scot, said that an Irishman would not have behaved in such a manner (*IWS* 2002, 271).

47. The Tralee magistrates in 1845 were Oliver Strokes, Esq.; Thomas Collis, Esq.; and T. Sarrow, Pierce Chute, Esq.

48. William Bedell (1571–1642) was born in Essex and educated at Cambridge. He served as provost of Trinity College between 1628 and 1629. He used his short tenure to strengthen the preparation of clerical students in the Irish language. When he was appointed bishop of Kilmore and Ardagh, he continued to work to produce liturgy in the Irish language. He commissioned an Irish translation of the Old Testament (A. Clarke 2009, 1:411–12).

49. John Gregg (1798–1878), born near Ennis, County Clare, was a graduate of Trinity College Dublin. Ordained in 1826, he became a prominent evangelist who was an Irish-speaking agent of the Home Mission; he was a well-known preacher. He built a congregation of some two thousand when he was chaplain to the Bethesda Chapel in Dublin. Appointed the bishop of Cork, Cloyne, and Ross, he built St. Finnbarr's cathedral (1865–78) (Andrews 2009, 4:245–46).

50. The modus operandi of the Irish Society was described in an article in the conservative *Dublin University Magazine*:

> A proper person is in the first instance employed to seek for individuals, in a particular district, who are competent to instruct in the primer of the Irish language; these are then engaged to teach their neighbors, when and how they can, generally in the hours of relaxation from labour, and in the cabins of the peasantry; and they are furnished with elementary books and portions of Scripture for the purpose. At the end of three or four months an inspection, by the person who engaged them, takes place; and the teachers are paid a sum, usually one shilling per head, for each person passing this inspection. The teaching of a pupil is generally completed within a year from his first commencement with the primer. There is a peculiarity in these schools, if they may be called, which must be noticed, as residents in the country are often surprised to hear of such beings reported to exist in the neighborhood and even in a flourishing state, while the facts of their existence is unknown to them. ("Protestant Conversion" 1845, 744)

51. Shortly before Nicholson arrived in Dingle, there were two instances of Catholics trying to reclaim their lands (December 1844 and February 1845). "Reports of Persecution in Dingle" regularly appeared in the pages of the *Achill Herald and Western Witness*.

52. There is an 1890 photograph of the colony in the Lawrence Collection (L_ROY_00142). Lydia Fisher, who published *Letters from the Kingdom of Kerry* in 1845 anonymously, was the daughter of Quaker author and educator Mary Leadbeater of Ballintore. Lydia Leadbeater married John Fisher, a prominent Limerick

Quaker. The refrain of the Irish folk song "Fill. Fill a rún," concludes, "Ní fhaca mé iontas go deo mar an sagairt Ó Dhomhnaill in a minister" (I never saw a greater wonder than Fr. O'Domhnaill as a minister).

53. Nicholson did not name Miss Rae, but Mrs. D. P. Thompson identified her in *A Brief Account of the Rise and Progress of the Change in Religious Opinion Now Taking Place in Dingle and the West of County Kerry* (1867, 63).

54. The friary was returned to the Irish Franciscans in 1969 (Garner 1981, 20–21).

55. Power Le Poer Trench (1770–1839), Church of Ireland archbishop of Tuam, served as agent on family estates in Galway in 1790, a position that carried with it the responsibility for the local yeomanry during the 1798 rebellion (Lunney 2009b, 7:468–69).

56. Daniel O'Connell gave John MacHale (1791–1881), the Catholic archbishop of Tuam (1834–81), the sobriquet "the Lion of the West," a name that referred to MacHale's passionate nationalism that championed the Irish language, Repeal, and later Home Rule. Although he was always an important figure in Irish nationalist movements, his position in the Irish Church declined when he fell out with Paul Cardinal Cullen, who was appointed archbishop of Dublin (1852–78). A moderate nationalist and ultramontanist, Cullen had strong support from Rome (Barr 2009, 4:6–10; Villiers-Tuthill 2000, 134).

57. John D'Arcy (1785–1832) founded the town of Clifden in 1815, the year he built his Gothic castle. The limestone and granite D'Arcy Monument was started shortly after D'Arcy's death, but it was not finished until the local heritage society completed it (Lavelle, O'Scanaill, and Previté 1993, 8–11).

58. Tim Robinson's description of the remains of a "marine temple of sea shells" suggests that it is the site of Nicholson's "fairy castle" Connemara (1990, 47).

59. Robinson also included the story of the robber and the Clifden-Roundstone road situated in the Half-Way House, where its owners robbed and murdered traveling packmen and threw the bodies into the lake. When some of the victims' bodies floated to the surface, the owners-robbers were tried and executed (1990, 56).

60. The Presbyterian presence began with the founding of Roundstone by the Scottish engineer Alexander Nimmo who built the village for Scottish fishermen in the 1820s; in 1840 he donated the land for the "kirk" that was demolished in the 1930s.

61. Thomas H. Mason included photographs taken in the 1930s of young women on the island of Inishere carrying seaweed in bags on their backs (1950, 104, 322).

62. The story that Sir Walter Raleigh brought potatoes to Ireland in the late sixteenth century and planted them at his home near Youghal, County Waterford, is a popular legend. How and when the potato arrived in Ireland is still a matter of

speculation; however, it has been established that potatoes were cultivated in County Wicklow by the middle of the seventeenth century (Zuckerman 1998, 19). By the nineteenth century, the agricultural laborer existed on a diet of potatoes.

63. Although Connemara Park personnel ask hill walkers not to climb Diamond Hill because of erosion, it is considered an easy assent that rewards the climber with a magnificent view of the Bens and the north Connemara coast (Lynam 1989, 14–15).

64. In his introduction to *The Mountains of Connemara*, climber Joss Lynam cautions his readers not to hesitate "to cut short your work if the weather turns nasty" (1989, x).

65. "Outrage Reports, Galway 11/487-29099" (1845), National Archives of Ireland.

66. Howe Peter Browne, the Second Marquess of Sligo (1788–1845), died on January 26, 1845. At his death, he was succeeded by his son George Browne, the Third Marquess (1820–96).

67. The Croagh Patrick pilgrimage, which continues today, is the subject of Máire MacNeill's magisterial study of the survival of the old Celtic calendar custom that has continued into the twenty-first century, *The Festival of Lughnasa* (1962).

68. Mac Neill points out that the earliest account of the legend of Saint Patrick banishing demons from the top of Croagh Patrick involved demon birds, not snakes (1962, 72–73). Twelfth-century visitor Giraldus Cambrensis and the Cistercian cleric Jocelin changed the snakes to birds (73). The bird version of the legend provided the basis for W. B. Yeats's play *At the Hawk's Well*.

69. Nangle attacked the Halls regularly in the pages of his *Achill Herald and Western Witness*. He also carried on a running feud with Lord Mounteagle and Stephen DeVere in the *Herald*.

70. MS 8449, National Library of Ireland Photographic Collection, Dugort.

71. Hall and Hall, *Ireland*, includes an image of the houses in the village of Dooagh, Achill (1840, 3:18, 43, 404). They are as Nicholson described them.

72. Dr. Adams was a licentiate of Kings and Queens College of Physicians. According to the records of the Dublin Lying-in Hospital, Dr. Adams was a certified practitioner of medicine (*Thom's Dublin Directory* 1846, 268). Nicholson appears to have based her impression of Adams on that single meeting. He emerges as the hero of the colony in Mealla Ní Ghiobúin's *Dugort, Achill Island, 1831–1861: The Rise and Fall of a Missionary Community* (2001, 62).

73. The custom of booleying (buaile or milking place) involved driving stock to summer pasturage in the mountains and staying in simple huts to do the milking. The custom continued in Achill until the 1940s (Meehan 2003, 161).

74. In 1842 Nangle listed fifty-one of the sixty-four families as originally Roman Catholic. The number of Catholic families among the converts rose to fifty-nine in 1843 (Ní Ghiobúin 2001, 32–33).

75. Edward Nangle mentioned the death of the Newport postmaster James Arthur in the *Achill Herald and Western Witness* on June 25, 1845, 65. He noted that Mrs. Arthur's annual salary of £18.5 was too small to pay for her husband's death (1845, 9). The Arthurs' son William was a minister of Westport's Methodist Church (Allen 1996, 64).

76. Later, O'Donnell's drivers were accused of evicting tenants. O'Donnell claimed not to know anything about the evictions, but Nicholson would have none of his excuses. Her view was that landlords were responsible for the people they employed (*Annals* 1998, 115; Hall and Hall 1843, 3:383, 385–86).

77. W. B. Yeats situates his late poem "The Man and Echo" in the Alt (1996, 345).

78. The Poor Law of 1838 was an effort to replace the patchwork system with a government system of workhouses funded by local poorhouse unions.

79. Nicholson published the full text of Nangle's letter in *Ireland's Welcome to the Stranger* (2002, 336–37). She identified the "respectable person in Birmingham" as English abolitionist, Chartist reformer, and philanthropist Joseph Sturge (1793–1859), telling her reader that Sturge told her that he had not seen the letter at the time of her visit to the Achill colony (*IWS* 2002, 336).

80. Mícheál ÓCléirigh (1590–1643), a member of a learned Irish Donegal family, was educated at the Irish College of St. Anthony at Louvian. Aedh Buidh Mac-an-Bhaird, OFM, the warden of St. Anthony's, encouraged Ó Clérigh to begin to collect the manuscripts that became the *Annals of the Four Masters*.

81. Nicholson was friendly with the daughters of Thaddeus O'Dowda of Bonniconlon, County Mayo, who befriended her when she stayed in Ballina in February 1848.

82. Nicholson's memory is not accurate here. She would have been sixteen in 1808; Scott wrote "Lady of the Lake" in 1810.

83. Nicholson later attended a dinner in famine-stricken Ireland where wine and brandy were served with the meal. Nicholson objected. "When these heralds of salvation heard a word of remonstrance they put on the religious cant, and cited me immediately and solemnly the Marriage of Cana and the tribunal of Timothy's stomach" (*Annals* 1998, 90). 1 Tim. 4:1–5 criticized false asceticism.

84. "Glimpses of Old Glasgow," http://gdl.cdlr.strath.ac.uk/airgli/airgli0128.htm.

85. There was also the later *A Treatise on Vegetable Diet, with Practical Results; or, A Leaf from Nature's Own Book,* published in Glasgow in 1848 by John M'Combe.

86. The speech was reported in the *Dundee Courier* on February 3, 1846 (Douglass 1979, 1:407).

87. George Bernard Shaw exploited the scenario for *Major Barbara* (1905), his own drama of ends and means.

88. UK Census for 1841, Paisley. Stewart's household also included Isabella Dawson (servant) and James Young.

89. Nicholson was mistaken. Sir Richard was Maud's second, not her third, husband. Nicholson and Griffin were not the only ones who were intrigued by the story of Maud. James Joyce included a reference to the "maid, wife and widow" in the "Wandering Rocks" chapter of *Ulysses* (1961, 223.16).

90. James Joyce was also intrigued by the poem. The lines from "The Bridal of Malahide" appear in the "Proteus," the "Wandering Rocks," the "Oxen of the Sun," and the "Circe" chapters of *Ulysses*.

91. MS A.9.2, vol. 22, no. 77, William Goodell to Asenath Nicholson, July 20, 1846.

5. "If This Cup May Not Pass Away from Me"

1. The first notice of the potato blight appeared in the *Dublin Evening Post* on September 9, 1845.

2. Christine Kinealy has pointed out that while the 1845 potato failure was treated as a single event, the "second, more widespread, blight of 1846 marked the beginning of the Famine" (1995, 345).

3. The passage, from Luke 24:32, describes the response of the disciples when Christ appears to them at Emmaus.

4. DeVesci Lodge stands at the corner of Carrickbrennan Road. The graveyard is now part of the property of the Christian Brothers' Monkstown Park School. James Webb's business premises were located at 15–16 Upper Bridge Street and 16–17 Corn Market.

5. There was an ancient graveyard at Carrickbrennan, but there were no other burial grounds until Deans Grange was established in 1863 (Pearson 1991, 71).

6. Helen Hatton mentions a number of accounts of dogs devouring the dead and dying, including Nicholson's story of an Achill girl attacked by starved dogs (*Annals* 1998, 136). The horror of a dog cooked for dinner appears in North Longford oral tradition, where it is said that Saint Patrick cursed the region with barrenness because a pagan chief of Sliabh Chairbre insulted the saint by serving him a dog for his dinner.

7. The story "An Effort for Ireland" describing the meeting "in behalf of the Suffering Millions in Ireland" held at Tammany Hall on Saturday, December 26, 1846, appeared in the *New York Tribune* on December 28, 1846.

8. Daniel Fanshaw (1788–1860), one of the wealthiest printers in New York, was the printer for the American Bible Society and the American Tract Society. He and his family lived on Williams Street until 1840, when he moved his family to Yorkville.

9. Were Nicholson to have seen the article titled "The Irish Heart" in the *New York Tribune* of January 2, 1847, she would have been reassured that the Irish servants in New York were doing more than their share to help their families and friends at home. Jacob Harvey visited houses in the city where people were drawing small drafts for Ireland. He calculated that the amount remitted to Ireland by "laboring Irish males and females during 1846" was $808,000. He commented on this generosity:

It is the natural instinct of the Irish peasant to share his mite—be it money or potatoes—for those still poorer than himself and he thinks he had just done a Christian duty, deserving of no special applause. It is fitting to exalt our estimate of human nature to record such a proof of the self-sacrifice and severe self-denial through which alone such a sum as is here $808,000 could in one year be remitted from their earnings by the Irish at labor and service in an around this city. Of what other people in the world, under like circumstances, can such a fact be truly stated. (*New York Tribune*, Jan. 9, 1847)

10. Nicholson did not visit County Cavan. She wrote at the end of *Ireland's Welcome to the Stranger* that her tour of Ireland "embraced all but the county of Cavan" (2002, 339).

11. This may be a reference to Psalm 137.

12. Nicholson's task was identical to Margaret Kelleher's in *The Feminization of Famine*, her study of female representation in famine literature. Kelleher asks the question, "Is it possible to depict the horrors and scale of an event such as the famine . . . ?" (1997b, 2).

13. Lamentation 2: "Mine eyes do fall with tears, my bowels are troubled, and my liver is poured upon the earth, for the destruction of the daughter of my people: because the children and the suckling swoon in the streets of the earth. 12: They say to their mothers, Where is corn and wine? When they swooned as the wounded in the streets of the city, when their soul was poured out into their mothers' bosom."

14. Nicholson's tall Liffey-side house has not been identified. The house may have been located at 30 Arran Quay.

15. Helen Hatton identified Nicholson as the field agent for the New York Relief Society (1993, 136). There does not appear to be confirmation of this designation.

16. Richard Davis Webb was printing the sheets for *Ireland's Welcome to the Stranger*, which was published by Webb and Chapman in Dublin and Chapman and Hall in London in the summer of 1847.

17. The wall along the Liffey is said to have been built at the time of the Bruce invasion in 1317 to replace the earlier wall, part of which still stands in Cook Street

(Gillespie 1973, 16). In 1975 the wall was rebuilt by the Dublin Corporation as a contribution to the European Architectural Year (Liddy 1987, 4).

18. Alfred John Webb (1834–1908) was the eldest son of Richard Davis and Hannah Waring Webb. Influenced by his parents' commitment to radical reform, Webb supported a number of causes, including the disestablishment of the Church of Ireland and women's suffrage. The trials of the Fenian prisoners turned Webb into a nationalist; he traveled for the Land League and was the treasurer of the Irish National League. He later became involved with Indian nationalism (Webb 1999, 19).

19. Nicholson may have met Webb through William Lloyd Garrison. Garrison had met the Irish Quaker printer at the Great Anti-Slavery Convention in London in 1840. Webb invited the American to visit him in Dublin before Garrison returned to America (Garrison 1973, 283).

20. In her note about the Davis picture in *America's Eye: Irish Painting from the Collection of Brian P. Burns*, Christina Kennedy of the Hugh Lane Municipal Gallery of Modern Art pointed out that occasions of this sort continued in Dublin during the Great Irish Famine. She also noted the difference between the painting and an engraving published in the *Illustrated London News* (Aug. 11, 1849) that indicates there was extensive redecorating of the castle during the famine in preparation for the visit of Queen Victoria (2000, 21).

21. Joseph Crosfield (1821–79), a Liverpool Quaker minister, traveled with William Forster to Ireland in 1846 and 1847. Part of his report of that trip was published as appendix 3 in the Society of Friends, *Transactions of the Central Relief Committee of the Society of Friends during the Famine in Ireland in 1846 and 1847* (1852, 145–47). William Edward Forster (1818–86), who had experience with soup kitchens in Norwich, volunteered his services to the London committee on November 25, 1846. He traveled for four and a half months in Ireland with Joseph Crosfield to report to London about famine conditions. He was elected to Parliament in 1861 and served as chief secretary for Ireland under the William Gladstone administration.

22. The relief supplies sent to Maria Edgeworth came under the auspices of William Rathbone, Father Mathew's patron, a man Nicholson likely met later in Liverpool. Like Nicholson, Edgeworth admired Father Mathew. Her 1840 letter to the secretary of the Irish Temperance Union referred to the remarkable improvement that "the pledge" brought to Edgeworthtown. She said, "I consider Fr. Mathew as the greatest benefactor to his country, the most true friend to Irishmen and to Ireland." Margaret Kelleher contrasted Nicholson's and Edgeworth's response to the problem of famine relief in *The Feminization of Famine* (1997b, 94–95).

23. While the letter's return address is 45 Hardwicke Street, it is more likely that Nicholson wrote the letter from the house of her friend Ethelinda Warren at 5

Hardwicke Street. Nicholson's letter was numbered 3198 on the National Archives Relief Papers. When the archives were housed in the old Public Record Office, its shelf list location was 1A-42-19. The author has not been to find the letter in the Bishop Street location. The letter is included with this caveat.

24. There is an engraving of the *Macedonia* in the *Illustrated London News* (Aug. 7, 1847, 3). The ship left New York on June 19, 1847, and arrived in Cork twenty-seven days later, on July 16, with a cargo of cornmeal, Indian meal, rice, beans, and clothes (DeKay 1995, 237). Theresa Mullally (1728–1803) established an orphanage for poor girls of St. Michan's parish who were taught a curriculum that would have had Nicholson's approval: catechism, reading, writing, arithmetic, housework, and lace making (Casey 2005, 92).

25. Maria Waring (1818–74) was Hannah Webb's younger sister. According to Richard Davis Webb's biographer Richard S. Harrison, Maria Waring, "an independent-minded young woman," found Nicholson "repulsive"; however, she was eager to learn from her about diet, household management, and family planning (Harrison 1993, 56–57).

26. Boston Public Library, MS A.1.2, vol. 17, p. 42, courtesy of the Trustees of the Boston Public Library/Rare Books.

27. Webb described Waring's scrupulousness and his response to the Tappan letter in his letter of September 18, 1847, to Maria Weston Chapman. MS A.9.2, vol. 23, p. 43, courtesy of the Trustees of the Boston Public Library/Rare Books.

28. See Kinealy 1995, 165–66; and Kinealy and MacAtasney 2000, 120–24. The Ladies' Relief Association applied successfully to the Central Relief Committee for a grant of five hundred pounds in May 1848 (Society of Friends 1852, 436). Dr. John Edgar, DD (1798–1866), a Presbyterian temperance advocate and philanthropist, established industrial schools in the West of Ireland (Holmes 2009, 3:573). He reported in "Ireland's Mission Field," a paper to the British Organization of the Evangelical Alliance in August 1852, that the Belfast Ladies sent enough money to establish schools staffed by female teachers in seven districts that served some two thousand pupils (Killen 1867, 267).

29. Mary Ann McCracken (1779–1866) organized a muslin business with her sister that was attentive to workers' interests, worked with Edward Bunting to promote a renaissance of interest in Irish harp music, and devoted herself to philanthropic interests, including the welfare of women and girls in the Belfast workhouse as well as the Belfast Ladies' Association.

30. In his essay "Asenath Nicholson's New Domestic Economy," Gordon Bigelow argues that Nicholson's economic solutions for Irish poverty is "directly parallel" to the idea promulgated by John Stuart Mill's *Principles of Political Economy* (1848). "Both suggest that a knowledge of national character is necessary before

any formulation of social and economic policy can proceed effectively" (Cohen and Curtin 1989, 155).

31. In a March 31, 1867, letter to the American abolitionist Maria Chapman, Richard Davis Webb described Maria Webb as a "good woman intensely evangelical" (MS A.9.2, vol. 32, p. 68, courtesy of the Trustees of the Boston Public Library/ Rare Books).

32. Maria Webb to Maria Weston Chapman, Dec. 2, 1847, MS A.9.2, vol. 6, p. 17, courtesy of the Trustees of the Boston Public Library/Rare Books.

33. Mary Ann McCracken would have known the Grimshaws because the Joys, the McCrackens, and the Grimshaws were pioneering Northern Ireland cotton manufacturers (McNeill 1960, 29–30). Samuel Lewis said Nicholas Grimshaw built his mill, the first cotton mill in Ireland, in Newwtownabbey in 1784. It employed more than two hundred people (1837, 715; see also Lunney 2009a, 4:293).

34. Susan Hewetson [sic] received a grant of ten pounds from the Central Relief Committee on January 13, 1847.

35. Rt. Rev. Patrick McGettigan was bishop of Raphoe from 1820 to 1861; the See of Raphoe was coterminous with County Donegal.

36. Lord George Hill (1801–79), fifth son of Arthur Hill and Mary Sandys, represented Carrigfergus after his career in the army and before he bought twenty-three thousand acres in Gweedore on the bleak northwestern coast of County Donegal. A resident landlord who hired the conscientious Francis Forster as his agent, Hill transformed the economy of the area by transforming the agricultural practices from the traditional rundale system to a system of individual ownership. He stood by his tenants during the Great Irish Famine. In 1855 Hill bought in Scottish graziers, and that initiative led to the theft and destruction of much of the stock. Nationalists and Conservatives took sides in the Gweedore grazier controversy. The poverty returned. Hill rode out that period, and calm returned by the end of the 1860s. Contemporary historical judgment tends to agree with Nicholson's opinion that Hill's improvements made improvements to the area but that the old rundale system promoted communal life (Hourican 2005, 4:697–98).

37. *Lord Hill's Facts from Gweedore* went into three editions: 1845, 1846, and 1854. James Tuke, who visited the Hill estate in 1847, contrasted conditions on Gweedore favorably with the circumstances on the Marquis of Conyngham's neighboring estate. See Tuke's *A Visit to Connaught in the Autumn of 1847* (1848). Francis-Nathaniel Conyngham was the Earl of Conyngham of Mount Charles from 1824 to 1832. Lieutenant Milward, RE, reported on January 2, 1847, that "the people on the Marquis of Conyngham's estate are the poorest. The property is much neglected; it comprises an immense tract of land principally waste, but a large portion of it could be easily reclaimed, however not a shilling has been spent on it." *Parliamentary Papers* 52 (1847): 89.

38. Among the items for a population of four thousand were a single cart, one plow, 243 stools, no pigs, one school, one priest and no other resident gentleman, no clock, no boots, no turnips, and no carrots; half the population were without shoes, and people and animals were on the edge of starvation (Hill 1846).

39. Both Mary Pierce and Gordon Bigelow have noticed that Nicholson was aware of the negative impact of Hill's consolidation on "clan and community" (Pierce 2010, 116–17). Bigelow added Kevin Whelan's argument that the rundale/clachan system was an effective and appropriate response to the conditions of an increasing rural population who were supported by a fragile agricultural economy (2003, 142).

40. There is a letter from Francis Forster appealing for aid for "the very poorest [parish] in this extensive country" (RLFC Famine Relief Commission Papers, 3/2/7). See also Bennett 1847, 82.

41. The image of dogs scavenging among the famine dead appears in other literature of the Great Irish Famine (Hatton 1993, 136; Killen 1867, 148) and Jeremiah O'Ryan's famine ballad "Ireland's Lament: A Poem" with its lines "Shroudless and coffinless they thickly lie / The famish'd dogs devou'd them in their graves" (Morash 1989, 69). Nicholson would have known the image of the flesh-devouring dogs from 1 Kings 14, 11; and 1 Kings 16, 4.

42. Nicholson cited Zechariah's "And the streets of the city shall be full of boys and girls playing in the street thereof" (8:5), his hopes for a restored Jerusalem that would be stable enough for children to play in the streets, to make a similar point about children's laughter in a postfamine Ireland.

43. William Howitt (1792–1879) and Mary Botham Howitt (1799–1888) collaborated on a number of writing projects, including Howitt's *Journal* (1847–49). Howitt's *Journal of Literature and Popular Progress* was launched by the Howitts in January 1847; it ran through vol. 3, no. 78 (June 24, 1848). It was absorbed in July 1848 by the *People's Journal*. There were two volumes. Articles by Nicholson included "Ireland at the Present Moment," 2 (1847): 141–42; and "Frightful Conditions and Prospects in Ireland," 2 (1847): 339–42. Nicholson's letter was published in Howitt's *Journal* 1 (1847): 141–42.

44. There was a second, similar, letter written to a friend of Nicholson's in Belfast that was dated Templecrone, August 19, 1847. The letter was published under the title "Destitution in Arranmore, Co. Donegal," in the *Londonderry Journal and Donegal Tyrone Advertiser*, Sept. 1, 1847, 3. The date of the letter suggests that Nicholson did not leave Templecrone immediately, but stayed on another two weeks. A note introduced Nicholson's letter. "The following is an extract from a letter received by a lady in Belfast, relative to the state of destitution of the wretched inhabitants of the island of Aranmore. To it we direct the most serious attention of the humane and charitable. The text of the letter follows":

ROSHINE LODGE, TEMPLECRONE,
AUGUST 19, 1847

My dear Friend,

I have just returned from the island of Arranmore which place I visited with the company with the kind and energetic Mr. Griffith. What I have there witnessed is beyond my power of language to express. We took a guide who was well acquainted with the different localities of the island; he led us from one scene of wretchedness, till I was obliged to say it is enough. Not one family appeared to have a morsel of food—nothing, but chickweed, not tops of turnips, sageweed, unless by some lucky chance, they have the good fortune to pick up a few shell fish. They did not ask us for anything; but, when they held their dishes, containing nothing but cold turnip tops, need I say the sight was most affecting? No one spoke; a kind of inanity, a stupid despairing look—was all that they manifested. The public relief fund is now all stopped. There is not a boiler in operation on the island. The funds are exhausted. Unless some charitable substance is immediately given, all must perish, indeed, speedy death would be a blessing compared to the lingering torments they now endure. The greater part of the island presents a scene of desolation. Here and there a patch of barley, the produce of the seed sent by the Irish Society. But scarcely a patch of potato is to be seen, and no wheat—they had no seed—in the spring, but if they had been possessed of any, they had not sufficient strength to put it is the ground, and what are they to do? On the mainland, the misery is nearly as great. You can form no idea of the awful state of the people. The house of Mr. Forster, with whom I am present staying, is surrounded by miserable beings crying and howling. How they have so long borne such a burden, I know not. Fr. Forster and Mr. Griffith are entitled to the greatest credit for their unerring exertions, but they must sink if not supported. I visited Gweedore—Lord George Hill's estate. I wish all Ireland was under such landlords; yet, all his tenants are not free from want, though none are in extreme suffering. But for Arranmore and Templecrone, I know not what is to be done. The poor people are dying in a most awful state. Your sincere friend, A. Nicholson

45. The Central Relief Committee sent Richard Davis Webb to Belmullet in May 1847 to investigate charges that the CRC grants were not being administered properly. According to Jonathan Pim's May 16, 1847, letter to Jacob Harvey in New York, Webb found no grounds for the report. Webb's second tour to Erris in February 1848 was also made at the request of the CRC. See also Grant 1991, 354–55.

6. "Misery without Mask"

1. "An Address of Thanks" published in the *Tyrawly Herald and Sligo Intelligencer* on September 16, 1847, praised Butler's temper, energy, and intelligence. On the boat trip between Achill and Erris, Butler told Nicholson that he feared drowning. It was an ironic foreshadowing. Nicholson reported that he drowned in an accident in 1848 during a visit to the Continent (*Annals* 1998, 91). The author was not able to discover the circumstances of Butler's fatal accident.

2. When the Savages' little daughter traveled to Westport, she was afraid that the trees along the road would fall on her (Society of Friends 1852, 199).

3. A note to Mrs. Stock's Clothing Application (1848) to the Central Relief Committee (#2157) described the Stocks as "active parties" in relief. Mrs. Stock wrote to Frances Carter, wife of the absentee landlord, asking for help. There is no record of a response (Nolan 1997, 114). Samuel Stock (d. 1866) was the grand-nephew of Bishop Joseph Stock of Killala, who wrote *What Passed at Killala* (1800), a loyalist's account of the 1798 French invasion that landed near Killala on August 22, 1798.

4. While Nicholson spelled her host's name "Bourne," it also appears as "Bourn" and "Bournes." Mary A. Strange's history of the family is titled *The Bourne(s) Families of Ireland* (1970).

5. Nicholson identified the homes of Samuel Stock, Samuel Bourne, and James O'Donnell as the three households of precarious comfort in the Rossport area.

6. The striking detail that she wanted to be buried locally among seventeen shipwrecked sailors may have been grafted to the story collected by Michael Corduff about sixteen Kilgalligan men who perished at Poll an Mhúirín Bharr an Tuair in 1839. The main feature in stories of the supernatural is that they are told about those who drown (Ó Catháin and O'Flannagan 1975, 142).

7. James Cormack of Rossport identified Stácaí Iorrais (the Stags of Broadhaven) in Broad Haven Bay as a destination for bird and egg hunting during the Great Irish Famine (Póirtéir 1995, 56).

8. A local famine story describes Anna NicGraith picking barnacles with a seven-year-old girl at Poirtín na gCurrach who was carried off by a wave and drowned after she managed to get the little girl to safety. That site carries Anna's name and the tradition that her cry was heard by fishermen around Carraig Anna (Ó Catháin 1975, 120–21).

9. In chapter 34 of Liam O'Flaherty's *Famine* (1937), a novel based on the author's research about the Great Irish Famine, the local landlord brings a large force of police to the Black Valley to seize the sheep of tenants who defaulted on their rent. Tenants alerted by barking dogs drive their sheep into the safety of the mountains. A furious Chadwick threatens the tenants with eviction (1984, 259–60).

10. Sir George Charles Bingham (1800–1888) was known for his cruelty to tenants and his antipathy to his Catholic tenants. Finlay Don quoted Bingham in *Landlords and Tenants in Ireland* (1881) as saying that he "would not breed paupers to pay priests" (Meehan 2003, 139).

11. Mr. S. was Samuel Stock; Mr. B. was William Bennett. Before leaving Erris, Bennett "left with the minister, and the neighboring agent of the principal proprietor, a considerable quantity of carrot, turnip and mangel-wurzel seed, for the benefit of such of the poor as they could influence and control" (1847, 31).

12. In fact, in 1847 the American government lent the New England Committee for the Relief of Ireland and Scotland the *Jamestown* to use as a relief vessel. This loan was the first instance when a ship of the line was made available to private citizens for a foreign voyage.

13. James O'Donnell was a local landlord who received four bushels of Indian corn and forty pounds from the Central Relief Committee for relief expenses for Erris.

14. Nicholson refers to the belief among the Congregationalists of her youth that man is "lost." Puritan followers of John Calvin believed that only those elected would be saved and saved only by God's grace.

15. Nicholson may be referring to the attack on landlords. In the autumn and winter of 1847, six landlords were killed and one badly wounded (Woodham-Smith 1962, 324).

16. Phineas slayed Zimri and Cozbi, who brought on plague by intermarrying with Midiamite women (Num. 25:6–18).

17. The curate was probably Samuel Stock's curate John Greene.

18. The letter is unsigned, but textual evidence suggests that Nicholson was the author of the letter.

19. A white coffin or coffin of white boards was a mark of a decent burial. Maurya's last speech in John Millington Synge's *Riders to the Sea* concludes, "Bartley will have a fine coffin out of the white boards and a deep grave surely. What more can we want than that? (1968, 27; McCormack 2006, 246–47, 249).

20. A Rose Wilson died in the rectory at Newport in 1873 at the age of seventy. She is buried in Newport Churchyard (*Thom's Dublin Directory* 1847, 299).

21. Walshe refused to pay his Poor Rate and took no part in local relief efforts (Nolan 1997, 114).

22. The Mullet villages of Tiraun, Mullaroghoe, and Clogher were cleared (*Dublin Evening Post*, Feb. 8, 1848; see Bowen 1970, 191).

23. Walshe objected to the bad press he received about the evictions, and an exchange of letters followed in the *Tyrawly Herald*.

24. Novelist and historian William Hamilton Maxwell (1792–1850) was born in Newry, County Down. As a boy, he saw two United Irishmen hanged. After

his ordination, he served in curacies before he was given the prebendary of Balla, County Mayo; however, he preferred to spend his days hunting and fishing, the activities that informed his best-known work, *Wild Sports of the West* (1832). See McCabe 2009, 4:447–48.

25. In 1996 there were still driftwood tree trunks on Daly land next to the Granuaile castle ruins.

26. Citing her source as the Archaeological Society founded in Dublin in 1840, Nicholson begins with David O'Dowda's sons David and James, who were killed during the Williamite Wars, David at the Boyne and James at Aughrim. David's fourth son, Dominick, continued the O'Dowda line. Thaddeus, Dominick's third son, joined the Austrian army and married a German, Antonia Wippler; their third son, James, was known as Baron O'Dowda. His godfather gave him a commission in the Imperial Army. Heir to an estate in Ballycollen, he improved the area with a road to Ballina and Castlene. Implicated as a rebel in 1798, he was executed at Killala. Nicholson knew James's son Thaddeus.

27. In 1998, during the observances of the bicentenary of the Rebellion of 1798, Taoiseach Bertie Ahern unveiled a memorial to James O'Dowda in Bonnicon-lon (McHale 1988–89, 11–20).

28. The *Tyrawly Herald* reported in January 1847 that the Ballina and Ardnaree Relief Committee had distributed 1,387 quarts of soup each day to 563 families of the expense of twenty-three pounds (Meehan 2003, 61).

29. While a link with Bourke has not been established, it is tempting to speculate that Walter Bourke, QC, who was admitted to the Connaught Bar in 1838, may be an ancestor of Mary Bourke Robinson (b. 1939), a native of Ballina, barrister, and senator representing Trinity College Dublin, who was elected president of the Republic of Ireland in 1990.

30. Alphonse de Lamartine (1790–1869) was the French writer and politician who helped found and declare the Second Republic in 1848. Nicholson would have admired him for his efforts to end slavery. When he was not a successful presidential candidate, he retired from politics.

31. None is better remembered in this regard than the Rev. Robert Potter, Church of Ireland curate at Louisburg. Potter worked closely with Patrick MacManus, parish priest of Kilgeever. Indeed, it was undoubtedly Potter and MacManus that the traveler Asenath Nicholson found having dinner together when she visited Louisburg in 1847. When she expressed surprise at the sight, the priest assured her he could be no other than a friend to the Church of Ireland curate who was such a warmhearted friend to the poor (*Annals* 1998, 137; Bowen 1970, 136). Shortly before he died of typhus fever, Potter wrote to the *Mayo Constitution* on January 19, 1847, to praise Father MacManus for his work and to say, "Thank God the clergy of the Roman Catholic and Protestant churches all meet each other throughout Ireland

in the broadfront platform of humanity like brothers and friends" (Bowen 1970, 136; Sheehy 1991, 124).

32. James Berry (1842–1914) published an account of Doolough in his *Tales of the West of Ireland* (1966, 39–42). His narrative is based on stories he heard from his parents' generation. In Berry's account four hundred people perish on the Doolough walk. Although the two accounts differ about the scale of the loss, the accounts agree on the sense of loss and the resentment of those individuals who did not do enough to help the poor. For many years, the human rights organization Afri sponsored a walk through the Doolough Pass in support of human rights; the eleventh walk in 1998 was called the *Ireland's Welcome to the Stranger* Walk. The 1998 walk program included an appreciation of Nicholson written by Margaret Kelleher. See also Lyons n.d., 63.

33. There is a monument to John Christopher Garvey to the right of the altar, a stone inscribed, "Erected by his afflicted widow to the memory of her beloved husband, John Christopher Garvey, JPBL, 1856 whose mortal remains repose near the altar of Murrisk. He died April 5, AD 1856/aged 48 years. Blessed are the dead which die in the Lord."

7. Back to Cork

1. Although it is most likely that Nicholson visited the Presentations, the Sisters of Mercy had also opened a convent in Tuam in 1846 at the invitation of Archbishop John McHale. They set about efforts to relieve famine distress by providing care and employment for poor girls. The Mercies are also remembered locally for their part in caring for cholera victims in 1847 (O'Connell 1950, 85).

2. At same time, Nicholson praised the Galway workhouse, its energetic and kind matron, its good food, and its policy of allowing more contact between parents and children than was permitted in other workhouses (*Annals* 1998, 146).

3. It was the Jesuits who had the Jesuit Piscatorial School in the Claddagh (Hatton 1993, 216).

4. The 1847 Destitute Poor (Ireland) Act (10 Vict., c.7), known popularly as the "Soup Kitchen Act," addressed the need to provide direct food relief for the poor. Although the act was passed in February, the program did not really begin until the summer of 1847.

5. The numbers of no-parent children admitted to the Cork Union workhouse between March 1848 and August 1850 were identified as 31 percent deserted children, 67 percent orphaned children, and 2 percent foundlings. The cohort of children made up 60 percent of the Cork Union workhouse in 1847 (O'Mahony 2005, 103, table 29.2).

6. Annals of the South Presentation Convent, Cork, 300.

7. Charles Gavan Duffy (1816–1903), Irish nationalist and statesman, was born in County Monaghan. He came of age during the period of nationalists' agitation for the Repeal of the Act of Union. Trained for the bar, he edited a Catholic paper in Belfast from 1839 to 1842, when he returned to Dublin and joined Thomas Davis and John Dillon in founding the *Nation*, which had a circulation of more than ten thousand by 1844. The following year he published the influential *Ballad Poetry of Ireland* (1845). The Young Irelanders broke with Daniel O'Connell when O'Connell called on the Repealers to eschew violence. Duffy joined other young Irelanders in the unsuccessful 1848 Rising and was transported to Van Diemen's Land (Tasmania). Duffy found great welcome in Australia, where he settled as a barrister in Melbourne and was elected to the legislature. Returning to Europe for medical treatment in 1874, he was appointed a Knight Commander of the Most Distinguished Order of Saint Michael and Saint George in 1877. (He had been knighted in 1873.) He established himself as a journalist in Nice, where he lived until his death in 1903. He is buried with the Young Irelanders at Glasnevin Cemetery in Dublin.

William Smith O'Brien (1803–64) was born at Dromoland, the O'Brien home in County Clare. His grandfather Sir Edward O'Brien had opposed the Act of Union. O'Brien was elected to Parliament from Clare in 1826; he later represented Limerick from 1835 to 1848. He joined Daniel O'Connell's Repeal Association in 1844 but left the association in 1846 over O'Connell's prohibition of the use of physical force. O'Brien subsequently joined the more radical nationalists to found the Irish Confederation, the small force of Confederates who staged an unsuccessful rising, really a skirmish, in Ballingarry, County Tipperary, on July 29, 1848. Tried for high treason in Clonmel, O'Brien's sentence of death was reduced to transportation to Van Diemen's Land. He was pardoned in 1854; however, he was forbidden to return to the United Kingdom. Two years later he was permitted to return to Ireland. He died at the age of sixty in Bangor, Wales, in June 1864.

8. Richard Boyle (1809–68), the Fourth Earl of Shannon (Park), would have lived in Castle Martyr during the Great Irish Famine.

9. Edward Walsh (1805–50) was born near Kiskeam, County Cork. A schoolteacher at Millstreet and later in Waterford, he is remembered as a nationalist poet and a friend of Charles Gavin Duffy, and his work appeared in the *Nation*. He is best known for his *Irish Jacobite Poetry* (1844) and *Irish Popular Songs* (1847). In 1848 he accepted a position as schoolmaster to young convicts at Spike Island. While he was a prisoner at Spike Island, John Mitchel met Walsh, an episode Mitchel described in his *Jail Journal* (1854). He saw a tall, shabbily dressed man approach him who grasped both of Mitchel's hands with reverence and said tearfully how he tried to get the chance to see Mitchel while he was at Spike Island. Mitchel recognized him as the author of "Mo Chaoibhín Chnó" (My Nutty Branch). Walsh went from Spike

Island to the schoolroom at the Cork workhouse. He died in Cork in 1850 (Mitchel 1921, 11).

10. The Levy Sheet Music Collection at Johns Hopkins University has a copy of the sheet music for "The Soldier's Grave," the full title of which is "The Soldier's Grave: Monody on the Death of Sir John Moore, Poetry by the Rev. Chas. Wolfe, the Music by Thomas Williams."

11. Charles Wolfe (1791–1821), a relative of Theobald Wolfe Tone, was born in Dublin, educated at Trinity College Dublin. He is best known for his poem "The Burial of Sir John Moore" (ca. 1814), describing the burial of Moore, where he fell after he was fatally wounded at the battle of Corruna (1809). Wolfe died in Cove on February 21, 1823. Some of the victims of the *Lusitania* are buried in the Clonmel graveyard. There is a memorial to Wolfe in St. Patrick's Cathedral in Dublin.

12. The entrance to Mount Patrick, the Mathew Tower, is located three miles east of Cork between Dunkettle and Little Island, almost across from Blackrock Castle. The restored tower is a private residence. The chimney piece has been damaged. The statue of Father Mathew outside the tower has been defaced in the same way; its head and arm are missing.

13. There is a story and an engraving of the dedication, held on October 30, 1843 ("Temperance Monument at Cork," *Illustrated London News*, Nov. 18, 1843, 1).

14. Nicholson's source for the line "Ireland, I love thee still" is a mystery. Christine Kinealy identified the lines in a late unpublished poem written by Maria Edgeworth to her sister Honora Beaufort in May 1949. The poem begins: "Ireland, with all thy faults, thy follies too, I love thee still" (2013, 158). Nicholson could not have known the poem because it did not appear until Augustus J. C. Hare published his edition of *The Life and Letters of Maria Edgeworth* in 1894. There is a single mention of a song with the title "Ireland, I Love Thee Still" in the report of a St. Patrick's Day concert in Ashburton, New Zealand, when a Mr. Higgins sang "Ireland, I Love Thee Still" as an encore to his rendition of "The Wearing of the Green" ("'The Wearing of the Green': St. Patrick's Day Annual Concert," *Ashburton Guardian*, Mar. 18, 1893, 2).

15. Nicholson sneered at Charles E. Trevelyan's *The Irish Crisis* (1848) when he asserted that there was not a single case of embezzlement among the two thousand hired relief officers (*Annals* 1998, 106). Nicholson responded that there were some hired officers who lived well while they were engaged to care for the hungry. She also criticized the upper-class women who picked through the clothes collected for the poor and appropriated the better garments for themselves.

16. Nicholson was thinking of the lines from Psalm 137, "If I forget thee, O Jerusalem, let my right hand forget her cunning. If I do not remember thee, let my tongue cleave to the roof of my mouth."

8. Peace and Progress, 1848–52

1. Unpublished letter to William Goodell, May 8, 1849, Oberlin Special Collections Library, Oberlin, OH.

2. *Vegetarian Advocate* (1848): 51. I am grateful to J. R. T. Gregory for this information. William Horsell (1807–63), who was associated with the Hydropathic Institution in Ramsgate, Kent, was a leading figure in the London Vegetarian Association. He or J. S. Hibberd, the horticulturist, who was joint editor of the *Vegetarian Advocate* (1848–51), wrote a favorable review of Nicholson's "Kitchen Philosophy." Horsell commented, "It contained some remarks which ought not to have appeared." There is a copy of the *Vegetarian Advocate* in the British Library.

3. The pamphlet was published in London by William Horsell in 1849. See J. Smith 1863, 247. The headnote to Bennett's section describes him as now living at Brooklam Lodge, Betchworth, near Reigate, Surrey. Bennett is also listed at the author of *Gilpin in London* (1430 b2). He edited *Pages from the Life of the Apostle Paul* (1873) with Elizabeth Bennett.

4. John Bunyan (1628–88), the author of *The Pilgrim's Progress* (1678, 1684), had little formal education. He became a member of the Baptist Church in 1653 and became a deacon and a preacher. Imprisoned for preaching without a license, he spent twelve years in the county jail in Bedford between 1660 and 1672.

5. Daniel Defoe, Isaac Watts, and William Blake are also buried there. The Friends' Burial Ground is nearby.

6. The grave marker has since been revived. Bunyan's recumbent effigy was restored in 1922 (Muirhead 1956, 135).

7. Bunyan's birthplace was destroyed in the late twentieth century; the site is marked with a stone pillar. The cottage where he lived after 1655 at 17 St. Cuthbert's Street was demolished in 1838. The 1910 Baedeker (383) says the cottage where Bunyan lived after his marriage was still extant.

8. The radical Lord Henry Brougham (1778–1868), a prominent abolitionist, served as lord chancellor in the ministry of Earl Grey and was a Francophile. In 1848 he was interested in becoming a naturalized citizen of France, but the Legislative Assembly required that he relinquish his peerage. He died at his villa near Cannes.

9. "The Landing at Boulogne," *Illustrated London News*, Apr. 1849, 365. An article about the Paris Peace Conference was also published in the *Friend* 7 (1849): 164–66.

10. There is a modern hospital on the site now.

11. See Jacques Louis David's painting *The Coronation of Emperor Napoleon I and the Crowning of Empress Josephine in Notre-Dame Cathedral in Paris, 2 December 1804* (1806–7). Nicholson would not have seen the painting at the Louvre because it was hung at Versailles in 1848.

12. Nicholson could not have visited the garden at the Château de Malmaison because, in 1848, Maria Cristina, dowager queen of Spain, who owned the property, did not open the gardens to the public. Daniel Osiris (1828–1907) bought the château from Maria Cristina and returned it, refurbished, to the state. It is a Napoleonic museum.

13. Alphonse Marie Louis de Prat de Lamartine (1790–1869) is better known for his influential *Méditationes Poétiques* (1820) and *Histoire des Girondiris* (1847) than for his political career. Although he was influential in establishing the Second Republic and served as minister for foreign affairs from February to May 1848, his political career was short-lived.

14. Burritt wrote:

If there is to be one man in America above any other, who ought to be present at that august demonstration, thou art the man—representing all the Christian philanthropies of America in your own character and labor. We look forward to an Assembly which shall make a profound impression upon the whole civilized world. The great Lamartine, and leading men of the French National Assembly will be there; Cobden, his compère, and many of the enlightened legislators from Germany, & other continental countries will be there, and hundreds of good men and true from both sides of the English Channel, and of the Atlantic. There you would meet probably 500 or 1000 of the purest men of England, many of whom would greet you as a long tried brother in works of love and liberty for men of every color and country. (Curti 1929, 55)

15. The Liberty League was founded by Arthur Tappan to put abolitionism on the political agenda. William Lloyd Garrison and the American Anti-Slavery Society had no confidence that abolitionism would be addressed by the political process.

16. William Rathbone (1819–1902), merchant and philanthropist, represented Liverpool in Parliament from 1868 to 1880. He was present at St. Patrick's Church on July 15, 1843, when Father Mathew gave the pledge to the city's children. It was the beginning of a friendship that lasted until the Capuchin's death in 1855. Rathbone shared Father Mathew's concern for the poor. He also supported nursing initiatives, particularly the education of nurses. Rathbone's nursing interest led him to ask Florence Nightingale to start a training school for nurses in Liverpool (Woodham-Smith 1951, 181).

17. The William Rathbone V section of the University of Liverpool's Rathbone Collection includes the Letterbook of the New England Relief Society, Liverpool (May 12, 1847–August 14, 1847).

18. May 8, 1849, letter to William Goodell. Nicholson may have been referring to the Naval and Military Bible Society that was founded in 1779.

19. Thomas Jones Barker (1815–82) was known primarily as a military painter. The National Portrait Gallery also owns Barker's *The Relief of Lucknow* (1857), his iconic painting of the defense of the British at Lucknow, an incident that occurred during the Indian Rebellion of 1857. Two Irish writers have written works based on Lucknow: Dion Boucicault wrote a play, "based on the letters of a lady," called *Jessie Brown; or, The Relief of Lucknow* (1858), and the twentieth-century novelist J. G. Farrell wrote *The Siege of Krishnapur*, volume 2 of his *Empire Trilogy*, that was based on the memories of the Lucknow survivors. *The Siege of Krishnapur* won the Booker Prize in 1973.

20. Baptist Noel (1798/1799–1873) was a Church of England clergyman known as a powerful, "silver-toned" preacher and prolific writer. He was particularly concerned with the spiritual needs of the urban poor. In 1836 he visited the Achill Mission on behalf of the English evangelicals and recorded his approval of the advances that Nangle had made with his colony in his *Notes on a Short Tour through the Midland Counties of Ireland in the Summer of 1836 with Observations on the Condition of the Peasantry* (1837).

21. Nicholson letter to William Goodell, May 8, 1849, William Goodell Family Papers, Record Group 30/029, Oberlin College Archives, Series II, 1813–1882, Box 1, Correspondence, 1826–1876, Incoming 1828–1850, Box 2.

22. Zachary Taylor (1785–1850), twelfth president of the United States, was elected as the Whig candidate for president in 1848. He died of cholera on July 9, 1850, and was succeeded by his vice president, Millard Fillmore.

23. Nicholson said that she heard from Elizabeth Griffith, the wife of Rev. Valentine Griffith, rector of Templecrone, County Donegal, in the spring of 1849; however, her letter said that the people of Arranmore had recovered, that they had received relief from England, and that "they had saved as much for seed as they could and not starve" (*Annals* 1998, 78).

24. Nicholson described the little school in Kilcommon in *Annals*. "Here is a humble cabin the kind Miss Carey commenced a little school to do what she could to keep alive the scattered lambs of that desolate parish in order that she might give them, through some relief society, a little food once a day and teach them to read. Her cabin was soon filled, and with these poor children received instruction, and for a year she continued her labor of love with but little remuneration and at last, with much regret, was obliged to return them to their mountain home—perhaps to perish" (*Annals* 1998, 98).

25. After his ordination in 1798, Leigh Richmond (1772–1827) went to the Isle of Wight to take up the curacy of the Church of England at Brading. The stories that he wrote were published by the Religious Tract Society in a collection titled *Annals of the Poor* (1814).

26. Nicholson says that she drank from the silver cup at the home of a Mr. O'Donol [*sic*]; however, she does not mention the incident in her Irish books (*LP* 1853, 161).

27. Nicholson would have been cheered by the sight of a later generation of donkeys working the tread wheel to raise well water continuing to charm children, and she would have approved of *There's More to Explore at Carisbrooke Castle* (1994), the English Heritage activity pamphlet designed for today's young visitors.

28. By 2000 Blackgang Chine, like Westport House, had morphed into a family theme park.

29. According to *The Isle of Wight Coastal Path*, tourists are cautioned about coastal erosion caused by the gault clay under the chalk cliffs, causing the land to slip in the wet weather. http://www.isle-of-wight-information.co.uk.

30. Sovereign Grace Publishers reissued *The Dairyman's Daughter and Other Personal Testimonies* in 2001, and it is available on the Safe-Haven Books Online website.

31. An engraving titled *Grave of the Dairyman's Daughter, Arreton, Isle of Wight* by Rock and Co., dated June 26, 1860, depicts the churchyard with the two Wallbridge graves. Elizabeth's has the longer inscription.

32. Mr. John T. Cooper, the owner of the Dairyman's Cottage in 2000, has marked the site with a sign. He said that before the cottage become known as the Dairyman's Cottage, it was known as "Spicer's." It is near the Fighting Cock Pub in Hale Commons. The building across the road was formerly a Methodist meetinghouse dated 1837. It is surprising that Nicholson did not make note of it.

33. The names appear in the Dairyman's Cottage guest book. When the author visited the Dairyman's Cottage in July 2000, John T. Cooper produced a photocopy of the guest book that included Nicholson's entry. Of the three guests, Nicholson might have known or known about Chase (1789–1882), a Presbyterian clergyman and educator who published a letter about the Fugitive Slave Act in the *Liberator*, the abolitionist paper once edited by Joshua Leavitt. Nicholson's entry is quoted with permission, courtesy of Carisbrooke Castle Museum.

34. The dating is a little confusing. Nicholson says in *Loose Papers* that she left London for Southampton and the Isle of Wight on July 29, 1849 (1853, 39).

35. Mr. Cooper said he thought that the armchair was bequeathed to Rev. James C. Richmond and that it served as the Chancel Chair in Richmond's church. Richmond's name appears in the cottage guest book on August 26 and September 16, 1849.

36. Theodore Frelinghuysen (1787–1862), an evangelistic Christian and ardent abolitionist, was the chairman of the American Tract Society between 1842 and 1846. He served in the US Senate from 1829 to 1835.

37. Nicholson's experience with cottage hospitality in Ireland was probably associated with the popular "hospitality rewarded" legend so popular in the Irish countryside.

9. Peace and Progress, 1850–51

1. Despite Burritt's reputation as a linguist, Paris conference attendees discovered that he was unable to ask for directions in French (Tyrrell 1987, 170).

2. Burritt's temperance sketch "The Influence of the Drunkard" was included in *The Miscellaneous Writings of Elihu Burritt* (1850, 96–97). In his journal for October 7, 1841, Burritt wrote of hearing Joshua Leavitt saying that he "listened to the most thrilling and powerful speeches. Mr. Leavitt of New York made a speech worthy of a statesman and orator, scholar and Christian" (Curti 1929, 14). See also Tolis 1968.

3. The matter of the disputed border was settled by the treaty that established the border at the latitude 54"40'. The controversy gave rise to the slogan "Fifty-Four Forty or Fight."

4. Letter from Manchester, February 6, 1847, to Quaker James Clark of Somerset, Joseph Sturge's cousin (Curti 1929, 45). See Tolis 1968, 162–65; and Webb 1999, 156.

5. There had been another unsuccessful rising in Paris the previous month, on June 13.

6. There was not unanimous admiration for Hugo's vision. John Greenleaf Whittier regarded Hugo as one of "the modern Satanic school" (Tyrrell 1987, 170). Honoré Daumier, who considered the Paris Peace Conference participants naive, lampooned the conference (Tyrrell 1987, 169). The National Portrait Gallery's exhibition *Peace Ridiculed: Caricatures by Honoré Daumier* (February 11–October 23, 2011) featured Daumier's series of satirical images of the leaders of the international peace movement. See also *Proceedings of the Second Generation* 1849. The secretaries of the congress were Elihu Burritt and Henry Richard. Asenath Nicholson is listed as a guest in appendix 4, "British Visitors."

7. http://american-miniatures.blogspot.com/2006/04/rogers-nathaniel-portrait-of-anne.html.

8. Burritt knew accommodations would be scarce. He wrote in his journal 14 on July 30, 1850, that "hotels are overflowing, we shall find it difficult to secure accommodations for all" (Burritt Collection, New Britain, CT, Library).

9. See the discussion of preparations for the Frankfurt meeting in Curti 1929, 178–83.

10. See the accounts of the Frankfurt meeting in *Friend* 8 (1850): 208.

11. The station was located on the site of the present Willy Brandt Platz.

12. My colleague Diana Ben-Merre has pointed out that the gambling scene reminds one of the opening scene of George Eliot's novel *Daniel Deronda* (1876).

13. She would have also approved of Thomas Wallace Knox's description of Wiesbaden as one of the "Gambling Hells of Germany" in his *Underground; or, Life below the Surface . . . Gambling and Its Horrors* (1876).

14. Nicholson spelled the name "Sterne," but it appeared as "Stern" in the English census of 1851.

15. US Census of 1910, Queens, Fourth Ward. If Nicholson's Frederick was eleven in 1850, he would have been born in 1839.

16. The British Library has a later edition of *Lights and Shades* that was published in 1858 in London by William Tweedie, 337 Strand.

17. The lines were reproduced in the fourth stanza of the poem "The Banks; or, Western Melodies—No.1" that was song to the air "Oh! Blame Not the Bard." The song appeared first in *Niles' Weekly Register* 16 (1819); it was reprinted in "The Postwar Nation Looks Forward" chapter of *The Early American Republic: A Documentary Reader* (Adams 2009, 62).

18. Roscommon-born James Wills (1790–1868) was educated at Trinity College Dublin. Although he was trained for the law, he became by turns a clergyman, a literary man (*Blackwood, University Magazine, Irish Quarterly Review*), a theologian, and a poet.

19. Christine Kinealy's analysis of the British response to the Great Irish Famine concurs with Nicholson's judgment of how crop failure turned into a famine (1995, 342–59).

20. The reviewer was referring to Rev. Sydney Godolphin Osborne's book *Gleaning in the West of Ireland* (1850) that was based on his visit to Ireland in the early summer of 1849. Like Nicholson, his outspoken views brought criticism.

21. Joseph Paxton was the landscape architect for the duke of Devonshire (Auerbach 1999, 47).

22. Men paid three guineas for a season ticket; women paid two.

23. The picture, painted between 1851 and 1852, is in the collection of the Victoria and Albert Museum.

24. There is an account of He Sing, the alleged Chinese mandarin who attended the exhibition opening, in Auerbach 1999, 178, 255.

25. The last paragraph of Nicholson's letter "Distress in Erris," writing to the *Tyrawly Herald and Sligo Intelligencer* (Dec. 2, 1847), begged for money to buy the supplies for women and children to produce cloth and clothing (*Annals* 1998, 102).

26. Nicholson's fictional characters may have been influenced by Henry Mayhew's popular novel *The Adventure of Mr. and Mrs. Sandboys and Family Who Came Up to London to "Enjoy Themselves"* (1851).

27. "In the early forties, Exeter Hall was the centre of the anti-slavery campaign, and the example once stated, its platform began to take into its particular care the cause of oppressed nationalities. Statesmen, weighing one policy against another, have had to ask, 'What will Exeter Hall say?'" (Howard 1907, 5).

28. The order of the daily services held at Exeter Hall at 11:00 a.m. and 6:30 p.m. included a psalm or hymn, a reading from scripture, a prayer, another psalm or hymn, a sermon, a third psalm or hymn, and a concluding prayer.

29. In the United States, the Evangelical Alliance was renamed the World Evangelical Fellowship in 1951. See Kessler 1968, 17.

30. In addition to meeting at the Crystal Palace, the two could have met at the home of Greeley's host, John Chapman, Nicholson's London publisher.

31. Charlotte Elizabeth was another admirer, but she had the good fortune to have lived in Clifden, near Bristol, in 1824 and knew Hannah More.

32. The British Library owns Hannah More's pencil drawing of Barley Wood.

10. Last Years

1. *Illustrated London News*, Aug. 31, 1850, 164. The eleven-hundred-ton ship was built in Boston in 1850 by the shipbuilding firm of Grinnell Minturn. An engraving of the ship appeared with the article (184). The *Cornelius Grinnell* was wrecked off the coast of New Jersey on January 13, 1853, when it ran aground in heavy surf off Squan or Squam Beach. The 234 people aboard were rescued by a surf car.

2. An advertisement for the United States Mail Steamers' New York–Liverpool service listed that fare range for cabin passages in 1855 (Gopsill 1855, 3).

3. Although there is no record of the day the *Cornelius Grinnell* departed in April 1852, we can estimate that the voyage took two weeks. In 1852 the *City of Glasgow* took fourteen days; by 1855 the Cunard Line iron-hulled paddlers made the trip from Liverpool to New York in nine days and ten hours.

4. These poor Irish probably belonged to the St. Patrick's parish founded in 1843, ten years before the Diocese of Brooklyn was created (Sharp 1954, 1:113). The parish later merged with St. Lucy's parish; the combined parish was absorbed by the parish of Mary of Nazareth on January 31, 2011 (Paul Vitello, "Two Catholic Churches in Brooklyn Will Close," *New York Times*, Nov. 15, 2010, A28). I am grateful to John Ridge for information about the Irish in Brooklyn.

5. William Goodell wrote "Slavery to Missouri," a poem about the Missouri Compromise, under the name "Edgar" in the *Providence Gazette*.

6. Northerners tend to pay little attention to the original Fugitive Slave Law of 1793; a second law was passed that carried penalties of fines and imprisonment for individuals who aided runaways. The Fugitive Salve Law hardened the resistance of the North to slavery.

7. http://www.oberlin.edu/archive/holdings/finding/RG30/SG29/biography .html.

8. In her book *Well-Behaved Women Seldom Make History*, Laurel Thatcher Ulrich argues that details are valuable to the writing of women's history because it is a way of accommodating contradiction, provides context, and "lead[s] us out of boxes created by slogans" (2008, 227).

9. In fact, a lady from near Castlegregory, County Kerry, produced a Skellig List composed in 1951. http://irelandsotherpoetry.wordpress.com/2008/03/28 /the-skellig-lists/.

10. The usual spelling of the Irish name is "Granuaile"; her name also appears in an English version as Grace O'Malley.

11. Anne Chambers includes the engraving in her biography of Granuaile (1998, 147).

12. While the Howth abduction is a staple of Granuaile lore, Anne Chambers cites the work of seventeenth-century historian Duald MacFirbis that establishes that the abductor was, in fact, Richard Bourke (Burke) (1998, 72).

13. A lithograph by François Courtin (1820–71) shows the building and its visitors in 1853–54 (Symmes 2005, 98–99).

14. Horace Greeley published *Art and Industry as Represented in the Exhibition at the Crystal Palace, New York 1853–4* (1853).

15. No. 93 Erie Street remains, but 95 was demolished to create the Pennsylvania Railroad's tunnel.

16. The Third Reformed Dutch Church has been replaced by St. Mary's High School.

17. Joseph Pascal Strong (1826–90) was born in Flatbush. Educated at Rutgers College's Dutch Reformed Seminary, he was ordained in 1850. He married Cornelia W. Heyer on June 18, 1851, in New York. He served as pastor of the Third Dutch Reformed Church in Jersey City from 1854 to 1856.

18. An 1857 *New York Directory* indicates that Sanger was still at the same business address but that he was living at 75 East Sixteenth Street. By 1859 Sanger had a business at 22 Cedar Street, but he had joined with his partners, William Cary and Samuel Emerson Howard, to found Cary, Howard & Sanger at 105–107 Chambers Street, the landmark cast-iron Italian Renaissance building designed by Gamaliel King and John Kellum in 1856–57. In 1865 Sanger became a director of the Tenth National Bank at 240 Broadway, a bank later taken over by Jay Gould, "the skunk of Wall Street." The 1870 census lists Sanger and his family as living on an estate valued at thirty thousand dollars on Warburton Avenue in Yonkers; his personal wealth was estimated at fifty thousand dollars.

19. The *Merck Manual* notes that specific infections, including typhoid fever, may be responsible for myofascitis (1997, 870). It should be noted, however, that the

record of her death is inaccurate in other respects. She was sixty-three, not sixty, and she was born in Vermont, not Massachusetts.

20. *Anti-Slavery Advocate* (London) 33 (June 1855): 1. The notice appeared in the *Ohio Anti-Slavery Bugle*.

21. Cemetery records indicate that John White purchased the grave in lot 2247 on January 7, 1848. On his death the title to the grave passed to his heirs.

22. *Friend* (Seventh Month, 1855): 122–23. It is tempting to think that W. B. Yeats may have been referring to Nicholson when he wrote about proselytism in the West of Ireland and mentioned a woman who described meetings in peasant cottages where she "was oppressed and slandered by the powerful because she was on this side of the poor" (1936, 12).

Afterword

1. The American edition of *The Bible in Ireland* was published by the John Day Company in 1927.

2. The reviewer was also critical of Sheppard's borrowing his title from Borrow's *The Bible in Spain*, a book he considered the work of a bigot (Cealtra 1926, 1164).

3. See also F. O'Connor 1959, 38–40, 129–31, 136–37; and 1967, 134–37, 138–39. The other "best description" was William Carleton's "Autobiography."

4. Accounts of travels to Ireland include John McVeagh, *Irish Travel Writing: A Bibliography* (1996); and Allison Lockwood, *Passionate Pilgrims: American Travellers in Great Britain, 1800–1914* (1981, 243–45).

References

Acts of Proceedings of the 84th Regular Session of the General Synod of the Reformed Church in America Convened in Asbury Park, New Jersey, June 1890. 1890. New York: Board of Publications of the Reformed Church in America.

Adams, Sean Patrick, ed. 2009. *The Early American Republic: A Documentary Reader.* Malden, MA: Wiley-Blackwell.

Aldwell, Cork Directory, 1844, 1845. 1846. Cork: Aldwell.

Allen, Donna. 1996. "Westport Methodist Church." *Cathair na Mart* 16: 62–65.

Anbinder, Tyler. 2002. *Five Points: The 19th Century New York City Neighborhood That Invented Tap Dance, Stole Elections and Became the World's Most Notorious Slum.* New York: Plume Book.

Andrews, Helen. 2009. "Gregg, John." In *Dictionary of Irish Biography*, 4:245–46. Cambridge: Cambridge Univ. Press.

Asbury, Herbert. 1928. *The Gangs of New York.* Garden City, NY: Garden City.

Auerbach, Jeffrey A. 1999. *The Great Exhibition of 1851: A Nation on Display.* New Haven, CT: Yale Univ. Press, 1999.

Augustine, Rev. Fr. 1947. *Footprints of Father Theobald Mathew, OFM, Cap., Apostle of Temperance.* Dublin: Gill.

Baedeker, Karl. 1910. *Great Britain: A Handbook for Travellers.* Leipzig: Karl Baedeker.

"The Bank or Western Melodies—No. 1." 2009. *Niles' Weekly Register* 16 (1819). In *The Early American Republic: A Documentary Reader*, edited by Sean Patrick Adams, 62. Malden, MA: Wiley-Blackwell.

Barr, Colin. 2009. "Mac Hale, John." In *Dictionary of Irish Biography*, 4:6–10. Cambridge: Cambridge Univ. Press.

Barron, Hal S. 1984. *Those Who Stayed Behind: Rural Society in Nineteenth-Century New England*. New York: Cambridge Univ. Press.

Bennett, William. 1847. *Narrative of a Recent Journey of Six Weeks in Ireland: In Connection with the Subject of Supplying Small Seed to Some of the Remoter Districts*. London: Charles Gilpin.

Berry, James. 1966. *Tales of the West of Ireland*. Edited by Gertrude M. Horgan. Dublin: Dolmen Press.

Bigelow, Gordon. 1999. "Asenath Nicholson's New Domestic Economy." In *Reclaiming Gender: Transgressive Identities in Modern Ireland*, edited by Marilyn Cohen and Nancy J. Curtin, 145–60. New York: St. Martin's Press.

———. 2003. "Esoteric Solutions: Ireland and the Colonial Critique of Political Economy." In *Fiction, Famine and the Rise of Economics in Victorian Britain and Ireland*, 134–43. New York: Cambridge Univ. Press.

Bowen, Desmond. 1970. *Souperism: Myth or Reality? A Study of Catholics and Protestants during the Great Famine*. Cork: Cork Univ. Press.

Bradford, Sarah H. 1961. *Harriet Tubman: The Moses of Her People*. New York: Corinth.

Brasher, Thomas L. 1970. *Whitman as Editor of the "Brooklyn Daily Eagle."* Detroit: Wayne State Press.

Brown, George Levi. 1905. *Pleasant Valley: The History of Elizabethtown*. Elizabethtown, NY: Post and Gazette Press.

Brown, Robert. 1889–90. *Paisley Poets: With Brief Memoirs of Them and Selections from Their Poetry*. Paisley: J. and J. Cook.

Bryan, Deirdre. 2009. "Nicholson, Asenath." In *Dictionary of Irish Biography*, edited by James McGuire and James Quinn, 6:916. Cambridge: Cambridge Univ. Press.

Burke's Irish Family Records. 1976. 2 vols. London: Burke's Peerage.

Burritt, Elihu. 1847. *Four Months in Skibbereen*. London: Charles Gilpin.

———. 1850. "The Influence of the Drunkard." In *Miscellaneous Writings of Elihu Burritt*, 96–98. 2nd ed. Worcester, MA: Thomas Drew.

Burrows, Edwin G., and Mike Wallace. 1999. *Gotham: A History of New York City to 1898*. New York: Oxford Univ. Press.

Carleton, William. 1834. Preface to *Tales of Ireland*. Dublin: Curry.

Carville, Geraldine. 1973. *The Heritage of Holy Cross*. Belfast: Blackstaff Press.

Casey, Christine. 2005. *Dublin: The City within the Grand and Royal Canals and the Circular Road with the Phoenix Park*. The Buildings of Ireland. New Haven, CT: Yale Univ. Press.

Centennial Committee. 1884. *Centennial Celebration of the Settlement of Chelsea, Vermont, September 4, 1884*. Keene: Sentinel.

Central Relief Committee, Dublin. 1865. *Distress in Ireland: Extracts from Correspondence*. Vol. 1. Dublin: Society of Friends.

Chadwick, Loraine. 2012. "Asenath Nicholson's Irish Journeys." In *Atlas of the Great Irish Famine, 1845–52*, edited by John Crowley, William J. Smyth, and Mike Murphy, 476–81. Cork: Cork Univ. Press.

Chambers, Anne. 1998. *Granuaile: The Life and Times of Grace O'Malley c. 1530–1603*. Dublin: Wolfhound Press.

Chaney, George Leonard. 1877. *Hollis Street Church from Mather Byles to Thomas Starr King, 1732–1861: Two Discourses Given in Hollis Street Meeting House, December 31, 1876, and January 7, 1877*. Cambridge: George H. Ellis.

Chatterton, Lady Henrietta. 1839. *Rambles in the South of Ireland during the Year 1838*. London: Saunders and Otley.

Chelsea Historical Society. 1984. *Chelsea, Vermont, 1784–1984: Shire Town*. Barre, VT: Chelsea Historical Society.

Chevigny, Bell Gale. 1976. *The Woman and the Myth: Margaret Fuller's Life and Writing*. Old Westbury, CT: Feminist Press.

Clarke, Aidan. 2009. "Bedell, William." In *Dictionary of Irish Biography*, 1:411–12. Cambridge: Cambridge Univ. Press.

Clarke, Frances. 2009a. "Chatterton, Henrietta (Georgiana)." In *Dictionary of Irish Biography*, 2:279. Cambridge: Cambridge Univ. Press.

———. 2009b. "Mulally, Teresa." In *Dictionary of Irish Biography*, 6:740–41. Cambridge: Cambridge Univ. Press.

Clubb, Henry. 1855. "The Late Asenath Nicholson." *Water-Cure Journal* 20, no. 2: 30–31.

Coleman, Ambrose, OP. 1933. "Book of the Month." Review of *The Bible in Ireland*. *Irish Rosary* 4 (June): 388–92.

Coleman, James. 1904. "Voyage of the *Jamestown*." *Cork Historical and Archaeological Society*, 2nd ser., 10, no. 61: 23–31.

Colgan, Maurice. 1999. Review of *Annals of the Famine in Ireland*. *Irish Studies Review* 7, no. 2: 246–48.

Colum, Padraic. 1927. "Breadless Ireland." Review of *The Bible in Ireland*. *Nation*, Apr. 20, 450.

Combre [Coombre], George. 1860. *A System of Phrenology*. New York: Harper & Bros.

Comstock, John Moore. 1944. *History of Chelsea*. Chelsea, VT: n.p.

Cooney, Dudley Levistone. 2006. *Sharing the Word: A History of the Bible Society of Ireland*. Blackrock: Columba Press.

Corwin, Edward T. 1902. "Joseph Pascal Strong." In *A Manual of the Reformed Church in America*, 756. New York: Board of the Reformed Church in North America.

Cross, Whitney R. 1950. *The Burned-Over District: The Social and Intellectual History of Enthusiastic Religion in Western New York, 1800–1850*. Ithaca, NY: Cornell Univ. Press.

Crowe, Catríona. 2003. Review of *Ireland's Welcome to the Stranger*. *Irish Economic and Social History* 30: 165–66.

Crowley, John, William J. Smyth, and Mike Murphy, eds. 2012. *Atlas of the Great Irish Famine, 1845–52*. Cork: Cork Univ. Press.

Cullen, Fintan. 2004. *The Irish Face: Redefining the Irish Portrait*. London: National Portrait Gallery.

Curti, Merle. 1929. *The American Peace Crusade, 1815–1860*. Durham, NC: Duke Univ. Press.

———. 1937. *The Learned Blacksmith: The Letters and Journals of Elihu Burritt*. New York: Wilson Erickson.

Daly, Mary. 1986. *The Famine in Ireland*. Dundalk: Dublin Historical Association.

D'Arcy, Gerard. 1969. *Portrait of the Grand Canal*. Wicklow: Transportation Research Associates.

Davis, Hugh. 1990. *Joshua Leavitt: Evangelical Abolitionist*. Baton Rouge: Louisiana State Univ. Press.

Davis, Richard. 1998. *Revolutionary Imperialist: William Smith O'Brien, 1803–1864*. Dublin: Lilliput Press.

De Brún, Pádraic. 1986. "Tralee's Voters in 1835." *Journal of the Kerry Archaeological and Historical Society* 19: 143–48.

Deignan, Tom. 2004. "A New Yorker in Famine Ireland." *Irish Voice* (Feb. 18–24): 10.

DeKay, James Tertius. 1995. *Chronicles of the Frigate* Macedonia, *1809–1922*. New York: W. W. Norton.

de Tocqueville, Alexis. 2003. *Recollections of the French Revolution of 1848.* Edited by J. P. Mayer and A. P. Kerr. New Brunswick, NJ: Transaction.

Diner, Hasia. 1996. "'The Most Irish City in the Union': The Era of Great Migration, 1844–1847." In *The Irish in New York*, edited by Ronald H. Bayer and Timothy J. Meagher. Baltimore: Johns Hopkins Univ. Press.

Dodge, Bertha S. 1987. *Vermont by Choice.* Shelbourne: New England Press.

Douglass, Frederick. 1994. "Appendix: My Bondage and My Freedom." In *Autobiographies.* New York: Library of America.

———. 1979. "Slavery in the Pulpit of the Evangelical Alliance." In *The Frederick Douglass Papers: Series One—Speeches, Debates and Interviews,* edited by John W. Blassingame, 1:407. New Haven, CT: Yale Univ. Press.

Dowling, A. 1978. *Johnstown, Galmoy and Urlingford Parishes.* Freshford: Wellbrook Press.

Dowling, P. J. 1968. *The Hedge Schools of Ireland.* Cork: Mercier Press.

Draper, James. 1860. *History of Spencer, Massachusetts, from its Earliest Settlement to the Year 1860.* Worcester, MA: Henry J. Howland.

The Dublin Almanac and General Register of Ireland for the Year 1845. 1845. London: Pettigrew and Oulton.

Dublin Post Office Annual Directory and Calendar. 1844. Dublin: John S. Folds.

Dun, Finlay. 1881. *Landlords and Tenants in Ireland.* London: Longmans, Green.

Elizabeth, Charlotte. 1838. *Letters from Ireland, MDCCCXXXVII.* London: R. B. Seeley and W. Burnside.

———. 1844. *The Works of Charlotte Elizabeth.* 2 vols. New York: M. W. Dodd.

Evans, Estyn. 1957. *Irish Folk Ways.* London: Routledge and Kegan Paul.

Everett, Nigel. 2000. *Wild Gardens: The Lost Demenses of Bantry Bay.* Bantry: Haford Press.

Farrow, G. 1993. *A History of Carisbrooke Church, St. Mary the Virgin.* 2nd ed. Newport: Biltmore Printer.

Fegan, Melissa. 2002. *Literature and the Great Irish Famine, 1845–1919.* Oxford: Clarendon Press.

Fisher, Lydia. 1847. *Letters from the Kingdom of Kerry in the Year 1845.* Dublin: Webb and Chapman.

Fitz, Connie Hendren. 1999. "Witness to Suffering: Witness to the Famine." Review of *Annals of the Famine in Ireland. Irish Literary Supplement* (Spring): 8.

Flayhart, William. 2000. *The American Line, 1871–1982.* New York: W. W. Norton.

Fletcher, Robert S. 1971. *A History of Oberlin College from Its Foundation through the Civil War.* Vol. 1. 1943. Reprint, New York: Arno Press.

Flynn, Peter. 1998. Review of *Annals of the Famine in Ireland. Studies* 87, no. 347: 320–22.

Foley, Patrick. 1903. *The Ancient and Present State of the Skelligs, Blasket Islands, Dunquin and the West of Dingle.* Baile Átha Cliath: An Cló Chumann.

Forbes, Robert Bennett. 1847. *The Voyage of the* Jamestown *on Her Errand of Mercy.* Boston: Eastburn Press.

Forster, T. C. 1846. *Letters on the Condition of the People of Ireland.* London: Chapman and Hall.

Fraser, James. 1844. *A Handbook for Travellers in Ireland.* Dublin: Curry.

Friel, Brian. 1999. *Essays, Diaries, Interviews, 1964–1999.* Edited by Christopher Murray. London: Faber and Faber.

Friel, Mary. 2004. *Dancing as a Social Pastime in the South-East of Ireland, 1800–1897.* Maynooth Studies in Local History 54. Dublin: Four Courts.

Fuller, Margaret. 1855. *Women in the Nineteenth Century and Kindred Papers Relating to the Sphere, Condition and Duties of Women.* Boston: J. P. Jewett.

"Funeral Service for a Christian Worker." 1889. *Homiletic Review* 18: 382.

Garner, William. 1981. *Ennis Architectural Heritage.* Dublin: An Foras Forbatha.

Garrison, William Lloyd. 1973. *No Union with Slave-Holders, 1841–1849: The Letters of William Lloyd Garrison, III.* Edited by Walter M. Merrill. Cambridge, MA: Belknap Press of Harvard Univ.

Gillespie, Elgy, ed. 1973. *The Liberties of Dublin.* Dublin: E. and T. O'Brien.

Gilmartin, Mary. 1999. "The Irish Travels of Asenath Nicholson in 1844–45." In *Text and Image: Social Construction of Regional Knowledges,* edited by Anne Buttimer, Stanley Brunn, and Ute Wardenga, 245–55. Leipzig: Selbstverlag Institut für Länderkunde.

Goodman, Matthew. 2008. *The Sun and the Moon: The Remarkable True Account of Hoaxers, Showmen, Dueling Journalists and Lunar Man-Bats in Nineteenth Century New York.* New York: Basic Books.

Gopsill, James. 1856. *Jersey City Directory, 1855; or, Directory of Jersey City for 1855–6.* Jersey City: Publications Office.

Graham, Sylvester. 1833. *A Lecture on Epidemic Diseases Generally and Particularly the Spasmodic Cholera, Delivered in New York in 1832.* New York: n.p.

Grant, Elizabeth, of Rothiemurchus. 1999. *The Highland Lady in Ireland: Journals, 1840–50.* Edited by Patricia Pelly and Andrew Tod. Edinburgh: Cannongate Books.

"Grants to Individuals." 1849. In *Hibernian Society Annual Report, 1842–1849.* Dublin: Hibernian Bible Society.

Greeley, Horace. 1851. *Glances at Europe: In a Series of Letters from Great Britain, France, Italy, Switzerland during the Summer of 1851.* New York: Dewitt and Davenport.

———. 1853. *Art and Industry as Represented in the Exhibition at the Crystal Palace, New York, 1853–4.* New York: Redfield.

Griffin, Gerald. 1926. *The Poetical Works of Gerald Griffin.* Dublin: James Duffy.

Griffiths, Mary E. 1946–47. "Emma Willard." *Connecticut Teacher*: 60–61, 78–79.

Groneman, Carol. 2002. "The Real Five Points." *New Yorker*, Dec. 9.

Guide to Killarney and Glengarriff. 1835. Dublin: W. Curry.

Guthrie, Charles John. 1897. *Life of Thomas Guthrie, D.D.* Edinburgh: Free Church of Scotland.

Gwynn, Stephen. 1929. "Bible Christian." In *Saints and Scholars*, 183–204. London: Thornton Butterworth.

Haber, Barbara. 2002. "Feeding the Great Hunger." In *From Hardtack to Home Fries: An Uncommon History of American Cooks and Meals.* New York: Free Press.

Hale, Thomas. 1884. "The Historical Address." In *Centennial Celebration of the Settlement of Chelsea, Vt.*, 28–98. Keene, NH: Sentential.

Hale, William Harlan. 1950. *Horace Greeley: Voice of the People.* New York: Harper.

Hall, Samuel, and Anna Hall. 1843. *Ireland: Its Scenery and Character.* 3 vols. London: Hall.

———. 1865. *A Week in Killarney.* London: Virtue Brothers.

Harrison, Richard S. 1991. *Cork City Quakers, 1655–1939: A Brief History.* Cork: Richard S. Harrison.

———. 1993. *Richard Davis Webb, Quaker Printer.* Skibbereen: Red Barn.

———. 1997. *A Biographical Dictionary of Irish Quakers.* Dublin: Four Courts Press.

Hastings, Thomas, and Lowell Mason. 1832. *Spiritual Songs for Social Worship.* Utica, NY: Gardiner Tracy.

Hatch-Hale, Ruth. N.d. *Genealogy and History of the Hatch Family.* Salt Lake City: Hatch Genealogy Society.

Hatton, Helen. 1993. *The Largest Amount of Good: Quaker Relief in Ireland, 1654–1921.* Montreal: McGill-Queens.

Haughton, Samuel. 1877. *Memoir of James Haughton.* Dublin: L. Ponsonby.

Hawell, Robert. 1980. *Panoramic View of New York from the East River, 1844. Metropolitan Museum of Art Bulletin* (Spring): 28–29.

Heads of Families at the First Census of the United States Taken in the Year 1790: Vermont. 1903. Spartanburg, SC: Reprint Co.

Heads of Families at the Second Census of the United States Taken in the Year 1800: Vermont. 1938. Barre: Vermont Historical Society.

Hewitt, John. 1991. "An Irishman in Coventry." In *Collected Poems,* edited by Frank Ormsby. Belfast: Blackstaff Press.

Hewitt, Nancy. 2001. "Sisterhood and Slavery: Transatlantic Antislavery and Women's Rights." In *Proceedings of the Third Gerda Lehrman Center International Conference.* New Haven, CT: Yale Univ. Press.

Hill, Lord George Augustus. 1846. *Facts from Gweedore: With Useful Hints to Donegal Tourists, Compiled from Notes by Lord G. H.* 2nd ed. Dublin: P. D. Hardy.

Holland, M. 1913. "A Forgotten Mathew Memorial." *Journal of the Cork Historical and Archaeological Society* 20, no. 99: 131–34.

Hone, Joseph M. 1934. "Asenath Nicholson." *Dublin Magazine,* Oct.–Dec., 37–41.

Hone, Philip. 1927. *The Diary of Philip Hone, 1828–1851.* Edited by Allan Nevins. 2 vols. New York: Dodd, Mead.

Hourican, Bridget. 2009. "Hill, Lord George." In *Dictionary of Irish Biography,* 4:696–98. Cambridge: Cambridge Univ. Press.

Howard, Percy. 1907. "The Passing of Exeter Hall." *Civil Service Observer* 13, no. 5.

Howitt, Mary. 1889. *An Autobiography.* Edited by Margaret Howitt. 2 vols. London: William Isbister.

Howra, David. 1986. *The Dream That Would Not Die: The Birth and Growth of the World Evangelical Fellowship, 1846–1986*. London: Paternoster Press.

Hughes, Sarah Forbes. 1899. *Letters and Reflections of John Murray Forbes*. 2 vols. Boston: Houghton Mifflin.

Hurley, John W. 2010. *Irish Gangs and Stick Fighting in the Works of William Carleton*. Dallas: Alamo Press.

Inis Cealtra [pseud.]. 1926. "A Rediscovered Writer on the Irish People." Review of *The Bible in Ireland*. *Catholic Bulletin* 16 (Nov.): 1164–78.

In Memoriam. 1879. *William Goodell: Born in Coventry, New York, October 27, 1792; Died in Janesville, Wisconsin, February 14, 1875*. Chicago: Guilbert and Winchell.

"Ireland and the Irish." 1847. Review of *Ireland's Welcome to the Stranger*. *Tait's Edinburgh Magazine* 14 (May): 640.

Jenkinson, Henry Irwin. 1873. *Epitome of Lockhardt's Life of Scott*. Edinburgh: Adam and Charles Black.

Johnson, Joan. 2000. *James and Mary Ellis: Background and Quaker Famine Relief in Letterfrack*. Dublin: Historical Committee of the Religious Society of Friends in Ireland.

Jordan, Thomas E. 2000. "The Quality of Life in Victorian Ireland, 1831–1901." *New Hibernian Review* 4, no. 1.

Joyce, James. 1961. *Ulysses*. New York: Modern Library.

Kavanagh, Art. 2004. *The Landed Gentry and Aristocracy of Kilkenny*. Bunclody, County Wexford: Irish Family Names.

Keane, Maureen. 1997. *Mrs. S. C. Hall: A Literary Biography*. Irish Literary Studies 50. Gerrard's Cross: Colin Smythe.

Kelleher, Margaret. 1997a. "Asenath Nicholson's Famine Annals." In *The Feminization of Famine: Expressions of the Inexpressible?*, 74–86. Cork: Cork Univ. Press.

———. 1997b. *The Feminization of Famine*. Cork: Cork Univ. Press.

———. 1998. Review of *Annals of the Famine in Ireland*. *Irish University Review* 26, no. 2: 393–95.

Kennedy, Christina. 2000. "The State Ballroom, St. Patrick's Hall, Dublin Castle." In *America's Eye: Irish Paintings from the Collection of Brian P. Burns*. Arts from Ireland, a Kennedy Center Festival. Washington, DC: John F. Kennedy Center for the Performing Arts.

Kennelly, Brendan. 1969. "My Dark Fathers." In *Selected Poems*. Dublin: Allen Figgis.

Kerrigan, Colm. 1992. *Father Mathew and the Irish Temperance Movement, 1838–1849*. Cork: Cork Univ. Press.

———. 1999. "Irish Temperance and United States Anti-Slavery: Fr. Mathew and the Abolitionists." *History Workshop* 31 (Sept.): 191–225.

Kessler, J. B. 1968. *A Study of the Evangelical Alliance in Great Britain*. Goes, Netherlands: Oosterban and LeCointre.

Killanin, Lord, and Michael Duignan. 1967. *The Shell Guide to Ireland*. 2nd ed. London: Ebury Press.

Killen, W. D. 1867. *Memoir of John Edgar, D.D.* Belfast: C. Aitchison.

Kinealy, Christine. 1995. *This Great Calamity: The Irish Famine*. 1994. Reprint, Boulder, CO: Roberts Rinehart.

———. 2013. *Charity and the Great Hunger in Ireland*. London: Bloomsbury Press.

Kinealy, Christine, and Gerard MacAtasney. 2000. *The Hidden Famine: Hunger, Poverty and Sectarianism in Belfast*. London: Pluto.

Kirby, Sheelagh. 1963. *The Yeats Country*. 2nd ed. Dublin: Dolmen Press.

Knox, Thomas Wallace. 1876. *Underground; or, Life below the Surface: Incidents and Accidents beyond the Light of Day; Startling Adventures in All Parts of the World; Minerals and the Mode of Working Them; Undercurrents of Society; Gambling and Its Horrors*. Hartford, CT: J. B. Burr.

Kohl, J. G. 1844. *Travels in Ireland*. London: Bruce and Wyld.

Krieg, Joann P. 2000. *Whitman and the Irish*. Iowa City: Univ. of Iowa Press.

Kuti, Elizabeth. 2005. *The Sugar Wife*. London: Nick Hern Books.

Lamartine, Alphonse de. 1857. *Les Confidences*. Translated by Eugène Plunkett. New York: Appleton.

Lavelle, Rory, Brendan O'Scanaill, and Anthony Previté. 1993. "D'Arcy Monument Is Back on the Map." *Journal of Clifden and Connemara Heritage Group* 1, no. 1: 8–11.

Le Duc, Thomas H. 1939. "Grahamites and Garrisonites." *New York State History* 20: 190–91.

Legg, Mary-Louise. 2009. "Webb, Alfred John." In *Dictionary of Irish Biography*, 10:817–18. Cambridge: Cambridge Univ. Press.

Lewis, Samuel. 1837. *A Topographical Dictionary of Ireland*. 2 vols. Dublin: S. Lewis.

Liddy, Pat. 1987. *Dublin Be Proud*. Dublin: Chadworth.

Lincoln, Colm. 1981. *Steps and Steeples*. Rev. ed. Cork: Mercier Press.

Lincoln, William. 1837. *History of Worcester, Massachusetts, from Its Earliest Settlement to September 1836*. Worcester, UK: Moses Philips.

Linn, William Alexander. 1981. *Horace Greeley*. 1903. Reprint, New York: Chelsea House.

"Literature." 1929. Review of *The Bible in Ireland*. *Advertiser* (Adelaide, Australia), June 29, 20.

Lloyd, David. 2005. "The Indigent Sublime: Specters of Irish Hunger." *Representations* 92, no. 1: 152–85.

Lockwood, Allison. 1981. *Passionate Pilgrim: American Travellers in Great Britain, 1800–1914*. Madison, NJ: Farleigh Dickinson Press.

Lockwood, Charles. 2003. *Bricks and Brownstones: The New York Row House, 1783–1929*. Rev. ed. New York: Rizzoli.

Loeber, Rolf, and Magda Loeber. 2006. *A Guide to Irish Fiction, 1650–1900*. Dublin: Four Courts.

Longworth's American Almanac, New York Register and City Directory, 1833. 1834. New York: Thomas Longworth.

Longworth's American Almanac, New York Register and City Directory, 1839–40. 1841. New York: Longworth.

Lucy, Ronan. 2010. "Cromwell's Foot Bridge." *Kerry Magazine* 20.

Luddy, Maria. 1995. *Women in Ireland, 1800–1918: A Documentary History*. Cork: Cork Univ. Press.

Lunney, Linda. 2009a. "Grimshaw, Nicholas." In *Dictionary of Irish Biography*, 4:293–94. Cambridge: Cambridge Univ. Press.

———. 2009b. "Trench Power Le Poer." In *Dictionary of Irish Biography*, 7:468–69. Cambridge: Cambridge Univ. Press.

Lynam, Joss. 1988. *The Mountains of Connemara: A Hill-Walker's Guide*. Roundstone: Folding Landscapes.

Lyne, Gerard. 2001. *The Landsdowne Estate in Kerry under W. S. Trench, 1849–72*. Dublin: Geography Publications.

Lyons, John. N.d. *Louisburgh: A History*. Louisburgh: Louisburgh Traders Association.

Lysaght, Moira. 1983. *Fr. Theobald Mathew, O.F.M. Cap: The Apostle of Temperance*. Dublin: Four Courts.

Lysaght, Patricia. 1996–97. "Perspectives on Women during the Great Irish Famine from Oral Tradition." *Béaloideas* 64–65: 63–130.

MacCurtain, Margaret. 2005. "Book Mark." Review of *Ireland's Welcome to the Stranger*. *World* 54, no. 3: 7.

Macintyre, Angus. 1965. *The Liberator: Daniel O'Connell and the Irish Party, 1830–1847.* London: Macmillan.

Mac Neill, Máire. 1962. *The Festival of Lughnasa.* London: Oxford Univ. Press.

Malcolm, Elizabeth. 1986. *Ireland Sober, Ireland Free: Drink and Temperance in Nineteenth Century Ireland.* Syracuse, NY: Syracuse Univ. Press.

Mason, Thomas. 1950. *The Islands of Ireland.* 3rd ed. London: Batsford.

Maxwell, Constantia. 1954. *The Stranger in Ireland.* London: Jonathan Cape.

Mayhew, Henry. 1851. *The Adventure of Mr. and Mrs. Sandboys and Family, Who Came Up to London to "Enjoy Themselves" and to See the Great Exhibition.* London: David Bogue.

McCabe, Desmond. 2009. "Hamilton, William." In *Dictionary of Irish Biography*, 4:447–48. Cambridge: Cambridge Univ. Press.

McCain, Mary Donoghue. 1999. Review of *Annals of the Famine in Ireland. New Hibernia Review* (Spring): 152–53.

McCarthy, B. G. 1951. "Thackeray in Ireland." *Studies* 41 (Mar.): 55–68.

McCormack, W. J. 2006. *Fool of the Family: A Life of J. M. Synge.* New York: New York Univ. Press.

McDonald, Theresa. 1992. *Achill 5000 B.C. to 1900 A.D.: Archaeology, History, Folklore.* Dublin: LAS.

McHale, Conor. 1988–89. "Colonial Baron James O'Dowda: Bonniconlon, 1765–98." *North Mayo Historical Society* 2, no. 2: 11–20.

McNamara, T. F. 1981. *Portrait of Cork.* Cork: Waterman.

McNeill, Mary. 1960. *The Life and Times of Mary Ann McCracken: A Belfast Panorama.* Dublin: Allen Figgis.

McVeagh, John. 1996. *Irish Travel Writing: A Bibliography.* Dublin: Wolfhound Press.

M'Dowall, John R. 1838. *Memoir and Select Remains of the Late Rev. John R. M'Dowall, the Martyr of the Seventh Commandment in the Nineteenth Century.* New York: Leavitt, Lord.

Meehan, Rosa. 2003. *The Story of Mayo.* Castlebar: Mayo County Council.

The Merck Manual of Medical Information. 1997. Whitehouse Station, NJ: Merck.

Miall, Charles S. 1889. *Henry Richard, M.P.: A Biography.* London: Cassell.

Military Minutes of the Council of Appointments of the State of New York, 1783–1821. 1901. Albany, NY: James B. Lyon, State Printer.

Miller, Perry. 1956. *Errand into the Wilderness.* New York: Harper.

Mitchel, John. 1921. *Jail Journal.* Dublin: M. H. Gill.

Moffitt, Miriam. 2008. *Soupers and Jumpers: The Protestant Missions in Connemara, 1848–1937.* Dublin: Nonsuch Press.

Moloney, Stephen J., O. Cist. N.d. *The History of Mount Melleray Abbey.* Cork: Paramount Printing House.

Moore, Thomas. 1915. *The Poetical Works of Thomas Moore.* London: Oxford Univ. Press.

Morash, Christopher. 1989. *The Hungry Voice: The Poetry of the Irish Famine.* Dublin: Irish Academic Press.

———. 1997. "Making Memories: The Literature of the Irish Famine." In *The Meaning of Famine,* edited by Patrick O'Sullivan, 40–55. London: Leicester Press.

Muirhead, Findlay, ed. 1924. *Short Guide to London.* London: Macmillan.

Murphy, Ignatius. 1973–74. "Pre-famine Passenger Service on the Lower Shannon." *North Munster Antiquarian Journal* 16: 70–83.

Murphy, Maureen. 1997. "Asenath Nicholson and the Famine in Ireland." In *Women and Irish History: Essays in Honour of Margaret MacCurtain,* edited by Maryann Gialanella Valiulis and Mary O'Dowd, 109–24. Dublin: Wolfhound Press.

———. 2004. "Asenath Nicholson." In *Oxford Dictionary of National Biography,* 36–38. Oxford: Oxford Univ. Press.

———. 2012. "Asenath Nicholson and Famine Folklore Tradition in Rossport, Co. Mayo." In *Sruthannaan Aigéin Thiar: Atlantic Currents; Féilscríbhinn do Shéamas ÓCatháin,* edited by Criostóir MacCarthaigh, 88–97. Dublin: Univ. College Dublin Press.

Myers, Jesse S. 1912. *Life and Letters of Dr. William Bennett.* St. Louis: C. V. Mosby.

Neeley, W. G. 1983. *Kilcooley: Land and People in Tipperary.* Belfast: Universities Press.

Nicholson, Asenath. 1926. *The Bible in Ireland.* Abridgement of *Ireland's Welcome to the Stranger.* Edited by Alfred Tresidder Sheppard. New York: John Day, 1927.

———. 1835. *Nature's Own Book.* 2nd ed. New York: Wilbur and Whipple.

————. 1846. *Nature's Own Book; or, Practical Results of a Vegetable Diet Illustrated by Facts and Experiments of Many Years' Practice*. Glasgow: W. S. Brown for private circulation.

————. 1848. *A Treatise on Vegetable Diet, with Practical Results; or, A Leaf from Nature's Own Book*. Glasgow: John M'Combe, 1848. London: Simpkin, Marshall.

————. 1850. *Lights and Shades of Ireland: In Three Parts*. Pt. 1, "Early History." Pt. 2, "Saints, Kings and Poets of the Early Ages." Pt. 3, "The Famine of 1847, '48 and '49." London: Houlston and Stoneman, 1850. London: Charles Gilpin.

————. 1853. *Loose Papers; or, Facts Gathered during Eight Years' Residence in Ireland, Scotland, England, France and Germany*. New York: Anti-Slavery Office.

————. 1998. *Annals of the Famine in Ireland in 1847, 1848 and 1849*. New York: E. French, 1851. Pt. 3, revision of author's *Lights and Shades of Ireland* (London, 1850). Edited by Maureen Murphy. Dublin: Lilliput Press.

————. 2002. *Ireland's Welcome to the Stranger*. Edited by Maureen O'Rourke Murphy. Dublin: Lilliput Press, 1847.

Ní Ghiobúin, Mealla. 2001. *Dugort, Achill Island, 1831–1861: The Rise and Fall of a Missionary Community*. Maynooth Studies in Local History 39. Dublin: Irish Academic Press.

Nissenbaum, Stephen. 1980. *Sex, Diet and Debility in Jacksonian America*. Westport, CT: Greenwood Press.

Niven, John. 1983. *Martin Van Buren: The Romantic Age of American Politics*. New York: Oxford Univ. Press.

Noel, Baptist Wriothesley. 1837. *Notes on a Short Tour through the Midland Counties of Ireland in the Summer of 1836 with Observations on the Condition of the Peasantry*. London: Nisbet.

Nolan, Rita. 1997. *Within the Mullet*. Naas: Leinster Leader.

Ó Broin, León. 1961. "The Search for Madden's Grave." *Studies* 50, no. 197: 88–91.

Ó Caoimhe, Tomás. 1990. *Killarney Cathedral*. Dublin: Easons.

Ó Catháin, Séamus, and Patrick O'Flannagan. 1975. *The Living Landscape: Kilgalligan, Erris, County Mayo*. Baile Átha Cliath: Comhairle Bhéaloideas Éireann.

Ó Cléirigh, Nellie. 1992. *Valentia: A Different Irish Island*. Dublin: Portobello Press.

O'Connell, Jarlath. 1950. "Tuam Schools in the Last Century." *Galway Reader* 2, nos. 3–4: 173–79.

O'Connor, Frank. 1959. *A Book of Ireland*. London: Collins.

———. 1966. *The Backward Look: A Survey of Irish Literature*. London: Macmillan.

———. 1967. "The Background of Modern Irish Literature." In *A Short History of Irish Literature: A Backward Look*, 134–39. New York: Putnam's Sons.

O'Connor, John. 1995. *The Workhouses of Ireland: The Fate of Ireland's Poor*. Dublin: Anvil.

O'Donoghue, D. J. 1912. *The Poets of Ireland*. Dublin: Hodges & Figgis.

O'Donovan, John. 2003. *Ordnance Survey Letters, Kilkenny*. Edited by Michael Herity. Dublin: Four Masters Press.

O'Faoláin, Seán. 1938. *King of the Beggars: Daniel O'Connell and the Rise of Irish Democracy*. New York: Viking Press.

O'Farrell, Fergus. 2009. "Daniel O'Connell and Iveragh." In *The Iveragh Peninsula: A Cultural Atlas of the Ring of Kerry*, edited by John Crowley and John Sheehan. Cork: Cork Univ. Press.

O'Flaherty, Liam. 1984. *Famine*. Dublin: Wolfhound Press, 1984.

O'Gallagher, Marianna. 1984. *Grosse Isle: The Gateway to Canada, 1832–1837*. Quebec: Carraig Books.

Ó Gráda, Cormac. 1999. *Black '47 and Beyond: The Great Irish Famine in History, Economy and Memory*. Princeton, NJ: Princeton Univ. Press.

Ó Macháin, Pádraig. 2004. *Six Years in Galmoy: Rural Unrest in Kilkenny, 1819–1824*. Dublin: Poodle Press.

O'Mahony, Michelle. 2005. *The Famine in Cork City: Famine Life at the Cork Union Workhouse*. Cork: Mercier Press.

Osborne, Sidney Godolphin. 1856. *Gleanings in the West of Ireland*. Boston: P. Donaghoe.

Ó Tuathaigh, Gearóid. 1984. "Aspects of Nineteenth Century Galway." In *Diarmuid Ó Cearbhaill, Galway, Town and Gown, 1484–1984*, 129–47. Dublin: Gill and Macmillan.

Parton, J. 1855. *The Life of Horace Greeley, Editor of the "New York Tribune."* New York: Mason Bros.

Paxman, Jeremy. 2010. *The Victorians*. London: BBC.

Payne, Daniel A. 1969. *Recollections of Seventy Years*. New York: Arno Press and the New York Times.

Pearson, Peter. 1991. *Dun Laoghaire: Kingston*. Dublin: O'Brien Press.

Pethica, James, and James C. Roy, eds. 1998. *"To the Land of the Free from This Island of Slaves": Henry Stratford Persse's Letters from Galway to America, 1821–1832*. Cork: Cork Univ. Press.

Pierce, Mary. 2010. "Land Issues in Donegal through the Eyes of Asenath Nicholson, William Allingham and Maud Gonne." In *A Garland of Words for Maureen O'Rourke Murphy*, edited by Munira Mutran, Laura P. Z. Izarra, and Beatriz Kopschitz X. Bastos, 115–26. São Paulo: Humanitas.

Pizer, Lawrence R. 2004. Review of *The Seventeenth Century Town Records of Scituate, Massachusetts*, by Jeremy Deportius Bangs. *New England Quarterly* 77, no. 2: 327–30.

Póirtéir, Cathal. 1995. *Echoes of the Famine*. Dublin: Gill and Macmillan.

Proceedings of a Meeting of Friends of Rev. John Pierpont and His Reply to the Charges of the Committee of the Hollis Street Society. 1839. Oct. 29.

Proceedings of the Annual Convention of the Episcopal Church. 1845. New York: Diocese of New York.

The Proceedings of the Second Generation Peace Congress Held in Paris on the 22, 23 and 24th of August 1849, Compiled by Documents. 1849. London: Charles Gilpin.

"Protestant Conversion in Ireland." 1845. *Dublin University Magazine* 25: 733–48.

Psalms and Hymns Selected for the Congregations Assembling in Exeter Hall during the Great Exhibition of 1851. 1851. London: J. Gadsby.

"A Puritanical Writer on the Famine." 1926. Review of *Lights and Shades of Ireland. Catholic Bulletin* 16 (Dec.): 1259–70.

Quinn, James. 2008. *John Mitchel*. Dublin: Univ. College Dublin Press.

Quinn, Peter. 1997. "The Tragedy of Bridget Such-a-One." *American Heritage* 48, no. 8: 36–49.

Reid, T. Weymss. 1888. *Life of the Rt. Hon. W. E. Forster*. London: Chapman and Hall.

Review of *Lights and Shades of Ireland*. 1852. *Northern Star and National Trade Journal* (Leeds) (Oct. 19).

Riach, Douglas C. 1976. "Daniel O'Connell and American Anti-Slavery." *Irish Historical Studies* 20, no. 77: 3–25.

Rice, C. Duncan. 1968. "The Anti-Slavery Mission of George Thompson to the United States, 1834–1835." *American Studies* 2, no. 1: 13–31.

Richard, Henry. 1865. *Memoirs of Joseph Sturge*. London: Partridge.

Richman, Jeffrey. 1988. *Brooklyn's Green-Wood Cemetery*. Brooklyn: Green-Wood Cemetery.

Richmond, Leigh. 1828. *Annals of the Poor: Containing the Dairyman's Daughter, the Negro Servant, and Young Cottager, a New Edition Enlarged and Illustrated, with an Introductory Sketch of the Author by the Rev. John Ayre*. London: Hatchard.

Robinson, Tim. 1990. *Connemara*. Pt. 1, "Introduction and Gazetteer." Roundstone: Folding Landscapes.

Rouse, Ruth, and Stephen C. Neill. 1967. *A History of the Evangelical Movement, 1517–1948*. Philadelphia: Westminster Press.

Russell, John Abraham. 1836. *Remains of the Late Rev. Charles Wolfe, A.B., with a Brief Memoir of His Life by the Rev. John A. Russell*. London: Hamilton Adams.

———. 1842. "Memoirs and Remains of Charles Wolfe." *Dublin University Magazine* 20 (Nov.): 618–34.

Russell, Mary. 1994. *The Blessing of a Good Thick Skirt: Women Travellers and Their World*. London: Flamingo Press.

Scott, Sir Walter. 1870. *The Waverly Novels; or, 'Tis Sixty Years Since*. Vol. 1. Edinburgh: Adams and Charles Black.

Sennett, Milton C. 1986. *Abolition's Axe: Beriah Green, Oneida Institute and the Black Freedom Struggle*. Syracuse, NY: Syracuse Univ. Press.

Sharp, John. 1954. *History of the Diocese of Brooklyn, 1853–1953*. New York: Fordham Univ. Press.

Shaw, Henry. 1988. *The Dublin Pictorial Guide and Directory of 1850*. Belfast: Friar's Bush Press.

Sheehy, David. 1991. "Archbishop Murray of Dublin and the Great Famine in Mayo." *Cathair na Mart: Journal of the Westport Historical Society* 11: 118–28.

Sheppard, Alfred Tresidder. 1926. "Asenath Nicholson and the Howitt Circle." *Bookman* (Nov.): 103–5.

Shryock, Richard H. 1931–32. "Sylvester Graham and the Popular Health Movement, 1830–1870." *Mississippi Valley Historical Review* 18: 174.

Simmons, Ernest J. 1940. *Dostoyevsky: The Making of a Novelist*. New York: Vintage.

Slater's Royal National Commercial Directory of Ireland. 1846. Manchester and London: Slater.

Smith, H. P., ed. 1885. *History of Essex County with Illustrations and Biographical Sketches of Some of Its Prominent Men and Pioneers.* Syracuse, NY: Mason.

Smith, Joseph. 2012. *A Descriptive Catalogue of Friends' Books; or, Books Written by Members of the Society of Friends, Commonly Called Quakers.* New York: Gale Sabin Americana.

Smith-Rosenberg, Carroll. 1985. *Disorderly Conduct Visions of Gender in Victorian America.* New York: Alfred A. Knopf.

Snyder-Grenier, Ellen. 1996. *Brooklyn: An Illustrated History.* Philadelphia: Temple Univ. Press.

Society of Friends. 1852. *Transactions of the Central Relief Committee of the Society of Friends during the Famine in Ireland in 1846 and 1847.* Dublin: Hodges and Smith.

Sonne, Conway B. 1987. *Ships, Saints and Mariners: A Maritime Encyclopedia of Mormon Migration, 1830–90.* Salt Lake City: Univ. of Utah Press.

Stearns, Bertha-Monica. 1932. "Reform Periodicals and Female Reformers, 1830–1860." *American Historical Review* 37, no. 4: 678–99.

Stock, Samuel. 1847. "Letter to Lord John Russell, October 28, 1847." *Howitts' Journal* 2 (Nov. 27): 341.

Strange, Mary A. 1970. *The Bourne Families of Ireland.* Orange Park, FL: Quintan.

Strong, Douglas M. 1928. "Goodell, William." In *Dictionary of American Biography*, 9:236–37. New York: Charles Scribner's Sons.

Sweeney, Douglas A. 2005. *The American Evangelical Story: A History of the Movement.* Grand Rapids, MI: Baker Academic.

Swords, Liam. 1999. *In Their Own Words: The Famine in North Connacht, 1845–1849.* Blackrock: Columba Press.

Symmes, Marilyn. 2005. *Impressions of New York Prints from the New York Historical Society.* New York: Princeton, Architectural Press.

Synge, John Millington. 1968. *Riders to the Sea.* In *Collected Works: Plays.* Bk. 1, edited by Ann Saddlemyer. London: Oxford Univ. Press.

Talmon, J. L. 1967. *Romanticism and Revolt: Europe, 1815–1848.* New York: Harcourt, Brace, and World.

Tappan, Lewis. 1870. *The Life of Arthur Tappan.* New York: Hurd and Houghton.

Taylor, Benjamin C. 1857. "History of the Third Dutch Reformed Church of Jersey City." In *Annals of the Classis of Bergen of the Reformed Dutch*

Church Including the Civil History of the Ancient Township of Bergen in New Jersey. New York: Board of Publication of the Reformed Protestant Dutch Church.

Thackeray, William Makepeace. 2005. *The Irish Sketchbook of 1842.* 1843. Reprint, Dublin: Nonsuch.

Thompson, Mrs. D. P. 1867. *A Brief Account of the Rise and Progress of the Change in Religious Opinion Now Taking Place in Dingle and the West of County Kerry.* 2nd ed. Dublin: Curry.

Thom's Dublin Directory for 1845. 1846. Dublin: Pettigrew and Oulton.

Thom's Dublin Directory for 1847. 1848. Dublin: Pettigrew and Oulton.

Tolis, Peter. 1968. *Elihu Burritt: Crusader for Brotherhood.* Hamden: Archon.

Townsend, Paul. 2002. *Father Mathew, Temperance and Irish Identity.* Dublin: Irish Academic Press.

Trevelyan, Charles E. 1848. *The Irish Crisis.* London: Longman Brown, Green & Longmans.

Trow's New York City Directory, 1857, for the Year Ending May 1, 1857. 1857. New York: John F. Trow.

Tuke, James. 1848. *A Visit to Connaught in the Autumn of 1847.* 2nd ed. London: Charles Gilpin.

Tyrrell, Alex. 1987. *Joseph Sturge and the Moral Radical Party in Early Victorian Britain.* London: Christopher Helin.

Ulrich, Laurel Thatcher. 2008. *Well-Behaved Women Seldom Make History.* New York: Vintage.

Van Deusen, Glyndon G. 1953. *Horace Greeley: Nineteenth Century Crusader.* New York: Hill and Wang.

Vecsay, Christopher. 1983. *Traditional Ojibwa Religion and Its Historical Changes.* Memoir Series no. 15. Philadelphia: American Philosophical Society.

Villiers-Tuthill, Kathleen. 2000. *Beyond the Twelve Bens: A History of Clifden and District, 1860–1921.* 2nd ed. Rathfarnham: Connemara Girls.

Watson's; or, The Gentleman's and Citizen's Almanack. 1844. Dublin: C. Hope.

Webb, Alfred John. 1999. *The Autobiography of a Quaker Nationalist.* Edited by Mary-Louise Legg. Cork: Cork Univ. Press.

Whelan, Irene. 2003. *The Bible War in Ireland: The "Second Reformation" and the Polarization of Protestant Catholic Relations, 1800–1840.* Dublin: Lilliput Press.

Whitman, Walt. 1984. "Wants." In *Notebooks and Unpublished Prose Manuscripts*. Vol. 1, *Family Notes and Autobiography: Brooklyn and New York*. Edited by Edward F. Grier. New York: New York Univ. Press.

Wilde, Jane Francesca Elgee. 1890. *Cures, Charms and Usages of Ancient Ireland*. London: Ward and Downey.

Winter, Ron, and Pat Winter. 1987. *Village Church of the Isle of Wight*. East Cowes: Forget-Me-Not Books.

Wood, C. J. 2009a. "Madden, Richard Robert." In *Dictionary of Irish Biography*, 6:216. Cambridge: Cambridge Univ. Press.

———. 2009b. *Travellers' Accounts as Source Material for Irish Historians*. Dublin: Four Courts Press.

Woodham-Smith, Cecil. 1951. *Florence Nightingale*. New York: McGraw-Hill.

———. 1962. *The Great Hunger: Ireland, 1845–1849*. New York: Harper and Row.

Woodring, C. R. 1952. *Victorian Samplers: William and Mary Howitt*. Lawrence: Univ. Press of Kansas.

Wright, Daniel S., and Kathryn Kish Sklar. 1999. *What Was the Appeal of Moral Reform to Antebellum Northern Women*. Binghamton: State Univ. of New York.

Wyatt-Brown, Bertram. 1969. *Lewis Tappan and the Evangelical War against Slavery*. Baton Rouge: Louisiana State Univ. Press.

Wyse, Jackson R. 1946. Review of *The Bible in Ireland*. Bell 11, no. 5: 990–94.

Yeats, W. B. 1936. *Dramatis Personae*. New York: Macmillan.

———. 1953. *The Autobiography of William Butler Yeats*. New York: Macmillan.

———. 1996. *The Collected Poems of W. B. Yeats*. Edited by Richard Finneran. New York: Simon and Schuster.

Ziegler, Valerie H. 1992. *The Advocates of Peace in Antebellum America*. Bloomington: Indiana Univ. Press.

Zuckerman, Larry. 1998. *The Potato: How the Humble Spud Rescued the Western World*. New York: North Point Press.

Index

Italic page number denotes illustration.

Other titles in Irish Studies